Lawrenceville Press

An Introduction to Computing Using Microsoft Works®

version 4 for Windows 95

Bruce Presley
Beth Brown

**All orders including educational, Canadian, foreign,
FPO, and APO may be placed by contacting:**

Lawrenceville Press, Inc.
P.O. Box 704
Pennington, NJ 08534-0704
(609) 737-1148
(609) 737-8564 fax

This text is available in both hardcover and softcover editions.

16 15 14 13 12 11 10 9 8 7 6 5 4 3

P | Preface

We believe the best way to introduce students to computing is with an introductory course that gives them considerable "hands-on" computer experience. This objective is best accomplished with an integrated software package such as Works that allows students to use a word processor, database, and spreadsheet. We also believe that an introductory course should include discussions about the roles computers play in modern society as well as a brief history of computing. These goals are accomplished by this text which is designed to serve both the needs of students who will complete only an introductory course and those who will go on to take subsequent computer courses. The emphasis of this text is on the concepts of computing and problem solving so that students learn how computers can be applied to a wide range of problems. The text is written to be used either in a one or two term course by students with little or no previous computer experience.

Designs and Features

Format: Each chapter contains numerous examples and graphics printed in a two color format to help students visualize new concepts. Important commands are listed on the first page of each chapter. Works menus are displayed in the margins for easy reference.

Objectives: An outline of the significant topics that should be emphasized is presented at the beginning of each chapter.

History of Computing: Before learning to use the applications software, Chapter One introduces students to a history of computing and covers the vocabulary needed to understand the concepts presented in later chapters.

Concepts of Applications: Each of the application areas begins with an introductory section which describes the application and its uses. In this way, students are taught the purpose of the application without being overly concerned with the specific software. If the student then goes on to use another software package, he or she will fully understand the general concepts behind each application.

Hands on Practice: In the applications chapters each new concept is presented, discussed, and then followed by a hands-on Practice which requires the student to test newly learned skills on the computer. The Practice sections also serve as excellent reference guides to review applications commands.

Chapter Summary: At the end of each chapter is an outline that briefly discusses the concepts covered in the chapter.

Vocabulary: A vocabulary section which defines the new terms used is given at the end of each chapter.

Review Questions: Numerous review questions are presented keyed to each section of the chapter, providing immediate reinforcement of new concepts. Answers to all review questions are included in the *Teacher's Resource Package* described below.

Exercises: Each of the applications chapters includes a set of exercises of varying difficulty appropriate for students with a wide range of abilities. Answers to all exercises are included in the *Teacher's Resource Package* described below.

Desktop Publishing: Chapter Twelve offers an introduction to desktop publishing using Microsoft Draw.

Internet and Ethical Implications: Chapter Thirteen offers an introduction to the Internet and its history. Also because computers play such an important role in modern society, this chapter discusses the social and ethical consequences of living in a computerized society. Telecommunication is explained and the Works communications application introduced.

Careers in Computing: It is hoped that many students will become interested in careers in computing based upon their experience in this introductory course. A section in Chapter Thirteen outlines different computer careers and the educational requirements needed to pursue them.

Appendices: Summaries of Works functions, making backups with Windows 95, and keyboarding skills are presented in appendices at the end of the text for easy reference.

Teacher's Resource Package

When used with this text, the Lawrenceville Press Teacher's Resource Package provides all the additional material required to offer students an excellent introductory computer applications course. These materials place a strong emphasis on developing the student's problem-solving skills. The Package divides each of the chapters in the text into lessons that contain the following features:

- **Assignments** – Suggested reading and problem assignments.

- **Teaching Notes** – Helpful information that we and our reviewers have learned from classroom experience.

- **Discussion Topics** – Additional material that supplements the text and can be used in leading classroom discussions.

- **Transparency Masters** – Diagrams of the different topics that can be copied onto film.

- **Worksheets** – Problems that supplement the exercises in the text by providing additional reinforcement of concepts.

- **Quizzes** – A short quiz that tests recently learned skills.

P

In addition to the material in the lessons, other features are included for each chapter:

- **Tests** – Two sets of comprehensive end-of-chapter tests as well as a midterm and final examination. Each test consists of multiple choice questions and "hands-on" problems that require work on the computer. A full set of answers and a grading key are also included.

- **Answers** – Complete answers for the review questions and exercises presented in the text.

Master Diskettes, included with the Package, contain the following files:

- **Data files** – All files the student needs to complete the practices and exercises in the text. These files allow students to work with large amounts of data without having to type it into the computer. Also included are the files needed to complete the worksheets, quizzes, and tests in the Package.

- **Tests** – The tests are also provided in word processing files so that they can be edited.

- **Answer files** – Answers to the practices, exercises, worksheets, quizzes, and tests.

Student data diskettes can be easily made by following the directions included in the Teacher's Resource Package. Student diskettes are also available in packs of 10.

As an added feature, the Package is contained in a 3-ring binder. This not only enables pages to be removed for duplication, but also allows you to keep your own notes in the Package.

Our Works Texts

The previous editions of our Works texts have established them as leaders in their field, with more than one million students having been introduced to computing using our "hands-on" approach. With this new Works edition, we have made significant improvements over our earlier Works texts. These improvements were based on the many comments we received, a survey of instructors who are teaching the text, and our own classroom experience.

This text presents material for Work's word processor, database, and spreadsheet in introductory, intermediate, and advanced chapters. The word processing chapters discuss such topics as footnotes and paragraph indents. The database chapters cover such topics as queries and reports. The spreadsheet chapters include charts. Other topics include the history of computers, desktop publishing, telecommunications, and the Internet.

As an additional feature the softcover edition now has an improved sewn lay-flat binding which keeps the text open at any page and gives the book additional strength.

Thousands of instructors have found the Teacher's Resource Package and its accompanying diskettes an integral part of their instructional materials. The latest edition includes new worksheets, tests, and quizzes.

As active teachers, we know the importance of using a well written and logically organized text. With this edition we believe that we have produced the finest introductory computer text and Teacher's Resource Package available.

P

Acknowledgments

The authors are especially grateful to the following teachers and their students who classroom tested an early version of this text as it was being written. Their comments and suggestions have been invaluable:

Dr. Mary K. Adkemeier, Fontbonne College, St. Louis, MO

Judy Boyd, Sanford H. Calhoun High School, Merrick, NY

Mary Ann Dougherty, South Brunswick High School, NJ

Kurt Douglas, Rangley High School, Rangely, CO

Dr. Cindy Emmans, Central Washington University, Ellensburg, WA

Calvin Gates, Lebanon High School, Lebanon, PA

Neil Hall, Bedford Community Schools, Bedford, IA

Jodi McMasters, Boca Raton, FL

Joanne Prell, College of DuPage, Glen Ellyn, IL

Sherry Reinking, IKM Community School, Manilla, IA

Jess Rollin, Clearfield County Vocational Technical School, Clearfield, PA

Walter Vestal, Ridgewood High School, Norridge, IL

Dr. Lila Waldman, Murray State University, Murray KY

Thanks are due Rick Dunn and Dot Bernier of Courier Book Companies, Inc. who supervised the printing of this text. Rachel Stern designed the imaginative cover. Graphics Illustrated updated the cover for this new edition. The new graphics for this edition were produced by John Gandour.

The success of this and many of our other texts is due to the efforts of Heidi Crane, Vice President of Marketing at Lawrenceville Press. She has developed the promotional material which has been so well received by instructors around the world, and coordinated the comprehensive customer survey which led to many of the refinements in this edition. Joseph DuPree and Robin Van Ness run our Customer Relations Department and handle the many thousands of orders we receive in a friendly and efficient manner. Richard Guarascio and Michael Porter are responsible for the excellent service Lawrenceville Press offers in shipping orders.

Elaine Malfas, a Lawrenceville Press author, created Chapter Twelve, made the many updates to Chapter One and Chapter Thirteen, and generated the complete Index for this text. We value her good sense of design and technical expertise.

P

Vickie Grassman, the newest member of our staff, has edited this entire text and did the research needed for this new edition. She also created Appendix B and provided all the screen captures for this text. We appreciate her efficiency and thoroughness.

A note of appreciation is due our colleagues Robert Kenyon, Nanette Hert, and Ruth Wagy in the Computer Science department of Saint Andrew's School. They helped test this text in their class and have offered valuable suggestions on ways in which it could be improved. Also, thanks are due Bari Attis of Saint Andrew's School. Her suggestions have helped to make our text more grammatically correct and easier to understand.

Finally, we would like to thank our students, for whom and with whom this text was written. Their candid evaluation of each lesson and their refusal to accept anything less than perfect clarity in explanation have been the driving forces behind the creation of *An Introduction to Computing Using Works*.

About the Authors

Bruce W. Presley, a graduate of Yale University, taught computer science and physics at The Lawrenceville School in Lawrenceville, New Jersey for twenty-four years where he served as the director of the Karl Corby Computer and Mathematics Center. Mr. Presley was a member of the founding committee of the Advanced Placement Computer Science examination and served as a consultant to the College Entrance Examination Board. Presently Mr. Presley, author of more than twenty computer textbooks, is president of Lawrenceville Press and teaches computing applications.

Beth A. Brown, a graduate in computer science of Florida Atlantic University, is director of development at Lawrenceville Press where she has co-authored several applications texts and their Teacher's Resource Packages and contributed in the development of several programming texts. Ms. Brown currently teaches computer applications and computer programming.

P

An Introduction to Computing Using Microsoft Works

T | Table of Contents

Chapter One - An Introduction to Computers

Chapter Two - Introducing the Word Processor

Chapter Three - Manipulating Text with the Word Processor

An Introduction to Computing Using Microsoft Works

T | Chapter Four - Advanced Word Processor Techniques

Chapter Five - Introducing the Database

Chapter Six - Manipulating Data with the Database

Chapter Seven - Reports and Advanced Database Techniques

Chapter Eight - Introducing the Spreadsheet

T

Chapter Nine - Manipulating Data with the Spreadsheet

Chapter Ten - Advanced Spreadsheet Techniques

Chapter Eleven - Integrating the Word Processor, Database, and Spreadsheet

T Chapter Twelve - An Introduction to Desktop Publishing

Chapter Thirteen - Telecommunications and the Social and Ethical Implications of Computing

Appendix A - Works Keyboard Commands and Functions

Appendix B - Windows 95 and Backups

Appendix C - Keyboarding Skills

An Introduction to Computing Using Microsoft Works

Chapter One
An Introduction To Computers

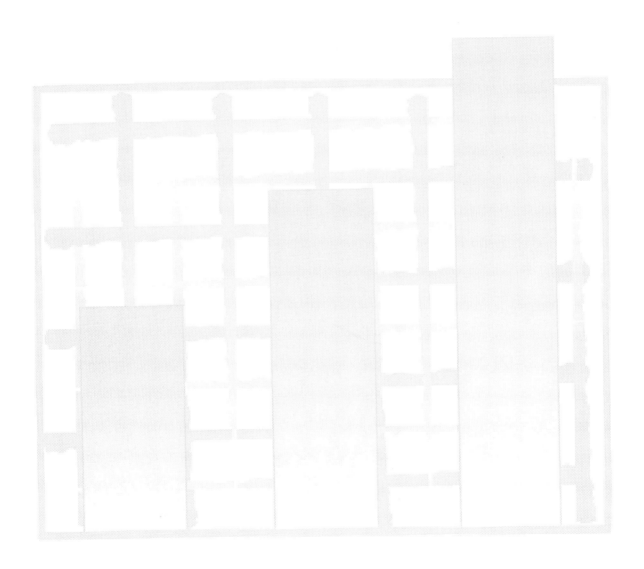

Objectives

After completing this chapter you will be able to:

1. Define what a computer is.

2. Discuss the history of computers.

3. Understand how computers work.

4. Name the types of components in a modern computer system.

5. Describe what software and hardware are.

6. Understand the advantages of using a computer.

1

This text is about computers: their history, how they process and store data, and the role they play in modern society. We will use a popular computer program named Works to teach you about word processors, databases, spreadsheets, graphics, and telecommunications. Each of these applications will be explained as we proceed.

There are three reasons for learning how to use a computer. The first and most important is to develop problem-solving skills. This is done by learning how to analyze a problem carefully, develop a step-by-step solution, and then use the computer as a tool to produce a solution.

A second reason for learning about computers is to become acquainted with their capabilities and limitations. Because you are a part of a computerized society, learning to use a computer is probably the best way to become familiar with one.

Finally, using a computer can be fun. The intellectual challenge of controlling the operations of a computer is not only rewarding but also an invaluable skill. The techniques learned in this class can be used both at home and on the job.

1.1 What is a Computer?

A *computer* is an electronic machine that accepts information (called *data*), processes it according to specific instructions, and provides the results as new information. The computer can store and manipulate large quantities of data at a very high speed and, even though it cannot think, it can make simple decisions and comparisons. For example, a computer can determine which of two numbers is larger or which of two names comes first alphabetically and then act upon that decision.

Although the computer can help to solve a wide variety of problems, it is merely a machine and cannot solve problems on its own. It must be provided with instructions in the form of a computer *program*. A program is a list of instructions written in a special language that the computer understands. It tells the computer which operations to perform and in what sequence to perform them. In this text the computer program we will use is called Works.

The History of Computers

1

Many of the advances made by science and technology are dependent upon the ability to perform complex mathematical calculations and to process large amounts of data. It is therefore not surprising that for thousands of years mathematicians, scientists, and business people have searched for computing machines that could perform calculations and analyze data quickly and accurately.

1.2 Ancient Counting Machines

As civilizations began to develop, they created both written languages and number systems. These number systems were not originally meant to be used in mathematical calculations, but rather were designed to record measurements like the number of sheep in a flock. Roman numerals are a good example of these early number systems. Few of us would want to carry out even the simplest arithmetic operations using Roman numerals. How then were calculations performed thousands of years ago?

Calculations were carried out with a device known as an *abacus* which was used in ancient Babylon, China, and throughout Europe until the late middle-ages. Many parts of the world, especially in the Orient, still make use of the abacus. The abacus works by sliding beads on a frame with the beads on the top of the frame representing fives and the beads on the bottom of the frame representing ones. After a calculation is made the result is written down.

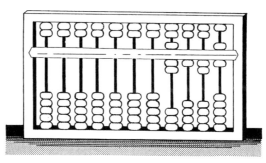

The abacus is a calculating device used throughout the Orient

1.3 Arabic Numerals

Toward the end of the middle ages, Roman numerals were replaced by a new number system borrowed from the Arabs, therefore called Arabic numerals. This system uses ten digits and is the system we still use today. Because the Arabic system made calculations with pencil and paper easier, the abacus and other such counting devices became less common. Although calculations were now easier to perform, operations such as multiplication and division were able to be done by only those few mathematicians who were well educated.

1.4 The Pascaline

One of the earliest mechanical devices for calculating was the *Pascaline*, invented by the French philosopher and mathematician Blaise Pascal in 1642. At that time Pascal was employed in the recording of taxes for the French government. The task was tedious and kept him up until the early hours of the morning day after day. Being a gifted thinker, Pascal thought that the task of adding numbers should be able to be done by a mechanism that operated similarly to the way that a clock keeps time.

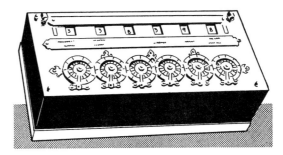

The Pascaline was a mechanical calculating device invented by Blaise Pascal in 1642

The Pascaline he invented was a complicated set of gears which could only be used to perform addition and not for multiplication or division. Unfortunately, due to manufacturing problems, Pascal never got the device to work properly.

1.5 The Stepped Reckoner

Later in the 17th century Gottfried Wilhelm von Leibniz, a famous mathematician credited with being one of the developers of calculus, invented a device that was supposed to be able to add and subtract, as well as multiply, divide, and calculate square roots. His device, the *Stepped Reckoner*, included a cylindrical wheel called the *Leibniz wheel* and a moveable carriage that was used to enter the number of digits in the multiplicand.

Though both Pascal's and Leibniz's machines held great promise, they did not work well because the craftsmen of their time were unable to make machined parts that were accurate enough to carry out the inventor's design. Because of the mechanically unreliable parts, the devices tended to jam and malfunction.

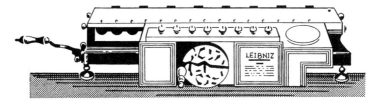

The Stepped Reckoner was another early attempt at creating a mechanical calculating device

1.6 The Punched Card

In 1810 Joseph Jacquard, a French weaver, made a revolutionary discovery. He realized that the weaving instructions for his looms could be stored on cards with holes punched in them. As the cards passed through the loom in sequence, needles passed through the holes and then picked up threads of the correct color or texture. By rearranging the cards, a weaver could change the pattern being woven without stopping the machine to change threads.

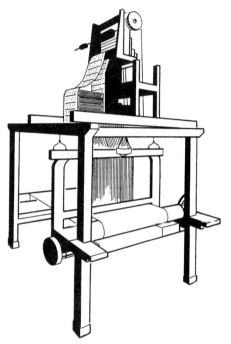

*Jacquard's loom was the first device to make use of
punched cards to store information*

The weaving industry would seem to have little in common with the computer industry, but the idea that information could be stored by punching holes on a card was to be of great use in the later development of the computer.

1.7 Babbage's Difference and Analytical Engines

In 1822 Charles Babbage began work on the *Difference Engine*. His hope was that this device would calculate numbers to the 20th place and then print them at 44 digits per minute. The original purpose of this machine was to produce tables of numbers that would be used by ship's navigators. At the time navigation tables were often highly inaccurate due to calculation errors. In fact, several ships were known to have been lost at sea because of these errors. However, because of mechanical problems similar to those that plagued Pascal and Leibniz, the Difference Engine never worked properly.

Undaunted, Babbage later planned and began work on a considerably more advanced machine called the *Analytical Engine*. This machine was to perform a variety of calculations by following a set of instructions, or *program*, entered into it using punched cards similar to the ones used by Joseph Jacquard. During processing, the Analytical Engine was to store information in a memory unit that would allow it to make decisions and then carry out instructions based on those decisions. For example, for comparing two numbers it could be programmed to determine which was larger and then follow different sets of instructions. The Analytical Engine was no more successful than its predecessors, but its design was to serve as a model for the modern computer.

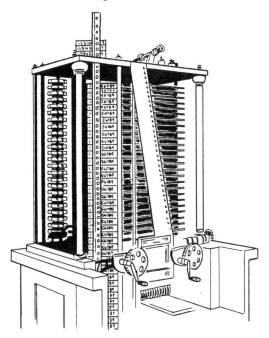

Babbage's Analytical Engine was a calculating machine that used punched cards to store information

Babbage's chief collaborator on the Analytical Engine was Ada, Countess of Lovelace, the daughter of Lord Byron. Interested in mathematics, Lady Lovelace was a sponsor of the Engine and one of the first people to realize its power and significance. She also tested the device and wrote of its achievements in order to gain support for it. Because of her involvement she is often called the first programmer.

Babbage had hoped that the Analytical Engine would be able to think. Lady Lovelace, however, said that the Engine could never "originate anything," meaning that she did not believe that a machine, no matter how powerful, could think. To this day her statement about computing machines remains true.

1.8 The Electronic Tabulating Machine

By the end of the 19th century, U.S. Census officials were concerned about the time it took to tabulate the continuously increasing number of Americans. This counting was done every 10 years, as required by the Constitution. However, the Census of 1880 took 9 years to compile which made the figures highly inaccurate by the time they were published.

To solve the problem, Herman Hollerith invented a calculating machine that used electricity rather than mechanical gears. Holes representing information to be tabulated were punched in cards similar to those used in Jacquard's loom, with the location of each hole representing a specific piece of information (male, female, age, etc.). The cards were then inserted into the machine and metal pins used to open and close electrical circuits. If a circuit was closed, a counter was increased by one.

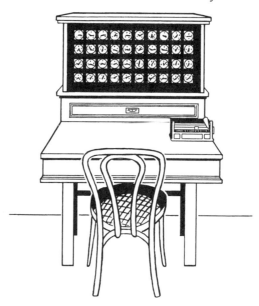

Herman Hollerith's tabulating machine, invented for the Census of 1880, used electricity instead of gears to perform calculations

Hollerith's machine was immensely successful. The general count of the population, then 63 million, took only six weeks to calculate, while full statistical analysis took seven years. This may not sound like much of an improvement over the nine years of the previous census, but Hollerith's machine enabled the Census Bureau to make a far more detailed and useful study of the population than had previously been possible. Based on the success of his invention, Hollerith and some friends formed a company that sold his invention all over the world. The company eventually became known as International Business Machines (IBM).

1.9 The Mark I

By the 1930s, key-operated mechanical adding machines had been developed which used a complicated assortment of gears and levers. Scientists, engineers, and business people, however, needed machines more powerful than adding machines; machines capable of making simple decisions such as determining which of two numbers was larger and then acting upon the decision. A machine with this capability is called a computer rather than a calculator. A calculator is not a true computer because, while it can perform calculations, it cannot make decisions.

The first computer-like machine is generally thought to be the *Mark I*, which was built by a team from IBM and Harvard University under the leadership of Howard Aiken. The Mark I used mechanical telephone relay switches to store information and accepted data on punched cards, processed it and then output the new data. Because it could not make decisions about the data it processed, the Mark I was not a real computer but was instead a highly sophisticated calculator. Nevertheless, it was impressive in size, measuring over 51 feet in length and weighing 5 tons! It also had over 750,000 parts, many of them moving mechanical parts which made the Mark I not only huge but unreliable.

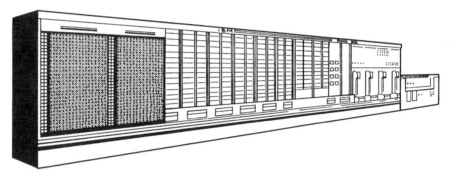

The Mark 1 was 51 feet long and weighed over 5 tons

1.10 ENIAC: The First Electronic Computer

In June 1943, John Mauchly and J. Presper Eckert began work on the Electronic Numerical Integration and Calculator, or *ENIAC*. It was originally a secret military project which began during World War II to calculate the trajectory of artillery shells. Built at the University of Pennsylvania, it was not finished until 1946, after the war had ended. But the great effort put into the ENIAC was not wasted. In one of its first demonstrations ENIAC was given a problem that would have taken a team of mathematicians three days to solve. It solved the problem in twenty seconds.

ENIAC was different from the Mark I in several important ways. First, it occupied 1500 square feet, which is the same area taken up by the average three bedroom house and it weighed 30 tons. Second, it used vacuum tubes instead of relay switches. It contained over 17,000 of these tubes, which were the same kind used in radios. Because the tubes consumed huge amounts of electricity the computer produced a tremendous amount of heat and required special fans to cool the room where it was installed. Most importantly, because it was able to make decisions, it was the first true computer.

Because it could make decisions, ENIAC was the first true computer

ENIAC had two major weaknesses. First, it was difficult to change its instructions to have the computer solve different problems. It had originally been designed to compute artillery trajectory tables, but when it needed to work on another problem it could take up to three days of wire pulling, replugging, and switch-flipping to change instructions. Second, the ENIAC was unreliable because the tubes it contained were constantly burning out.

Today, much of the credit for the original design of the electronic computer is given to John Atanasoff, a math and physics professor at Iowa State University. Between 1939 and 1942, Atanasoff, working with graduate student Clifford Berry, developed a working digital computer on the campus at Iowa State. Unfortunately, their patent application was not handled properly, and it was not until almost 50 years later that Atanasoff received full credit for his invention, the *Atanasoff Berry Computer* (ABC). In 1990, he was awarded the Presidential Medal of Technology for his pioneering work, and some of his early devices were exhibited at the Smithsonian.

1.11 The Stored Program Computer

In the mid 1940s, John von Neumann developed the idea of storing computer instructions in a central processing unit, or *CPU*. This unit consisted of different elements to control all the functions of the computer electronically so that it would not be necessary to flip switches or pull wires to change the instructions. Now it would be possible to solve many different problems by simply typing in new instructions at a keyboard. Together with Mauchly and Eckert, von Neumann designed and built the *EDVAC* (Electronic Discrete Variable Automatic Computer) and the *EDSAC* (Electronic Delay Storage Automatic Computer).

With the development of the concept of stored instructions, or programs, the modern computer age was ready to begin. Since then, the development of new computers has progressed rapidly, but von Neumann's concept has remained, for the most part, unchanged.

Based on von Neumann's concept, all computers process information, or *data* by carrying out four specific activities:

1. Input data
2. Store data while it is being processed
3. Process data according to specific instructions
4. Output the results in the form of new data.

The next computer to employ von Neumann's concepts was the UNIVersal Automatic Computer, or *UNIVAC*, built by Mauchly and Eckert. The first one was sold to the U.S. Census Bureau in 1951.

Computers continued to use many vacuum tubes which made them large and expensive. UNIVAC weighed 35 tons. These computers were so expensive to purchase and run that only the largest corporations and the U.S. government could afford them. Their ability to perform up to 1,000 calculations per second, however, made them popular.

1.12 The Transistor

It was the invention of the transistor that made smaller and less expensive computers possible, with increased calculating speeds of up to 10,000 calculations per second. Although the size of the computers shrank, they were still large and expensive. In the early 1960s, IBM, using ideas it had learned while working on projects for the military, introduced the first medium-sized computer named the model 650. It was still expensive, but it was capable of handling the flood of paper work produced by many government agencies and businesses. Such organizations provided a ready market for the 650, making it popular in spite of its cost.

One transistor replaced many tubes, making computers smaller, less expensive, and more reliable

These new computers also saw a change in the way data was stored. Punched cards were replaced by magnetic tape and high speed reel-to-reel tape machines. Using magnetic tape gave computers the ability to read (access) and write (store) data quickly and reliably.

1.13 Programming Languages

Another important advance occurring in the 1960s was the development of programming languages. Previously, computers had to be programmed by rewiring different switches to their ON or OFF positions. The first programming languages, referred to as low-level languages, used 0s and 1s to represent the status of the switches (0 for OFF and 1 for ON). The lowest-level language was called *machine language* and consisted of directly typing in 0s and 1s, eliminating the time-consuming task of rewiring. However, accurately typing instructions consisting of only 0s and 1s is extremely difficult to do, and high-level languages were then developed that allowed programmers to write in English-like instructions that the computer translated into 0s and 1s. One of the first popular high-level languages was Fortran (FORmula TRANslator) which had intuitive commands such as READ and WRITE.

One of the most widely used high-level programming languages has been COBOL. COBOL was first developed by the Department of Defense in 1959 to provide a common language for use on all computers. In fact, COBOL stands for COmmon Business Oriented Language. The designer of COBOL was Grace Murray Hopper, a Commodore in the Navy at the time. Commodore Hopper was the first person to apply the term *debug* to the computer. While working on the Mark I computer in the 1940s, a moth flew into the circuitry, causing an electrical short which halted the computer. While removing the dead moth, she said that the program would be running again after the computer had been "debugged." Today, the process of removing errors from programs is still called debugging.

A number of new high-level languages have been developed since that time. Basic is a popular language with easy to understand commands. C is a popular programming language designed by Bell Labs. Developed by the Swiss computer scientist Niklaus Wirth to teach the fundamentals of programming, Pascal is a language used by many schools and universities. The latest language developed by the Department of Defense is named Ada, after the first programmer, Ada the Countess of Lovelace.

1.14 Integrated Circuits

The next major technological advancement was the replacement of transistors by tiny integrated circuits or *chips*. Chips are blocks of silicon with logic circuits etched into their surfaces. They are smaller and cheaper than transistors and can contain thousands of circuits on a single chip. Integrated circuits also give computers tremendous speed allowing them to process information at a rate of millions of calculations per second.

Chips are covered by intricate circuits that have been etched into their surfaces and then coated with a metallic oxide that fills in the etched circuit patterns. This enables the chips to conduct electricity along the many paths of their circuits. Because there are as many as millions of circuits on a single chip, the chips are called integrated circuits.

Integrated circuits are so small that they must be housed in special plastic cases that have metal pins coming out of them. The pins allow the chips to be plugged into circuit boards that have wiring printed on them.

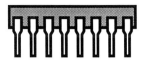

A typical integrated circuit chip (approximately half an inch wide and 1.5 inches long)

One of the most important benefits of using integrated circuits is to decrease the cost and size of computers. The IBM System 360 was one of the first computers to use integrated circuits and was so popular with businesses that IBM had difficulty keeping up with the demand. Computers had come down in size and price to such a point that smaller organizations such as universities and hospitals could now afford them.

1.15 Mainframes

Mainframe computers are large computer systems that cost many hundreds of thousands, if not millions, of dollars. Mainframes can carry out many different tasks at the same time. They are used by large corporations, banks, government agencies, and universities. Mainframes can calculate a large payroll, keep the records for a bank, handle the reservations for an airline, or store student information for a university—tasks that require the storage and processing of huge amounts of information.

Mainframe computers are large, often requiring their own rooms

Most people using mainframes communicate with them using *terminals*. A terminal consists of a keyboard for data input, and a monitor for viewing output. The terminal is connected by wires to the computer, which may be located on a different floor or a building a few blocks away. Some mainframe computers have hundreds of terminals attached and working at the same time.

1.16 The Microprocessor and the Microcomputer

The most important advancement to occur in the early 70s was the invention of the *microprocessor*, an entire CPU on a single chip. In 1970, Marcian Hoff, an engineer at Intel Corporation, designed the first of these chips.

The small microprocessor made it possible to build a computer called a microcomputer that fit on a desktop. The first of these was the ALTAIR in 1975. In 1977, working originally out of a garage, Stephen Wozniak and Steven Jobs designed and built the Apple computer.

Fast advances in technology made microcomputers inexpensive and therefore available to many people. Because of these advances almost anyone could own a machine that had more computing power and was faster and more reliable than either the ENIAC or UNIVAC. As a comparison, if the cost of a sports car had dropped as quickly as that of a computer, a new Porsche would now cost about one dollar.

1.17 The Personal Computer

Microcomputers, often called *personal computers* (PCs), can cost as little as a few hundred dollars and fit on a desktop. During the past few years their processing speed and their ability to store large amounts of data have increased to the point where some microcomputers now rival older mainframe computers. The computer you will use is a microcomputer.

A microcomputer consists of several *hardware* components:

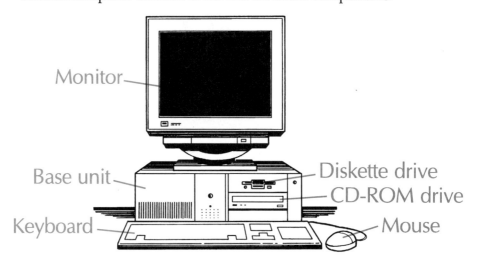

A microcomputer combines a keyboard, monitor, disk drives, and a mouse in a desktop-sized package

The base unit of a microcomputer contains the CPU and data storage devices such as a diskette drive, a CD-ROM drive, and a *hard disk* which is a disk drive completely contained inside the base unit. The keyboard, mouse, and disk drives are used to input data, and the monitor is used to view input and output. A microcomputer also has *software* which are programs that tell a computer what to do.

Many businesses and schools have *networked* their microcomputers. In a network, microcomputers are connected so that data can be transmitted between them. Because a network can include a large number of computers, it can perform many of the functions of a mainframe. As network technology progresses, the distinction between a mainframe computer and networked microcomputers is rapidly becoming blurred.

1.18 The Components of a Microcomputer

Microcomputers contain four types of components:

1. **Input Devices:** tools from which the computer can accept data. A keyboard, disk drives, and a mouse are all examples of input devices.

2. **Memory:** chips inside the computer where data can be stored electronically.

3. **Central Processing Unit (CPU):** a chip inside the computer that processes data and controls the flow of data between the computer's other units. It is here that the computer makes decisions.

4. **Output Devices:** a device that displays or stores processed data. Monitors and printers are the most common visual output devices and disk drives are the most common storage output devices.

This diagram illustrates the direction in which data flows between the separate components:

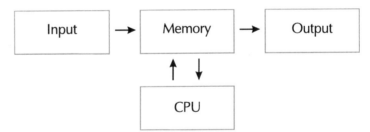

Notice that all information first flows through the CPU. Because one of the tasks of the CPU is to control the order in which tasks are completed, it is often referred to as the "brain" of the computer. However, this comparison with the human brain has an important flaw. The CPU only executes tasks according to the instructions it has been given; it cannot think for itself.

1.19 Memory

Computers have two types of memory contained on chips, *ROM* and *RAM*. Read Only Memory, or ROM, contains the most basic operating instructions for the computer. It is a permanent part of the computer and cannot be changed. The instructions in ROM enable the computer to complete simple jobs such as placing a character on the screen or checking the keyboard to see if any keys have been pressed.

Random Access Memory, or RAM, is temporary memory where data and instructions can be stored. Data stored here can be changed or erased. When the computer is first turned on, this part of memory is empty and, when turned off, any data it stores is lost. Because RAM storage is temporary, computers use disks as auxiliary memory storage. Before turning the computer off, the data stored in RAM can be saved as output on a disk so that it can be used again at a later time.

1.20 The Central Processing Unit

The Central Processing Unit (CPU) directs all the activities of the computer. It can only follow instructions that it gets from ROM or from a program in RAM. In following these instructions, the CPU guides the processing of information throughout the computer.

A CPU chip many times more powerful than the Mark I measures about 2 inches by 2 inches

The Arithmetic Logic Unit, or *ALU*, is the part of the CPU where the "intelligence" of the computer is located. It can perform only two operations: adding numbers and comparing numbers. How does the computer subtract, multiply, or divide numbers if the ALU can only add and compare numbers? The ALU does this by turning problems like multiplication and division into addition problems. This would seem to be a very inefficient way of doing things, but it works because the ALU is so fast. For example, to solve the problem 5×2, the computer adds five twos, $2 + 2 + 2 + 2 + 2$, to calculate the answer, 10. The ALU is so fast that the time needed to carry out a single addition of this type is measured in *nanoseconds* (billionths of a second). The other job of the ALU is to compare numbers and then determine whether a number is greater than, less than, or equal to another number. This ability is the basis of the computer's decision-making power.

1.21 Bits and Bytes

The electrical circuits on a chip have one of two states, OFF or ON. Therefore, a system was developed that uses two numbers to represent the states: 0 for OFF and 1 for ON. A light switch is similar to a single computer circuit. If the light is off, it represents a 0, and if on, a 1. This number system, which uses only two digits, is called the *binary* (base 2) number system. Each 0 or 1 in the binary code is called a *bit* (BInary digiT) and these bits are grouped by the computer into 8-bit units called *bytes*.

Humans find a system with ten digits, 0 to 9, easier to use primarily because we have ten fingers. The computer uses binary digits to express not only numbers, but all information, including letters of the alphabet. Because of this a special code had to be established to translate numbers, letters and characters into binary digits. This code has been standardized for computers as the American Standard Code for Information Interchange, or *ASCII*. In this code, each letter of the alphabet, both uppercase and lowercase, and each symbol, digit, and special control function used by the computer is represented by a number. The name JIM, for example, is translated by the computer into the ASCII numbers 74, 73, 77. In turn, these numbers are then stored by the computer in binary:

Letter	ASCII	Binary code
J	74	01001010
I	73	01001001
M	77	01001101

Each ASCII code requires one byte in memory. Note how eight 0s and 1s are used to represent each letter in JIM in binary form.

The size of the RAM memory in a computer is also measured in bytes. For example, a computer might have 8MB of RAM. In computers and electronics *MB* stands for *megabytes* where mega represents 2^{20} or 1,048,576 bytes and *GB* stands for *gigabytes*, which is 2^{30} bytes. Bytes are sometimes described as *kilobytes*, for example 256K. The *K* comes from the word *kilo* and represents 2^{10} or 1024. Therefore, 64K of memory is really 64×2^{10} which equals 65,536 bytes.

1.22 Storage Devices

Most microcomputers today have three disk drives: a diskette drive, a CD-ROM drive, and a hard disk drive. The diskette drive and CD-ROM drive are accessible from outside the base unit, and the hard disk is completely contained inside the base unit. All three types of disks are used to store files so that they can be reused:

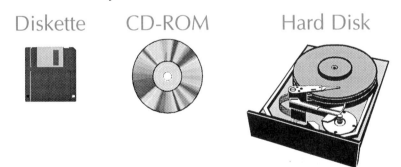

Diskette   CD-ROM   Hard Disk

Data can be stored on a diskette, a CD-ROM, or a hard disk

Sometimes called a floppy disk, diskettes are made of a mylar (thin polyester film) disk that is coated with a magnetic material and then loosely encased in hard plastic. Each diskette has a capacity of 1.44MB. The CD-ROM drive reads data from CD-ROMs (an acronym for compact disc, read-only memory). The discs are made of mylar with a reflective coating that is sealed in clear, hard plastic. Each CD-ROM can store over 600 megabytes of data, equal to the storage capacity of over 430 diskettes. Hard disks are made of an aluminum disk coated with a magnetic material. Unlike diskettes and CD-ROMs, hard disks are permanently installed inside the hard disk drive. Each hard drive may have multiple disks inside, and therefore have large storage capacities of 1GB or more.

Although the files on a CD-ROM are permanent and cannot be changed, the files stored on diskettes and hard disks can be added to, deleted, and modified.

1.23 Operating Systems

All microcomputers use an operating system to create a *user friendly* environment. An *operating system* is software that allows the user to communicate with the computer using the keyboard and mouse. This software automatically runs when the computer is turned on. Operating systems include Windows 95, MS-DOS (Microsoft Disk Operating System) and Unix (used with many mainframes).

Some operating systems, such as Windows 95, are a special kind of program known as a *graphical user interface*, or GUI (pronounced "gooey"). When a GUI is running it provides the user with pictures called *icons* that are used to run other programs. The Windows 95 screen is called the *Desktop* and displays icons and the Start button. The Start button displays a list of commands from which other programs can be run. Each running program is displayed in its own area of the screen called a *window*, discussed in Chapter Three.

1.24 Applications Software

One of the most useful ways in which a computer can be used is to run commercially produced *applications software*. This is software written by professional programmers to perform specific applications or tasks. Applications software is designed to communicate to the computer through a specific operating system. In this text we will use an applications program named Works, designed to work with Windows 95, which includes three common applications: word processing, database, and spreadsheet.

Word processors allow us to enter text from the keyboard into the computer and then manipulate it electronically. We will be able to insert and delete text, correct mistakes, move text, and perform numerous other functions all on the computer screen. The text can then be printed.

Databases allow us to store and manipulate large quantities of data using the computer. For example, a database can store the names, addresses, grades and extracurricular activities for all of the students in a school. It will be possible to add or delete data and produce printed reports using the database.

Spreadsheets primarily store numeric data which can then be used in calculations. We will use a spreadsheet to store a teacher's grades and then calculate student averages. The primary advantage of a computerized spreadsheet is its ability to automatically update the calculations should the data it stores be changed.

One common factor shared by these three applications is their ability to store data on disk in a *file*. A file is simply a collection of data stored on a disk in a form the computer can read. Unlike the computer's RAM memory, data placed in a file is not erased when the computer's power is turned off. This way, the applications program can access the information again and again.

A major advantage of Works is that it is an *integrated* program. This means that a single program performs all three applications, allowing data stored in a file by one application to be transferred to another. Later in this course you will produce a database file of names and addresses and then use this file in conjunction with a word processor file to produce personalized letters to everyone in the database file.

Besides integrated programs like Works there are numerous other applications programs available. There are programs that can be used by musicians to produce musical scores and then play them on a synthesizer, programs that assist an architect in designing a building, programs that produce the special effects graphics that you see in the movies and on television, and much more. This book, for example, has been created and typeset using applications software.

As we progress in this text the usefulness of applications software will become increasingly obvious. With computers becoming more widely used, applications software is being written to assist people in almost every profession. Learning to use Works will give you an idea of how the computer and applications software can be applied to help solve many types of problems.

1.25 Advantages of a Computer

Although computers cannot think, they do have some advantages over the human brain. For example, suppose you were given a list of ten numbers (input) and were asked to first, remember them (memory), second, calculate their average (process), and third, write down the average (output). In so doing, you would perform the same four tasks as a computer. Now suppose you were given 100 or 1,000 numbers and asked to calculate the average. Chances are you would get confused and tired performing all the calculations. The computer would have none of these problems. It would accurately remember all of the data and be able to quickly calculate the answers. The computer, therefore, has three important advantages over the human brain:

1. Reliable memory, with the ability to store and recall large amounts of data over long periods of time.
2. Speed, which enables it to process data quickly.
3. The ability to work 24 hours a day without rest.

Remember, however, that as reliable and fast as a computer is, it is only as smart as the instructions it is given by a program.

Chapter Summary

A computer is an electronic machine that accepts data, processes it according to specific instructions, and provides results as new information.

Humans have searched for a machine to calculate and record data for thousands of years. The earliest of these devices were mechanical, requiring gears, wheels and levers, and were often unreliable. The advent of electricity brought about machines which used vacuum tubes, and were capable of performing thousands of calculations a minute. The unreliability of the vacuum tube lead to the development of the transistor and integrated circuit. Von Neumann's concept of the central processing unit allowed computers to solve many different problems by simply typing new instructions at a keyboard. Computers became much smaller when vacuum tubes were replaced with transistors in the 1960s. A further reduction in size and cost came with the development of integrated circuits, also called chips. Programming languages were developed so programmers could write English-like instructions that the computer could translate.

Mainframes are large, expensive computers that can carry out many tasks at the same time. However, with the invention of the microprocessor, today's microcomputers rival the performance of older mainframes. All computers have several parts in common: (1) input devices (keyboard, mouse, disk drive) for entering data and commands, (2) memory for storing commands and data, (3) a central processing unit for controlling the operations of the computer, and (4) output devices (monitor, printer) for viewing the processed information. In general, a computer is a machine which accepts information, processes it according to some specific instructions in the form of software, and then returns new information as output.

Today's microcomputer makes use of a CPU on a chip, the microprocessor, which controls the actions of the computer. Memory chips come in two forms, RAM, which can be erased and used over, and ROM, which is permanent. Because the contents of RAM are lost when the computer's power is turned off, disks are used to store data. The CPU contains a special device called the Arithmetic Logic Unit (ALU) which performs any math or comparison operations.

The computer uses binary digits grouped into bytes to express all information. The ASCII code translates numbers and letters into binary digits. The diskette drive, CD-ROM drive, and hard disk drive all store files so that they can be reused.

We will be using the Microsoft Works application software with the Windows 95 operating system to introduce the word processor, database, and spreadsheet.

Vocabulary

Abacus - Ancient counting device which used beads on a frame.
ALU - Arithmetic Logic Unit, the part of the CPU that handles math operations.
Applications software - Commercially produced programs written to perform specific tasks such as word processing.
ASCII - American Standard Code for Information Interchange, the code used for representing characters in the computer.
Binary - Number system used by all computers. Uses only two digits (base 2).
Bit - Binary Digit, a single 0 or 1 in a binary number.
Byte - A group of 8 bits.
Chips - Tiny integrated circuits etched into blocks of silicon.
CPU - Central Processing Unit, the device which electronically controls the functions of the computer.

Data - Information either entered into or produced by the computer.

Debug - To remove errors from a computer program.

Desktop - The Windows 95 screen.

File - Collection of data stored on a disk in a form the computer can read.

GUI (Graphical User Interface) - An operating system that contains icons that are used to run other programs.

Hardware - Physical devices which make up the computer and its peripherals.

Icon - A picture on the screen used to run other programs.

Input - Data used by the computer.

Integrated program - A single program that performs multiple applications.

K, kilobyte - Measurement of computer memory capacity. 1024 bytes.

Keyboard - Device resembling a typewriter used for inputting data into a computer.

Machine language - Computer program written in binary code, just 0s and 1s.

MB, megabyte - Measurement of computer memory capacity. 1,048,576 bytes.

Memory - Electronic storage used by the computer.

Microprocessor - CPU on a single chip.

Monitor - Television-like device used to display computer output.

Nanosecond - Billionths of a second.

Output - Data produced by a computer program.

Operating System - Software that allows the user to communicate with the computer using the keyboard and mouse.

Program - Series of instructions written in a special language directing the computer to perform certain tasks.

PC - Personal Computer, a small computer employing a microprocessor.

RAM - Random Access Memory. Memory which the computer can both read and write.

ROM - Read Only Memory. Memory from which the computer can only read.

Software - Computer programs.

Window - The area of the screen where a program is displayed.

Windows 95 - The operating system used to run Works.

Reviews

Sections 1.1 — 1.10

1. What is a computer program?

2. Was Pascal's Pascaline a computer? Why or why not?

3. Why didn't early calculating devices work well?

4. a) What was the first calculating machine to make use of punched cards?
   b) What were the cards used for?

5. If successful, could Babbage's Analytical Engine have been considered a computer? Why or why not?

6. Why did scientists and business people want computers rather than calculators?

7. What is the primary difference between a computer and a calculator?

8. a) The Mark I was considered a calculator rather than a computer. Why?
   b) Why was the Mark I unreliable?
   c) What was the most important difference between the ENIAC and Mark I?

Sections 1.11 — 1.16

9. John von Neumann made one of the most important contributions to the development of modern computers. What was this contribution and why was it so important?

10. What made early computers so expensive?

11. What two innovations made the IBM Model 650 superior to earlier computers?

12. High-level programming languages such as Fortran and Basic were developed in the 1960s. Why were they important?

13. a) What is an integrated circuit?
    b) In what ways is it superior to transistors?

14. What invention made the microcomputer possible?

15. Compare a microcomputer with ENIAC. What advantages does the microcomputer have?

16. List three jobs which could best be performed on each of the following computers:
    a) mainframe computer
    b) microcomputer

Sections 1.17 — 1.25

17. List five hardware components of a personal computer.

18. Suppose you were to use a computer to store the names of all the students in your school and then print only those names beginning with the letter "P." Explain how each of the four activities needed to process data would be performed.

19. a) What is computer hardware?
    b) What is software?

20. Which of the four types of components in a microcomputer would be used to perform each of the following tasks?
    a) display a column of grade averages
    b) calculate grade averages
    c) store electronically a set of grades
    d) type in a set of grades
    e) decide which of two grades was higher
    f) store a set of grades outside the computer

21. What is the primary difference between the two types of memory in a computer?

22. How would the computer solve the problem 138×29?

23. Why do computers use binary numbers?

24. a) What is a bit?
    b) A byte?
    c) A K?

An Introduction to Computing Using Microsoft Works

25. How does the computer store a person's name in memory?

26. How many bytes of RAM are in a 4MB computer?

27. List three types of disk drives.

28. a) What is an operating system?
    b) List three operating systems.

29. What is an icon and what is it used for?

30. What is a GUI?

31. What is applications software?

32. What is a word processor used for?

33. What is a database used for?

34. What is a spreadsheet used for?

35. List three advantages of a computer.

36. a) List three tasks for which a computer would be better than a human working without a computer. Tell why the computer is better.
    b) List three tasks for which a human would be better than a computer. Tell why the human is better.

1

An Introduction to Computing Using Microsoft Works

Chapter Two
Introducing the Word Processor

Save

Exit Works

Close

Open

Print

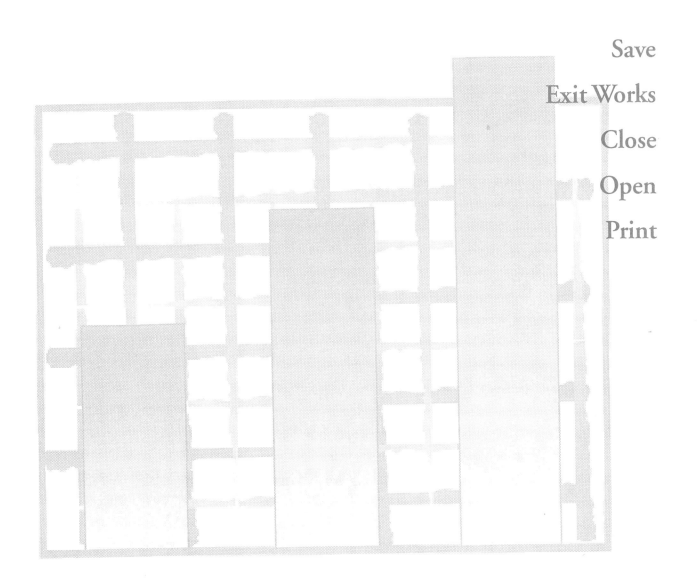

Objectives

After completing this chapter you will be able to:

1. Describe a word processor.

2. Explain why the word processor is ideal for producing a variety of different documents.

3. Start Works and create a word processor file.

4. Use the word processor to enter and modify text.

5. Select menus from the Menu bar and choose different commands from them.

6. Save a file.

7. Close a file.

8. Open a file.

9. Use the scroll bars to view a document.

10. Print a word processor file.

11. Exit Works properly.

2

This chapter describes what a word processor is and why it is a powerful tool for preparing documents. You will learn how to use the Works word processor to create, edit, print, and save documents.

2.1 What is a Word Processor?

A *word processor* is a computer application that is used to produce easy to read, professional-looking documents. It is a powerful tool that can be used to easily make changes (edit) in a document and to modify the look (format) of a document in a number of different ways. A document created in the word processor is edited electronically on the computer screen and printed later. A word processor document can be saved and then recalled at any time so that changes can be made or another copy printed.

Using a word processor allows you to easily refine a document until what has been written truly reflects what you wish to say. To correct an error or make an editing change, only those words requiring changes need to be retyped. Words, phrases, and whole paragraphs can be moved, copied, changed, or deleted. It is even possible to copy text·from one document to another so that lengthy paragraphs or several pages of text can be included in the document without having to retype them.

With a word processor, a document can be viewed on the screen as it will appear when printed. This provides flexibility in deciding how a document should look. Does the document look better with a half-inch margin or an inch margin? Should text be double spaced or single spaced?

2.2 How To Use This Text

Throughout this text new commands and procedures are introduced in a two step process. First, the command or procedure is discussed. Each discussion section describes how to use the command and gives examples of when the command should be applied. The discussion is followed by a section titled *Practice*. Each Practice leads you through a step-by-step example of how to use the command. You will perform the steps given in a Practice on the computer using Works. Practices also serve as reviews of the steps required to perform specific tasks.

Because the discussion sections explain the details of a command or procedure, you should read them carefully before proceeding to the Practices. When performing a Practice, do every step in order as directed. Also, do not skip any Practices—because they are all related, skipping one may mean that you do not get the correct result at the end of the next.

2.3 Using the Mouse

The computer comes equipped with a special input device called a *mouse* that is used to perform a variety of tasks:

The mouse

When the mouse is in use, the *mouse pointer* is displayed on the screen. One common shape of the mouse pointer is an arrow:

The mouse pointer

Sliding the mouse along the top of the table causes the mouse pointer to move on the screen; slide the mouse to the left and the mouse pointer moves to the left, slide the mouse to the right and the mouse pointer moves to the right.

Pointing

Moving the mouse to place the pointer on an object on the computer screen is called *pointing*. In this text, when we say to point to an object on the screen, we mean to move the mouse until the mouse pointer is placed on the object.

Clicking

An object on the computer screen can be selected by pressing the left button on the mouse and releasing it quickly. This type of selection is called *clicking*. When we say to select, or click, on an item, we mean to point to it and then press and release the mouse button.

Double-Clicking

A special form of clicking is the *double-click*. As the name implies, double-clicking means to point to an object and then press the left mouse button twice in rapid succession.

Dragging

The last mouse technique is called *dragging*. When we say to drag, we mean to hold the left mouse button while moving the mouse. In some cases, an object can be moved by dragging it. To drag an object, point to it and then hold down the left mouse button while moving the mouse. When the object is in the desired location, release the mouse button. When we say to drag an object, we mean to point to it, hold the left mouse button and move the mouse.

2.4 Starting Works

Before Works can be started, the computer must have Windows 95, the disk operating system, loaded into memory. When the computer is turned on Windows 95 is automatically loaded from the computer's hard disk (inside the base unit) to the computer's memory in a process called *booting*.

The Windows 95 screen contains the Microsoft Works 4.0 icon:

Microsoft
Works 4.0

Double-clicking on the Microsoft Works icon starts the program.

If the Microsoft Works icon is not displayed on the Windows 95 screen, Works can be started by clicking on the Start button in the lower-left corner of the Windows 95 screen and then pointing to Programs. Pointing to Programs displays the names of the programs on the computer. Pointing to Microsoft Works 4.0 displays a group of items related to Microsoft Works. Clicking on Microsoft Works 4.0 in this group starts Works.

Practice 1

In this Practice you will boot the computer and then start Microsoft Works. The following instructions assume that the Microsoft Works 4.0 icon is displayed on your Windows 95 screen. If you are using Works on a network, ask your instructor how to start Works.

1) BOOT THE COMPUTER

    a. Turn on the computer and the monitor. After a few seconds, the computer automatically loads Windows 95 from disk.

    b. After Windows 95 has booted, the Microsoft Works icon is displayed on your screen:

Microsoft
Works 4.0

2) RUN THE WORKS PROGRAM

    a. Point to the Microsoft Works icon by moving the mouse until the mouse pointer is on the icon:

Microsoft
Works 4.0

    b. Double-click on the Works icon by pressing the left mouse button twice in rapid succession.

c. The Works program runs and displays a copyright screen:

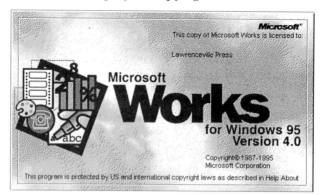

d. After a few seconds, the copyright screen is replaced by the Works Task Launcher dialog box, described in the next section.

2.5 Creating a New Document

A new, empty word processor document is created using the Works Task Launcher dialog box which is displayed after Works is started. Clicking on the Works Tools tab displays the following options:

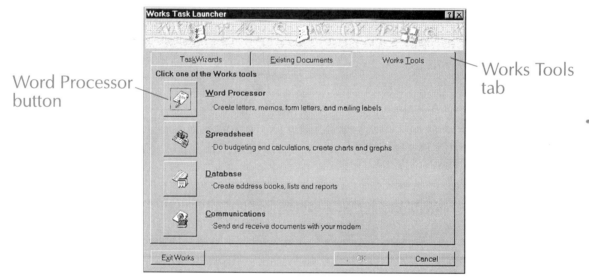

A new document is created using the Works Task Launcher dialog box

Clicking on the Word Processor button creates a new, empty word processor document.

An Introduction to Computing Using Microsoft Works

2.6 The Word Processor Screen

Word processor documents are displayed on the word processor screen. The screen below displays a new, empty word processor document. There are several features that will be important as you learn to use the word processor:

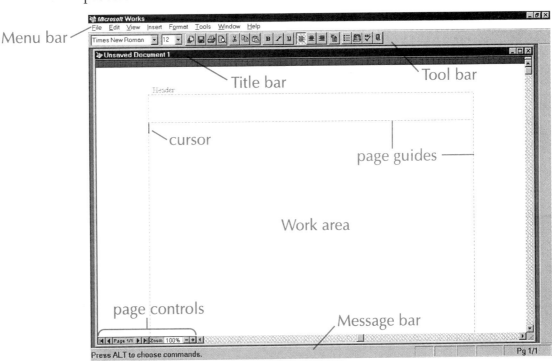

The Works word processor screen

Along the top of the screen is the *Menu bar*. Each word in the Menu bar is the name of a pull-down *menu* which contains commands that will be discussed later. The *Tool bar* provides shortcuts to some commonly used commands. Below the Tool bar is the *Title bar* which displays the name of the document. The name Unsaved Document 1 shown on the screen above is used temporarily by Works until you name the document. In the lower-left corner of the screen are *page controls*, also discussed later. Along the bottom of the screen is the *Message bar* which displays information about the command being executed.

The *Work area* is where text is entered and edited. Dotted lines called *page guides* indicate the boundaries of the Work area. The *cursor* is a blinking vertical line that indicates where the next character typed will be placed. It is always located in the Work area, and in a new word processor document the cursor is located in the upper-left corner of the body of Work area. At the top of the Work area is the Header area which is discussed in Chapter Three.

2.7 The Computer Keyboard and Word Processing

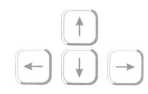

The cursor can be moved in a document's Work area, without erasing or entering text, by using the *cursor control keys*. Because these keys are marked with arrows (up, down, left, and right), they are also called *arrow keys*. The arrow keys can only be used to move the cursor where text has already been entered. To move the cursor down one line, press the key marked with a down arrow. Similarly, to move the cursor up, left, or right, use the key marked with the appropriate arrow. Each of the arrow keys is a *repeat key*, meaning that it will continue moving the cursor as long as it is held down.

To insert new text, the cursor control keys are used to place the cursor where the new text is to appear, and then the new text is typed. Any text following the insertion is moved to the right.

The Backspace key (sometimes marked with just an arrow) is used to erase a character. Pressing Backspace erases the character directly to the left of the cursor. When a character is deleted, any characters to its right are automatically moved over to fill the gap made by the deleted character. Do not confuse the Backspace key with the left-arrow key. Both move the cursor to the left, but Backspace erases characters and left arrow does not.

The Escape key (marked Esc) is used to cancel (escape from) the computer's current operation. The specific effect that pressing the Escape key will have depends on the operation being performed.

In the word processor, the Enter key is used to end a paragraph or to terminate any line that does not reach the right side of the screen. When Enter is pressed the cursor moves to the next line. Enter may also be used to instruct Works to accept a dialog box option (as will be explained later).

The Delete key (sometimes marked Del) is also used to erase a character. Pressing Delete erases the character directly to the right of the cursor. Any characters to the right of the deleted character are automatically moved over to fill the gap made by the deleted character.

Practice 2

In this Practice you will enter text into a new word processor document and then edit it by using the arrow and Backspace keys. Works should be started and the Works Task Launcher dialog box displayed from the last Practice.

1) CREATE A NEW WORD PROCESSOR DOCUMENT

    a. In the Works Task Launcher dialog box, click on the Works Tools tab.

    b. Click on the Word Processor button. A new, empty word processor document is displayed. Locate the Menu bar, Tool bar, Title bar, page guides, cursor, mouse pointer, and Message bar on your screen.

An Introduction to Computing Using Microsoft Works

2

2) TYPE THE FOLLOWING LINE INTO THE DOCUMENT

Carefully type the following line. Hold down the Shift key to generate the capital letter and exclamation point (!):

Hello, world!

Do not press Enter.

3) DELETE THE EXCLAMATION POINT

Press the Backspace key once to erase the exclamation point. Works automatically moves the cursor into the space formerly occupied by the erased character.

4) MOVE THE CURSOR WITHOUT ERASING ANY TEXT

Move the cursor to the right of the letter r by pressing the left-arrow key twice.

5) DELETE THE LETTER "r"

Press the Backspace key once. Note how the letters ld have moved over to fill the area where the letter r appeared. The document now contains the letters Hello, wold.

6) INSERT A CHARACTER

Press the R key. An r is inserted at the current cursor position, and Hello, world is now displayed.

7) MOVE THE CURSOR TO THE END OF THE LINE

Press the right-arrow key until the cursor is to the right of the d in world. Press the right-arrow key again several times. Works does not allow the cursor to be moved beyond the text.

8) DELETE ALL OF THE LETTERS IN THE LINE

Press the Backspace key to erase the d. Continue to hold down the Backspace key until all of the letters have been deleted.

9) ENTER THE FOLLOWING POEM

Type the following poem pressing the Enter key as indicated. Use the Backspace and arrow keys to correct any typing errors that you have made:

Jack and Jill went up the hill	*Enter*
to fetch a pail of water.	*Enter*
Jack fell down and broke his crown,	*Enter*
and Jill came tumbling after.	

Your document should be similar to the one shown on the next page.

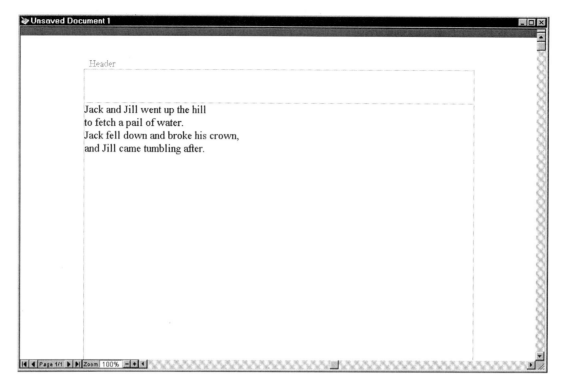

10) EDIT THE POEM

Insert new text and use the Backspace and arrow keys as necessary to make the following changes:

- Insert BIG and a space before the word pail
- Change the word water to gold
- Change the word crown to arm
- Change came tumbling after to stood up and laughed

<u>Check</u> - The edited poem should appear as follows:

> Jack and Jill went up the hill
> to fetch a BIG pail of gold.
> Jack fell down and broke his arm,
> and Jill stood up and laughed.

2.8 Using Menus

At the top of the word processor screen is the Menu bar. Each word on the bar is the name of a pull-down menu from which different commands can be selected. Clicking on a menu name displays the commands of that menu. For example, clicking on the word "File" displays the File menu:

An Introduction to Computing Using Microsoft Works

2

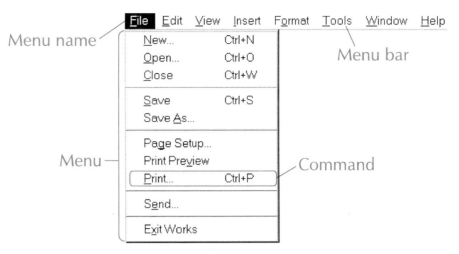

Menu name

Menu bar

Menu

Command

Menus are lists of commands

Pointing to a command on the menu highlights it. Highlighted commands are shown in reversed text (white letters on a dark background). Clicking on the highlighted command executes it. Clicking outside the menu or pressing the Escape key removes the menu from the screen.

On the menu, several commands have three dots (…) following the command name (New and Open are examples). This means that a dialog box asking for more information will appear when this command is executed. There are times when certain menu commands are displayed in dim text, meaning that these commands cannot be selected at this time.

Commands and menus may also be selected using the keyboard. Notice that one letter in each of the menu names is underlined. Pressing and holding the Alt key while pressing the underlined letter once displays that menu. For example, holding down the Alt key while pressing the F key displays the File menu. In this text, we denote this sequence of keystrokes as Alt+F, meaning to hold down the Alt key while pressing the F key once.

Each command in a displayed menu also has an underlined letter. Pressing that letter when the menu is displayed executes the command. To execute the Save command from the File menu Alt+F S is pressed.

2.9 Saving a Document

A new document is stored in the computer's memory until it is *saved*. When a document is saved a copy of what is currently stored in the computer's memory is placed on the computer's internal hard disk or on a diskette. The computer also retains the document in memory so that there are now two copies, one in memory that is displayed on the screen and one saved on disk.

It is important to save a document often because the computer's memory can only store data while the computer is turned on. When the computer is turned off any data in memory is lost. Once a document has been saved, it can later be loaded into memory for further editing or printing.

Another reason for saving a document is to prevent its accidental loss. A momentary power interruption can wipe everything out of the computer's memory. Even bumping the power cord may cause the memory to be erased. It is therefore a good practice to save a document repeatedly. It is also important to save before attempting to print because a problem involving the printer could cause the document to be lost.

Documents saved on disk are called *files* and must be given names to identify them. *Filenames* can be up to 255 characters long and can contain uppercase and lowercase letters, numbers, and spaces. Colons (:) and some other special characters may not be used. Examples of filenames are Letter, CHAPTER 5, and 2nd Memo. It is important to give a file a name that describes what it contains. For example, a file containing a letter to Suzy Lee is better named Suzy Letter or Letter to Suzy Lee rather than just Letter.

To save a document, select the Save command from the File menu. The Save As dialog box is displayed the first time a document is saved:

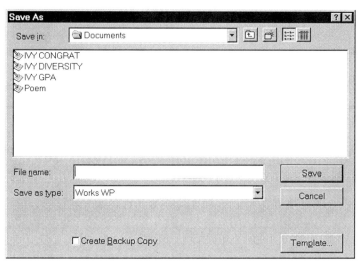

The Save command displays this dialog box

When this dialog box is displayed, type a descriptive name and then click on Save. A copy of the document is then placed on the disk using the name you supplied.

It is important to realize that any editing changes made to a previously saved file are not stored unless the file is saved again. It is also important to realize that saving an edited file *overwrites* the original copy on disk.

2.10 Using Diskettes

Files are often saved to diskette. It is important to handle diskettes carefully because they store files in a magnetic format that is vulnerable to dirt and heat. Observing the following rules will help to ensure that your diskettes give you trouble-free service:

1. Keep diskettes away from electrical and magnetic devices such as computer monitors, television sets, speakers, and any type of magnet.

2. Do not expose the diskette to either extreme cold or heat.

3. Store diskettes away from dust, dirt, and moisture.

4. Never touch the diskette's magnetic surface because this can damage it, destroying valuable data.

2.11 Dialog Boxes

A *dialog box* offers a group of options from which you may choose. Its purpose is to supply the information Works needs to execute a command. A dialog box can be removed without applying selected options by clicking on the Cancel button or by pressing the Escape key.

buttons

A common dialog box element is the *button.* Clicking once on a button initiates an action. In the Save As dialog box, clicking on the Save button saves a word processor document to disk.

Most dialog boxes display a default button. The *default button* has a solid outline, like the Save button in the Save As dialog box. The default button may be selected by pressing Enter.

entry boxes

Another common dialog box element is the entry box. An *entry box* is used to type information that may be needed by the command. For example, in the Save As dialog box, the File name entry box is used to tell Works the name of the file.

Each option in a dialog box has an underlined letter. Pressing and holding the Alt key and then pressing the underlined letter selects that option. For example, pressing Alt+S when the Save As dialog box is displayed selects the Save button.

2.12 Exiting Works

Whenever you want to stop using Works, the exit procedure should be performed. If Works is not properly exited, files in memory can be damaged or lost. **Never turn the computer off before following the exit procedure.** The proper way to exit Works is by selecting the Exit Works command from the File menu.

If you have created a new file or made editing changes to a previously saved file, Works informs you that any new information will be lost if the file is not saved before exiting:

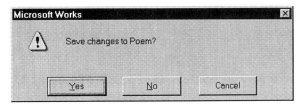

Works displays a warning if you attempt to exit
without saving a new or modified file

To save the changes, select the Yes button. If you do not wish to save the new version, select the No button and the previously saved version will remain unchanged. If the Exit Works command is selected by accident, select Cancel in the dialog box to return to the word processor.

Practice 3

In this Practice you will save the file created in Practice 2 using the name Poem. The document should still be displayed from the last Practice.

1) SELECT THE SAVE COMMAND FROM THE FILE MENU

   a.   On the Menu bar, click on the word File. The File menu is displayed.
   b.   Point to the Save command in the displayed menu. Save is highlighted.
   c.   Click on Save to execute the Save command. Works displays a dialog box prompting you to enter a filename for the document.

2) ENTER THE NAME OF THE FILE TO BE SAVED

   a.   The cursor is already in the File name entry box. Type Poem as the filename:

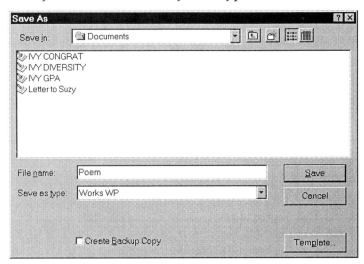

   b.   Press Enter to select the Save button. A copy of the file in memory is stored on the hard disk using the name Poem. Note that the filename Poem is displayed in the Title bar.

3) PROPERLY EXIT WORKS

   a.   On the Menu bar, click on File to display the File menu.
   b.   Point to the Exit Works command. Exit Works is highlighted.
   c.   Click on Exit Works to execute the command.

   The screen clears and the Windows 95 screen is again displayed, indicating that Works has been exited and that the computer is now ready to run a new program.

2.13 Word Wrap

When a word processor is used, it is not necessary to determine if the next word will fit on the end of the current line or if it must go on the next line. As you type, Works determines if there is sufficient room for a word at the end of a line. If there is not, the word is automatically moved to the beginning of the next line. This process is called *word wrap*.

The advantages of allowing Works to determine the arrangement of words on a line can be seen when deleting or inserting text. When new text is added to a line, any words to their right are moved over. If there is not enough room on the current line, those words which do not fit are moved to the next line. There may be a "domino" effect as words move from one line to the next. Similarly, when text is deleted, words are moved up from the lines below.

Because of the word wrap process, the Enter key should be used only to end a line of text. For example, you can specify the end of a paragraph by pressing the Enter key which moves the cursor to the beginning of the next line. Pressing Enter again creates a blank paragraph containing one line. Therefore, to end a paragraph and insert a blank line before the next paragraph, press the Enter key twice.

2.14 Closing Files

You will often need to work on more than one file after starting Works. When this is the case, the current file that you are working on should be saved and then *closed*. Closing a file means that it is removed from the screen and is no longer in the computer's memory. Selecting the Close command from the File menu closes the displayed file. If you attempt to close a file that has been edited but not saved, Works warns you before proceeding:

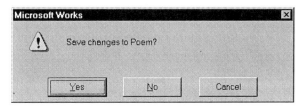

Works displays a warning before closing a modified file

If you wish to save the changes before closing, select the Yes button. If instead you wish to close the file without saving the edited version, select the No button. Cancel reverses the Close command and returns the cursor to the Work area.

It is a good practice to close any open files when you are finished working with them. Closed files are no longer in the computer's memory and therefore cannot be accidentally changed.

Practice 4

In this Practice you will create a document that has long lines of text in order to see how word wrap works.

1) START WORKS

Double-click on the Microsoft Works icon to start Works.

2) CREATE A NEW WORD PROCESSOR FILE

a. In the Works Task Launcher dialog box, click on the Works Tools tab.
b. Select the Word Processor button. A new, empty word processor document is displayed.

3) ENTER THE FOLLOWING STORY

Type the story below, allowing Works to determine the end of lines. Press Enter only at the end of a paragraph or line which does not reach the right margin such as in the dinner menu. Use the Enter key to create a blank line between each paragraph. Note that your lines will wrap at different positions than the text displayed below:

The annual Red Cross fund-raising dinner will be held in the main ballroom of the Downtown Hilton at 7:30 p.m. next Saturday night. Music for dancing will be provided by the Thom Steves Trio. All community members are invited.

The menu for the evening's event will be:

Fruit cup
Roast duck a l'Orange with wild rice stuffing
Garden salad
Mint parfait

After dinner, a reception will take place in the hotel's Algonquin Room. Dancing will continue until 11:30 p.m.

Review the text and use the Backspace and arrow keys to correct any typing errors.

4) SAVE THE FILE NAMING IT NEWS STORY

a. From the File menu, select the Save command. The Save As dialog box is displayed.
b. Type News Story and select the **Save** button. A copy of the document is saved on disk using the filename News Story.

5) EDIT THE STORY

Insert new text and use the Backspace and arrow keys as necessary to make the following changes to News Story:

- Insert the name of your town and a space before the words "Red Cross." Note how the rest of the paragraph is adjusted to make room.
- The location of the event was wrong. It will be held at the Eastside Sheraton, not the Downtown Hilton.
- The dessert has been changed from a Mint parfait to Double chocolate chip ice cream.
- The event will end at 11:00 p.m., not 11:30.

6) CREATE A NEW PARAGRAPH

a. Place the cursor just before the "A" that begins the sentence "All community members...."
b. Press Enter twice to insert a blank line and create a new paragraph.
c. At the end of the new paragraph, type a space and add the following sentence:

Tickets are $25.00 per person and are available from Mrs. Mitchell in the Red Cross office during regular business hours.

7) ADD A HEADLINE TO THE STORY

a. Move the cursor to the very beginning of the body of the document and type the following:

FUND RAISER TO BE HELD AT THE EASTSIDE SHERATON

Note how the rest of the text moves to the right to make room for the new text.

b. Press the Enter key twice to terminate the headline and insert a blank line between it and the rest of the story.

8) SAVE THE FILE AGAIN TO RETAIN THE EDITING CHANGES

From the File menu, select Save. The edited News Story is saved and the old file is overwritten and cannot be recovered.

Check - The completed document should be similar to the following:

FUND RAISER TO BE HELD AT THE EASTSIDE SHERATON

The annual Lawrenceville Red Cross fund-raising dinner will be held in the main ballroom of the Eastside Sheraton at 7:30 p.m. next Saturday night. Music for dancing will be provided by the Thom Steves Trio.

All community members are invited. Tickets are $25.00 per person and are available from Mrs. Mitchell in the Red Cross office during regular business hours.

The menu for the evening's event will be:

Fruit cup
Roast duck a l'Orange with wild rice stuffing
Garden salad
Double chocolate chip ice cream

After dinner, a reception will take place in the hotel's Algonquin Room. Dancing will continue until 11:00 p.m.

9) CLOSE THE FILE

From the File menu, select the Close command. The screen clears and the Works Task Launcher dialog box is displayed.

2.15 Opening a File

A saved file that has been closed must be loaded from disk to the computer's memory before it can be edited. This process is called *opening a file*. To open a file, select the Open command from the File menu which displays a dialog box similar to the following:

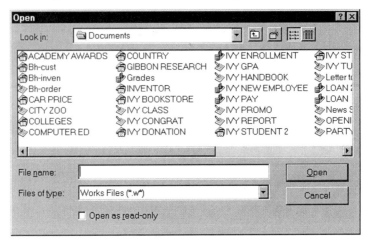

Saved documents are displayed in the Open dialog box

To open a document, click on its filename and select Open to transfer a copy of the document to the computer's memory and display it on the word processor screen.

2.16 Using the Tool Bar

Commonly performed actions such as saving a file can be performed using buttons on the Tool bar:

The Tool bar is used to execute commonly performed actions

Each button on the Tool bar represents a different action. Pointing to a button (not clicking) displays a balloon that describes the action that button will perform:

Balloons on the pointer indicate what a button is used for

Clicking on a button performs an action. Two commonly used buttons are described below. Other buttons are introduced when their corresponding command is introduced.

The Save button is clicked to save a document. If the document is new and has not yet been named, clicking on the Save button displays the Save As dialog box.

The Task Launcher button is clicked to display the Works Task Launcher dialog box.

An Introduction to Computing Using Microsoft Works

2.17 Printing a Document

Printing involves sending a copy of a document from the computer's memory to the printer. To do this, the computer must be connected to a printer. It is also important to make sure that the printer is turned on, is online, and that paper is positioned correctly. Before printing a document it should be saved because a problem involving the printer could cause the document to be lost.

To print a document, select the Print command from the File menu to display the Print dialog box. Your print dialog may be different depending on the printer you have selected, but you will be able to specify which pages to print and how many copies to make:

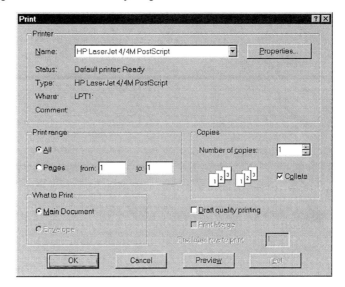

The Print dialog box

Because the default values are most normally used, you will usually just select the OK button to begin printing. If more than one copy of the document is to be printed, type the number required in the Number of copies box and then select OK.

The Print button on the Tool bar may also be used to print a document. However, clicking on this button does not display the Print dialog box. When the Print button is clicked one copy of the document is printed using the default settings.

Practice 5

In this Practice the News Story file will be opened, edited, and then re-saved. Works should be running. If not, start Works by following the instructions given in Practice 1.

1) OPEN NEWS STORY

    a. In the Works Task Launcher dialog box, click on Cancel. The dialog box is removed.
    b. From the File menu, select the Open command. The Open dialog box is displayed.
    c. In the Open dialog box, click on News Story.
    d. Select the Open button. A copy of News Story is transferred to the computer's memory and is displayed on screen.

2) EDIT THE FILE

Insert and delete text as necessary to make the following changes:

- The event will start at 7:00 p.m.
- The Schmenge Brothers Orchestra, not the Thom Steves Trio, will provide the evening's entertainment.
- Guests will have the choice of Fruit cup or lime sherbet for an appetizer.

3) USE THE TOOL BAR TO SAVE THE MODIFIED NEWS STORY

a. Point (do not click) to a button on the Tool bar. Note the balloon describing the action of the button. You may need to place the pointer near the bottom of the button.

b. Point to the Save button (⬛). Click on the Save button. The modified News Story is saved on disk, overwriting the old version.

Check - When complete, the modified document should be similar to:

FUND RAISER TO BE HELD AT THE EASTSIDE SHERATON

The annual Lawrenceville Red Cross fund-raising dinner will be held in the main ballroom of the Eastside Sheraton at 7:00 p.m. next Saturday night. Music for dancing will be provided by the Schmenge Brothers Orchestra.

All community members are invited. Tickets are $25.00 per person and are available from Mrs. Mitchell in the Red Cross office during regular business hours.

The menu for the evening's event will be:

Fruit cup or lime sherbet
Roast duck a l'Orange with wild rice stuffing
Garden salad
Double chocolate chip ice cream

After dinner, a reception will take place in the hotel's Algonquin Room. Dancing will continue until 11:00 p.m.

4) PRINT NEWS STORY

a. From the File menu, select the Print command. The Print dialog box is displayed.

b. Note the Number of copies option is 1. Select OK to print 1 copy of News Story.

c. From the File menu, select Close. News Story is removed from the screen.

2.18 Moving the Cursor

When the mouse pointer is moved within the page guides of the Work area, it changes from the arrow shape to the text or *I-Beam pointer* (I). Clicking the I-Beam pointer in a document moves the cursor to that position. Using the I-Beam pointer to move the cursor is a helpful technique when working with long documents. Because this technique is often used before inserting text, it is sometimes called creating an *insertion point*.

In the Practices, the arrow keys were used to move the cursor one character at a time. To move the cursor directly to the beginning of the word to its left, press Ctrl+left arrow. Similarly, pressing Ctrl+right arrow moves the cursor directly to the beginning of the word to its right. Press the Home key to move the cursor to the beginning of the line of text it is in. The End key moves the cursor to the end of the line of text it is in.

2.19 Screen Scroll

Most documents are too long to be displayed entirely on the screen. Bringing hidden parts of a document into view is called *screen scroll*. The scroll bars on the right side and bottom of the window are used to scroll a document:

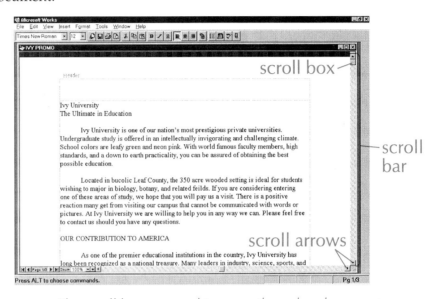

The scroll bars are used to move through a document

Clicking on the arrows in the vertical and horizontal scroll bars will move the document accordingly. Any text scrolled off the screen is not lost, it is just not displayed at that time.

Clicking once on the down arrow moves the document in the Work area up one line. Clicking once on the up arrow moves the document down one line. When working with long documents it can be time consuming to move in such small increments. The document can be scrolled in larger increments by dragging the scroll box. For example, dragging the scroll box to the middle of the scroll bar displays the middle of the document. The scroll arrows can then be used to make fine adjustments. Clicking on the scroll bar above or below the scroll box scrolls the document by one screen towards the top or bottom of the document.

The cursor does not move when the scroll bars are used to scroll a document. To move the cursor when scrolling, the keyboard must be used. The up-arrow and down-arrow keys move the cursor one line at a time, scrolling the document when necessary. The Page Up and Page Down keys scroll the document one screen towards the top or bottom of the document. To move the cursor directly to the first character in a document, press Ctrl+Home. Pressing Ctrl+End moves the cursor directly after the last character in the document.

Practice 6

In this Practice a document will be scrolled and the cursor moved by using the mouse. A previously created word processor file named SCROLL will be opened. Each line in SCROLL is numbered to help demonstrate screen scroll. Start Works if you have not already done so.

1) OPEN SCROLL

    a. If the Works Task Launcher dialog box is displayed, click on Cancel to remove it.
    b. From the File menu, select Open. The Open dialog box is displayed.
    c. Click on SCROLL to highlight it.
    d. Select the Open button. SCROLL is opened.

2) MOVE THE CURSOR TO THE BOTTOM OF THE SCREEN

Press the down-arrow key until the cursor is on the last line in the currently displayed screen. The document is automatically scrolled.

3) SCROLL DOWN 5 LINES USING THE SCROLL ARROW

Click the pointer on the down arrow (▼) in the vertical scroll bar 5 times. Note that each time the down arrow is selected, a line scrolls off the top of the screen, and the next line in the document appears from the bottom.

4) PLACE THE CURSOR IN THE LAST LINE IN THE DOCUMENT

    a. Point to the scroll box in the vertical scroll bar.
    b. Drag the scroll box to the bottom of the scroll bar.
    c. Release the button. The last line in the document, line number 90, is displayed.
    d. Move the pointer into the Work area. The I-Beam pointer is displayed.
    e. Move the I-Beam pointer within the text of line number 90.
    f. Click the left mouse button. The cursor is moved to the position of the I-Beam pointer.

5) SCROLL TO THE FIRST LINE IN THE DOCUMENT

    a. Click on the up arrow in the vertical scroll bar and hold down the button. The screen will scroll as long as the button is held down. Note how the scroll box moves in the bar as the screen scrolls. Also note that the cursor does not move as the document is being scrolled.
    b. When line 1 is displayed, release the button.

6) SCROLL THE DOCUMENT

    a. Drag the scroll box to the middle of the scroll bar. The middle of the document is displayed.
    b. Click the I-Beam pointer within the text of line number 50 to place the cursor.
    c. Press the up-arrow key until line 1 is again displayed.

7) EXIT WORKS

From the File menu, select Exit Works. Select No in the displayed dialog box.

2 | Chapter Summary

Professional looking documents can be produced quickly and efficiently using a word processor. Word processor documents can be changed easily; text can be inserted, deleted, or modified without retyping the entire document. A document can be saved and later recalled so that it can be further edited or another copy printed.

Works uses a mouse as a special input device. An object is selected on the screen by pointing to the object and then pressing the left mouse button once (clicking). Some objects are selected by double-clicking which is pressing the button twice in rapid succession. Dragging is the technique of holding down the mouse button while moving the mouse.

The computer needs the Windows 95 operating system to run. Once Windows 95 is loaded, the Works program can be started by double-clicking on the Microsoft Works icon. Icons are small pictures that are used to run programs and perform tasks. After Works loads, an opening copyright screen is displayed followed by the Works Task Launcher dialog box. The Works Task Launcher dialog box is used to create a new word processor document.

A new word processor document is created by clicking on the Word Processor button displayed in the Works Tools options of the Works Task Launcher dialog box. Along the top of the word processor screen is the Menu bar. Each word in the Menu bar is the name of a pull-down menu. A menu is displayed by clicking on its name. Below the Menu bar is the Tool bar. The Tool bar contains buttons that are clicked to execute commands or to perform an action. In the center of the screen is the Work area which is enclosed by page guides and contains the cursor. At the bottom of the word processor screen is the Message bar. It displays information about the command being executed.

Cursor control keys, also called arrow keys, are used to move the cursor through the document without changing any of the text. The Backspace key is used to remove the character to the left of the cursor. The Escape key is used to remove a dialog box or menu from the screen. The Enter key is used to end a paragraph or accept a dialog box option.

Menus contain commands. Clicking on the menu name displays its list of commands, and clicking on the desired command executes that command. Command names that include three dots (…) display a dialog box where information is entered for the command. A command can also be executed using the Alt key.

A document can be saved to a computer's hard disk or to a diskette by executing the Save command from the File menu. When a file is saved it is given a name of up to 255 characters which is then used to identify it. Each filename must be unique. To avoid possible data loss, a file must be saved before printing. Printing a document is accomplished by executing the Print command from the File menu.

Dialog boxes contain buttons and sometimes entry boxes. The default button has a solid outline and can be selected by clicking on it or by pressing the Enter key. Information can be typed into an entry box. The Alt key can also be used to select dialog box options.

Works determines if there is sufficient room for a word at the end of a line. If there is not, the word is automatically moved to the beginning of the next line in a process called word wrap. When new words are added to a line, any words to their right are automatically moved over. Deleting words moves existing words to the left to fill any empty space.

To remove a file from the computer's memory it must be closed by using the Close command from the File menu. This frees computer memory and protects the file from loss caused by an accident such as a power failure. Previously created files can be opened by selecting the Open command. To exit Works the Exit Works command from the File menu is executed.

The word processor screen displays a limited number of lines of a document at a time. Bringing hidden parts of a document into view is called screen scroll. The scroll bars below and on the right of the word processor screen are used to scroll through a document.

This chapter discussed the commands and procedures necessary to produce a word processor document. The major steps in producing such a document are:

1. Boot Windows 95 and load the Works program.
2. Display the word processor file on the screen—either by creating a new file or opening a previously created file.
3. Enter or edit the document.
4. Save the document.
5. Print the document if desired.
6. Close the document.
7. Exit Works.

Vocabulary

Alt key - A key that can be used to select commands from a menu. May also be used to select dialog box options.

Arrow keys - Four keys that move the cursor up, down, right, and left on the screen without changing any text. Also called cursor control keys.

Backspace key - A key that erases the character directly to the left of the cursor.

Boot - To turn on the computer and load Windows 95 from disk into the computer memory.

Button - Dialog box option that is used to initiate an action. Buttons are selected by clicking on them with the mouse.

Cancel button - Button available in most dialog boxes that removes the dialog box and returns to the Works screen without making changes.

Character - Any letter, number, or symbol that can be displayed on the computer screen.

Clicking - Placing the mouse pointer on an object and quickly pressing and releasing the left mouse button once.

Closed file - A file that has been removed from the screen and computer's memory.

Cursor - A blinking vertical line on the screen which indicates where characters entered from the keyboard are placed.

Cursor control keys - Keys used to move the cursor without having any effect on the text. See also Arrow keys.

Default - An option that is preselected. It will be used if no other option is chosen.

Delete key - A key that erases the character directly to the right of the cursor.

Dialog box - Used to select options required by a command.

2

Document - Any material that can be typed into the word processor, such as a letter, research paper, or story. Also called a file. See File.

Double-clicking - Placing the mouse pointer on an object and pressing the left mouse button twice in rapid succession.

Dragging - Holding down the left mouse button while moving the mouse.

Enter key - Key used to indicate the end of an entry or to select the default option in a dialog box. In word processing Enter is pressed at the end of each paragraph.

Entry box - Dialog box option that is used to type information into.

Escape key - A key used to cancel (escape from) the Works current operation.

Exit - To end the Works program, remove it from memory, and return to Windows 95.

File - A document that is stored on disk.

Filename - A name for a file stored on disk, up to 255 characters in length. Colons (:) and some other special characters may not be used in filenames.

I-Beam pointer - The shape of the mouse pointer when moved onto the text of a document. Clicking the mouse places the cursor at the position of the I-Beam pointer.

Icon - A small picture that when double-clicked starts a program or performs a task.

Insertion point - The position of the cursor.

Menu - A list of commands.

Menu bar - A horizontal bar at the very top of the screen showing names of available menus.

Message bar - Displays information about the command being executed.

Mouse - Input device that is used to move the mouse pointer and perform a variety of tasks.

Mouse pointer - A shape displayed on the screen when the mouse is in use.

Opening a file - The process where a saved file is transferred from disk to the computer's memory and displayed on the word processor screen.

Page guides - Dotted lines that indicate the boundaries of the Work area.

Pointing - Placing the mouse pointer on an object located on the screen.

Print - To send a copy of the document currently displayed on screen to the printer.

Repeat key - A key that repeats its action when held down. The left-arrow key is one example of a repeat key.

Save - Transfer a document from the computer's memory to the computer's hard disk or to a diskette.

Screen scroll - Bringing hidden parts of a document into view.

Scroll - Using the scroll bars, keyboard, or mouse to bring hidden parts of a document into view.

Scroll bars - Used to display different parts of a document, they are located at the bottom and on the right of the screen.

Text - Any character or group of characters in a document.

Title bar - A bar at the top of the document used to display the filename.

Tool bar - Provides shortcuts to commonly performed commands and actions.

Windows 95 - The disk operating system used to run Works.

Word processor - Computer application that allows text to be entered, edited, printed, and saved.

Word wrap - Process Works uses to decide whether to keep a word on the current line, or move it to the next line based on the amount of space left on the line.

Work area - Area of the word processor screen where text is entered and edited. Page guides enclose the Work area.

Works Task Launcher dialog box - Contains options for creating new files.

Reviews

Sections 2.1 — 2.6

1. List three reasons to use a word processor.

2. How can a word processor be used to easily refine what you have written?

3. Name three different types of organizations that could benefit from using word processors. Explain how each would benefit.

4. What is pointing and how is it done?

5. a) What is clicking?
   b) What is double-clicking?

6. List the steps required to drag an object.

7. What is Windows 95 and what is it used for?

8. What is meant by "booting" the computer?

9. What is the Microsoft Works icon used for?

10. What must be done in the Works Task Launcher dialog box to create a new word processor document?

11. What is the Work area of the word processor screen used for?

12. What is the cursor?

Sections 2.7 — 2.14

13. What is each of the following keys used for?
    a) Escape key
    b) Enter key
    c) Backspace key

14. How may the cursor be moved down 3 lines and then 10 places to the right without affecting text?

15. What does pressing the Enter key do when typing text in the word processor?

16. What is the difference between pressing the Backspace key four times and the left-arrow key four times when the cursor is located in the middle of a line of text?

17. List the steps required to change the word "men" to "people" in the sentence:

    > Now is the time for all good men to come to the aid of the party.

18. a) How is a menu displayed?
    b) How can a menu be removed from the screen without executing a command?

19. a) What is a file?
    b) Why is a file given a name?
    c) What limitations are placed on the names which may be given to a file?

20. List three reasons why it is important to save a word processor document.

21. If you are working on a word processor document and the power goes off, how can you retrieve the document if it has not been previously saved on disk?

22. When a file is saved where does it go? Is it removed from the computer's memory?

23. a) If a previously saved file is edited will the changes be automatically made to the file on disk, or must the file be saved again?
    b) What happens to an original file if an edited version of the same file is saved?

24. a) Why is it important to take good care of a diskette?
    b) What should be avoided when handling or storing a diskette?

25. What is a dialog box and what is it used for?

26. If you display a dialog box by mistake how can you remove it from the screen?

27. How can the default button be selected without using the mouse?

28. How can the Alt key be used to select a dialog box option?

2

29. a) Why is it important to exit Works properly?
    b) List the steps required to exit Works starting from the word processor screen so that the document currently being worked on is saved.

30. What is word wrap?

31. a) What happens to a file when it is closed? Is it automatically saved?
    b) Why is it important to close a file when you are finished working with it?

Sections 2.15 — 2.19
32. List the steps required to transfer a previously saved file from disk into the computer's memory?

33. What is the Tool bar used for?

34. How can a document be saved without using the Save command from the File menu?

35. a) Why is it important to save a document before printing it?
    b) What menu and command is used to print a document?

36. What is the shape of the mouse pointer when the pointer is within the page guides of a document?

37. How can the mouse be used to move the cursor?

38. a) What is screen scroll?
    b) Describe two ways to scroll through a document.

39. Describe how to use only the mouse to scroll to the end of a document and place the cursor in the last sentence.

40. What is the quickest way to move the cursor from the last sentence of a document to the first character in the document?

1. In a new word processing document create the letter below:

September 26, 1997

Mrs. Joan Kugler
123 Main St.
Reedsburg, WI 53959

Dear Joan:

I am writing to thank you for installing the CD-ROM drive on my computer. It's truly amazing to have so many reference books on a single compact disc.

Yesterday my manager praised me for the speech I wrote for her. The facts I retrieved from the CD were all timely, accurate, and interesting. I didn't tell her how easy it was to do.

Also, instead of calling the post office to get a zip code, I now look it up in seconds on the CD. Did you know that some staff members are asking management to add more CD-ROM drives to the Spring Budget Proposal?

You have improved the productivity of our entire department. Thanks again for all your help.

Sincerely,

Brian Esser
Administrative Assistant

---

a) Save the letter naming it Thank You.

b) Edit the letter as follows:

- Delete the word truly in the last sentence of the first paragraph.
- Delete the sentence I didn't tell her how easy it was to do.
- Change calling the post office to going to the mailroom
- Change some staff members to many of my co-workers
- Replace Brian Esser with your name.
- Add the following sentences to the beginning of the third paragraph:

Sometimes my manager asks me to quickly add new information to a memo or report. Having so many facts at my fingertips is great.

c) Save the modified Thank You and print a copy.

2

2. Word processors can be used to create documents that store a variety of information. It is interesting to think about how famous people in the past might have used a word processor.

a) In a new word processor document enter each of the sayings below. Press Enter twice at the end of each line to insert a blank line between each paragraph:

> An apple a day keeps the doctor away.
>
> A penny for your thoughts.
>
> Every cloud has a silver lining.
>
> A penny saved is a penny earned.
>
> Early to bed, early to rise, makes a man healthy, wealthy and wise.

b) Save the file naming it Benjamin in honor of Benjamin Franklin who wrote many of the famous sayings that appear above.

c) Check the document on screen for any errors and make the necessary corrections. Save the modified Benjamin to retain any changes you made.

d) Print a copy of Benjamin.

e) Edit the sayings as follows:

Saying 1: change apple to orange
Saying 2: change penny to dollar
Saying 3: change silver to gold
Saying 4: change penny to quarter (twice)
Saying 5: change man to person

f) Save the modified Benjamin and print a copy.

3. Your cousin is visiting you from out of town. The word processor can be used to create lists of directions that your cousin can follow to go from your house to various places.

a) In a new word processor document create lists of directions to the following places:

- Your school. Be sure to describe what time school gets out and where your cousin should meet you.
- A local fast food restaurant.
- The closest grocery store to your house. Include a list of items that your cousin should pick up for dinner.
- Your video rental club. Be sure to include your membership number in the directions so that your cousin can rent some videos.
- Your cousin is not the brightest person in the world. Leave complete instructions describing how to use your VCR to play a video.

b) Save the file naming it Directions and print a copy.

4. A. Student is interested in attending Ivy University and needs a letter of application.

a) In a new word processor document create the letter below that requests information and an application from Ivy U.

September 26, 1997

Ivy University
Admissions Department
1 College Court
Newton, IA 63343

Dear Admissions Department:

I am interested in attending Ivy University. I will graduate in 1998 and plan to major in medical communications. I have been president of the Student Congress for 4 years and captain of the Debate Team for 2 years. I have varsity letters in three sports and was a member of the All-State gymnastics and swim teams. My current grade point average is 3.95.

Please send a course catalog and application to me at this address:

A. Student
223 Main Street
Anytown, USA 11111

Thank you very much.

Sincerely,

A. Student

---

b) Check the document on screen for errors and make any necessary corrections.

c) Save the letter naming it College Apply and print a copy.

d) Modify the letter to contain your personal information as follows:

- Change the college name and address to a school you would like to attend. Be sure to also change the school name in the first sentence.
- Change the major in the second sentence to one of your choice.
- Change the activities listed in the letter to activities you have participated in.
- Change the GPA in the letter to your GPA.
- Change the name and address near the end of the letter to your name and address. Be sure to also change the name in the closing.

e) Save the modified College Apply and print a copy.

An Introduction to Computing Using Microsoft Works

2

5. Your local newspaper has an opening for an arts critic. In a new word processor document create a review of the last movie, concert, play, art show, or similar event that you attended. Save the file naming it Critic. Check your document on screen for errors and make any corrections. Save the modified Critic and print a copy.

6. A word processor can be used as a diary. In a new word processor document create a journal entry describing what you did last week. Add your plans for the upcoming weekend. Check your document on screen for errors and make any corrections. Save the file naming it Diary and print a copy.

7. Your English teacher has asked you to write an original essay entitled "How I spent my summer vacation." In a new word processor document create a 2 or 3 paragraph essay on this topic. Check your file on screen for errors and make any corrections. Save the file naming it Summer Essay and then print a copy.

8. In a new word processor document produce an advertisement for an upcoming dance or other special event. Be sure to include the date, time, location of the event, and cost (if any). Check your document on screen for errors and make any corrections. Save the file naming it Advertisement and print a copy.

9. Your science teacher has asked you to write a one page biography summarizing the life of the scientist you most admire. Include in the essay at least two references to outside sources. (Chapter Four will show you how to insert footnotes into a document.) In a new word processor document create the biography. Save the file naming it Science Bio. Check your document for errors and make any corrections. Save the modified Science Bio and print a copy.

10. You have opened a specialty retail store. Your store could be a jewelry store, clothing store, sporting goods store, or anything else you wish.

   a) In a new word processor document create a flyer that will be sent to prospective customers announcing your grand opening. Be sure to include the name, address, and phone number of your store, as well as a list of some of the special items you will be selling. Also include the date and time of the grand opening. Save the file naming it Grand Opening. Review the document and make any necessary corrections. Save the modified Grand Opening.

   b) Your promotions manager has suggested having a special sale at the grand opening. At the top of the flyer add the headline, 20% OFF AT THE GRAND OPENING, FANTASTIC ITEMS AT FANTASTIC PRICES! Save the modified Grand Opening and print a copy.

11. You are enrolled in an independent study of Shakespeare and your instructor wants a schedule listing topics and due dates for your research papers.

   a) In a new word processor document create a schedule using the following memorandum as a guide, substituting your own name (use the same layout, or arrangement):

   > Memorandum
   >
   > To: Kevin Dumont, English Department
   > From: Daniel Booksmith, student
   > Date: January 3, 1997
   > Subject: Shakespeare topics and due dates
   >
   > The following schedule outlines the research paper topics and due dates for my independent study in Shakespeare:
   >
   > Paper Topic Due Date
   > Hamlet 1/15
   > Henry V 2/5
   > Macbeth 2/26
   > Julius Caesar 3/11
   > Romeo and Juliet 4/1
   >
   > One week before each due date I will submit an outline containing a specific topic and a list of sources for each paper.

   b) Save the file naming it Shakespeare Schedule.

   c) Check your memo for errors and make any necessary corrections. Save the modified Shakespeare Schedule and print a copy.

12. Gibbons are apes that have a slender body with long arms and inhabit trees. Dr. Peter Helvetica and Dr. Lauren Williamson are studying the white-handed gibbons on Bashibashi Island. They have used the word processor to create a funding proposal for their gibbon research.

   a) Open RESEARCH and make the following changes:

   - In the second sentence of the first paragraph delete the phrase of lesser and greater apes.
   - In the same sentence insert the word primate before the word studies.
   - In the last sentence of the first paragraph change the words partial funds to total funding.
   - In the second sentence of the second paragraph insert the word particular between the words unique to this and group.
   - In the same paragraph insert the following sentence before the last sentence: From a primate database, behavioral statistics are easily obtained and readily comparable.

   b) Save the modified RESEARCH.

   c) Use the following steps to print only page 1:

   - Select the Print command from the File menu to display the dialog box.
   - Select the Pages option. The page range options are already set to print only page 1 of the document.
   - Select OK to print only the first page of this long document.

2

13. Businesses use word processors for everything from letters and memos to advertising material.

    a) In a new word processor document create the following letter. Substitute your name for that of the president at the end of the letter, and your initials for JP:

1 Paradise Garden
Newtown, FL 33445

June 10, 1997

Mr. Philip Crando
Italian Tours, Ltd.
14 Dunkin Drive
Key West, FL 33040

Dear Mr. Crando:

Thank you for the info you gave me during our telephone conversation this morning. As I explained, the head of our accounting department, Mr. Gordon Sharp, will leave Fast Track Publishing at the end of November, and the company would like to give him a trip to Italy as a retirement present.

We know that Mr. Sharp would like to spend the holiday season traveling, and I understand you have three tours planned for that time of the year. I look forward to receiving the price information and brochures you said were available.

Sincerely,

Janet Printmore
President

JP/jj

    b) Check the file for errors and make any necessary corrections. Save the file naming it Crando.

    c) A co-worker has read the draft of your letter and proposed the following corrections:

- Change the word info to advice and suggestions in the first paragraph.
- Add the sentence Your company was recommended to us as a leader in tour packages of Italy. at the end of the first paragraph.
- Add the words and his wife after Mr. Sharp in the second paragraph.
- Add a new paragraph before the closing which states Please contact me at 555-9825 if you have any questions. Thank you.

    d) Save the modified Crando and print a copy.

14. You are responsible for a newsletter about recycling. In a new word processor document create the following article for the newsletter:

Autos, Autos, Everywhere

We all know that automobile exhaust pollutes the air, but did you know that vehicles are the source of many other forms of pollution? For instance, one pint of motor oil that seeps into the ground can create an oil slick over a whole acre of a stream, river, or ocean. Taking your used motor oil to a recycling center (or making sure your garage recycles it) can clean up our water.

Another big source of pollution is tires. Keeping them under-inflated makes them wear faster (and costs you money in poor gas mileage). As tires wear, small pieces break off, scattering along the roadways. Eventually, dumps fill up with the hundreds of millions of tires that are discarded each year, because only a small percentage are recycled. By buying your tires from a dealer who recycles the worn-out tires, you help the world to be a cleaner, safer place to live.

An added bonus for our efforts is that recycling produces new products at less cost and energy than it takes to produce the same items from raw materials. Everyone benefits from recycling!

Check your article for errors and make any corrections. Save the document naming it Recycle News and print a copy.

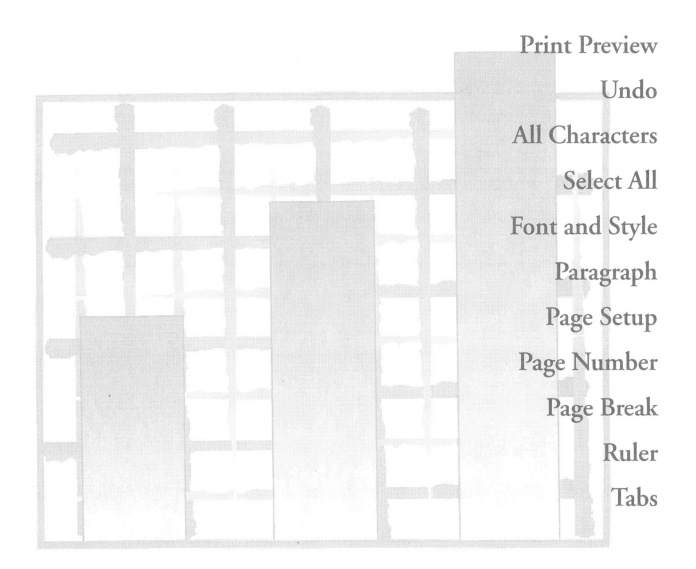

Chapter Three
Manipulating Text with the Word Processor

Print Preview

Undo

All Characters

Select All

Font and Style

Paragraph

Page Setup

Page Number

Page Break

Ruler

Tabs

3

Objectives

After completing this chapter you will be able to:

1. Manipulate a window.

2. Preview a document before printing.

3. Make special symbols visible, such as Enter and space characters.

4. Select text by highlighting blocks.

5. Apply character formats, such as different fonts and sizes.

6. Use the page controls to view different pages.

7. Apply paragraph formats, such as alignment and line spacing.

8. Apply page formats, such as margins.

9. Create headers and footers in a document.

10. Use page numbers and understand pagination.

11. Create tables using tabs, and set tab stops.

3

Chapter Two introduced the commands necessary to create, edit, save, and print word processor documents. In this chapter, formatting options are covered that improve the appearance and readability of word processor documents. These formatting options will be used to:

- change the way text appears, such as bold, underline, italic, and different fonts and sizes.

- change the way paragraphs appear, such as alignment, line spacing, tabs, and tab stops.

- control the arrangement of text on the page, such as margins, headers and footers, and pagination.

Other Works features such as windows and print preview are also discussed.

3.1 Using Windows

Each Works document is displayed in its own *window*. All document windows have similar features. For example, the vertical scroll bar you used in the last chapter is displayed on the right of all document windows. Other important window features are shown below:

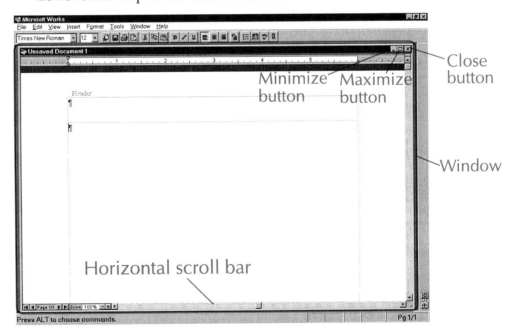

All document windows in Works have several common features

Close button

You can close a document by clicking on the document window's *Close button* in the upper-right corner. Closing a window closes the file in it and removes the window from the screen.

Maximize button

Clicking on the *Maximize button* in the upper-right corner of a window expands the window. When a window has been maximized, a *Restore button* () is displayed. Clicking on this button restores the window to its original size.

Minimize button

The *Minimize button*, also in the upper-right corner of a window, is used to reduce the window to an icon. The Minimize button will not be used in this text. However, if a window is minimized it can be restored to its previous size by double-clicking on the icon.

Horizontal scroll bar

The Work area can be scrolled horizontally to display information that is currently off the screen to either side. To scroll horizontally, click on the right or left arrow of the horizontal scroll bar or drag the scroll box.

3.2 Previewing a Document

Print preview is a Works feature that allows you to view a document on the screen as it will appear when printed. This enables you to see the effects of formatting without actually having to print the document.

When the Print Preview command is selected from the File menu, Works displays a print preview screen similar to the following:

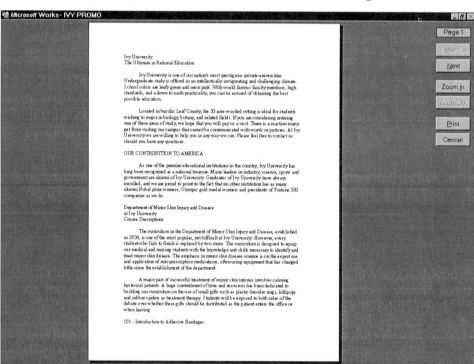

In print preview, Works displays a page as it will appear when printed

The print preview screen contains several buttons. The Next button is used to view the next page of the document. The Previous button displays the previous page in the document. The Zoom In and Zoom Out buttons are used to change the magnification of the preview. Zooming in allows you to look at a document's formatting in more detail. Selecting the Print but-

An Introduction to Computing Using Microsoft Works

ZOOM

ton displays the print dialog box. Selecting Cancel or pressing the Escape key returns you to the word processor screen.

When the mouse pointer is moved onto the document preview, the pointer shape changes to a magnifying glass. Clicking the magnifying glass on the document page magnifies that portion of the page.

A document may also be previewed by clicking on the Print Preview button on the Tool bar (🔍).

··

Practice 1

The Practices in this chapter use a promotional file for Ivy University named IVY PROMO.

1) START WORKS

   a. Following the directions given in Chapter Two, boot Windows 95.
   b. Double-click on the Microsoft Works icon to start Works. The Works Task Launcher dialog box is displayed.
   c. Click Cancel to remove the dialog box.

2) MAXIMIZE IVY PROMO

   a. From the File menu, select Open. The Open dialog box is displayed.
   b. Using the scroll arrows if necessary, locate IVY PROMO in the files list.
   c. Double-click on IVY PROMO to open it.
   d. In the upper-right corner of the document window, click on the Maximize button (□) to increase the document's window size. Note how the Title bar now appears at the top of the screen.

3) PRINT PREVIEW IVY PROMO

   a. From the File menu, select the Print Preview command. The print preview screen is displayed with the first page of IVY PROMO.
   b. Click once the Zoom In button to make the text more readable. Although the document is magnified on the screen, it will not be enlarged when printed.
   c. Click once the Zoom Out button to return to the default magnification.

4) SCROLL THE DOCUMENT IN PRINT PREVIEW

   a. Select the Next button. The second page of IVY PROMO is displayed.
   b. Continue to select the Next button until the last page of IVY PROMO is displayed. How many pages are there?
   c. Select Cancel to return to the word processor screen.

3.3 The Undo Command

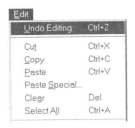

When using Works, there may be times when you execute a command or perform an action by mistake. For this reason, the effects of the last command can be reversed by executing the Undo command from the Edit menu. Undo only affects the command just executed; it is not possible to reverse the effect of the second or third previous command. There are also some commands that cannot be reversed. Print is an obvious example—the document has already been printed.

3.4 The All Characters Command

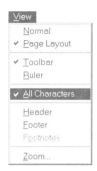

Some characters, such as spaces, are shown as white space in a document. Therefore, an editing change that leaves two spaces between a word instead of one may be difficult to see. To show symbols for these characters, select the All Characters command from the View menu:

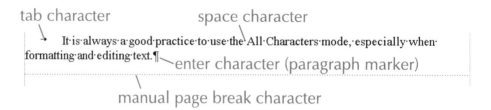

tab character   space character

It·is·always·a·good·practice·to·use·the·All·Characters·mode,·especially·when· formatting·and·editing·text.¶

enter character (paragraph marker)

manual page break character

The tab character and manual page break character are discussed later.

These symbols are shown on the screen as an aid in formatting and do not appear when the document is printed. To remove the symbols, select All Characters again. The characters are replaced by the appropriate white space and the symbols are no longer displayed on the screen. It is always a good practice to use the All Characters mode, especially when formatting and editing text.

3.5 Selecting and Deleting Blocks of Text

In the last chapter the Backspace key was used to remove text one character at a time, but for large amounts of text this can be time consuming. To speed deleting, first select the text to be removed. *Selected text* is shown highlighted on the screen:

→ Ivy·University·is·one·of·our·nation's·most·prestigious·private·universities.· Undergraduate·study·is·offered·in·an·intellectually·invigorating·and·challenging·climate.· School·colors·are·leafy·green·and·neon·pink.·With·world·famous·faculty·members,·high· standards,·and·a·down·to·earth·practicality,·you·can·be·assured·of·obtaining·the·best· possible·education.¶

The third sentence is highlighted

Next, press the Backspace key or Delete key to remove all of the selected text.

The easiest way to select text is by dragging the I-Beam pointer over the desired text to form a *highlighted block*. This highlighted block can contain a single character to several pages of text. When using this technique, be careful to include in the highlight only the text to be deleted. Another reason to be careful is that pressing a key replaces a highlighted block with the typed character. To remove the highlight, click the mouse anywhere in the document or press an arrow key.

There are several other methods for highlighting text:

- Double-clicking on a word highlights it. The highlight extends from the first character to the last and includes the space after the word.

- Holding down the Shift key and clicking the mouse in the Work area highlights the text from the cursor position to the position where the mouse was clicked.

- Holding down the Shift key and pressing an arrow key extends a highlight from the original cursor position in the direction of the arrow key.

- Placing the mouse pointer to the left of a document where the pointer changes to an arrow shape and then clicking once highlights the line to the right of the pointer. Double-clicking highlights the entire paragraph to the right of the mouse pointer.

- The entire document can be highlighted by executing the Select All command from the Edit menu.

Practice 2

In this Practice you will select and delete highlighted blocks of text. Undo will be used to restore a deleted block. Start Works and open IVY PROMO if you have not already done so.

1) SHOW ALL CHARACTERS

From the View menu, select the All Characters command if it has not already been selected (as indicated by a check mark). Note the space, tab, and paragraph markers in the document.

2) SELECT TEXT BY DRAGGING

a. Place the pointer in the paragraph at the beginning of the document which begins "Ivy University is one...."

b. Drag the mouse (hold down the left button and move the mouse) several words to the right. A highlighted block is created, and each character the pointer passes over is included in the block.

c. Release the button. The highlight remains.

3) REMOVE THE HIGHLIGHT

Click on any text. The highlight is removed.

4) SELECT A BLOCK OF TEXT

a. Place the pointer over a word and double-click the mouse button. The entire word is highlighted.

b. Press the up-arrow key to remove the highlight.

5) HIGHLIGHT THE ENTIRE DOCUMENT

a. From the Edit menu, execute the Select All command. All the text is highlighted.
b. Click on any text to remove the highlight.

6) HIGHLIGHT A SENTENCE

a. In the first paragraph of the body, place the cursor just to the left of the "S" in "School colors are…."
b. Move the I-Beam pointer, **but do not click**, after the space following the period at the end of the sentence. Make sure that the I-Beam pointer is just to the left of "With."
c. Hold down the Shift key and click. A highlight is created from the current cursor position to the pointer position. Be sure the space after the end of the sentence is included in the highlight.

7) DELETE THE HIGHLIGHTED BLOCK

Press the Delete key. All of the highlighted text, the entire sentence, is deleted and the highlight removed.

8) DELETE AND RESTORE THE NEXT PARAGRAPH

a. Move the arrow pointer outside the Work area to the left of the paragraph which begins "Located in…."
b. Double-click the mouse. The entire paragraph is highlighted.
c. Press the Delete key. The paragraph is removed.
d. From the Edit menu, select the Undo command. The paragraph is restored.

9) SAVE IVY PROMO

From the File menu, select Save. IVY PROMO is saved.

In future Practices, any of these highlighting techniques may be used when directed to select blocks of text.

3.6 Formatting Documents

The way text appears on a page is called its *format*. A document's format includes the size of its margins, the alignment of text within those margins, and the spacing between lines and paragraphs. Formatting also includes the placement of text on the page, as in tables composed of columns, and methods of emphasizing text such as underlined or bold (darker) characters.

Works allows you to format documents by selecting commands and options. Each formatting option is associated with a specific level: character, paragraph, or page. These levels describe how the format will affect a document. *Character formats* affect only the currently highlighted text, which can be a single character, a word, or several sentences. When a *paragraph format* is applied it affects the entire paragraph that contains the cursor, and only to that paragraph. When a *page format* is applied, the changes affect the entire document.

An Introduction to Computing Using Microsoft Works

3.7 Character Formats - Style

Style refers to the way in which a character is emphasized. Selecting the Font and Style command from the Format menu displays the Format Font and Style dialog box which has a number of style options:

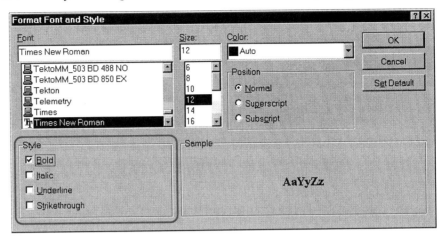

The Style options are used to emphasize characters

The Style section of the dialog box contains check box options. With *check boxes* (☑), any number of the listed options may be selected at the same time. In the dialog box above, the Bold option has been selected.

Two steps are required to emphasize text:

1. Highlight the text to be emphasized. The block can be created using any of the methods discussed in Section 3.5.
2. Execute the Font and Style command, click on the desired check box option(s), and select OK.

Bold text is printed darker so that words and phrases stand out on the page. It is most frequently used for titles and headings.

Italic text is slanted and is mostly used for emphasis. It is sometimes used for headings.

<u>Underlined text</u> is often used in footnotes and endnotes for referring to titles of publications.

~~Strikethrough~~ is commonly used to indicate editing changes.

Multiple styles can be applied to the same text. For example, a title can be bold and underlined at the same time. Remember, the text to be formatted must be highlighted before the format is applied.

The Bold (**B**), Italic (*I*), and Underline (<u>U</u>) buttons on the Tool bar may also be used to apply character styles to selected text.

Practice 3

In this Practice text will be formatted. The bold, italic, and underline styles will be used. Start Works and open IVY PROMO if you have not already done so. Use the All Characters command to display special symbols if they are not already displayed.

1) BOLD THE TITLE

 a. Highlight the "Ivy University" title at the top of the document.
 b. From the Format menu, select the Font and Style command. The Format Font and Style dialog box is displayed.
 c. In the Style section, click on the Bold check box.
 d. Select OK to remove the dialog box and apply the style.
 e. Click anywhere to remove the highlight. The emphasized text is shown bold on the screen.

2) ITALICIZE THE NEXT LINE USING THE TOOL BAR

 a. Highlight the text in the next line, the subtitle which begins "The Ultimate...."
 b. On the Tool bar, click on the Italic button (⬚). The emphasized text is shown italic on the screen.
 c. Click anywhere to remove the highlight.

3) UNDERLINE THE FIRST SENTENCE IN THE NEXT PARAGRAPH

 a. Highlight the sentence that starts "Ivy University is one of...."
 b. On the Tool bar, click on the Underline button (⬚). The text is underlined.
 c. Click anywhere to remove the highlight.

4) REMOVE UNDERLINING FROM PART OF THE SENTENCE

 a. Place the cursor after the "y" in "University" in the first sentence.
 b. Press and hold the Shift key.
 c. Continue holding the Shift key while pressing the right-arrow key. A highlight is created.
 d. Continue holding the Shift key while pressing the right-arrow key until the remaining portion of the sentence is highlighted.
 e. On the Tool bar, click on the Underline button.
 f. Click anywhere to remove the highlight. Only "Ivy University" is underlined.

<u>Check</u> - The title should be bold, the next line italicized, and the "Ivy University" in the first sentence underlined:

> **Ivy·University**¶
> *The·Ultimate·in·Education*¶
> ¶
> →   <u>Ivy·University</u>·is·one·of·our·nation's·most·prestigious·private·universities.·
> Undergraduate·study·is·offered·in·an·intellectually·invigorating·and·challenging·climate.·

5) SAVE IVY PROMO

Save the modified IVY PROMO. The next time IVY PROMO is opened, the bold, italic, and underlined text will be present.

3

3.8 When to Apply Formats

Any new text inserted inside existing formatted text will automatically be given the same format. For example, a character inserted between two bold characters is automatically made bold. This leads to a very common error. Suppose you are creating a new document and want to have a bold headline. After typing the headline, you highlight the text and make it bold. When you press Enter and begin to type the next paragraph, it is also bold. In fact, all of the paragraphs that you create from this point on will be bold! This is probably not what you wanted.

This problem can be solved by highlighting everything but the original title and deselecting any applied styles. However, the problem is best avoided by following this simple rule:

> **Type all of the material for your document first and then apply the desired formatting.**

3.9 Character Formats - Fonts

A *font* or *typeface* refers to the shape of characters. The letters in this paragraph are shaped differently from the letters in the footer at the bottom of this page because they are in a different font.

Selecting the Font and Style command from the Format menu displays a dialog box which has a number of font options:

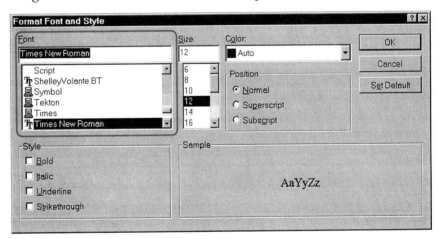

The Font options are used to change the shapes of characters

The Font section of the dialog box contains a scrollable *list*. To select an item from a list simply click on it. The scroll bar on the right side of the list is used to view hidden items in the list.

Two steps are required to change the font of text:

1. Highlight the desired text.
2. Execute the Font and Style command, select the desired font, and select OK.

A font can change the look of an entire document because some fonts take up less space on the page than others. The default Works font is named Times New Roman. There are also special fonts that contain only tiny pictures called *dingbats*. Wingdings is an example of this kind of font. Examples of these fonts and others are shown below:

Times New Romans	This is Times New Roman. ABCDEF abcdef 1234567890
Helvetica	This is Helvetica. ABCDEF abcdef 1234567890
Courier	This is Courier. ABCDEF abcdef 1234567890
Wingdings	
Symbol	Τηισ ισ Σψμβολ. ΑΒΧΔΕΦ αβχδεφ 1234567890
Arial	This is Arial. ABCDEF abcdef 1234567890

The Font Name list on the Tool bar is a *collapsible list* that can also be used to change the font of highlighted text. Clicking on the down arrow on the right of the Font Name list displays a list of available fonts. Clicking on the desired font in the list selects it.

Times New Roman ▼

3.10 Character Formats - Size

Characters can also be displayed in different sizes. Character size is measured in *points*, and there are 72 points to an inch. For example:

This is an example of 9 point Helvetica.
This is an example of 10 point Helvetica.
This is an example of 12 point Helvetica.
This is an example of 14 point Helvetica.
This is an example of 18 point Helvetica.

Selecting the Font and Style command from the Format menu displays a dialog box which has a number of size options:

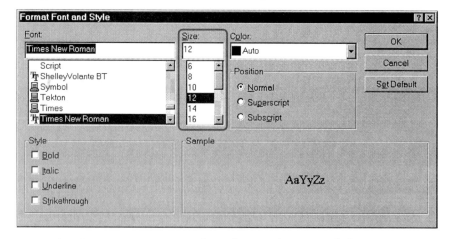

The Size options are used to change the size of characters

Changing the size of text affects the look of a document and can help distinguish between headings and regular text.

Two steps are required to change the font size of text:

1. Highlight the desired text.
2. Execute the Font and Style command, select the desired size, and select OK.

The collapsible Font Size list on the Tool bar may also be used to change the font size of highlighted text. Clicking on the down arrow on the right of the Font Size list displays a list of available point sizes. Clicking on the desired size in the list selects it.

Practice 4

In this Practice fonts and font sizes will be changed to emphasize text. Start Works and open IVY PROMO if you have not already done so. Use the All Characters command to display special symbols if they are not already displayed.

1) INCREASE THE FONT SIZE OF THE TITLE

a. Highlight the title at the top of the document, "Ivy University."
b. From the Format menu, select Font and Style. The Format Font and Style dialog box is displayed.
c. In the Size list, click on the down scroll arrow until 18 is displayed in the list.
d. Click on 18 and select OK. The highlighted text is now bold and 18 points.
e. Click anywhere to remove the highlight.

2) CHANGE THE FONT OF THE NEXT LINE

a. Highlight the very next line which begins "The Ultimate in...."
b. On the Tool bar, click on the down arrow of the collapsible Font Name list. A list of available fonts is displayed.
c. Press the up-arrow key to scroll through the list until Arial is visible. Click on Arial. The highlighted text is now in Arial.
d. Click anywhere to remove the highlight.

Check - The title should be bold and 18 point text and the next line italicized Arial:

Ivy·University¶
The·Ultimate·in·Education¶

3) SAVE IVY PROMO AND PRINT THE FIRST PAGE

a. Save IVY PROMO. The next time IVY PROMO is opened the formatted text will be present.
b. From File menu, select Print. The Print dialog box is displayed.
c. Click on the Pages option. The from and to options should already display a 1.
d. Select OK to print the file. Only the first page of the document will be printed. Note how the text in the printout resembles that shown on the screen.
e. Save IVY PROMO again.

3.11 Character Formats - Superscripts and Subscripts

A *superscript* is a section of text which is raised slightly above the current line while a *subscript* is printed slightly below the current line. For example:

> In her 9th Street laboratory, Dr. Sulfuric proved that the formula for water is H_2O.

The "th" after the 9 is a superscript, and the "2" in H_2O is a subscript.

Selecting the Font and Style command from the Format menu displays the Format Font and Style dialog box. The Position section of the dialog box contains radio button options. With *radio buttons* (◉), only one of the listed options may be selected at a time.

To create superscripts and subscripts, two steps are required:

1. Highlight the desired text.
2. Execute the Font and Style command, click on the desired radio button option, and select OK.

Footnotes and endnotes are usually marked with superscripted text. A special method for creating these marks is described in Chapter Four.

Character Format Review

Type all the material for your document first. Next, highlight the text to be emphasized. Execute the Font and Style command from the Format menu and then select the desired option(s).

3.12 Using the Page Controls

Rather than scrolling a document one screen at a time, the *page controls* can be used to scroll the document one page at a time. The page controls are located in the lower-left corner of the document window:

Page indicator

The page controls can be used for scrolling a long document

The page indicator displays which page of a document is currently displayed and the number of pages in the document. To scroll to the previous page in a document, click the ◀ control. The leftmost page control (◀◀) is clicked to scroll directly to the first page of the document. To scroll to the next page in a document, click the ▶ control. The rightmost page control (▶▶) is clicked to scroll directly to the last page in the document. When the page controls are used to scroll a document, the cursor is moved to the top of the displayed page.

3

Practice 5

In this Practice you will create superscripts and subscripts and use the page controls. Start Works and open IVY PROMO if you have not already done so. Use the All Characters command to display special symbols if they are not already displayed.

1) LOCATE THE 211 COURSE DESCRIPTION

Superscripts and subscripts are needed on page 2 of the document. Click once on the ▶ page control to scroll to the next page. Note that the page indicator displays Page 2/3. Locate the description for course 211. The "th" in "20th" needs to be superscripted.

2) CREATE THE SUPERSCRIPTS

a. Highlight the "th" in "20th."
b. From the Format menu, select Font and Style. The Format Font and Style dialog box is displayed.
c. In the Position section, click on the Superscript radio button.
d. Select OK. The highlighted text is placed slightly above the surrounding text.

Check - Your document should be similar to:

211·-·Adhesive·Bandages·and·Tooth·Decay¶
An·in-depth·seminar·on·inappropriate·adhesive·bandage·use·in·dentistry,·perhaps·the·greatest·medical·scandal·of·the·20th·century.¶

3) LOCATE THE FACULTY LIST

Scroll so that Dr. Scalp's description near the bottom of page 2 is visible. We will create the subscripts for the chemical formula so that it appears correctly.

4) CREATE THE FORMULA SUBSCRIPTS

a. In the formula H2O2, highlight the first "2."
b. From the Format menu, select Font and Style. The Format Font and Style dialog box is displayed.
c. In the Position section, click on the Subscript radio button.
d. Select OK. The highlighted text is placed slightly below the surrounding text.
e. Highlight the next "2" in the formula.
f. Repeat steps (b) through (d) to subscript the 2.

Check - Your document should be similar to:

Dr.·Phineas·Itchee·-·Department·Chair,·Specialist·in·Botanical·Skin·Irritants,·President·of·Regional·Association·of·Skin·Health·(RASH).¶
Dr.·Christine·Scalp·-·Specialist·in·Chemistry·of·Shampoo·and·author·of·You·and·Shampoo.·Awarded·patent·for·conditioning·shampoo·formula·that·contains·H$_2$O$_2$.¶
Dr.·Holly·McCleen·-·Specialist·in·Acne·Studies·and·author·of·How·to·Wash·Your·Face.¶

5) SAVE IVY PROMO

3.13 Paragraph Formats - Alignment

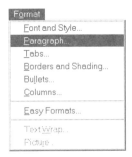

There are four ways to align text in a paragraph relative to the margins: left, centered, right, and justified. Selecting the Paragraph command from the Format menu displays the Format Paragraph dialog box. Selecting the Indents and Alignment tab displays the following options:

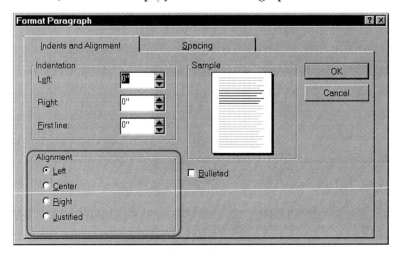

The Alignment options are used to change paragraph alignment

The Left, Center, Right, and Justified options can be selected from the Alignment section of the Format Paragraph dialog box. The Left Align (▤), Center Align (▤), and Right Align (▤) buttons on the Tool bar can also be used to format a paragraph.

Selecting an alignment option affects only the paragraph that the cursor is in. Multiple paragraphs can be formatted together by highlighting them first, and then applying the desired alignment.

Left

> Left aligned, the default, means that each line of text begins at the left margin. The right edge of the paragraph is jagged. This is the format most often used in letters or research papers.

Centered

> Centered is the alignment most often used for headings and titles. Each line of a centered paragraph is equidistant from the left and right margins.

Right

> Right aligned is the opposite of left aligned. Each line of a right-aligned paragraph is flush with the right margin while the left edge of the paragraph is jagged. This format is used infrequently, but can be found in some advertisements and catalogs.

Justified

> Justified creates straight paragraph borders at both margins. When a paragraph is justified, Works places extra space between words on each line of text so that it extends from the left margin to the right margin. Justified formats are common in newspapers and books—this textbook, for example.

3.14 Paragraph Formats - Line Spacing

The amount of space between lines in a paragraph can be controlled. Single spacing places text on each line of the page and double spacing inserts a blank line between lines of text. Double spacing can make a document more readable, leaving room for notes to be written between lines. Examples of both formats are shown below:

Single spacing

> This paragraph is single spaced. There is little space between the lines for notes or comments, but more information can be placed on each page. Most printed text, including this book, is single spaced.

Double spacing

> This paragraph is double spaced. Note how space is left between
>
> each line for notes or comments. Double spacing is used mostly for
>
> academic papers and drafts.

Like alignment, spacing changes affect only the paragraph that currently contains the cursor, or all of the paragraphs in a highlighted block. This allows one paragraph in a document to be single spaced and another double spaced. Single spacing is the default.

Executing the Paragraph command from the Format menu and selecting the Spacing tab in the dialog box displays the following options:

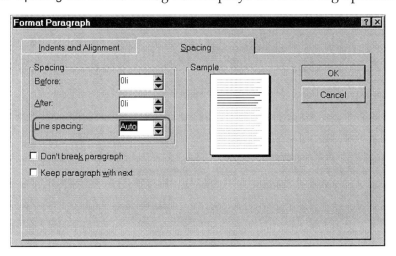

The Format Paragraph dialog box is used to control line spacing

Typing 2 in the Line spacing box and then selecting OK double-spaces the paragraph containing the cursor.

Paragraph Format Review

Type all the material for your document first. Next, place the cursor in the paragraph to be formatted. Execute the Paragraph command from the Format menu and then select the desired option.

Practice 6

In this Practice you will use alignment and spacing options to format IVY PROMO. Start Works and open IVY PROMO if you have not already done so. Use the All Characters command to display special symbols if they are not already displayed.

1) CENTER THE FIRST TWO LINES IN THE DOCUMENT

    a. In the page controls, click on the ◄ page control to scroll directly to page 1 if it is not already displayed.
    b. Click the I-Beam pointer in the title at the top of page 1 to place the cursor.
    c. On the Tool bar, click the Center Align button (▤). The title is centered on the screen and the Center Align button is highlighted in the Tool bar.
    d. Place the cursor in the next line of the document (the subtitle).
    e. On the Tool bar, click the Center Align button. The paragraph that contains the subtitle is centered.

2) JUSTIFY THE FIRST PARAGRAPH

    a. Place the cursor in the paragraph that begins "Ivy University is one of...."
    b. From the Format menu, select the Paragraph command. The Format Paragraph dialog box is displayed.
    c. In the Format Paragraph dialog box, click on the Indents and Alignment tab.
    d. In the Alignment section, select the Justified radio button.
    e. Select OK. The paragraph containing the cursor is justified.

3) DOUBLE SPACE THE SECOND PARAGRAPH

    a. Place the cursor in the second paragraph, which begins "Located in...."
    b. From the Format menu, select Paragraph. The Format Paragraph dialog box is displayed.
    c. Select the Spacing tab. Line spacing options are displayed.
    d. The Line spacing option should already be highlighted. If not, double-click in the Line spacing entry box to highlight the current setting.
    e. Type 2 to replace the current value.
    f. Select OK. The paragraph containing the cursor is double spaced.

4) RIGHT ALIGN THE SECOND PARAGRAPH

    a. The cursor should still be in the paragraph which begins "Located in...."
    b. On the Tool bar, click on the Right Align button (▤). The paragraph is right aligned. This paragraph now has two formats: right alignment and double spacing.

3

Check: Your document should be similar to the following:

Ivy·University¶
The·Ultimate·in·Education¶

¶

→   Ivy· University· is· one· of· our· nation's· most· prestigious· private· universities.· Undergraduate· study· is· offered· in· an· intellectually· invigorating· and· challenging· climate.· With· world· famous· faculty· members,· high· standards,· and· a· down· to· earth· practicality,· you·can·be·assured·of·obtaining·the·best·possible·education.¶

¶

→   Located·in·bucolic·Leaf·County,·the·350·acre·wooded·setting·is·ideal·for·students·

wishing·to·major·in·biology,·botany,·and·related·fields.·If·you·are·considering·entering·

one·of·these·areas·of·study,·we·hope·that·you·will·pay·us·a·visit.·There·is·a·positive·

reaction·many·get·from·visiting·our·campus·that·cannot·be·communicated·with·words·or·

pictures.·At·Ivy·University·we·are·willing·to·help·you·in·any·way·we·can.·Please·feel·free·

to·contact·us·should·you·have·any·questions.¶

---

5) UNDO THE LAST COMMAND

From the Edit menu, select Undo. The effect of the previous command (right alignment) is undone, and the paragraph is returned to its original alignment.

6) PREVIEW THE MODIFIED DOCUMENT

a. On the Tool bar, click on the Print Preview button ( ) to view the modified document. Note how the different paragraphs are aligned and spaced.

b. Select Cancel to return to the word processor screen.

7) JUSTIFY THE BODY OF THE DOCUMENT

a. Place the cursor in the paragraph which begins "Located in bucolic…."

b. Use the scroll bar to scroll to the very end of the text in the document.

c. Hold down the Shift key and click in the last paragraph that begins "We hope that…." A highlighted block is created that contains text from every paragraph but the centered titles and the first paragraph of the body.

d. From the Format menu, select Paragraph. Select the Indents and Alignment tab to display the alignment options.

e. In the Alignment section, select Justified.

f. Select OK. Click anywhere in the text to remove the highlight.

8) PREVIEW AND THEN SAVE IVY PROMO

a. Print Preview the document and note the justified paragraphs. Select Cancel to return to the word processor screen.

b. From the File menu, select Save. When IVY PROMO is next used, all of the body paragraphs will be justified.

3.15 Page Formats - Margins

Margins are shown on screen as the white region outside the page guides. Changes to the margins have an inverse affect on the amount of text that a page can contain. Widening the left and right margins decreases the number of characters that fit on a line and narrowing the left and right margins increases the line's capacity. Similarly, larger top and bottom margins decrease the number of lines of text a page can contain and decreasing the top and bottom margins increase the page's capacity. Works' default margin settings for an 8.5 inch by 11 inch page are 1.25 inches on the left and right and 1 inch on the top and bottom:

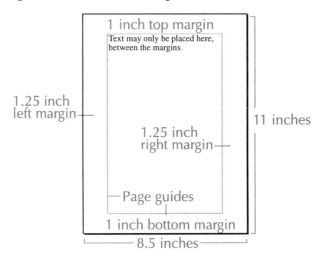

The length of a line that will fit across a page is determined by subtracting the size of the left and right margins from the width of the page. Using the default margins yields a line of text that is 6.0 inches long (8.5 – 1.25 – 1.25 = 6.0).

Selecting the Page Setup command from the File menu displays a dialog box that indicates the current margins:

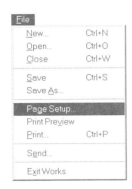

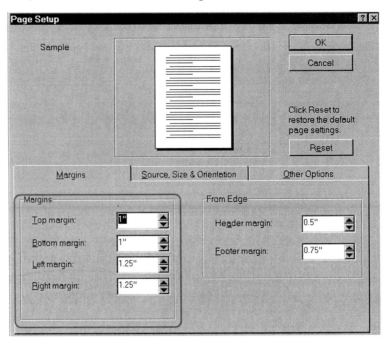

Top, bottom, left, and right margins each have their own entry box. To change a margin, simply type the desired measurement into the appropriate entry box and then select the OK button. For example, to change the bottom margin to 0.75 inches, double-click on the value in the Bottom margin box, type the new value, 0.75, and select OK.

Practice 7

In this Practice the margins of IVY PROMO will be changed. Start Works and open IVY PROMO if you have not already done so. Use the All Characters command to display special symbols if they are not already displayed.

1) CHANGE THE MARGINS

a. From the File menu, select the Page Setup command. The Page Setup dialog box is displayed. Click on the Margins tab if the margin options are not displayed.
b. Double-click on the "1.25" in the Left margin box to highlight the measurement.
c. Type 2.5 to replace the old value.
d. Double-click on the "1.25" in the Right margin box. Type 2 to replace the old value.
e. Select OK. The document now has a left margin of 2.5 inches and a right margin of 2 inches. Note how there is more white space on the left and right of the document. Also notice the page indicator—there are now 4 pages in the document.

2) PRINT PREVIEW IVY PROMO

Print preview the document. Scroll to the first page in the document if it is not already displayed. Note how much more room appears on the left and right of the page because the margins have been increased:

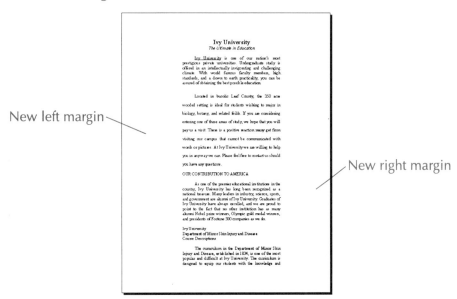

New left margin

New right margin

3) CHANGE THE MARGINS

The document is easier to read with larger margins because the line length of the text is shorter.

a. Return to the word processor screen.
b. From the File menu, select Page Setup to display the Page Setup dialog box.
c. Change the Left and Right margins to 1.5 inches. Select OK.
d. Save IVY PROMO.

3.16 Page Formats - Headers and Footers

Word processor documents can be made more informative by including text at the top and bottom of each page. Information that is automatically displayed at the top of each page is called a *header*. Similarly, information displayed at the bottom of each page is called a *footer*. Headers and footers are often used to indicate the current page number, the document or author's name, and other information.

The header is displayed at the top of a document page:

Header

To place text in the header, simply click the I-Beam pointer in the header area and type the desired text. Information in the header can be formatted like any other text. To move the cursor from the header, click the I-Beam pointer in the main body of the text. To change or edit an existing header, click in the header to place the cursor and then make changes as with any other text.

The footer is displayed in an area at the bottom of a document page:

Footer

As with header text, simply click the cursor in the footer to enter or edit footer text.

It is important to understand that there can be only one header and one footer per document and that text entered in the header or footer on one page is displayed on every page of the document.

3.17 Including Page Numbers

Executing the Page Number command from the Insert menu places a page number marker at the current cursor position. The marker appears as *page* and is replaced by the appropriate number when the document is printed or previewed.

When a page number marker is placed in a header or footer, the header or footer changes for each page in the document to display the appropriate page number. This technique is often used to print the appropriate page number at the bottom of each page in a document.

Headers and footers displaying page numbers may be easier to understand if the page number marker is placed after the word "Page." For example, Page *page*. A document with such a footer will show Page 1 at the bottom of page 1, Page 2 at the bottom of page 2, and so on.

3

Practice 8

In this Practice you will create a header and footer for the IVY PROMO document. Start Works and open IVY PROMO if you have not already done so. Use the All Characters command to display special symbols if they are not already displayed.

1) CREATE A HEADER

a. Click on the 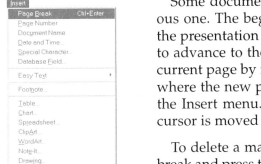 page control to display the top of page 1 if it is not already displayed. Note the header area.
b. Click the I-Beam pointer in the header area. The cursor is displayed in the header.
c. Type Promotional Information. These words will now appear at the top of every page in the document.
d. Highlight all of the header text and then display the Font Size list on the Tool bar. Click on 10 in the list. The header text is now 10 point.

2) CREATE A FOOTER

a. Scroll to the bottom of page 1. Note the footer area.
b. Click the I-Beam pointer in the footer area. Type Page and press the spacebar once.
c. From the Insert menu, select the Page Number command. A page number marker is inserted at the cursor position.
d. With the cursor still in the footer text, click on the Center Align button on the Tool bar. The footer text is centered.

3) PREVIEW THE DOCUMENT

a. From the File menu, select Print Preview. Page one of IVY PROMO is displayed.
b. Zoom in and note how the page number code has been replaced by a 1.
c. Select the Next button to preview page 2. Note the page number is a 2.
d. Preview the rest of the document and then return to the word processor screen.

4) SAVE IVY PROMO

3.18 Page Formats - Pagination

When using a word processor, it is not necessary to determine how many lines of text will fit on a printed page. Works automatically inserts *page breaks* where one page ends and the next begins. This process is called *pagination*. A document's pagination is automatically updated to reflect margin changes, text edits, etc.

Some documents require starting a new page before filling the previous one. The beginning of a new chapter, a change in subject matter, or the presentation of a table or chart are all examples. You can force Works to advance to the next page regardless of the number of lines left on the current page by inserting a *manual page break*. To do this, place the cursor where the new page is to start and select the Page Break command from the Insert menu. A dotted line is displayed and text to the right of the cursor is moved to the next page.

To delete a manual page break, place the cursor to the left of the page break and press the Delete key. The document is repaginated and text from the next page is moved up to fill the current page.

In this Practice you will view a document's pagination and insert manual page breaks. Start Works and open IVY PROMO if you have not already done so. Use the All Characters command to display special symbols if they are not already displayed.

1) INSERT A MANUAL PAGE BREAK

    a. Scroll to the beginning of the document.

    b. Place the cursor just before the "L" in the second paragraph that starts "Located in bucolic Leaf County...."

    c. From the Insert menu, select the Page Break command. Text to the right of the cursor is moved to the next page.

    d. Scroll up to view page 1. A dotted line indicates a manual page break.

    e. Note the page indicator displays 4 pages instead of the original 3.

2) PREVIEW IVY PROMO

    a. From the File menu, select Print Preview. Page 1 of IVY PROMO is displayed.

    b. Note the blank space at the bottom of page 1 as a result of the manual page break.

    c. Return to the word processor screen.

3) DELETE THE MANUAL PAGE BREAK

    a. Place the cursor just to the left of the dotted page break line.

    b. Press the Delete key. Text from page 2 is moved up to page 1. The number of pages in the document is again 3.

4) INSERT A MANUAL PAGE BREAK

Manual page breaks are used to control the placement of text in a document. The faculty members information appears at the bottom of page 2. It would be better placed at the top of page 3 together with the faculty members description.

    a. Scroll so that the bottom of page 2 is displayed.

    b. Place the cursor just to the left of "Ivy University," the first line of the subtitle.

    c. From the Insert menu, select Page Break. Text to the right of the cursor is moved to the next page.

5) SAVE, PRINT, AND CLOSE IVY PROMO

    a. Save the modified IVY PROMO.

    b. Print the entire document and then close the file.

3.19 Tabs and Tab Stops

Tabs are used to position text within a line. When the Tab key is pressed the cursor and any text to the right are moved over to the position of the next tab stop. *Tab stops* are locations specifying the length of the tab character (how far it moves the cursor).

In the Works word processor, default tab stops are located at every half inch and are generally used for indenting text from the margin. For example, when beginning a new paragraph, pressing Tab once indents the first line half an inch. The paragraphs in the body of IVY PROMO have been formatted this way.

Tabs are also used to create tables consisting of columns of data. Rather than using the default tab stops, new tab stops are usually created at the desired intervals for the table.

A tab character is deleted the same as any character by placing the cursor to the right of the tab and pressing the Backspace key. The text is automatically moved to the left to fill the space previously created by the tab.

3.20 The Ruler

A ruler can be displayed above the Work area of the word processor to gauge the placement of tab stops, margins, and indents. (Indents are discussed in Chapter Four.) To display the Ruler, the Ruler command from the View menu is selected. The Ruler measures from the edge of the page guides, with each vertical line representing one eighth of an inch, and full inches indicated by a number.

Practice 10

In this Practice you will format a document. Tabs will be used to indent text. If you have not already done so, start Works.

1) OPEN A WORD PROCESSOR FILE

a. If the Works Task Launcher dialog box is displayed, click on Cancel to remove it.
b. From the File menu, select Open. The Open dialog box is displayed.
c. Scroll through the files list until News Story is displayed. News Story was created in the Practices in Chapter Two.
d. Double-click on News Story to open a copy of the document. News Story is displayed on the screen.
e. From the View menu, select All Characters to display all characters if they are not already showing.

2) DISPLAY THE RULER

If the Ruler is not displayed, select the Ruler command from the View menu. The Ruler is displayed above the Work area.

3) USE THE TOOL BAR TO CHANGE THE TITLE ALIGNMENT

a. Place the cursor anywhere in the title (the first line of the document).
b. On the Tool bar, click on the Center Align button. The title is now centered.

4) INDENT THREE PARAGRAPHS WITH TABS

a. Move the cursor to the beginning of the paragraph that starts "The annual…."
b. Press the Tab key. A tab character is inserted and its symbol (→) displayed on the screen. The paragraph is now indented to the first tab stop at 0.5 inches.
c. Move the cursor to the beginning of the next paragraph and indent it like the first.
d. Use the Tab key to indent the line that begins "The menu…."

5) INDENT THE MENU

   a. Move the cursor to the beginning of the first menu item, "Fruit cup or lime sherbet."

   b. Press the Tab key twice. The line is indented 1 inch. Note the position of the first character in the line in relation to the Ruler.

   c. Follow parts (a) and (b) to indent the remaining menu items.

   d. Indent the last paragraph of News Story with one tab.

<u>Check</u>: When complete, News Story should appear similar to the following:

FUND·RAISER·TO·BE·HELD·AT·THE·EASTSIDE·SHERATON¶

¶

→   The·annual·Lawrenceville·Red·Cross·fund-raising·dinner·will·be·held·in·the·main· ballroom·of·the·Eastside·Sheraton·at·7:00·p.m.·next·Saturday·night.·Music·for·dancing·· will·be·provided·by·the·Schmenge·Brothers·Orchestra.··¶

¶

→   All·community·members·are·invited.·Tickets·are·$25.00·per·person·and·are· available·from·Mrs.·Mitchell·in·the·Red·Cross·office·during·regular·business·hours.·¶

¶

→   The·menu·for·the·evening's·event·will·be:¶

¶

→   →   Fruit·cup·or·lime·sherbet¶

→   →   Roast·duck·a·l'Orange·with·wild·rice·stuffing¶

→   →   Garden·salad¶

→   →   Double·chocolate·chip·ice·cream¶

¶

→   After·dinner,·a·reception·will·take·place·in·the·hotel's·Algonquin·Room.·Dancing·

6) SAVE, PRINT, AND THEN CLOSE NEWS STORY

   a. Save the modified News Story.

   b. On the Tool bar, click on the Print button (🖨) to print one copy of News Story.

   c. Close News Story.

3.21 Setting Individual Tab Stops

A tab stop can be set at any position on the Ruler. When a tab stop is set Works automatically ignores the default stops to the left. That is, setting a tab stop at 1.4 inches automatically removes the default stops at 0.5 and 1.0 inches. The default stop at 1.5 inches is not affected.

When the Tab key is pressed, a tab is inserted and text to the right of the tab is aligned at the next tab stop. A left-aligned tab stop aligns the beginning of the text at the stop, and is marked with a **L** on the Ruler. Right-aligned (◢), center-aligned (▲), and decimal-aligned (⬥) tab stops can also be created. A right-aligned tab stop aligns the end of the text at the stop, and a center-aligned tab stop centers the text equidistant over the stop. Decimal tabs are used with numbers and align the decimal point at the stop. Examples of each stop are shown with the corresponding Ruler:

3

→	Left	→	Right	→	Center	→	Decimal¶
→	Name	→	Tristan	→	Brown	→	10.04¶
→	Address	→	Delray	→	FL	→	334.444¶
→	Phone	→	123-4567	→	(407)	→	1234¶

Tab stops are indicated by markers on the Ruler

Tab stops are set by selecting the Tabs command from the Format menu which displays the following dialog box:

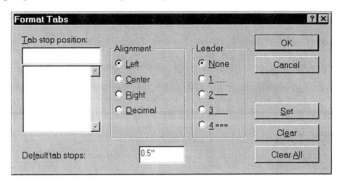

Multiple tab stops can be set at the same time using this dialog box

The Tab stop position is typed and then the appropriate Alignment selected. Selecting Set creates a tab stop at that position. This procedure can be repeated to create as many tab stops as desired. After all tab stops have been created, OK is selected to remove the dialog box.

To remove a specific tab stop, select it from the Tab stop position list in the Format Tabs dialog box and then select Clear. A tab stop can also be removed by dragging its marker from the Ruler into the Work area. Any text which was aligned at that stop is automatically reformatted.

It is important to realize that tab stops are a paragraph format like paragraph alignment or line spacing. That is, when tab stops are created, they are set for the current paragraph only. Any paragraphs before or after are not affected. This makes it possible for different paragraphs to have different sets of tab stops. As the cursor is moved through the text, the Ruler changes to show the tab stops set for the current paragraph. Like all formatting commands, the same set of tab stops can be applied to a number of paragraphs together by highlighting first and then setting the stops.

Practice 11

In this Practice you will set and delete tab stops to create a formatted table. Start Works and open IVY PROMO. Use the All Characters command to display special symbols if they are not already displayed.

1) LOCATE THE STUDENT DIVERSITY TABLE

Scroll to the Student Diversity section, located near the end of the document. This table has been entered using the Tab key and default tab stops. There is a single tab between each column—one tab between "Area" and "Students," another between "Students" and "Percentage of Student Body," and so on for the entire table. However, because tab stops have not yet been set, this table is not easy to read.

2) ADD A LINE TO THE UNFORMATTED TABLE

a. A line of data needs to be added to the table. Place the cursor at the end of the South America line, after "10.47%," but before the Enter character.
b. Press Enter. A new line is added to the table.
c. Press the Tab key once to indent the line. Type Other.
d. Press Tab again and type 49.
e. Press Tab and type 0.90%. Each line in this table was entered similarly. The table should be similar to:

```
→   Area → Students   →   Percentage·of·Student·Body¶
→   Africa→213 → 3.87%¶
→   Asia → 471 → 8.56%¶
→   Europe→689 → 12.52%¶
→   North·America   →   3,503→63.68%¶
→   South·America   →   576 → 10.47%¶
→   Other→49 → 0.90%¶
→       →   5,501→100.00%¶
```

3) HIGHLIGHT THE TABLE

a. We want to set three tab stops that are the same for the entire table. So that we only have to enter the tab stops once, we will highlight the table first. Any tab stops created then affect the entire highlighted block. Place the cursor anywhere in the title of the table, "Area Students Percentage of Student Body."
b. Drag the mouse slowly down the table. When the highlight is in the last line of the table (5,501), release the button. Any tab stops now set will affect each highlighted line in the table.

4) SET THE TAB STOPS FOR THE TABLE

a. From the Format menu select the Tabs command. The Format Tabs dialog box is displayed.
b. The first column of the table needs to be left aligned at ¾ inch. In the Tab stop position box, type 0.75. The Alignment should be Left.
c. Select the Set button to add the Tab stop to the list.
d. The second column of the table needs to be right aligned at 3 inches. In the Tab stop position box, type 3.
e. In the Alignment section, select the Right radio button.
f. Select the Set button to add the Tab stop to the list.
g. The last column needs to be right aligned at 4¼ inches. In the Tab stop position box, type 4.25.
h. In the Alignment section, select the Decimal radio button.
i. Select the Set button to add the Tab stop to the list.
j. Select OK. The table is now formatted and easy to read.

5) CHANGE AN EXISTING TAB STOP

Note the alignment of the title "Percentage of Student Body" in the title. It would be better if it were centered over the column of numbers.

a. Place the cursor in the title.
b. From the Format menu select Tabs. The Format Tabs dialog box is displayed.
c. In the Tab stop position list, select 4.25".
d. Select the Clear button to remove the tab stop.
e. In the Tab stop position box, type 4.5.
f. In the Alignment section, select Center.

An Introduction to Computing Using Microsoft Works

3

    g. Select the Set button to add the Tab stop to the list.
    h. Select OK. The title is centered over the column of numbers.
    i. Click anywhere to remove the highlight.

Check - Your table and Ruler should be similar to:

| | 1 | | 2 | | 3 | | 4 | | 5 | |

→ Ivy·University·prides·itself·on·having·a·diverse·student·body.·Our·students· come·from·around·the·country·and·the·world·to·study·here.·The·following·table· shows·the·global·breakdown·of·our·students:¶
¶

	Area	→	Students	→	Percentage·of·Student·Body¶
→	Africa	→	213	→	3.87%¶
→	Asia	→	471	→	8.56%¶
→	Europe	→	689	→	12.52%¶
→	North·America	→	3,503	→	63.68%¶
→	South·America	→	576	→	10.47%¶
→	Other	→	49	→	0.90%¶
→		→	5,501	→	100.00%¶

¶
In·Conclusion¶
¶
→ We·hope·that·you·have·enjoyed·this·brief·description·of·Ivy·University·and· that·you·plan·to·visit·us·soon.¶

6) SAVE AND PRINT IVY PROMO

    a. Save the modified IVY PROMO.
    b. From the File menu, select Print and print the entire document. Note on the printed copy all of the formatting options created in this chapter: headers, footers, paragraph formats, text formats, fonts and styles, tab stops, etc.
    c. Close IVY PROMO.
    d. If the Task Launcher dialog box is displayed, click on the Exit Works button. The Windows 95 screen is displayed.

Chapter Summary

This chapter explained how a word processor document can be formatted to improve its appearance and readability. Works displays each open file in a window which can be closed, maximized, minimized, and scrolled.

A document can be previewed by executing the Print Preview command from the File menu. In print preview, a document is displayed on the screen as it will appear when printed.

To reverse the effects of the last command, the Undo command from the Edit menu is used.

The All Characters command from the View menu is used to display normally invisible characters using symbols. This can be especially useful when editing a document.

A highlighted block of text is created by dragging the mouse over the text. When a formatting command is executed, the format is applied to the highlighted block. A highlighted block can be deleted by pressing the Backspace key or Delete key.

A specific arrangement of text is called a format. There are three levels of formats in Works: character, paragraph, and page. Each level describes how the format will affect a document.

The Font and Style command from the Format menu displays a dialog box with options that can be used to emphasize characters. Text to be formatted is first highlighted and then the appropriate option selected. Bold, italic, and underline styles are common character formats. Text can also be made to appear superscripted or subscripted using options from this dialog box. The Bold, Italic, and Underline buttons on the Tool bar can also be used to format text.

The Font and Style command is also used to change the font and size of highlighted text. Collapsible lists on the Tool bar can also be used to change the font or font size of selected text.

The page controls in the lower-left corner of a document window are used to scroll a document one page at a time. Scrolling with the page controls moves the cursor to the top of the displayed page.

The Paragraph command from the Format menu contains options for changing the alignment of a paragraph. Left alignment creates a straight left border and a jagged right border. Right alignment is the opposite, creating a straight right border and a jagged left border. Centering positions a line equidistant from the left and right margins. Justified alignment creates straight borders at both margins. The Left Align, Right Align, and Center Align buttons on the Tool bar may also be used to change a paragraphs alignment. When alignment is set, it affects the paragraph containing the cursor or all the paragraphs in a highlighted block.

The Paragraph command from the Format menu also contains options to control the line spacing of a paragraph. Line spacing applies to all the lines in the current paragraph or in all the paragraphs in a selected block.

Margins are the white region outside the page guides. Works' default margin settings can be changed using the Page Setup command from the File menu. When a margin is changed it affects the whole document.

A header is text displayed at the top of each page and a footer is text displayed at the bottom of each page. Page numbers and information such as a title or name can be printed in either. A header or footer is created by clicking the I-Beam pointer in the header or footer area and then entering the text. The current page number can be printed in a header by placing the cursor in the header and selecting the Page Number command from the Insert menu. The page number marker (*page*) that is displayed at the cursor position is replaced by the actual page number when a document is printed or previewed.

Pagination is the process by which Works determines how many lines of text will fit on a printed page. During this process Works inserts page breaks to mark the end of one page and the beginning of another. When it

3

is necessary to end the current page, a manual page break can be inserted using the Page Break command from the Insert menu. Pressing the Delete key removes the page break to the right of the cursor.

Tabs are characters used to position text within a line. Tab stops are locations specifying the position of the tab character. There are several types of tab stops—left, right, center, or decimal aligned. Individual tab stops are set using the Tabs command from the Format menu.

Vocabulary

Alignment - Position of paragraph text relative to the margins. Left, right, centered, or justified.

All Characters command - Used to display symbols for normally invisible characters as an aid to editing.

Block - A highlighted section of text that may contain anything from a single character to an entire document. A block can be created by dragging the mouse over the desired text. Any applied formatting affects the currently highlighted text.

Bold text - Character format that makes text appear darker. Used for making words or phrases stand out on a page.

Centered alignment - Alignment format that positions text evenly between the left and right margins.

Character - Any letter, number, or symbol that can be displayed on the computer screen.

Character format - Formatting option that affects the currently highlighted characters. Character formats include font (i.e. Arial), size (i.e. 12 point), and style (i.e. bold).

Close button- Square button containing an X in the upper-right corner of a window. Clicking it closes the current window and file.

Delete text - A highlighted block that is removed from a document.

Dingbat - A small picture found in some special fonts such as WingDings.

Double space - Formatting a paragraph so that there is a blank line between each line of text.

Font - Shape of a set of characters.

Footer - Information that is printed at the bottom of each page.

Format - The way that text appears on a page, including options such as margins, fonts, emphasized text, and headers and footers.

Header - Information that is printed at the top of each page.

Highlighted text - Text that has been selected. Highlighting is usually done by dragging or clicking the mouse.

Horizontal scroll bar - Used to display the part of a document that is currently off the screen to either side.

Italic text - Character format that makes text appear slanted. Sometimes used for headings.

Justified alignment - Paragraph format in which each line of text is made to extend from the left margin to the right by adding extra space between words.

Left alignment - Default paragraph format where text is even with the left margin, while the right side is ragged.

Manual page break - A page break that is inserted to force text onto the next printed page.

Margin - The white area outside the page guides.

Maximize button - Button located in the upper-right corner of a document window. Used to expand the window to fill the screen.

Minimize button - Button located in the upper-right corner of a document window. Used to reduce a document window to an icon.

Page break - The location where one printed page ends and another begins.

Page controls - Located in the lower-left corner of the document window. Used to scroll document one page at a time.

Page format - Formatting option that affects the entire document, such as margins.

Page indicator - Part of the page controls in the lower-left corner of the document window. Displays current page number and total number of pages.

Page Number command - Used to insert a page number marker at the current cursor position. Often inserted in a header or footer to display the page number of each page in a document.

Pagination - Process by which Works determines where one page ends and another begins.

Paragraph alignment - How text is printed in relation to the margins: left (default), right, centered, or justified.

Paragraph format - Formatting option that affects the paragraph containing the cursor or the highlighted paragraphs. Paragraph formats include alignment, spacing, and tab stops.

Point - The unit used to measure character size. There are 72 points per inch.

Print Preview command - Used to view a document as it will appear when printed.

Restore button - Button displayed in the upper-right corner of a document window in place of the Maximize button when a window has been maximized. Used to restore a window to its original size.

Right alignment - Paragraph format where text is set even with the right margin while the left side is ragged.

Ruler - An area below the Menu bar and Tool bar showing the placement of tab stops.

Selected text - Text that is shown highlighted on the screen.

Single space - The default paragraph format where each line of text is placed so that there is no space in between.

Subscript - Text printed slightly below the normal line.

Superscript - Text printed slightly above the normal line.

Tab stop - A location specifying the position of the tab character.

Tabs - Characters used to position text within a line. Used to create tables or to indent the first line of a paragraph.

Typeface - Also commonly referred to as font. See font.

Underlined text - Character format that puts a line under text. Used to emphasize text.

Undo command - Reverses the effect of the last command issued.

Window - Area of the screen where a file is displayed.

3 Reviews

Sections 3.1 — 3.5

1. a) What is a window?
   b) List the steps required to expand a window.

2. How can you view each page of a document as it will appear when printed?

3. If you make a mistake in formatting a paragraph and realize it before performing a second command, what is usually the fastest method of correcting the error?

4. What normally invisible characters are displayed on the screen when the All Characters command is selected?

5. a) What is meant by a highlighted block?
   b) How can you tell which text is selected?

6. What is one reason for creating a highlighted block?

7. List two methods that can be used to highlight a paragraph of text.

8. List the steps required to delete the second paragraph in a five paragraph document.

Sections 3.6 — 3.12

9. What is a document's format?

10. a) What is meant by formatting text?
    b) List three publications in which you have seen formatted text and describe the formats used (in terms of margins, headers and footers, pagination, and paragraph alignment).

11. List the steps required to bold the first line of text and underline the second line in a word processor document.

12. What is a font? List 5 of the fonts available on your computer.

13. a) What is character size measured in?
    b) How many points are there in an inch?

14. List the steps required to format the title of a document to bold, 24 point Arial type.

15. List the steps required to superscript the word *aid* and subscript the word *party* in the sentence:

    > Now is the time for all good people to come to the aid of the party.

16. How can the page controls be used to scroll directly to the last page in a document?

Sections 3.13 — 3.14

17. a) What is meant by justified text?
    b) List the steps required to justify a paragraph.

18. a) What is meant by centered text?
    b) What type of text is usually centered?

19. a) What is meant by text that is left aligned?
    b) What types of documents are usually formatted using left alignment?

20. What is the easiest way to justify all of the paragraphs in a document?

21. After centering and bolding a document title, you discover that you have also accidentally centered and bolded the first two paragraphs. How do you remove these formats from the paragraphs?

22. a) What is double spacing?
    b) Why might you want a document to be double spaced?

23. a) List the steps required to double space only the second paragraph in a document that contains five paragraphs.
    b) How can a double spaced paragraph be returned to single spacing?

24. a) What are margins?
    b) What are the default (standard) Works margins?

25. a) List the steps required to change the margins of a document so that the left margin is 2 inches and the right margin 3 inches.
    b) How long is a line of text after these margins have been set? (Assume an 8.5 x 11 inch sheet of paper.)

26. a) What is a header?
    b) What is a footer?
    c) What type of information is typically included in a header or footer?

27. List the steps required to have Works print the header "My Summer Vacation" and a footer containing the page number on each page of a document.

28. a) What is meant by pagination?
    b) What does a page break indicate?
    c) Explain two situations when you might want to control the pagination in a document.
    d) How can you create a page break?
    e) How can you remove the page break set in part (d)?

29. a) What are tabs used for?
    b) What is a default tab stop?
    c) What are default tab stops often used for?

30. What is the Ruler used for?

31. Explain the purpose of the following tab stops:
    a) left aligned
    b) right aligned
    c) center aligned
    d) decimal aligned

32. a) List the steps required to set a center aligned tab stop at 2¼ inches.
    b) How can the tab stop described in part (a) be removed?
    c) How can you tell where tab stops have been set?

33. List the steps required to change a center-aligned tab stop at 2.5" to a left-aligned tab stop at 3".

3

3 | Exercises

1. The file named COMPUTER ED contains information about computers in education.

   a) Open COMPUTER ED and make the changes noted below:

Justify all paragraphs

Computers in Education   *Center and bold title in 18 point Arial*

Over the past ten years it has become obvious that computers will play an increasingly important role in education. The invention of the microcomputer has made it possible for schools to purchase large numbers of computers at affordable prices. Now that computers are available for student use, educators have been discussing how they should be used. Below are a few examples of how schools are using their computers.

Computer Aided Instruction   *Bold subtitle in 14 point Arial*

Underline 2nd sentence

Computer programs have become available which instruct students in different academic disciplines. These programs have been especially effective in instructing students in languages and mathematics. When used with elementary school students, computer aided instruction (CAI) has been found to keep students interested in a subject while entertaining them at the same time. This is especially true of programs that employ multimedia -- integrating the computer with devices such as CD players and video disks. Mrs. Groves, a teacher at West Lawrence Elementary School, said, "When used as part of a complete learning system, computers help reinforce skills learned in the classroom."

Applications Programs   *Bold subtitle in 14 point Arial*

Many students are now taking courses which introduce them to applications software. They are taught how to use word processing, database, and spreadsheet software. Most students find that knowing how to use such software can help them in their other courses. Mr. Ronald Johnson of Ivy University said, "Our students are especially interested in learning how to use integrated software like Microsoft Works and ClarisWorks."

Writing Programs   *Bold subtitle in 14 point Arial*

Italicize "BASIC" and "C++"

Students who would like to pursue careers in computing often elect to take courses that teach them how to write computer programs. The languages most often learned are BASIC and C++. Besides teaching programming, these courses teach valuable problem-solving skills.

Lawrence Township Computer Usage   *Bold subtitle in 14 point Arial*

The following table shows the number of computers in Lawrence Township schools and percentage by manufacturer:

Manufacturer	Number	Percent
Apple II 35	7.9%	
IBM and clones	187	42.3%
Macintosh	212	48.0%
Other 8	1.8%	

b) Create a footer that prints the page number. Right align the footer text.

c) Format the table at the bottom of the document with the following tab stops:

- 3 inch right aligned tab stop (for the number of computers)
- 4¼ inch decimal aligned tab stop (for the percentage of computers)

d) Bold the table titles.

e) Save the modified COMPUTER ED and print a copy.

2. The file named OPENINGS contains several lines that could be used to start a short story. Open OPENINGS.

a) Choose one of the lines, delete the rest, then write a short paragraph using the remaining line as the opening line.

b) Justify and double space the paragraph.

c) Create a title, then format it as 18 point and bold.

d) Create a header showing your name. Center the header text.

e) Save the modified OPENINGS and print a copy.

3. The SuperSub sandwich shop has just opened a new store in this area. They are creating a flyer and need your help to improve its appearance. Open SUPERSUB.

a) Center and bold the flyer's heading.

b) Change the font for the heading and increase its size to 18 points.

c) Format all occurrences of the word "SUPER" in SUPERSUB as superscript. Format all occurrences of the word "SUB" in SUPERSUB as subscript.

d) Bold each occurrence of the word SUPERSUB.

e) Justify the entire body of the advertisement (do not justify the title).

f) Change the font of all the occurrences of the word "FREE" so it stands out.

g) Insert a superscripted asterisk (*) after the words "absolutely FREE" in the first paragraph. Type the following text in a new paragraph at the very bottom of the flyer:

*Availability and number of customers may make the offer null and void. No refunds, rainchecks, or apologies.

Format the text in the new paragraph in a different font and size.

h) Save the modified SUPERSUB and print a copy.

3

4. In Chapter Two, Exercise 5 you wrote a review of a movie or concert and saved it in a file named Critic.

   a) Open Critic and make a bold, centered headline that has the name of the event you reviewed.

   b) Italicize any titles in the review, such as the title of a movie, an album or song title, etc.

   c) The paper's editors like all submissions to be doubled spaced. Format the body of your review to conform with their wishes.

   d) Create a header that prints CRITIC'S CHOICE. Center the header text.

   e) Justify the body of the review so that it looks more like a newspaper article.

   f) Save the modified Critic and print a copy.

5. Tables make information easier to read and understand. It is a simple process to use tabs to create tables in documents.

   a) In a new word processor document create the following table. Precede the first column and separate the opponent column from the record column with a single tab character. After entering the data, set a left aligned tab stop at 1 inch and a right aligned tab stop at 3 inches so that the table appears similar to the following:

Opponent	Record
Audubon	7-4
Cherry Hill East	7-4
Cherry Hill West	4-7
Collingswood	2-8
Gulf Stream	6-5
Haddon Heights	10-1
Pine Crest	8-1

   Note: Your table will not look like the one above until tab stops have been set.

   b) Save the document naming it Table.

   c) Bold the column titles.

   d) Add a third column as shown below. Separate it from the second using a single tab character. After entering the new data, set a centered tab stop at 3¾ inches for the entire table:

Opponent	**Record**	**Division**
Audubon	7-4	I
Cherry Hill East	7-4	IV
Cherry Hill West	4-7	IA
Collingswood	2-8	III
Gulf Stream	6-5	IV
Haddon Heights	10-1	V
Pine Crest	8-1	I

   e) Save the modified Table and print a copy.

6. In Chapter Two, Exercise 4 you created a file named College Apply that contains an application letter for a college. Open College Apply and follow the directions below to create a table in the application letter:

   a) Insert two blank lines after the first paragraph of the body of the letter.

   b) Using single tab characters to precede the first column and separate the remaining columns, enter the table below:

Year	Semester	GPA	Special Activities
1995	Fall	3.6	President of Student Congress
1996	Spring	3.9	Captain of Debate Team
1996	Fall	4.0	All-State Swim Team
1997	Spring	3.95	All-State Gymnastics Team

   Note: Your table will not look like the one above until tab stops have been set.

   c) After entering the data, set the following tab stops for the entire table:
      - At ½" create a left aligned tab stop (for the Year)
      - At 1½" create a centered tab stop (for the Semester)
      - At 2½" create a decimal aligned tab stop (for the GPA)
      - At 3¼" create a left aligned tab stop (for the Special Activities)

   d) Save the modified College Apply.

   e) Bold the column titles.

   f) Double space the first paragraph of the letter.

   g) Save the modified College Apply and print a copy.

7. Red Barn petting zoo needs a listing of their farm animals. In a new word processor file create the following table, preceding the first column and separating the remaining columns with a single tab character:

Name	Color	Gender	Type
Betsey	Black/White	F	Guernsey cow
Bluebell	Brown	F	Ayrshire cow
Lucy	Brown	F	Morgan horse
Sandy	Tan/White	F	Mustang horse
Toby	White	F	Shetland pony
Harriot	Red	F	Shetland pony
SusieQ	Red	F	Jersey Red hen
Harry	Red	M	Maine Red rooster
Marylou	White	F	Long Island duck
Larry	White	M	Long Island duck

   Note: Your table will not look like the one above until tab stops have been set.

   a) After entering the data, Set the following tab stops for the entire table:
      - At ½" create a left aligned tab stop (for the Name)
      - At 1½" create a left aligned tab stop (for the Color)
      - At 2¾" create a center aligned tab stop (for the Gender)
      - At 3¼" create a left aligned tab stop (for the Type)

   b) Save the file naming it Red Barn.

c) Create a title above the table which reads: Red Barn Farm Animal Inventory

d) Bold and center the title, then bold the column headings.

e) Change the top and bottom margins to 0.75".

f) Add the Location column shown below. Separate it from the fourth column using a single tab character. After entering the new data, set a centered tab stop at 5¼" for the entire table:

Red Barn Farm Animal Inventory

Name	Color	Gender	Type	Location
Betsey	Black/White	F	Guernsey cow	Farm Stall A1
Bluebell	Brown	F	Ayrshire cow	Farm Stall A2
Lucy	Brown	F	Morgan horse	Farm Stall A3
Sandy	Tan/White	F	Mustang horse	Farm Stall B1
Toby	White	F	Shetland pony	Farm Stall B2
Harriot	Red	F	Shetland pony	Farm Stall B3
SusieQ	Red	F	Jersey Red hen	Barn Yard
Harry	Red	M	Maine Red rooster	Barn Yard
Marylou	White	F	Long Island duck	Farm Pond
Larry	White	M	Long Island duck	Farm Pond

g) Save the modified Red Barn and print a copy.

8. The Ivy University literary magazine would like to print the essay you wrote for Chapter Two, Exercise 7. Open Summer Essay and make the following changes:

a) Create a title that describes your essay. Bold and center the title, then change the point size and font of the title.

b) Double space the body of the essay.

c) Create a header showing your name. Left align the header.

d) Create a footer that prints the page number. Center the page number.

e) Change the top and bottom margins to 0.75".

f) Save the modified Summer Essay and print a copy.

9. The memo you wrote in Chapter Two, Exercise 11 needs to be formatted. Open Shakespeare Schedule and make the following changes:

a) Create a header showing the course title: Independent Study of Shakespeare. Center the header.

b) Format the word "Memorandum" as bold and italic.

c) Underline the words "To," "From," "Date," and "Subject."

d) Italicize the "Paper Topic" and "Due Date" titles.

e) Edit the listing of research papers so that there is a single tab before each paper topic and each due date. Delete any spaces that were previously used to separate the columns.

f) Set the following tab stops for the entire table:
- Centered at 2 inches (for the paper topic)
- Right aligned at 4 inches (for the due date)

The tabs stops could be improved, so they will be changed in the next step.

g) Modify the previous tab stops for the entire table to:
- Right aligned at 2 inches
- Left aligned at 4 inches

h) Delete the tab stops and create new ones for the entire table:
- Left aligned at 1½ inch
- Right aligned at 3¾ inches

i) Insert a blank line between the column titles and the column information.

j) Save the modified Shakespeare Schedule and print a copy.

10. Open Science Bio, which contains the biography you wrote in Chapter Two, Exercise 9 and make the following changes:

a) Create a header showing your name. Center the header text.

b) Create a footer showing the page number. Right align the footer text.

c) Change the top and bottom margins to 0.75".

d) Center, bold, and underline the title of your paper.

e) Double space the body of the biography.

f) Save the modified Science Bio and print a copy.

11. In Chapter Two, Exercise 8 you created an advertisement for an upcoming event in a file named Advertisement. Open Advertisement and make the following changes:

a) Create a header showing your name.

b) Use at least four different formatting options such as tabs, centering, fonts, sizes, and styles to make the advertisement more attractive.

c) Save the modified Advertisement and print a copy.

12. The Gibbon Research Proposal you corrected in Chapter Two, Exercise 12 needs further refinement before it is finished. Open RESEARCH and make the following changes:

a) Center the paragraphs from "A PROPOSAL FOR RESEARCH" up through and including the "University of Eastern Florida" paragraph.

b) Bold the first three paragraphs of the proposal (the first two titles).

c) Change the top and bottom margins to 0.75".

d) Create a footer that prints the word Page followed by the page number.

e) Underline the headings: "Summary," "Purpose and Description," "White-handed Gibbons," and "Computerized Guide."

f) Place the cursor in the space above the title "BUDGET" on page 2 and insert a page break.

g) Center the "BUDGET" title and make it bold and a larger point size.

h) Set the following tab stops for the lines containing dollar values:
  • Left aligned at 1 inch
  • Decimal aligned at 5 inches

i) In the "Notes" section on page 3 insert a tab before each of the funding/support items.

j) Save the modified RESEARCH and print a copy.

13. The store opening you announced in Chapter Two, Exercise 10 needs to be formatted. Open Grand Opening and make the following changes:

a) Bold all occurrences of the store name.

b) Use appropriate paragraph alignment throughout the flyer.

c) Use appropriate tabs throughout the flyer.

d) Since this is a flyer, increase the font size of all the text so that the information fills the page.

e) Save the modified Grand Opening and print a copy.

14. City Zoo keeps a list of their animals in the word processor. Open CITY ZOO and make the following changes:

a) Set the following tab stops for the entire table (including column titles):
  • create a 2.5" center aligned tab stop (for the Number/Gender)
  • create a 3.5" left aligned tab stop (for the Type)
  • create a 4" left aligned tab stop (for the Location)
  • create a 6" right aligned tab stop (for the Staff)

b) Bold all the column titles in the table.

c) Center the title "City Zoo Catalog" and make it a different font and larger size.

d) Create a footer that prints Dr. Deborah Lynn - President of City Zoo. Center the footer.

e) Below the listing add the following legend:

Animal Type
M - Mammal
R - Reptile
B - Bird
I - Insect
F - Fish

f) Save the modified CITY ZOO and print a copy.

15. You are to produce a questionnaire that could be used to survey students in your school.

    a) In a new word processor document create a list of at least six survey questions. Each question should be on a separate line to leave room for responses. Include questions concerning personal statistics, favorite course in school, favorite movie or band, and anything else you would like to know.

    b) Save the questionnaire naming it Survey Form.

    c) At the top of the questionnaire, create the title Student Survey and make it bold, centered, and in a larger font size.

    d) Change the font of the entire questionnaire. Double space the survey questions.

    e) Create a header that includes your name and the name of the file.

    f) Save the modified Survey Form and print a copy.

16. Open the file Recycle News which you created in Chapter Two, Exercise 14. Improve your article's appearance by making the following changes:

    a) Bold the headline and increase its size to 14 points.

    b) Add your byline (by *your name*) under the headline. Format the byline as italics.

    c) Justify the body of the article.

    d) Add a header with the words Recycle News centered and bolded.

    e) Add a footer with the word Page and a code for the page number. Center the footer text.

    f) Save the modified Recycle News and print a copy.

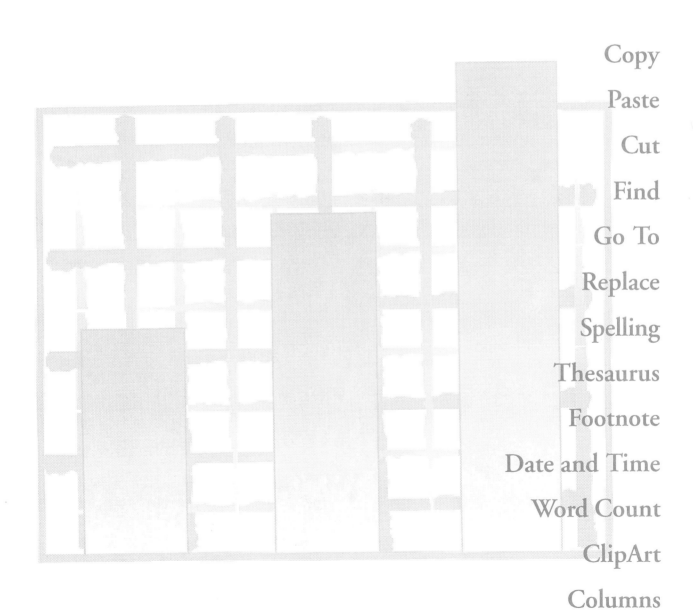

Chapter Four
Advanced Word Processor Techniques

Copy

Paste

Cut

Find

Go To

Replace

Spelling

Thesaurus

Footnote

Date and Time

Word Count

ClipArt

Columns

Objectives

After completing this chapter you will be able to:

1. Copy and move highlighted blocks of text.

2. Use the Control key for command and formatting shortcuts.

3. Find and replace text using the Find and the Replace commands.

4. Use the Go To command to display a specific page.

5. Use the spelling checker to check the spelling of a document.

6. Use the thesaurus to suggest synonyms for words.

7. Indent paragraphs and create hanging indents for bulleted lists.

8. Create and edit footnotes.

9. Time stamp documents.

10. Use the Word Count command to count the words in a document.

11. Add graphics to a document and change the graphic's size.

12. Insert special characters such as ® and ¢ into a document.

13. Create a multi-column document.

4

T his chapter discusses some of the advanced features of the word processor. Editing commands such as Cut, Copy, and Paste are introduced. Specialty features, such as the spelling checker, are also covered.

4.1 Copying and Pasting Blocks of Text

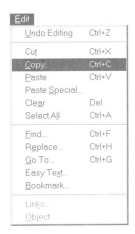

There are times when text needs to be repeated in a publication. Rather than typing the text multiple times, it can be duplicated by using the Copy and Paste commands from the Edit menu.

When the Copy command (Ctrl+C) is executed, highlighted text is copied to a special area of memory called the *Clipboard*. When the Paste command (Ctrl+V) is executed, a copy of the Clipboard contents is placed at the current cursor position. If the cursor is positioned within existing text, any text after the cursor is automatically moved to make room for the pasted text.

Creating a copy of text is a four step process:

1. Highlight the text to be copied.
2. Execute the Copy command.
3. Place the cursor where the copied block is to be inserted.
4. Execute the Paste command. A copy of the highlighted block is placed at the cursor position.

On the Tool bar, click the Copy button () to execute the Copy command, and click the Paste button () to execute the Paste command.

4.2 Moving Text

The Cut command (Ctrl+X) is used to move highlighted text from one place in a document to another. For example, a sentence can be removed from one paragraph and placed in a paragraph on the next page. Text that is cut is removed from the document and placed on the Clipboard. Any text after the cut text is automatically moved up to fill the space.

Moving text is a four step process:

1. Highlight the text to be moved.
2. Execute the Cut command. The highlighted text is removed from the screen.
3. Place the cursor where the moved block is to be inserted.
4. Execute the Paste command. The previously cut text is placed at the cursor position.

On the Tool bar, the Cut button () is clicked to cut text.

4.3 Using the Control Key

The Control key (Ctrl) is located at the bottom of the keyboard, next to the spacebar. One application of this key is to execute commands without using the mouse. For example, in the File menu the Save command has the shortcut Ctrl+S next to it:

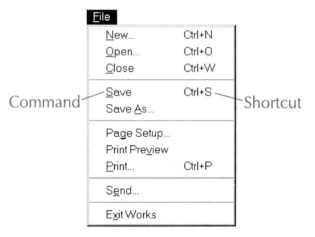

Command — Shortcut

Control key shortcuts are listed next to the command names in the menu

This means that holding down the Control key and pressing S once (written in this text as Ctrl+S) executes the Save command without first displaying the menu. This shortcut can save time because you do not have to take your hands off the keyboard.

Another use for the Ctrl key is to apply formatting. This can be faster than executing the appropriate command and then selecting options from a dialog box. Control key shortcuts are listed below for commands and formatting options previously discussed:

Print	Ctrl+P	Copy	Ctrl+C
Undo	Ctrl+Z	Paste	Ctrl+V
		Cut	Ctrl+X
Bold	Ctrl+B	Left align	Ctrl+L
Italic	Ctrl+I	Center align	Ctrl+E
Underline	Ctrl+U	Right align	Ctrl+R
		Justify	Ctrl+J
Single-space	Ctrl+1		
Double-space	Ctrl+2		
Superscript	Ctrl+Shift+=(equal sign)		
Subscript	Ctrl+=(equal sign)		

4

In this Practice you will use the Cut, Copy, and Paste commands and the Clipboard. A high-lighted block of text will be moved and another sentence copied.

1) START WORKS AND OPEN IVY PROMO

a. Following the directions given in Chapter Two, start Works. The Works Task Launcher dialog box is displayed.
b. Click on Cancel to remove the dialog box.
c. From the File menu, select Open. In the Open dialog box, double-click on IVY PROMO to open it. Use the All Characters command to display special symbols if they are not already displayed.

2) HIGHLIGHT THE TEXT TO BE MOVED

Highlight the sentence which begins "There is a positive reaction…" in the second paragraph. In the highlight, include the space after period at the end of the sentence, but do not include the space before the "T" at the beginning of the sentence.

3) MOVE THE HIGHLIGHTED BLOCK

a. From the Edit menu, select the Cut command. The text is removed from the screen and placed on the Clipboard.
b. Place the cursor before the "W" that begins the sentence "With world famous…" in the first paragraph.
c. From the Edit menu, select the Paste command. The sentence is inserted at the cursor position.

4) HIGHLIGHT THE TEXT TO BE COPIED

You will place a copy of the first sentence at the end of the document.

Highlight the sentence which begins "Ivy University is one of our nation's…" in the first paragraph. In the highlight, include the space after period at the end of the sentence, but do not include the tab before the "I" at the beginning of the sentence.

5) COPY THE HIGHLIGHTED BLOCK

a. On the Tool bar, click on the Copy button (🖺).
b. Scroll to page 3 and place the cursor at the beginning of the last sentence in the document, but after the tab character that begins the sentence.
c. On the Tool bar, click on the Paste button (🖺). The sentence is inserted in the last paragraph of the document:

> ¶
> In·Conclusion¶
> ¶
> → Ivy·University· is· one· of· our· nation's· most· prestigious· private· universities.·
> We· hope· that· you· have· enjoyed· this· brief· description· of· Ivy· University· and· that·
> you·plan·to·visit·us·soon.¶

d. Scroll to the top of the document and verify that the original sentence is still there.

6) SAVE IVY PROMO

4.4 Finding Text in a Document

The Find command is used to scan a document for *search text*. This text may be a single character, word, or phrase. Selecting the Find command from the Edit menu (Ctrl+F) displays a dialog box where search text is typed:

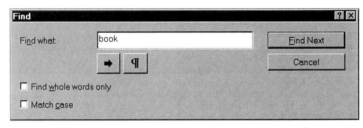

Search text is typed in the Find what entry box

In this case, the word "book" has been entered as the search text. When Find Next is selected, Works starts searching from the current cursor position and continues through the document looking for the search text. If a match is found, Works stops scanning and highlights the text. To continue searching the document, the Find Next button is selected again. If the search text is not found, a message similar to the following is displayed:

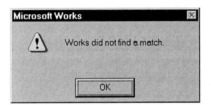

Works could not find the search text

The Find whole words only option in the Find dialog box is used when occurrences of the search text that are not part of another word are to be found. For example, a search for the will not only find the but also they, theory, and another unless Find whole words only is selected.

The Match case option is used when text with the same capitalization as the search text is to be found. For example, with Match case selected a search for CAT will not find Cat or cat. A very precise find can be performed by using the Match case and Find whole words only options together.

On some occasions, text that matches the search text may be displayed behind the Find dialog box. When this occurs, the Find dialog box can be moved by dragging its Title bar. Clicking on the Close button of the dialog box terminates the search and the last search text found is left highlighted.

4.5 Finding Special Characters

Special characters such as tab and paragraph characters can also be found using the Find command. For example, suppose you wish to locate only occurrences of the word Because if it is at the beginning of a paragraph. If all paragraphs in the document are indented with a single tab, a more precise search would include the tab character before the word because. To do this, click on the Tab button (➡) and then type the rest of the search text:

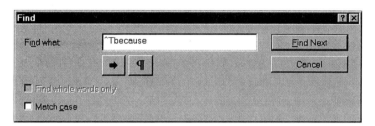

Find Next highlights the next "because" preceded by a tab

The tab character appears as ^T in the Find what entry box. Similarly, a paragraph marker (enter character) can be found by clicking on the Paragraph button (¶). The enter character appears as ^P in the Find what box.

4.6 Going to a Specific Page

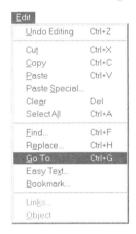

Executing the Go To command from the Edit menu (Ctrl+G) displays the Go To dialog box:

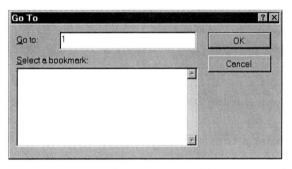

Go to page may be used to move quickly to a specific page

Typing a page number in the Go to entry box and then selecting OK moves the cursor to the top of that page. This can be much quicker than using the arrow keys or scroll bars, especially when the document is long.

A benefit of this command is that it can be used to limit the amount of text that is checked by the Find command. For example, if you wish to locate the occurrence of text, such as a name, which is on page 15 or later, you can use the Go To command to move the cursor to the top of page 15. Executing the Find command begins a search from the current cursor position.

In this Practice the Find and Go To commands will be used. You will begin by searching for each occurrence of the word "bandage" in the Ivy University promotional file. Start Works and open IVY PROMO if you have not already done so.

1) EXECUTE THE FIND COMMAND

    a. Make sure that the cursor is at the beginning of the IVY PROMO document.

    b. From the Edit menu, select the Find command. The Find dialog box is displayed.

2) FIND SEARCH TEXT

Type the word Bandage (with a capital "B") in the Find what box and select the Find Next button. There is a slight pause as Works searches the document. The first "bandage" found is in the course description for class 101. Note that "Bandage" is highlighted in the text. The plural "Bandages" is found because "Bandage" is part of the word.

3) REPEAT THE FIND USING THE SAME SEARCH TEXT

    a. In the Find dialog box, select the Find Next button to highlight the next occurrence of the same search text.

    b. Select Find Next a third time. Works highlights the word "bandage" with a lower-case "b" even though the search text is "Bandage."

    c. Continue to select Find Next until Works displays a message asking if you want to continue searching from the beginning of the document. The message is displayed because the Header text has not yet been searched.

    d. Select No to remove the dialog box.

    e. Remove the Find dialog box by clicking on its Close button. Note how the last occurrence of bandage remains highlighted in the text.

4) GO DIRECTLY TO THE TOP OF PAGE 1

    a. From the Edit menu, select the Go To command. The Go To dialog box is displayed.

    b. Type 1 in the Go to box and select OK. The cursor is placed at the beginning of the document and page 1 is displayed.

5) MODIFY THE SEARCH TEXT

    a. Press Ctrl+F to execute the Find command. The previously entered text is displayed and highlighted in the Find what box.

    b. Click on the Match case option so that only "Bandage" with a capital "B" will be found.

    c. Select the Find Next button. Note how the found text has an uppercase "B."

    d. Continue to select Find Next until Works displays a message asking if you want to continue searching from the beginning of the document. Select No. Note how a more specific search has been created by using the available options.

    e. Close the Find dialog box.

6) SEARCH FOR A SPECIAL CHARACTER

a. Use the All Characters command from the View menu to display symbols for normally invisible characters if they are not already displayed.

b. We want to locate all occurrences of the word "Ivy" which begin a paragraph. We can do this by searching for a tab and then the word. Use the Go To command to move the cursor to the beginning of the document.

c. Display the Find dialog box. Click on 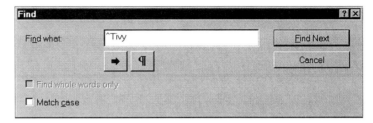 to replace the current search text with a tab. Remember highlighted text is replaced by a typed character, in this case a tab character. Type the word ivy.

d. Click on the Match case option to deselect it. Your dialog box should look like the following:

e. Select Find Next to start the search. The first "ivy" located is in the first sentence of the first paragraph. Note how the tab symbol is also highlighted.

f. Continue to select Find Next until Works displays a message asking if you want to continue searching from the beginning of the document. Select No.

g. Close the Find dialog box.

4.7 Replacing Text

The Replace command from the Edit menu (Ctrl+H) is used to locate text and then replace it with another piece of text you supply called the *replace text*. This makes it easy to create different versions of a document. For example, Works could be used to create a letter requesting an admissions interview with Ivy University. After printing the letter, the Replace command could then be used to change each occurrence of "Ivy University" to "Trenton State" and the new letter printed. Then "Trenton State" could be changed to "New Brunswick College" and so on. Thus, all the letters could be easily created without having to type each one separately.

The Replace command displays a dialog box similar to the following:

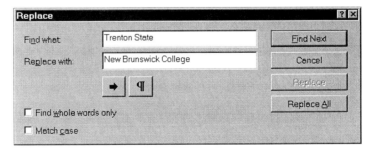

Works will search for "Trenton State" and replace it with "New Brunswick College"

Tab and paragraph characters may be used in either the search or replace text. The Find whole words only option is used when occurrences of the search text that are not part of another word are to be replaced. The Match case option is used when text that has the same capitalization as the search text is to be replaced.

Find Next must be selected to find the first occurrence of the search text. The Replace command starts at the current cursor position. After the first occurrence has been found, the Replace button is no longer dimmed. Selecting Replace replaces the currently highlighted text with the replace text and then finds the next occurrence of the search text. This is usually the best procedure because each replacement can be verified before it is made. The Replace All button is used to automatically replace all occurrences of the search text with the replace text.

Practice 3

Ivy University is considering updating its image by changing its name. In this Practice you will use the Replace command to change each occurrence of "Ivy University" to "Modern College" in IVY PROMO. If you have not already done so, start Works and open IVY PROMO.

1) EXECUTE THE REPLACE COMMAND

a. Make sure the cursor is at the beginning of IVY PROMO.
b. From the Edit menu, select the Replace command. In the dialog box, search text and options may be displayed from the last Practice.
c. Type Ivy University for the Find what text, replacing any old search text.
d. Press the Tab key once to move the cursor to the Replace with box. Type Modern College.

2) REPLACE EACH OCCURRENCE

a. Select the Find Next button to highlight the first occurrence of Ivy University.
b. Works moves the cursor to the first occurrence of Ivy University and highlights it.
c. Select the Replace button to replace the highlighted text with Modern College and highlight the next occurrence of Ivy University.
d. Select Replace. Works changes the highlighted occurrence and then highlights the next occurrence of the find text.
e. For each Ivy University found, click on the Replace button to make the replacement and then locate the next occurrence. When Works displays a message asking if you want to continue searching from the beginning of the document, select No.
f. Select the Close button to remove the dialog box. Scroll through the document to verify the changes.

3) REPLACE ALL OCCURRENCES OF MODERN COLLEGE

a. University officials have decided against the name change. From the Edit menu, select Replace.
b. Type Modern College in the Find what box and Ivy University in the Replace with box.
c. Select the Replace All button. All occurrences of "Modern College" are changed to "Ivy University."
d. Select the Close button to remove the dialog box. Scroll through the document to verify the changes.

4) SAVE IVY PROMO

4.8 Using the Spelling Checker

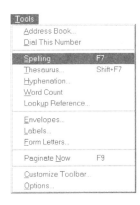

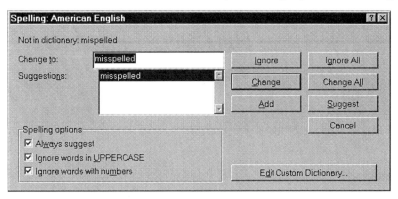

One of the most useful features of a word processor is its ability to check the spelling of the words in a document. In Works, this is accomplished by using the Spelling command from the Tools menu (F7) or the Spelling Checker button on the Tool bar ( ). When the spelling in a document is checked, each word in the document is compared to words in a dictionary file. If a word is not in the dictionary it is displayed in a dialog box:

The Spelling dialog box displays words not found in the Works dictionary

From the Spelling dialog box you can type a correction in the Change to box or select a correctly spelled word from a list of suggestions, and then select the Change button to make the correction in the document.

Because the dictionary file does not contain every word in the English language, it is possible that the spelling command will not find a correctly spelled word, such as a proper name or abbreviation. When this happens, Ignore can be selected to ignore the word. If the word is one that you will use often, such as your name, you can have Works add it to its dictionary file by selecting Add.

After Works has checked the entire document, including any header, footer, and footnotes, a dialog box appears indicating that the spelling check is complete. Selecting OK removes the dialog box.

If the Spelling dialog box obscures the word currently in question, the dialog box can be moved by dragging its Title bar.

To limit the number of words checked by the spelling checker, first highlight the block of text to be checked. Works then checks only the highlighted words when Spelling is executed. For example, a single word can be checked by first highlighting it and then clicking on the Spelling Checker button.

Practice 4

Ivy University is about to have 50,000 copies of its promotional file printed. In this Practice you will use the Spelling checker to verify the spelling in that document before sending it to the print shop. Start Works if you have not already done so and open IVY PROMO.

1) EXECUTE THE SPELLING COMMAND

From the Tools menu, select the Spelling command. There is a slight pause as Works checks the spelling. Works finds a word that may be misspelled and displays it in the Spelling dialog box.

2) CORRECT THE MISSPELLED WORDS

a. Works finds the word "feilds" and suggests the word "fields."
b. Because "fields" is the word we want, select the Change button to accept the suggested spelling and have it replace the misspelled word in the file. Works makes the correction and continues to check the spelling.
c. Works finds the word "proffessional" and suggests the spelling "professional." Because "professional" is the word we want, select the Change button to accept the suggested spelling and have it replace the misspelled word in the file. Works makes the correction and continues to check the spelling.

3) SKIP THE PROPER NAMES

a. The next word in question is "Phineas." Select Ignore to ignore this proper name.
b. Continue to Ignore any proper names.
c. When the spelling check is finished a dialog box is displayed. Select OK to remove the dialog box.

4) SAVE IVY PROMO

4.9 Using the Thesaurus

Using a *thesaurus* can help make your writing more interesting. A thesaurus is a collection of *synonyms* which are words that have similar meanings. For example, chilly is a synonym for cool. Works contains a thesaurus that can supply synonyms for many words and phrases. To display a list of synonyms for a word, highlight the word and then select the Thesaurus command from the Tools menu (Shift+F7):

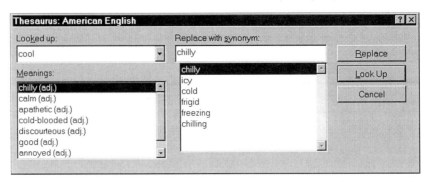

The Thesaurus command displays synonyms for a selected word

Because words can have different definitions, Works provides a list of meanings identified by their parts of speech (adjective, noun, verb, etc.). The Replace with synonym list corresponds to the highlighted meaning. Highlighting a different meaning changes the list of synonyms.

Selecting Replace replaces the word in the document with the highlighted meaning or synonym. Selecting Cancel removes the dialog box, leaving the word in the document unchanged.

Works displays additional synonyms for any of the suggested synonyms or meanings by highlighting the word in the list and selecting Look up. This procedure may be continued for as many words as desired.

Like the dictionary, Works uses a file for its thesaurus which does not contain every possible word. If the selected word cannot be found, a dialog box similar to the following is displayed:

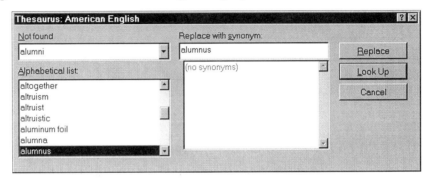

Works provides suggestions when a selected word is not found

Messages like this may be the result of highlighting a misspelled word. To avoid this, it is a good practice to spell check a document before using the thesaurus.

It is important to realize that the thesaurus will only replace the highlighted word or phrase. For example, the word "bucolic" might appear five times in a document. However, only the highlighted one will be replaced with the selected synonym. Multiple occurrences can be replaced using the Replace command.

Practice 5

In this Practice you will use the thesaurus to suggest synonyms for two words. Start Works and open IVY PROMO if you have not already done so.

1) LOCATE THE WORD TO BE CHANGED

Double-click on the word "major" in the sentence which begins "A major part of successful treatment..." near the bottom of page one.

2) EXECUTE THE THESAURUS COMMAND

a. From the Tools menu, select the Thesaurus command. The Thesaurus dialog box is displayed.

b. The definition of major that is being used in the sentence is most similar to "important." In the Meanings list, click on the word important. Your Thesaurus dialog box should look similar to the following:

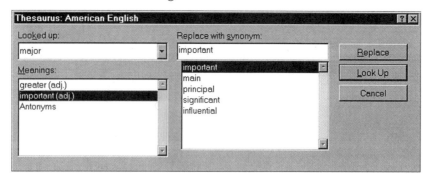

3) SELECT THE DESIRED SYNONYM AND REPLACE THE WORD

a. From the group of synonyms, click on significant to select it.
b. Select the Replace button. The word "major" is replaced with "significant" and the dialog box is removed.

4) CHANGE THE WORD "COMMON"

a. Double-click on the word "common" in the description for course 101 to select it.
b. Execute the Thesaurus command. "Common" has many meanings.
c. Select the meaning "ordinary" to get a new list of synonyms.
d. Select the meaning "prevalent" to get another list of synonyms.
e. Select "universal" from the list of synonyms.
f. Select Replace. The word common is replaced by universal.

5) SAVE IVY PROMO

4.10 Paragraph Formats - Indents

Margin settings apply to the entire document and cannot change from paragraph to paragraph. However, it is possible to decrease the width of the text lines in a specific paragraph by using *indents*. Indents are often used to set off a paragraph, such as a quotation.

The default indents are 0 inches, meaning that lines extend from the left margin to the right margin. Specifying left and right indents causes a paragraph to have a shorter line length:

This is a normal paragraph. Each full line extends from the left margin to the right margin.

    This paragraph is indented. The lines of text extend from the left to the right indent, making a shorter line length.

Executing the Paragraph command from the Format menu displays the Format Paragraph dialog box. Selecting the Indents and Alignment tab displays the following options:

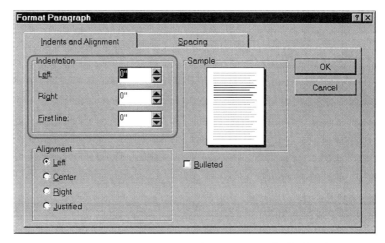

Indents may be set using the Paragraph dialog box

The left indent amount is typed in the Left entry box and the right indent is typed in the Right entry box. For example, to indent a paragraph by 1 inch on the both the right and left, type 1 in the Right box and 1 in the Left box and then select OK.

Setting an indent affects only the paragraph that contains the cursor. Multiple paragraphs can be formatted together by highlighting them first and then applying the indents.

Indents can also be set by dragging markers on the Ruler:

Right indent

Left indent

The indent markers are displayed on the Ruler

Dragging an indent marker changes the indent for either the paragraph that contains the cursor or for the highlighted block of paragraphs. This method of changing indents is usually less precise than using the Paragraph command.

- -

Practice 6

In this Practice you will change paragraph indents. Start Works and open IVY PROMO if you have not already done so.

1) CREATE PARAGRAPH INDENTS

    a. If the Ruler is not displayed, select Ruler from the View menu.

    b. Place the cursor in the paragraph which begins "Inline skating has strained…," the quote below the faculty listing on page 3. Note the indent markers in the Ruler.

    c. From the Format menu, select Paragraph. In the dialog box, select the Indents and Alignment tab to display indent options if they are not already displayed.

    d. In the Indentation section, type 1 for the Left indent.

    e. Press the Tab key to highlight the Right indent option. Type 0.75 for the right indent.

    f. Select OK. Note how the lines of the paragraph are shorter. Also, look at the Ruler and see that the indent markers have been changed to reflect the new indents.

2) CHANGE THE RIGHT INDENT

    a. Be sure the cursor is still in the quote paragraph.

    b. In the Ruler, drag the right indent marker to the 5 inch mark. Note how the right indent of the paragraph changes.

3) SAVE IVY PROMO

<u>Check</u> - Your screen should be similar to:

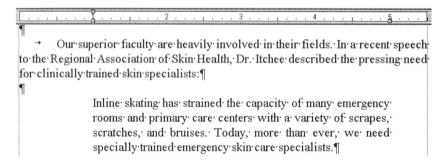

4.11 Hanging Indents and Bulleted Lists

The *hanging indent* is a special type of indent that is often used for lists, outlines, or bibliography entries in a research paper. Below is a bibliography entry using a hanging indent:

Canine, Butch S. <u>My Life as a Dog: A True-Life Story</u>.
New York: Sirius Press, 1993.

Notice how the first line of the paragraph sticks out from the rest of the paragraph.

A hanging indent is created by formatting a paragraph with a left indent and a negative first line indent. For example, to create a half inch hanging indent, select the Paragraph command from the Format menu and then select the Indents and Alignment tab. For the Left indent type 1 and for the First line indent type –0.5:

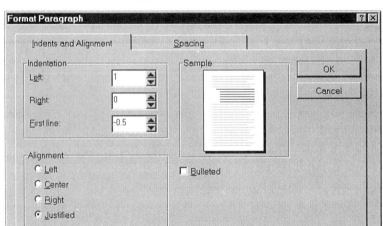

These measurements will produce a half inch hanging indent

The first line indent is relative to the left indent. Therefore, the first line will stick out ½" to the left of the rest of the paragraph.

An Introduction to Computing Using Microsoft Works

On the Ruler, a first line indent can be created by dragging the first line indent marker. Dragging the left indent marker also moves the first line indent marker, even when the two are separated. Dragging the left indent marker while holding down the Shift key moves it independently of the first line indent marker.

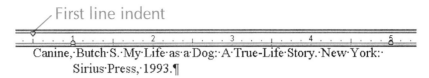

Canine, Butch S. My Life as a Dog: A True-Life Story. New York: Sirius Press, 1993.¶

A negative first line indent creates the hanging effect

One use for the hanging indent is in the creation of *bulleted lists*. In a bulleted list, a special character such as an asterisk (*) is used to introduce each item:

Today's Lunch Specials

* *Pizza Bianca* - A delicate blend of four imported cheeses with fresh Italian herbs on a thin, crispy crust.
* *Insalata di Pollo* - Oak grilled chicken breast served with fresh salad greens, mozzarella, roasted peppers, and olives in a light vinaigrette.
* *Veal Chop* - Mesquite grilled with mushrooms.

In a bulleted list each item is a separate paragraph formatted with a hanging indent. A tab after the bullet character aligns the text of the first line with the rest of the paragraph:

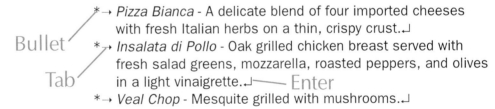

Bulleted lists do not show order of importance within the list; each item is equally important. However, *numbered lists* show a priority of importance and should be used, for example, when listing steps in a recipe. Tabs and hanging indents are also used to create numbered lists such as the following recipe:

1. Pour chicken broth into saucepan and bring to a boil.
2. Add noodles and cook for 5-7 minutes, stirring occasionally.
3. Reduce heat and add chicken chunks. Let simmer for 3-4 minutes.
4. Serve immediately with crackers.

Numbers are used as the "bullets" for this recipe because each step logically follows the previous one.

In this Practice you will create a bulleted list in the course description of IVY PROMO using hanging indents. Start Works and open IVY PROMO if you have not already done so. Use the All Characters command to display special symbols if they are not already displayed.

1) SCROLL TO THE COURSE DESCRIPTIONS

Scroll to the course descriptions and place the cursor in the paragraph describing course 101, which begins "A comprehensive survey…."

2) CREATE A HANGING INDENT

a. From the Format menu, select Paragraph. In the Format Paragraph dialog box, se-lect the Indents and Alignment tab to display the indent options.
b. In the Left entry box, type 0.75.
c. In the First line entry box, type –0.25.
d. Select OK. The first line of the paragraph hangs out to the left of the second and third lines of the paragraph:

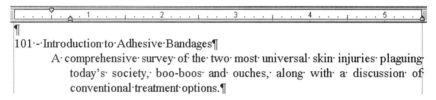

3) ADD THE BULLET

a. Move the cursor to the left of the first character in the current paragraph, the "A" in "A comprehensive survey…."
b. Type an asterisk (*) as a bullet.
c. Only the bullet should hang out from the rest of the paragraph. Press the Tab key to insert a tab between the bullet and the "A." This aligns the text in the first line with the rest of the indented paragraph. The course description paragraph is now a bulleted list:

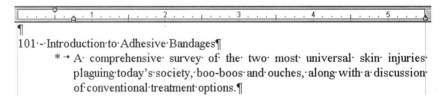

4) FORMAT THE NEXT COURSE DESCRIPTION

a. Place the cursor in the paragraph describing course 102, which begins "Proper use of…."
b. On the Ruler, drag the left indent marker (the bottom marker) to the 0.75" mark.
c. On the Ruler, drag the first line indent marker (the top marker) to the left to the 0.5" mark.
d. Place the cursor at the beginning of the paragraph, type a bullet (*), and then press Tab to align the text. The course description for 102 now has the same format as course 101.

5) FORMAT THE REMAINING COURSES

Follow the instructions in steps 2 and 3 to format the six remaining course descriptions.

6) SAVE IVY PROMO

4.12 Creating Footnotes and Endnotes

Research papers and reports often include *footnotes* to document sources. Selecting the Footnote command from the Insert menu displays the following dialog box:

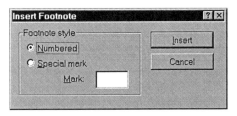

The Insert Footnote dialog box

Numbered is the default option. Selecting Insert adds a number at the current cursor position and then adds the same number at the bottom of the page. The cursor is automatically placed to the right of the footnote number at the bottom of the page so that the footnote can be entered:

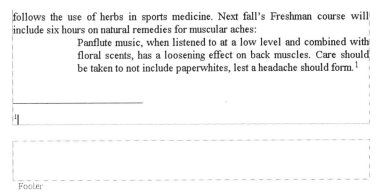

A short horizontal line separates footnotes from the rest of the text

Footnote text can be edited and formatted like any other text. To return the cursor to the document, simply click the I-Beam pointer in the text. To place the cursor back in the footnote, click the I-Beam pointer in the footnote text.

Works sequentially numbers footnotes. A document's footnotes are automatically renumbered when one of its footnotes is moved, copied, or deleted. To delete a footnote simply delete the footnote number in the text which also removes the reference from the bottom of the page.

Endnotes appear separately on the last page of a document, and can be used instead of footnotes. To document sources in endnotes, select the Page Setup command from the File menu. In the Page Setup dialog box, select the Other Options tab to display the following:

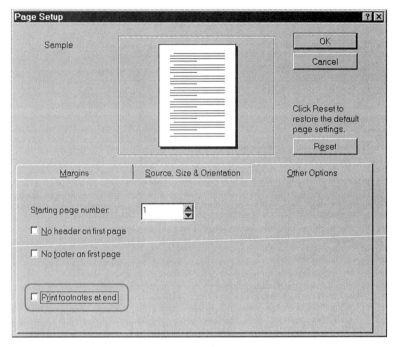

The Page Setup dialog box is used to display footnotes as endnotes

Existing footnotes are converted to endnotes when the Print Footnotes at end option is selected.

Practice 8

In this Practice you will create a footnote. Start Works and open IVY PROMO if you have not already done so. Use the All Characters command to display special symbols if they are not already displayed.

1) LOCATE THE TEXT TO FOOTNOTE

In the middle of page 3, the quote by Dr. Itchee that starts "Inline skating…" needs to be properly referenced. Place the cursor at the end of the quote, just after the period ending "…skin care specialists."

2) EXECUTE THE FOOTNOTE COMMAND

a. From the Insert menu, select the Footnote command. A Footnote dialog box is displayed.
b. Select Insert to accept the Numbered style. Works inserts a "1" in the text and moves the cursor to the bottom of the page where the footnote text may be entered. Note the horizontal line separating the reference from the rest of the text.

3) ENTER THE FOOTNOTE TEXT

Type the following text:

Dr. Phineas Itchee, "Keynote Address," 15th Annual RASH Conference, Crane Hotel, Cincinnati, 15 Oct. 1996.

An Introduction to Computing Using Microsoft Works

4) FORMAT THE FOOTNOTE TEXT

   a. Highlight the "th" in "15th."
   b. Use the keyboard Ctrl+Shift+= (equal sign) to superscript the text.
   c. With the cursor in the footnote text, drag the first line indent marker to the 0.5" mark on the Ruler. The footnote is indented by ½ inch.

Check - The footnote should look similar to the following:

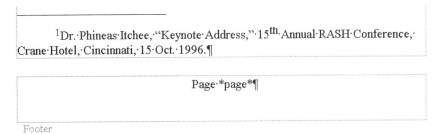

[1]Dr.·Phineas·Itchee,·"Keynote·Address,"·15th·Annual·RASH·Conference,·Crane·Hotel,·Cincinnati,·15·Oct.·1996.¶

Page·*page*¶

Footer

5) SAVE AND PRINT IVY PROMO

Save IVY PROMO and then print a copy of the entire document.

4.13 Time Stamping Files

It is easier to keep track of document revisions when printouts have a time stamp. A *time stamp* can include the current date and the current time.

The Date and Time command is an easy way to create a time stamp. Selecting Date and Time from the Insert menu displays the following dialog box:

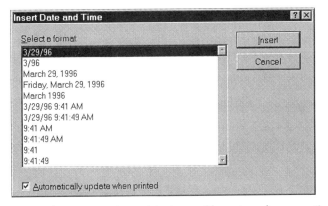

A date and time can be added to a file using these options

Selecting a date, time, or date and time format and then Insert places a time stamp, similar to the one below, at the cursor position:

   6/27/96 8:35 PM

These dates and times are not composed of separate characters, but are instead codes. When the file is opened or printed, the date and time codes are automatically updated.

Placing a time stamp in the header or footer of a document is often better because the information appears on each page.

4.14 Counting Words

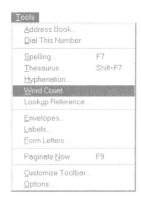

It can be useful to know the number of words contained in a document. For example, journalists often *write for space*, which means writing to fill a precise amount of newspaper or publication space. Some student assignments also require a certain number of words. Selecting the Word Count command from the Tools menu displays a dialog box with the number of words in the document:

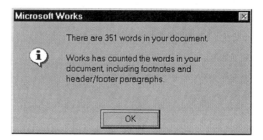

The Word Count command is used to display the number of words in a document

To display the word count for a portion of a document, simply highlight the desired text before executing the Word Count command.

Practice 9

In this Practice you will add a time stamp to IVY PROMO and determine the number of words in the document. Start Works and open IVY PROMO if you have not already done so.

1) INSERT A TIME STAMP IN THE HEADER

    a. Scroll to display the header of the document if it is not already showing.

    b. Place the cursor in the header just to the right of "Information." Press the spacebar once to enter a space.

    c. From the Insert menu, select the Date and Time command. The Insert Date and Time dialog box is displayed.

    d. Click on the date and time format that appears similar to 1/1/97 9:00 AM, the sixth format in the list. Select Insert. The current date and time is inserted at the cursor position.

    e. Drag the pointer over the date stamp and attempt to highlight just the day. Because the displayed code is for the actual date, it is impossible to highlight just a character—either the entire code is highlighted or nothing is.

2) DETERMINE THE NUMBER OF WORDS IN THE DOCUMENT

    a. Click the I-Beam pointer in the main body of the text to place the cursor.

    b. From the Tools menu, select the Word Count command. A dialog box is displayed. How many words does IVY PROMO contain?

    c. Select OK to remove the dialog box.

3) DEMONSTRATE HOW THE TIME STAMP IS UPDATED

    a. Save IVY PROMO.

    b. The time stamp will be updated each time the document is opened or printed. Carefully note the current time, especially the minutes.

    c. From the File menu, select Print. Select the Pages option. The From and To boxes should already contain 1. Select OK to print the first page only. The header printed at the top of the page reflects the time of printing, not the time the stamp was placed in the header. Also, the time stamp in the document has been updated on the screen.

4.15 Adding Graphics to a Document

A word processor document that includes graphics is usually more interesting and informative. Because of this, Works includes *clip art* which are graphic images that have been previously created. Selecting the ClipArt command from the Insert menu displays a dialog box with clip art. Clicking on an image and then selecting Insert places the image at the cursor position.

A clip art image can be moved and copied like text, and can also be resized. However, all of these actions require the image to first be selected by clicking on it once which displays dotted lines and handles for resizing:

Graphics can be added to and resized in a word processor document

Dragging a handle changes the size of the image. Executing the Cut or Copy command places the selected image on the Clipboard. Clicking anywhere in the document other than on the image removes the handles.

Formatting features such as paragraph alignment and tab stops can be used to change the placement of a graphic. More information about graphics and their creation and use is given in Chapter Twelve.

4.16 Inserting Special Characters

There are characters available for your use that do not appear on a specific key on the keyboard. One example is the copyright symbol, ©.

In Chapter Two you learned that the Alt key can be used to execute commands. The Alt key can also be used to create special characters such as those in the following table:

• Alt+0149	™ Alt+0153	÷ Alt+0247	é Alt+0233
© Alt+0169	½ Alt+0189	¢ Alt+0162	£ Alt+0163
® Alt+0174	¼ Alt+0188	¥ Alt+0165	× Alt+0215

To create these special characters, the Alt key must be held down while typing four numbers on the *numeric keypad* of the keyboard:

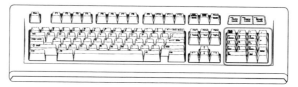

The numeric keypad is a group of number keys on the keyboard

For example, to create the • symbol, press and hold the Alt key and then press the 0, 1, 4, and 9 keys on the numeric keypad. When the Alt button is released the • symbol is displayed at the cursor position.

The symbols created by the Alt key combinations depend on the font used. The symbols shown on the previous page are for the Times New Roman font, the default Works word processor font.

Practice 10

In this Practice you will insert clip art and add a special character. Start Works and open IVY PROMO if you have not already done so.

1) INSERT A PICTURE

a. Place the cursor just to the left of "Ivy" in the first line (the title) of the document, if it is not already there.
b. From the Insert menu, select the ClipArt command. The ClipArt dialog box is displayed.
c. Scroll if necessary to display the apple clip art image. Click on the apple clip art to select it.
d. Select Insert. The apple clip art is placed before the title.
e. Press the right arrow key once to move the cursor just before the title.
f. Press the Enter key to move the title to the next line. Note how the graphic is centered because the paragraph is formatted for center alignment.

2) CHANGE THE SIZE OF THE GRAPHIC

a. Move the I-Beam pointer so that it is on top of the graphic.
b. Click the mouse button. The dotted lines and handles around the graphic indicate that it is selected.
c. Point to the handle in the lower-right corner of the graphic. The I-Beam pointer changes to a double-headed arrow shape with the word RESIZE just below it.
d. With the double-headed arrow pointer on the handle, drag the handle upward and to the left a little. Note how the dotted lines move with the mouse to indicate the size of the graphic. When the graphic is about ¼ the original size, release the mouse button.

3) INSERT A SPECIAL CHARACTER

a. Move the cursor to the end of the subtitle at the top of the document, the line which reads "The Ultimate in Education." The blinking cursor should be displayed just before the Enter character at the end of the line.

b. To create a registered symbol (®) you will need to hold down the Alt key and then press four keys on the numeric keypad, one at a time. Hold down the Alt key and then press the 0, 1, 7, and 4 keys on the numeric keypad. Release the Alt key. The registered symbol is displayed.

<u>Check</u> - The first page of your document should look similar to the following:

4) SAVE, PRINT, AND CLOSE IVY PROMO

4.17 Columns

Columns are commonly used in newspapers, newsletters, magazines, and similar publications to make text easier to read. To format a document for multiple columns, select the Columns command from the Format menu:

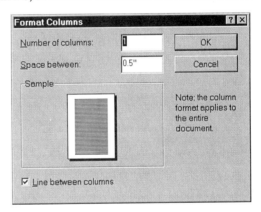

Text is placed into columns using the Columns command

In the Number of columns entry box, type the desired number of columns per page. The amount of space between the columns is specified in the Space between entry box. Works uses these two options and the page margins to determine the width of the columns. For example, increasing the value in Space between decreases the width of the columns. The Line between columns check box is selected to have Works draw a line between the columns. Selecting OK applies the column formatting to the entire document.

In this Practice you will format a document for multiple columns. Start Works if you have not already done so.

1) OPEN COURSE OFFERINGS

    a. If the Works Task Launcher dialog box is displayed, click on Cancel to remove it.
    b. From the File menu, select Open.
    c. In the Open dialog box, select COURSE OFFERINGS.
    d. Select Open. COURSE OFFERINGS contains the course descriptions for the Department of Minor Skin Injury and Disease at Ivy University.
    e. From the View menu, select All Characters to display special symbols, if they are not already showing.

2) CREATE A HEADER

    a. Place the cursor in the header.
    b. Type the following text for the header pressing the Enter key as indicated:

Ivy University	*Enter*
Department of Minor Skin Injury and Disease	*Enter*
Course Descriptions	

    c. Highlight the header text and then click on the Center Align button on the Tool bar to center all of the header text.
    d. Highlight all of the header text, and then select Font and Style from the Format menu. The Format Font and Style dialog box is displayed.
    e. Select the appropriate options to make the header text bold and 14 point.
    f. Select OK.

3) FORMAT THE DOCUMENT FOR TWO COLUMNS

    a. Place the cursor in the main body of text.
    b. From the Format menu, select the Columns command. The Format Columns dialog box is displayed.
    c. In the Number of columns entry box, type 2.
    d. Select OK. The text in the document is placed in two columns. Note how the header remains formatted as one column. Changing the number of columns in a document does not affect headers and footers.

4) MODIFY THE WIDTH BETWEEN THE COLUMNS

    a. From the Format menu, select Columns. The Columns dialog box is displayed.
    b. In the Space between entry box, type 0.75.
    c. Select OK. The columns of text are reformatted with more space between them.

5) PREVIEW, SAVE AND THEN PRINT COURSE OFFERINGS

    a. Print preview the document. Note the line between the columns:

> **Ivy University**
> **Department of Minor Skin Injury and Disease**
> **Course Descriptions**
>
> *101 - Introduction to Adhesive*
> *Bandages*
> A comprehensive survey of the
> two most common skin injuries
> plaguing today's society,
> boo-boos and ouches, along
> with a discussion of
> conventional treatment options.
>
> greatest medical scandal of the
> 20th century.
>
> *335 - Advanced Adhesive Bandage*
> *Application*
> This award winning course,
> known affectionately as Ad
> Band, prepares our students to

    Select Cancel to return to the word processor screen.

    b. Save the modified COURSE OFFERINGS and print a copy.

    c. Close COURSE OFFERINGS and exit Works.

4.18 Where can you go from here?

The last three chapters have introduced you to the concepts of word processing. You can now create, edit, format, and print word processor documents. The Works word processor has other options not discussed in this text which you may want to explore using the online help or *The Works Companion* supplied by Microsoft.

A powerful feature of Works is its ability to integrate the information stored in a database with a word processor document to produce personalized form letters. This process is called *mail merge* and is described in Chapter Eleven. Chapter Eleven also describes how to integrate charts into a word processor document.

There are many different word processor programs available, some of which have options and features not included in Works. Some of the more popular packages are Microsoft Word and WordPerfect. Because you have learned how to use the Works word processor, you will easily be able to learn and use other word processors.

Chapter Summary

A highlighted block can be moved or copied using commands from the Edit menu. To copy a highlighted block of text to another location in the document, the Copy command is executed, the cursor moved to the desired location, and the Paste command executed. To move a highlighted block of text from one location to another in a document, the above procedure is used except the Cut command is executed rather than Copy. When text is Cut or Copied it is placed on the Clipboard.

The Control key is used to execute commands without using the mouse. For example, the Save command can be executed by pressing Ctrl+S. This means the Control key (Ctrl) is held down and the S key pressed. Control key shortcuts are displayed beside the command in the menu. The Ctrl key can also be used to apply some formatting.

The Find command searches a document for a particular combination of characters called search text. The Replace command replaces the search text with the replace text. Searches start from the current cursor position. The Go To command can be used to move the cursor to the top of a designated page.

Two of the most powerful features of the Works word processor are the spelling checker and thesaurus. The Spelling command compares the words in a document to a dictionary file. A word that is not in the dictionary file is displayed in a dialog box where a correctly spelled word can be selected or the word in question edited. The Thesaurus command lists synonyms for a highlighted word and then allows the word to be replaced with one of the synonyms.

Indents are used to decrease the width of the text lines in a paragraph. A hanging indent has a first line indent that hangs out to the left over the lines in the rest of the paragraph. Bulleted and numbered lists are created with hanging indents.

Footnotes are created using the Footnote command from the Insert menu. Works automatically places the appropriate number at the bottom of the page containing the footnote. When a footnote number is deleted from the text, its corresponding footnote is removed from the bottom of the page and any remaining footnotes renumbered. Footnotes can be converted to endnotes by selecting the Print footnotes at end option in the Page Setup dialog box. Endnotes appear on the last page of a document.

The Date and Time command from the Insert menu is used to include a date and time code in a document. The code is automatically updated whenever the document is printed or previewed. If these codes are included in the header or footer the time stamp will be printed on every page of the document.

The Word Count command from the Tools menu is used to display the number of words in a document.

A document can be made more interesting by including clip art. Works provides many different clip art images that can be placed in a document by using the ClipArt command from the Insert menu. A selected graphic is resized by dragging on its handles.

Special characters such as the ® and © symbols can be added to a document using the Alt key and the numeric keypad.

Columns can make a document easier to read. The Columns command from the Format menu is used to create columns. The Format Columns dialog box allows you to specify the number of columns and the amount of white space between columns.

Vocabulary

Alt key - Used with keys on the numeric keypad to create special characters such as ©.

Bulleted list - List created with a hanging indent and a tab character where each item is set off by a special character.

Clip art - A graphic image that has been previously created.

ClipArt command - Inserts a previously made graphic at the cursor position.

Clipboard - Area in memory where Cut or Copied text is stored.

Columns command - Formats a document into multiple columns with a specific amount of space in between.

Control key - Used to execute menu commands without using the mouse.

Copy command - Copies highlighted text to the Clipboard without removing the text from its original location.

Cut command - Removes a highlighted block and places it on the Clipboard.

Date and Time command - Inserts a time stamp at the current cursor location.

Endnote - Used to document a source. Appears on the last page of a document.

Find command - Searches a document for specified text.

Footnote - Used to document a source. Appears at the bottom of the page containing the foot-noted material.

Go To command - Used to move the cursor to the top of a specified page.

Hanging indent - First line of a paragraph that hangs out to the left over the lines below it. Created with a negative first line indent.

Indent - Paragraph formatting option that decreases the width of text lines.

Numbered list - List created with a hanging indent and a tab character where each item is set off by a number that indicates each item's order in the list.

Numeric keypad - Group of number keys on the keyboard.

Paste command - Copies text from the Clipboard to the document at the cursor location.

Replace command - Searches a document for specified text and replaces it with other specified text.

Replace text - Text entered by the user that is to take the place of search text.

Ruler command - Used to display the Ruler above the Work area.

Search text - Text to be found that is entered by the user.

Spelling command - Checks the spelling of a document for words not found in the Works dictionary and allows them to be changed.

Synonym - A word that has the same or similar meaning as another word.

Thesaurus - A collection of synonyms.

Thesaurus command - Lists words with meanings similar (synonyms) to a highlighted word.

Time stamp - A marker in a document that automatically displays the current date and/or time when a file is opened or printed.

Write for space - Writing to fill a precise amount of newspaper or publication space.

Reviews

Sections 4.1 — 4.7

1. a) What is meant by duplicating text?
   b) List the steps required to copy the second paragraph in a document to a point directly after the fourth paragraph.

2. a) What is meant by moving text?
   b) What is the difference between moving and duplicating text?

3. Explain what the Clipboard is used for.

4. How can the Control key be used to execute a command? Give an example.

5. a) What is meant by finding search text?
   b) Give three examples of where you might use the Find command.

6. List the steps required to find each occurrence of "Jerome" in a document.

7. In a search for the word hat how can you avoid finding the word that?

8. List the steps required to precisely search for the word The at the beginning of each paragraph if each paragraph begins with a tab.

9. What is the fastest way to move the cursor to the top of page 12 in a 15-page document?

10. What is replace text?

11. Why is it better to use the Replace button repeatedly instead of the Replace All button in the Replace dialog box?

Sections 4.8 — 4.11

12. a) List the steps required to have Works check the spelling of a document starting at the beginning of the document.
    b) What does Works do when it finds what it considers a spelling error?
    c) Is it possible that Works might indicate an incorrect spelling of a word when a word is spelled correctly? What should be done if this occurs?

13. a) What is a thesaurus?
    b) What is a synonym? Give an example.
    c) List the steps required to have Works list the synonyms for the word "house" in a word processor document.

14. What is an indent and when might one be used?

15. List the steps required to format a paragraph with half-inch left and right indents.

16. List the steps required to format a paragraph with a hanging indent of –0.25 inches.

17. Explain how indents are used to create a numbered list.

18. When would a numbered list be used instead of a bulleted list?

Sections 4.12 — 4.18

19. a) What is a footnote used for?
    b) List the steps required to create a footnote in a document.
    c) Where are footnotes displayed in a document?
    d) How can a footnote be edited?

20. How are footnotes converted to endnotes?

21. a) What is a time stamp and why might it be used?
    b) How can a time stamp be inserted in a document?

22. What command is used to determine the number of words in a document?

23. List the steps required to add clip art to a document.

24. How can a bullet (•) be added at the cursor position?

25. a) How can a document be formatted with three columns?
    b) How can a three column document be converted to a two column document?

4 | Exercises

1. The file named PARTY gives directions to a party, but the steps are listed out of order. Open PARTY and use the Cut and Paste commands to place the directions in proper order. Be sure there is a blank line between each step. Save the modified PARTY and print a copy.

2. The Copy command is useful when text must be repeated in a document.

   a) Use the Copy and Paste commands to create a file that contains your name 40 times, each on a separate line. Hint: Consider using a text block with more than 1 line.

   b) At the end of the file have Works print the current date and time.

   c) Save the file naming it My Name and print a copy.

3. This summer you are going on a vacation to Phoenix, Arizona for a whole month. You need to start planning now so that you will be ready. Bulleted lists can be very useful for planning.

   a) In a new word processor document, type the following:

   List of clothing to pack for Phoenix vacation:

   b) Save the file naming it Phoenix.

   c) Below the "List of clothing…" sentence, make a bulleted list of clothing items that you need to pack for your vacation. Be specific by including the color, fabric, size, etc. For example "long sleeve blue cotton Ivy University sweatshirt." Be sure to make hanging indents for the bulleted list.

   d) Change the indents of your list to ½ inch for the left indent and –¼ inch for the first line indent.

   e) Make the list very narrow by changing the left margin to 3" and the right margin to 3.5".

   f) Use the spelling checker to check the spelling and make any corrections.

   g) Use the thesaurus to find a synonym for vacation and replace it.

   h) Save the modified Phoenix and print a copy.

4. The research proposal last modified in Chapter Three, Exercise 12 needs further refinement. Open RESEARCH and make the following changes:

    a) On page two of the proposal is a numbered list (1-3) that outlines the phases of the development of a computerized guide to be used by the study. Create hanging indents for these phases using the following indents:

        - ¾ inch left indent
        - –½ inch first line indent
        - ½ inch right indent

        Insert a tab between the number and the text for each indented paragraph.

    b) Use the spelling checker to check the spelling and make any necessary corrections.

    c) Use the Find command to find the word incalculable and then use the thesaurus to replace it with a synonym.

    d) Replace all occurrences of Archaeological with Anthropological and all occurrences of Archaeology with Anthropology.

    e) Locate the sentence that begins "Years two through…" and move the entire sentence to a new location below phase 3. Separate the two paragraphs with a blank line.

    f) Save the modified RESEARCH and print a copy.

5. The scientist's biography last modified in Chapter Three, Exercise 10 needs to be refined. Open Science Bio and make the following changes:

    a) Modify the biography, if necessary, to include information from two outside sources. Create proper footnotes for these references using the Footnote command.

    b) Use the spelling checker to check the spelling and make any necessary corrections.

    c) Use the thesaurus to change three words you believe could be improved. Italicize the new words.

    d) Save the modified Science Bio and print a copy.

6. The review last modified in Chapter Three, Exercise 4 needs to be refined. Open Critic and make the following changes:

    a) The school newspaper needs to know when the copy of your review was printed. Have Works print the current date and time in a footer.

    b) Create left and right indents of 0.5 inches for the first paragraph of your review.

    c) Use the spelling checker to check the spelling and make any necessary corrections.

    d) Format the document with two columns. Increase the space between columns to one inch to allow for easier reading.

    e) The school newspaper needs to keep track of the number of words in an article. Add a paragraph at the end of your article that states the number of words in your article.

    f) Save the modified Critic and print a copy.

7. You created a document containing directions to a number of different places in Chapter Two, Exercise 3. Unfortunately, your cousin is having a hard time reading and following these directions. Open Directions and make the following changes:

    a) Use the spelling checker to check the spelling and make any necessary corrections.

    b) Separate the directions into individual lettered steps and use hanging indents to make them easier to read. Create a left indent of 0.75 inches, a 0.5 inch right indent, and a first line indent of –0.25 inches. Use the following example as a guide:

        a. Go South on Sibley Avenue until you come to a stop sign. Turn right.

        b. After about one mile you will cross a bridge. Gargantuan Gulch will be on your left.

    c) Have Works print the current date and time in the header.

    d) Save the modified Directions and print a copy.

8. You last modified a college application letter in Chapter Three, Exercise 6. Open College Apply and make the following changes:

    a) Replace all occurrences of the school's name with New Brunswick College. Change the college address to 101 Main Street, Sometown, US, 10101.

    b) Use the spelling checker to check the spelling and make any necessary corrections.

    c) Save the modified College Apply and print a copy.

9. The file named COMPUTER ED contains information about computers in education, and was last modified in Chapter Three, Exercise 1. Open COMPUTER ED and make the following changes:

    a) This document contains information to be presented at the Conference of American Education. Create a header with the conference name.

    b) Create 0.5 inch right and left indents for the paragraph that begins "Computer programs have become…."

    c) Move the entire last section concerning Computer Usage (including the subtitle and table) to its new location after the indented paragraph. The section titled Lawrence Township Computer Usage should now be the third section of the document. Be sure each section is separated by a blank line.

    d) Save the modified COMPUTER ED and print a copy.

10. Open Grand Opening last modified in Chapter Three, Exercise 13 and make the following changes to create a more effective selling tool:

    a) Use the spelling checker to check the spelling and make any necessary corrections.

    b) To make the flyer look more exciting, format the body of the flyer with right and left indents of 0.75 inches.

    c) Save the modified Grand Opening and print a copy.

11. Ivy University is launching a new campaign to attract students. Open IVY PROMO which contains a promotional advertisement for IU and make the following changes:

   a) Ivy's English department has pointed out that the term "A huge" is too informal to be used in this important document. Search for "huge" and then replace it with a more appropriate word using the thesaurus.

   b) Create hanging indents for the list of faculty members of the Department of Minor Skin Injury and Disease. Make the left and right indents 0.5 inches. Create a first line indent of –0.25 inches.

   c) Aside from Dr. Itchee, two other faculty members have published works, Dr. McCleen and Dr. Scalp. Find their names in the faculty list and create the following footnotes for their works:

      [1]Dr. Chris Scalp, <u>You and Shampoo</u> (Pennington: Lawrenceville Press, 1989).
      [2]Dr. Holly McCleen, <u>How to Wash Your Face</u> (New York: Maple, Snow & Daughters, 1991).

      In the footnotes and in the text, underline the titles of the works.

   d) Create a 0.5 inch first line indent for the new footnote references.

   e) Save the modified IVY PROMO and print a copy.

12. In Chapter Three, Exercise 3 you assisted in the design of a flyer for the SuperSub store opening. Open SUPERSUB and make the following changes:

   a) Replace all occurrences of best with greatest.

   b) Insert the following sentences below the paragraph which begins: "Lemonade isn't the only thing…." Be sure to press Enter after each dessert.

      Here are some of Nanny's favorites:
      Pure Chocolate Dream Cream Pie with chocolate crust and fudge frosting.
      New York Cheesecake with bits of cream cheese, raspberries in syrup, and chocolate shavings.
      Fresh Strawberry Pie on a graham cracker crust topped with whole strawberries and homemade vanilla ice cream.

   c) Create a bulleted list of the desserts with left and right indents of 0.75 inches and a first line indent of –0.25 inches.

   d) Italicize the dessert names in the list.

   e) Use the spelling checker to check the spelling of the entire document.

   f) Save the modified SUPERSUB and print a copy.

13. City Zoo needs more work done on the animal inventory you created for them in Chapter Three, Exercise 14. Open CITY ZOO and make the following changes:

    a) The Staff column should include the caretaker's name for each animal. Copy each staff member's name into the proper location for the remainder of the list.

    b) The heading "Location" is not very descriptive. Replace it with a more descriptive name from the thesaurus.

    c) Scroll down to the bottom of the catalog and insert two blank lines. Then copy the title of the catalog and insert it at the bottom of the page. Under the title, enter the address and phone number of the zoo, and then center the four lines:

City Zoo Catalog
2323 Big Cat Bend
Long Boat Key, FL 33548
(555) CITY ZOO or 248-9066

    d) Save the modified CITY ZOO and print a copy.

14. Fax machines are used daily by many businesses. A fax cover sheet is used to tell the receiver where the fax came from. In a new word processor file, create a fax cover sheet for an imaginary company that includes at least the following:

    • The name, address, telephone number, and fax number of your company.
    • Date and time stamps.
    • A message area for the sender.

Choose appropriate fonts, styles, and sizes for the cover sheet. Save the file naming it Faxcover and print a copy.

15. In Chapter Three, Exercise 16 you modified an article for a recycling newsletter. The editor has read your article and suggested ways to make it more effective. Open Recycle News and make the following changes:

    a) Above the headline "Autos, Autos, Everywhere" insert a graphic of a car.

    b) Insert a blank line after the second paragraph which ends "safer place to live", then add the information below. Format the items as a bulleted list. Use a 0.5" left indent, a 0.25" right indent, and a first line indent of –0.25 inches. The new information should look similar to:

> Here are three easy things you can do:
> • Don't throw away your used motor oil. Leave it at a garage that recycles or take it to a recycling center.
> • Keep your tires properly inflated so that they will last longer.
> • Buy your new tires from a dealer who recycles the worn-out tires.

    c) Use the spelling checker to check the spelling and make any necessary corrections.

    d) To make this look more like a newsletter, format the document as two columns.

    e) Save the modified Recycle News and print a copy.

16. In a new word processor document create a two-page newsletter on any topic. Save the document naming it Newsletter and print a copy when complete. Be sure to use the spelling checker to check the spelling of the document. Your newsletter should contain the following:

- At least four different stories.
- At least one table of information. Be sure that tabs and tab stops are used to align the information in the tables.
- A header with the title of the newsletter.
- A footer with a centered page number.
- Two advertisements.
- Justified paragraphs.
- Correct spelling.
- At least one footnote.
- At least two clip art images.
- Multiple columns per page (like a newspaper).
- Appropriate character formatting. The titles of each article should be bold and in a larger point size than the text of the article. Titles of books, magazines, songs, etc. should be italicized.

An example newsletter is shown below:

Ivy University
CAMPUS NEWS
Weekly news from around campus and beyond...
April 16, 1996

Gill Hall Renovations to Commence Early Next Week

The renovations to Gill Hall will start at 8 a.m. next Monday. Residents are advised that the water will be turned off between 8 and 10 a.m. the entire week. Concessions to not use the restroom facilities at that time must therefore be made.

The restroom facilities will be renovated first, followed by all hallway floors and walls. The dorm lounge will be renovated last. Three new computer terminals with color printers will be installed in the renovated dorm lounge.

The Gill Hall renovations are from the Hazel B. Gladoff memorial fund. Gladoff lived in Gill Hall for her four years at Ivy U in the early 1950s. She is survived by her husband, Barry, and her son Adam.

It's Time
To Sign Up
For Intramurals

Sign up for next semester's teams NOW. Lists are posted by the Information Desk in the gymnasium.

Photography Workshop Offered

The Studio Arts department is offering a two day workshop this weekend on black and white photography.

The first in a 1 month series, the workshop will focus on photographing nature. The next workshop, to be held the following week, will focus on developing black and white film. The workshops are free to students, faculty, and staff who have not taken Photography 101 or later. A camera and film are requited. The workshop will take place from 11 a.m. to 3 p.m. this Saturday and Sunday.

Nina Johnson, photography coordinator, said "This is a good opportunity for students to try out photography, and see if they are truly interested before they take the intense, one semester course."

Editorial - Dana Thompson

I am glad to see Thom Steves was re-elected for the third time as Student Congress President. Steves' impressive record and dedicated campaign staff helped him defeat his opponents. Based on Steves' past performance, we should look forward to another year of Student Congress working for the students.

This Week at IVY U
Monday
    V. Football at home   3:00 p.m.
    Open Mike Night, Ivy Cafe 6:30 p.m.
Wednesday
    Women's Soccer at home   6:00 p.m.
    Movie Night, Auditorium   9:00 p.m.
Friday
    50¢ Pizza, Ivy Cafe   All day
    V. Men's Soccer at Iona   6:00 p.m.

Varsity Men's Soccer 6-0
Ivy's varsity men's soccer team, the *Oak Leaves*, have a winning season so far. This is their best record ever. According to Coach Smith, "The extra two months of training this summer has really paid off." *(continued next page)*

Page 1

Chapter Five
Introducing the Database

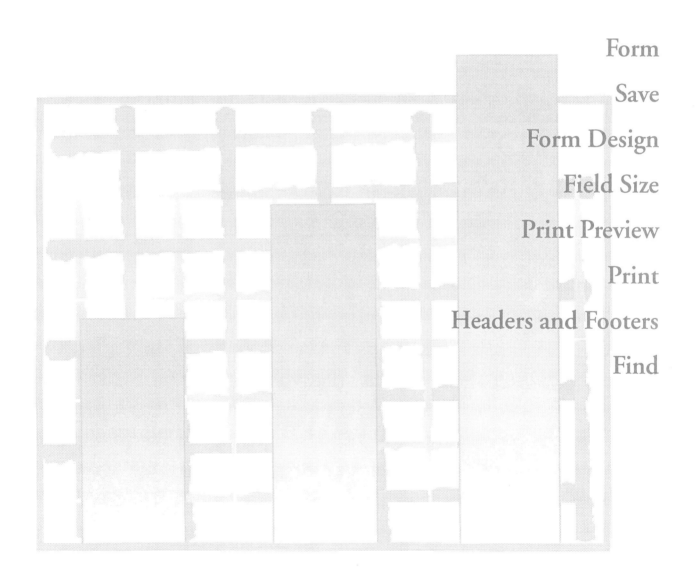

Form

Save

Form Design

Field Size

Print Preview

Print

Headers and Footers

Find

Objectives

After completing this chapter you will be able to:

1. Describe a database.

2. Define records, fields, and entries.

3. Plan and design a database.

4. Create a database and modify its form design.

5. Display a database in Form view and Form Design view.

6. Save and print a database.

7. Use labels on a form.

8. Enter records into a new database.

9. Use the record controls to view a specific record.

10. Use Find to display specific records.

5

This chapter provides an introduction to databases and describes how they can be used to organize and store information. Attention is given to understanding what a database is, and also to the planning and design considerations that make databases efficient and easy to use. This chapter also explains the step-by-step process of creating and modifying a Works database, from paper and pencil sketches to computerized printouts.

5.1 What is a Database?

As you discovered using the word processor, the computer is a powerful tool for storing and manipulating information. Its speed and storage capabilities make the computer an ideal tool for managing large amounts of information in the form of databases.

A *database* is a group of related pieces of information. Almost all businesses and organizations use databases in some way: a bank to store the account information of its depositors, and a school to store student records. Department and grocery stores use databases to keep track of the different items they have for sale, their prices, and how many of each are in stock. A major advantage of using a computer is its ability to rapidly search a large database for a specific piece of information.

Databases can be used to organize any information: addresses, inventories, payrolls, research data, and more. Any information that can be stored in a list or on individual forms can be put into a database. Many historians refer to our present time as the "Information Age" primarily because of the ability databases have given us to store and manipulate huge amounts of information.

5.2 Database Structure

All databases have the same structure and the same words are used to describe that structure. A *record* is information about a single item in a database. For example, Ivy University uses a database to organize student information. In their database, a record is the information about a single student. Information within a record is divided into *fields*. Each field has a *field name* that describes its contents. The data stored in an individual field in a single record is called an *entry*. For example, First Name, Last Name, and GPA are the names of three separate fields in an Ivy U database record. The entries for the fields in the database vary from record to record.

For example, the GPA entry for student Sam Adams is 1.5; the same field in the record for student Roberta Poisson contains an entry of 4.0. The order and placement of fields in a record is referred to as its *form*. It is important to note that each record in a database has the same form, but that the entries vary from record to record. The following illustrates the structure of a database:

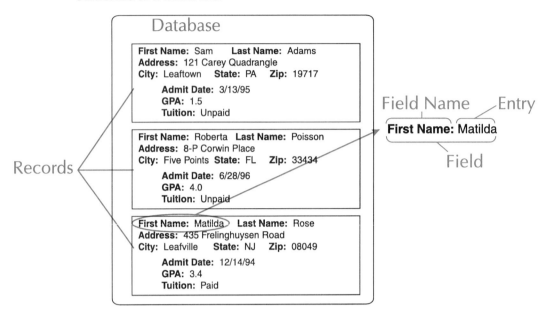

The size of a record depends on the number of fields it contains. A record may have as few as one or two fields, such as a name and phone number, or there may be hundreds of fields in each record.

5.3 Database Fields

Each field in a record is identified by its field name. In Works, field names may be up to 15 characters long and can contain spaces. For example, in the Ivy U database First Name is a field name which contains a space and is less than 15 characters long.

Fields are classified by the *type* of data they store. Fields that store characters (letters, symbols, words, a combination of letters and numbers, etc.) are called *text fields*. In the Ivy U student database, the name and address for each student are stored in text fields. Fields that store only numeric values are called *number fields*. Ivy U's student database stores grade point averages (GPA) in a number field. Fields that store a date or time are called *date fields* and *time fields*. At Ivy U, the student's admission date is stored in a date field.

Because number fields are used to store many different kinds of entries, the way their entries appear can vary. For example, a field storing dollar amounts, another storing GPAs, and a third storing percents are all number fields. However, each of these fields display their values differently. An entry of 2.1 in the three fields would be displayed as $2.10, 2.1, and 210%. The appearance of date and time field entries can also vary. Their entries can be displayed in short form (1/15, 10:12) or long form (January 15, 1997, 10:12:30 AM).

5.4 Planning a Database

A great deal of time and thought should go into the planning of a database before it is created. Careful planning saves time and eliminates frustration later. There are four steps for planning a database:

1. **Determine what data should be stored in a record.** This is best accomplished by examining the needs of the different users of the database. Start by creating a list on paper of the data available. Eliminate any information that is not directly related to the overall purpose of the database.

2. **Examine the specific uses of the database.** Do these uses require any information that is missing from the current list? Is there a need for a complete mailing address or will a street address be enough? Will there be a need to separate the first name from the last? Is a phone or fax number required? Make any changes required to the list produced in step 1.

3. **Create a list of appropriate field names, their types, and appearances.** Using the list of categories from step 2, create descriptive field names and determine the field types (text, numeric, date, etc.) and appearances (one decimal place, dollar amount, percent, etc.) for each field.

4. **Sketch the form on paper.** This helps to show where potential problems may occur.

Careful planning requires information about both the user of the database and how the database will be used. Most databases are accessed by more than one user, and each user has different requirements. For example, the dean's office needs access to student names and GPAs, and the admission's office needs access to student names and addresses. Therefore, the database must contain at least fields for all of this information.

Planning a database makes it easier for each user to get the fullest use from the stored information and avoids having to waste time later making major modifications to the database.

In the sections that follow, we will use the four steps for planning a database to create the Ivy U student database in Works.

5.5 Planning Records and Fields

The first two steps in planning a database are answering the questions "What information should be stored?" and "What operations will be performed with that information?" These are the two most important questions when designing a database.

Deciding what information to store depends on what the database will be used for. A student database would not contain information about faculty salaries or how many desks are in certain classrooms, only information that is directly related to the students. Therefore the Ivy U student database should include the following information:

Student Name
Address
Date student was admitted
Current GPA
Has tuition been paid?

The database will contain one record for each student which stores information for only that student.

Next, the operations performed on the database should be considered. Ivy University keeps its student records in order by last name. Therefore, the Student Name category needs to be expanded to First Name and Last Name:

First Name
Last Name
Address
Date student was admitted
Current GPA
Has tuition been paid?

Finally, the administration would like to be able to mail warning letters to each student who has a low GPA. In order to use the database to produce complete mailing labels, the Address category must be expanded to Street address, City, State (or province), and Zip code (or postal code):

First Name
Last Name
Street address
City
State
Zip code
Date student was admitted
Current GPA
Has tuition been paid?

Several problems have been avoided by carefully considering the uses for this database before it is created. For example, the ability to produce mailing labels is valuable. Had this not been planned for, a great deal of work would have to be done to later modify the database.

5.6 Choosing Field Names and Types

The third step in planning a database is creating a list of field names. Each field must have a distinct name to distinguish it from the other fields in a record. A well-chosen field name describes the data stored in that field. Below are good examples of field names for the student database using the list of categories created in Section 5.5:

Data	Field name
First name	First Name
Last name	Last Name
Street address	Address
City	City
State	State
Zip code	Zip
Date student was admitted	Admit Date
Current GPA	GPA
Has tuition been paid?	Tuition

Choosing the shortest possible name that accurately describes the contents of the field is best. This is why the name Address rather than Street Address was chosen to represent the street address field. It is a good idea to use complete words instead of numbers or abbreviations as field names to avoid confusion. First Name, for example, is better than 1st Name, F. Name, and No. 1 Name.

After creating the list of field names, the type of data each field will contain and the way that data will be displayed needs to be determined. For example, First Name will contain text. The GPA field will store only numbers and is therefore a number field that should be displayed to one decimal place. The Zip field is text because many countries use letters as well as numbers in their codes. The field names, their types, and their appearance for the student record database are as follows:

Field names and their types
First Name (text)
Last Name (text)
Address (text)
City (text)
State (text)
Zip (text)
Admit Date (date displayed in short form)
GPA (number displayed to one decimal place)
Tuition (text)

Practice 1

Mega Music, a national retail store that specializes in CDs, cassette tapes, music videos, and other accessories has hired you to computerize their customer mailing list. The list of categories below is a result of the first two steps for planning a database. To complete the third step of planning a database, on a piece of paper write down appropriate field names and indicate the type (text, number, date, or time) and appearance for each field based on the categories below:

Customer's name
Customer's mailing address
Is the customer male or female?
What type of music do they like?
Why did they make the purchase (gift, personal, work, etc.)?
When was the sale made?
Customer's account number
How many items did they purchase?
How did they pay for the purchase?

5.7 Creating a New Database

To create a new database, the Database button is selected from the Works Task Launcher dialog box. When a new database is created, the Create Database dialog box is automatically displayed:

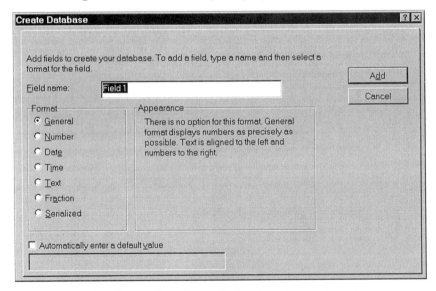

The Create Database dialog box is displayed
when a database is created

Fields are defined by typing a field name, selecting the appropriate type, and then selecting the Add button. For example, consider the Ivy U student database discussed previously. To create the First Name field, type First Name in the Field name box, select Text as the type, and then select the Add button. When a number, date, or time field is created a display option from the Appearance list must also be selected. For example, to create the GPA field, type GPA in the Field name box, select Number as the type, select 1234.56 from the Appearance list, and type 1 in the Decimal places box:

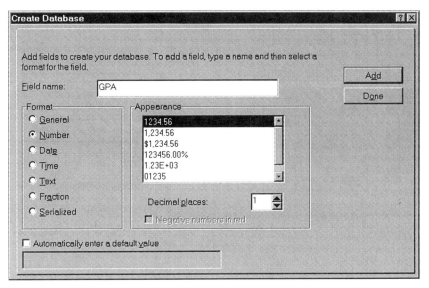

A display option must be selected for number fields

Select the Add button to add the GPA field to the database.

After all the fields have been added, select the Done button to remove the Create Database dialog box and display the database is List view:

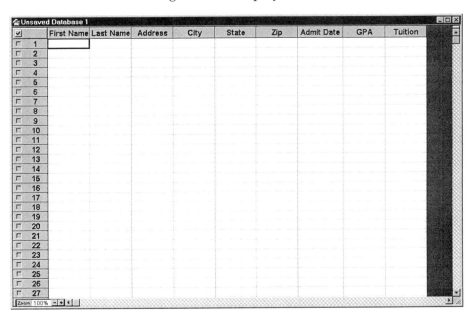

The new Ivy U student database in List view

In *List view* the fields of a database are displayed in columns. List view is most useful for comparing records to one another.

5.8 Form View

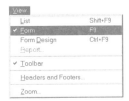

Form view displays all the fields for a single record. This view is best for entering records into the database. The database may be viewed this way by selecting the Form command from the View menu or clicking on the Form View button on the Tool bar (▣).

The default record form in a new database is all the fields placed one below the other in the order in which they were entered. Later in this chapter, we will discuss how the form can be changed. The Form view screen below shows the default form of the new Ivy student database:

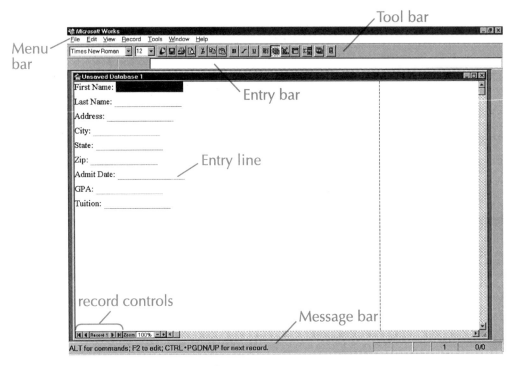

The Form view screen

The Menu bar and Tool bar are used like those in the word processor. The *Entry bar* below the Tool bar displays the selected field's entry. The *record controls* display the record number of the record displayed on the screen and is discussed later in this chapter. The *Message bar* displays the number of records that have entries, as well as the total number of records in the database. The Message bar also displays information about the command being executed. The dotted line on the right side of the records indicates the right edge of the page. To the right of each field name is an *entry line* where data for that field is displayed.

5.9 Saving a Database

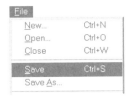

Executing the Save command from the File menu (Ctrl+S) or clicking on the Save button on the Tool bar (▣) saves the database. Once a database has been saved, it may be opened later and its records displayed, printed, or changed. After saving a database, it should be closed if no longer needed by selecting the Close command from the File menu (Ctrl+W).

An Introduction to Computing Using Microsoft Works

Practice 2

In this Practice you will create the student database described in Section 5.7.

1) CREATE A NEW DATABASE

    a. Following the directions given in Chapter Two, start Works.

    b. In the Works Task Launcher dialog box, click on the Works Tools tab if the Works Tools options are not already displayed.

    c. Select the Database button. The Create Database dialog box is displayed.

2) DEFINE FIVE FIELDS

    a. Type First Name in the Field name entry box.

    b. Select Text in the Format section and then select the Add button to define the First Name field.

    c. Repeat steps (a) and (b) to define the following fields:

Field Name	Field Type
Last Name	Text
Address	Text
City	Text
State	Text
Zip	Text

3) DEFINE THE ADMIT DATE FIELD

    a. Type Admit Date in the Field name entry box.

    b. Select Date in the Format section. Notice that the Appearance section now contains a list of display options.

    c. The display option similar to 1/1/96 should already be selected. Select Add to define the Admit Date field.

4) DEFINE THE GPA FIELD

    a. Type GPA in the Field name entry box.

    b. Select Number in the Format section. The Appearance section now contains a list of display options.

    c. The GPAs are to be displayed to one decimal place. Select the display option 1234.56 if it is not already selected and then type 1 in the Decimal places box.

    d. Select Add to define the GPA field.

5) DEFINE THE TUITION FIELD

    a. Type Tuition in the Field name entry box.

    b. Select Text in the Format section and then select the Add button to create the Tuition field.

    c. Select the Done button to remove the Create Database dialog box and display the database in List view.

6) DISPLAY THE DATABASE IN FORM VIEW

From the View menu, select the Form command. All the fields for one record are displayed on the Form view screen. Note how all the fields are placed one below the other on the left side of the screen.

7) SAVE AND THEN CLOSE THE NEW DATABASE

   a. From the File menu, select Save. The Save As dialog box is displayed.
   b. In the File name entry box, type Student. Select Save.
   c. From the File menu, select Close. The database is removed from the screen and the Works Task Launcher dialog box is displayed.

5.10 Form Design

The fourth step in planning a database is making sketches of the form using paper and pencil. A good form has related fields grouped together (like parts of an address) and more important and frequently used fields placed first. A sketch of the Student database form could look similar to the following:

A sketch of the Student database form—note how the address and university information are grouped separately

Form design also includes determining the length of the field entry lines. For example, to fully display a Last Name field entry, the Last Name field line will normally be longer than the First Name field line.

Labels should also be considered when designing the form. *Labels* are text that identify the database or give added information about a field. For example, on the form sketch above, Student Database is a label describing the database. The label (U for Unpaid, P for Paid) is used to describe the Tuition field entry.

Practice 3

In this Practice you will sketch three forms for two different databases, Ivy University's student enrollment and Mega Music's customer list. Use the sketch in Section 5.10 as an example.

   a. Ivy University wants to see record form sketches for their student database. Sketch three different forms, experimenting with field groupings and order, using the fields entered in Practice 2.

   b. Mega Music now wants to see some ideas on record forms. Using the field names you created in Practice 1, sketch three different forms, experimenting with field groupings and order.

An Introduction to Computing Using Microsoft Works

5

5.11 Form Design View

In *Form Design view* fields can be moved and resized and labels added. To display the database in this view, select the Form Design command from the View menu or click on the Form Design button on the Tool bar (🖼). The Student database in Form Design view appears like the following:

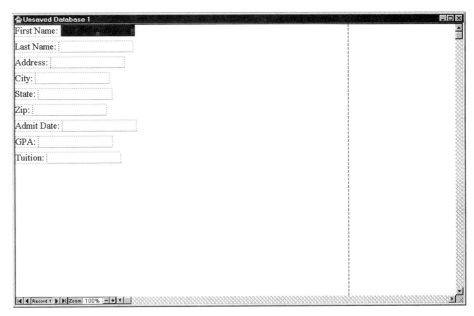

The record form can be changed only in Form Design view

5.12 Changing Entry Line Widths on the Form

In a new database, field entry lines usually need to be resized. The length of a field's entry line only determines the number of characters displayed on the screen, not the number of characters actually stored in that field. For example, a field storing Shakespeare will display Shake if the field is sized to display 5 characters and Shakespe if it is sized to display 8 characters.

The best length for a field entry line is one that displays the field entries entirely but is not excessively long. For example, a First Name field that can display only 5 characters may be too short, while 30 characters is probably too long. Somewhere between 10 and 15 characters is probably best. In Form Design view, entry lines are displayed as a box. When the mouse pointer is placed on an entry box and clicked once, the entry box is highlighted and square *handles* appear:

A selected entry box displays handles

These handles indicate that the entry box is *selected*. Dragging the width handle changes the width of the entry box. Shown below are examples of fields with different entry box widths:

First Name:
Last Name:

Field widths can vary from field to field

A selected field's width can be changed more precisely by executing the Field Size command from the Format menu to display the Format Field Size dialog box:

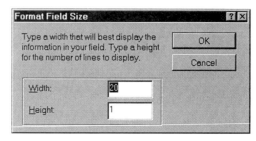

The Format Field Size dialog box

Typing the desired width and selecting OK changes the field's width.

5.13 Moving Fields on the Form

In a new database, fields must be moved on the form to match the form design sketched when planning the database. In Form Design view, a field is moved by dragging it to its new location:

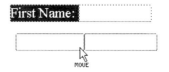

First Name:

A field is moved by dragging it

More than one field can be moved at a time by first selecting them as a group. To select multiple fields together, hold down the Ctrl key and click on the desired fields. The selected fields can be moved by dragging on one of the fields in the group. Moving fields this way maintains the original spacing. To deselect a field, hold down the Ctrl key and click on the field. Clicking the mouse in an empty space on the form deselects any highlighted fields.

5.14 Using Labels on the Form

Labels should be added to a form to describe the database and supply information about fields. In Form Design view, a label is added by clicking the mouse to place the cursor on the form, typing the label, and then pressing the Enter key. A colon (:) cannot end a label because Works will interpret the label as a field name. To move a label on the form, drag it to its new location. To delete a label, first click on it to select it and then press the Delete key.

An Introduction to Computing Using Microsoft Works

5

In this Practice you will modify the Student database form by changing field entry line widths, moving fields, and adding labels. Start Works if it is not already running and open Student.

1) CHANGE THE WIDTH OF THE FIRST NAME ENTRY BOX

    a. From the View menu, select the Form Design command. The database is displayed in Form Design view.

    b. Click on the First Name entry box if it is not already selected. The selected entry box displays handles.

    c. Drag the width handle to the left, narrowing the entry box to approximately two-thirds of its original width. Your field should be similar to:

First Name: ▮▮▮▮▮
Last Name: ▢▢▢▢▢▢▢

Note - If you accidentally moved the field, select Undo from the Edit menu.

2) CHANGE THE WIDTH OF THE OTHER FIELDS

Use the procedure described in step 1 to change the widths of the remaining fields so that they are similar to:

First Name:
Last Name:
Address:
City:
State:
Zip:
Admit Date:
GPA:
Tuition:

3) MOVE THE LAST NAME FIELD

Click on the Last Name field to select it. Drag the Last Name field, being careful not to drag on a handle, and place it next to the First Name field:

First Name: Last Name:

Note - If you accidentally resized the field, select Undo from the Edit menu.

4) MOVE THE OTHER FIELDS

Use the procedure described in step 3 to position the remaining fields so that they are similar to:

First Name: Last Name:
Address:
City: State: Zip:
Admit Date:
GPA:
Tuition:

5) MAKE ROOM FOR A LABEL

To make the database more descriptive, we would like to place a label at the top of the form. To do this we must first move the fields to make room for the label.

a. Click on the First Name field. The field is selected.
b. Hold down the Ctrl key and click on the Last Name field. Both the First Name and Last Name fields are selected.
c. Hold down the Ctrl key and click on the remaining fields. All the fields on the form are selected. Release the Ctrl key.
d. Drag the Tuition field straight down about 1 inch. All the selected fields are moved at once to make room at the top of the form for a label.
e. Click on any blank space on the form. The fields are no longer selected.

6) ADD LABELS TO THE FORM

a. Click the mouse above the First Name field at the top of the screen. The cursor is displayed on the form.
b. Type Student Database for a label and press Enter. The label is displayed highlighted.
c. Drag the label so that it is centered above the fields. Click on any blank space on the form to remove the highlight.
d. Click the mouse to the right of the Tuition field to place the cursor.
e. Type (P for Paid, U for Unpaid) to label the field entry and press Enter.
f. Move the label if necessary so that it is even with the tuition field. Click on any blank space on the form to remove the highlight.

<u>Check</u> - When complete your form should similar to the following:

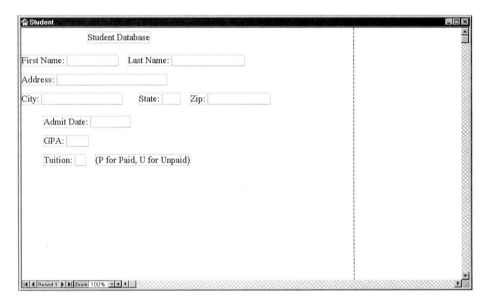

7) SAVE AND PRINT THE DATABASE

a. From the View menu, select Form. The database is displayed in Form view.
b. From the File menu, select Save.
c. From the File menu, select Print. In the Print dialog box, select OK. An empty record is printed. The database form matches the database form design sketched when planning the database.

5.15 Entering Records

It is best to enter records in Form view because it displays all the fields for only one record at a time. In a new database, Form view displays an empty record 1 ready to receive data. In the displayed record, there is a selected field called the *active field* that is ready to receive an entry.

To enter a record, its fields are selected one at a time and entries typed. An active field's entry appears on the Entry bar and on the entry line as it is being typed. Pressing the Tab key enters the data and makes the next field active. To cancel data entry the Escape key is pressed, leaving the cell blank. Pressing the Enter key enters the data and keeps the current field active. When the last field in a record is active, pressing Tab displays the next record in the database with its first field selected. To change an existing entry select the field and then type the new entry.

Any field on the form can be selected by clicking on it. To select a previous field press Shift+Tab.

5.16 Using the Record Controls

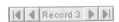

The record controls are used to scroll through the database. To display the previous record, click the ◀ control. The next record is displayed by clicking the ▶ control. The ◀◀ record control is clicked to display the first record in the database, and the ▶▶ record control is clicked to display the last record in the database.

5.17 Printing a Database

The Print Preview command from the File menu or the Print Preview button on the Tool bar (🔍) are used to view the database as it will appear when printed. To print the database, the Print command from the File menu is selected to display its dialog box. Selecting the OK button prints all records. To print only the active record, select the Current record only option in the bottom of the dialog box before selecting OK.

A database can also be printed by clicking on the Print button (🖨) on the Tool bar. When the Print button is used, the Print dialog box is not displayed and all the records in the database are printed. Before printing, it is a good practice to first save the database.

Information such as the creator's name, the date, or the filename can be included in a header or footer to provide more informative printouts. To include a header or footer in a printout, the Headers and Footers command from the View menu is selected and then the desired text typed in the displayed dialog box.

Practice 5

In this Practice you will enter three student records and print the Student database. Start Works and open the Student database if you have not already done so.

1) ENTER A STUDENT'S FIRST NAME

a. If the database is not displayed in Form view, select Form from the View menu.
b. The record controls display Record 1 indicating that the first record of the database is displayed on the screen. The first field of the record should already be active.
d. Type Sam. If you make a mistake, press the Escape key to erase the current entry so that you can retype the entry. Press the Tab key when you are done to enter the data into the field and select the next field, Last Name.

2) ENTER THE STUDENT'S LAST NAME

a. Type Adams.
b   Press the Tab key. Adams is placed in the Last Name field and the Address field selected.

3) COMPLETE THE STUDENT RECORD

Use the procedure in step 2 to complete the entries for the record:

Address: 121 Carey Quadrangle
City: Leaftown
State: PA
Zip: 19717
Admit Date: 3/13/95
GPA: 1.5
Tuition: U

Pressing Tab after typing the data in the Tuition field displays the next, empty record in the database.

4) ADD THE NEXT TWO RECORDS

Enter the next two records:

First Name: Roberta
Last Name: Poisson
Address: 8-P Corwin Place
City: Five Points
State: FL
Zip: 33434
Admit Date: 6/28/96
GPA: 4.0
Tuition: U

An Introduction to Computing Using Microsoft Works

First Name: Matilda
Last Name: Rose
Address: 435 Frelinghuysen Road
City: Leafville
State: NJ
Zip: 08049
Admit Date: 12/14/96
GPA: 3.4
Tuition: P   *Press Enter after typing the Tuition field entry*

Pressing Enter after typing the data in the Tuition field keeps the current field selected.

5) USE THE RECORDS CONTROLS

a. Click on the ◄ record control. The first record in the database is displayed.
b. Click on the ► record control. The next (second) record in the database is displayed.
c. Click on the right record control again. The last record in the database is displayed.

6) PRINT THE DATABASE

a. Save modified Student.
b. From the File menu, select Print. The Print dialog box is displayed. Note the All records option. It should be selected.
c. Select OK. The database with the three records is printed.

7) CLOSE STUDENT

5.18 Using the Find Command

The records of a database can be *searched* to locate specified information. To search a database, execute the Find command from the Edit menu (Ctrl+F) to display a dialog box where the information to be found is typed:

Text, numbers, dates, and times can be searched for using the Find command

Type text (characters, words, or phrases), numbers, a date, or a time in the Find what entry box and then select OK to start searching the database from the current record. When a match is found, the record is displayed on the screen with the matching entry selected. Select the Find command again to display the Find dialog box with the last search text already in the Find what entry box, and then select OK to continue the search from the current record.

Practice 6

In this Practice you will use the Find command to locate specified information in the records of a large database called IVY STUDENT.

1) OPEN IVY STUDENT

    a. Open IVY STUDENT. Note that there are 80 records in this database as indicated in on the far right of the Message bar.

    b. Display the database in Form view if it is not already.

    c. Use the record controls to display the first record if it is not already showing.

2) FIND THE RECORDS FOR STUDENTS WITH A GPA OF 4.0

    a. From the Edit menu, select the Find command. The Find dialog box is displayed.

    b. Type 4.0 and then select OK. The first occurrence of 4.0 is found in the record for Amy Freitas.

    c. From the Edit menu, select the Find command. The Find dialog box is displayed with 4.0 already in the Find what entry box.

    d. Select OK. The next record that contains 4.0 is for Alma Lee.

    e. Repeat steps (a) through (d) until all the records for students with a GPA of 4.0 are found. How many are there?

3) PRINT THE RECORDS FOR STUDENTS FROM NEW MEXICO

    a. Display the first record of the database.

    b. From the Edit menu, select Find. The Find dialog box is displayed.

    c. Type NM and then select OK. The first occurrence found is in the record for Jack Portillo.

    d. From the File menu, select Print. The Print dialog box is displayed.

    e. In the Print dialog box, select the Current record only option. Select OK. Only the NM record is printed.

    f. From the Edit menu, select Find. The Find dialog box is displayed with NM already in the Find what entry box.

    g. Select OK. The next record that contains NM is for Odessa Greenmaiden. The NM found was not in the State field. Therefore, we will not print her record.

    h. Use the Find command to find the remaining NM record(s) and then print only those record(s).

4) CLOSE IVY STUDENT AND EXIT WORKS

Chapter Summary

The speed and storage capabilities of the computer make it an ideal tool for managing large amounts of information in the form of databases. Databases are used by many organizations (businesses, governmental agencies, educational institutions, etc.) to organize information.

A database is an organized collection of related information that is divided into records, each of which stores a complete set of data about a specific item. Each piece of data within a record is called a field and the arrangement of the fields within a record is called its form. The data stored in an individual field in a single record is called an entry.

A field name and type is required for each field. Fields that store letters or a combination of letters and numbers are called text fields, while fields that store only numeric values are called number fields. Date and time fields store dates or times. Number, date, and time field entries can be displayed in many different ways.

Time should be spent planning a database before it is created. The four steps for planning a database are determining what data should be stored in each record, examining the specific uses of the database, creating a list of appropriate field names, and sketching the form. A form can be made more informative by including labels on it. In a well-designed database the form should not need to be changed frequently. A hastily designed database usually requires a large amount of work to reorganize after it has been created.

When creating a new database, you must first define the fields by assigning them a name and type (text, number, time, date). The way in which a number, date, or time field will appear must also be decided. A new database is displayed in List view. However, it is best to display a database in Form view to enter records. In Form view, all the fields for only one record are displayed. The form is modified from Form Design view. In Form Design view, a field's entry line is changed by clicking on the entry box to select it and then dragging the width handle. A field can be dragged to move it on the form.

A record is entered by making each of its fields active and then typing the field entry. The field entry appears on the entry line and on the Entry bar below the Tool bar. Clicking the mouse on a field or pressing the Tab key makes a field active. Pressing Tab when the last field on the form is active displays the next record in the database. In a new database, the next record will be a blank, empty record. The record controls above the Message bar indicate the number of the current record and can be used to display a specific record. The Message bar displays the total number of records in the database.

A database is saved by executing the Save command from the File menu or clicking the Save button on the Tool bar. The Print command from the File menu or the Print button on the Tool bar is used to print records in a database. Works prints all the records that contain entries unless the Current record only option is selected in the Print dialog box. The Print Preview command is used to view a record on screen as it will appear when printed. Headers and footers can be included on the printout by selecting the Headers and Footers command from the View menu and typing the desired information in the entry box.

A database can be searched for specific information by using the Find command from the Edit menu. The Find command displays the first record after the current record that contains the search information in any of the fields.

Vocabulary

Active field - The currently selected field.

Database - A group of related pieces of information.

Date field - A field that stores a date.

Enter key - Used to enter data into a field and keep the current field active.

Entry - The data stored in an individual field in a single record.

Entry bar - Displays the selected field's entry.

Entry line - Location where data for a field is displayed. Displayed to the right of a field name in Form view.

Field - A specific piece of information stored in each record, such as Last Name.

Field name - Name used to identify a field.

Field type - A field is classified by the kind of data it holds, such as text, numeric, time, or date.

Field width - The amount of space to display the field's entry.

Find command - Used to display a record that contain specific information in any field.

Form - The order and placement of fields in a record.

Form Design view - View in which a database's form can be modified.

Form view - View in which all the fields for only one record are displayed. Best view for entering records.

Handle - Used to resize a field in Form Design view.

Label - Text included on the database form that is used to identify the database or give added information about a field.

List view - View in which the fields of a database are displayed in columns.

Message bar - Displays the number of records that have entries as well as the total number of records in the database. Located at the bottom of the screen.

Number field - A field that contains only numeric values.

Record - Information about a single item in a database.

Record controls - Indicates the number of the currently displayed record. May also be used to display a record.

Search - To locate specific information in a database.

Selected field - A field that displays handles in Form Design view indicating that it can be resized or moved. Also, a field that is shown highlighted in Form view indicating that an entry can be made.

Tab key - Used to make the next field in a record active.

Text field - A field that stores characters such as letters, symbols, words, etc.

Time field - A field that stores a time.

Type - See field type.

5 Reviews

Sections 5.1 — 5.3

1. What capabilities of the computer make it an ideal tool for managing databases?

2. Why do historians refer to our present time as the "Information Age"?

3. a) What is a database?
   b) What is a record?
   c) What is a field?
   d) What is a field name?
   e) What is an entry?
   f) What is a form?

4. What determines the size of a record?

5. Can a database be used to store the following information? Why or why not?
   a) the white pages in a phone book
   b) the yellow pages in a phone book
   c) patient files in a doctor's office
   d) items on a grocery list
   e) a school yearbook

6. The following information is found in the white pages of a phone book:

   Capeletti, Rhoda 7 Adams St. 212-0987
   Caputti, J. 80 Scarlet Ct. 123-4567
   Neldon, Karl 25 Potomac St. 555-1234

   a) What information would constitute a single record?
   b) List the separate fields in such a record.
   c) What information does each field store?

7. What fields would be used to store the information in a doctor's patient files?

8. List three government agencies that might use a database, and explain what information each agency would store in its database.

9. a) What is the difference between text and number fields?
   b) What is a date field? What is a time field?

10. How many text, number, and date fields are there in the database shown in Section 5.2?

Sections 5.4 — 5.6

11. a) Why is it important to plan a database before using the computer?
    b) List the four steps for planning a database.

12. Why might it be better to store the first name and last name of students in separate fields in the Ivy U student database?

13. a) What should be considered when choosing a field name?
    b) Why should abbreviations and numbers be avoided in field names?

14. Determine appropriate field names, types, and appearances for the following data:
    a) a person's name
    b) a phone number
    c) the color of a car
    d) an item's price
    e) whether an item is on sale or not
    f) the day a person was born

15. a) What information should be stored in a car inventory database for an automobile dealership?
    b) Describe a record from such a database including the names, types, and appearances of each field.

Sections 5.7 — 5.14

16. List the steps required to create a new Works database that has a text field, number field, and date field.

17. What is the difference between displaying the database in Form view and List view?

18. How do you save a database?

19. Using appropriate field names, sketch two different forms for a car inventory database at an automobile dealership.

20. Why do you display a database in Form Design view?

21. a) How can the width of a field entry line be changed?
    b) Does changing the width of a field entry line change the amount of data the field can store? Explain.

22. a) What does a new database form look like?
    b) How can the form be changed?
    c) How can a field be moved on the database form?
    d) What are labels used for?
    e) How can a label be added to a form?

Sections 5.15 — 5.18

23. a) What is meant by the active field?
    b) The text Josephine was entered into a First Name field but only Jose is displayed. What happened to the undisplayed part of the name?
    c) What must be done to display the complete name in part (b)?

24. A database has been created which contains four fields—Item, Product Number, Price, and Department. Explain how entries are made in the first record of the database.

25. Is it possible to enter data into certain fields and leave others empty in the same record?

26. After entering the first record in a database, how can the next record be displayed for data entry?

27. a) How can you tell what the number is of the currently displayed record?
    b) Where is the total number of records in the database displayed?
    c) What are two ways the record controls can be used to scroll the database?

28. There are 5 records in a database. How can you print only record 2?

29. List the steps required to find the text New in a database.

5 Exercises

1. Many people use a database as an address book. You will create a database to store information about your friends.

    a) On a piece of paper create a list of categories for your address book. Be sure to include at least the full name, complete mailing address, and phone number for each person.

    b) It would be useful to store birthdays in your database. Add this category to the list.

    c) Using your categories, create a list of field names and types and determine the appropriate appearance of any number, date, and time fields.

    d) Create two different sketches of the database form experimenting with order, groupings, and spacing. Be sure to include appropriate labels.

    e) Using Works, create the database. Pick the best form sketch from part (d) and modify the database form to match. Save the database naming it Address.

    f) Enter records for three of your friends. Save the modified Address and print a copy.

    g) Use the Find command to display the records of those friends who live in the same city as you, and then print only those records.

2. Everybody wants to be an author. You will create a database to store information about books that your friends might someday write. For example, a friend who likes to talk on the phone may write a book entitled *Is There Life Beyond The Telephone?* The purpose of this database is to create a catalog of your friends and their works which will then be sent to different publishers.

    a) On a piece of paper create a list of categories for your author database. In addition to the author's name and the title of his or her work, publishers will want a phone number and a complete mailing address where they can contact the author.

    b) It would be helpful to know the subject area of each publication. Examples of subject areas include fiction, science fiction, mystery, education, humor, drama, romance, western, sports, etc. Add this field to your list of categories.

    c) Using your categories, create a list of field names and types and determine the appropriate appearance of any number, date, and time fields.

    d) Create two different sketches of the database form experimenting with order, groupings, and spacing. Be sure to include appropriate labels.

    e) Using Works, create the database. Pick the best form sketch from part (d) and modify the database form to match. Save the database naming it Author Catalog.

    f) Enter records for three authors. Have a least one of your friends author a mystery. Save the modified Author Catalog and print a copy.

    g) Use the Find command to display the records of those authors who wrote a mystery book, and then print only those records.

3. The specialty store you announced in the Exercises for Chapters Two and Three needs a database for its inventory. Use the flyer you created in Chapter Three, Exercise 13 as a guide for the data to be included in the database.

    a) On a piece of paper create a list of data categories that describe the items in the inventory of your store. Categories could include item name, department, cost, price, etc.

    b) Be sure to include an item number, quantity on hand, amount ordered, and a price for each item in your inventory. If you have not included these categories, add them to your list created in part (a).

    c) Using your categories, create a list of field names and types and determine the appropriate appearance of any number, date, and time fields.

    d) Create two different sketches of the database form experimenting with order, groupings, and spacing. Be sure to include appropriate labels.

    e) Using Works, create the database. Pick the best form sketch from part (d) and modify the database form to match. Save the database naming it Store.

    f) Enter information for four items in the store.

    g) Save the modified Store and print a copy.

4. In the previous exercise you created a database file for the inventory of your store. Using the Store database as a guide, you will create a database to record the store's sales activity.

    a) On a piece of paper create a list of data categories for the store's daily sales log. Be sure there is a category for each of the following: item number, item name, department, price, quantity sold, method of payment (cash, credit card, check), and date of purchase.

    b) Using your categories, create a list of field names and types and determine the appropriate appearance of any number, date, and time fields.

    c) Create two different sketches of the database form experimenting with order, groupings, and spacing. Be sure to include appropriate labels.

    d) Using Works, create the database. Pick the best form sketch from part (c) and modify the database form to match. Save the database naming it Store Log.

    e) Enter information for three different items that were sold today.

    f) Save the modified Store Log and print a copy.

An Introduction to Computing Using Microsoft Works

5. An adventure comic book company has hired you as a database consultant. They would like to use a database to organize the information about each character.

   a) On a piece of paper create a list of categories for the comic database. Be sure there is a category for each of the following: superhero name, "real life" name (i.e. Clark Kent is Superman), special power or advantage, partner, and the role of the character (i.e. crime fighter, villain, assistant, etc.).

   b) Most comic book characters have promotional items available for sale such as T-shirts, action figures, and other toys. The company would like to add a category that contains the best-selling promotional item for each character. Add this category to the list you created in part (a).

   c) Using your categories, create a list of field names and types and determine the appropriate appearance of any number, date, and time fields.

   d) Create two different sketches of the database form experimenting with order, groupings, and spacing. Be sure to include appropriate labels.

   e) Using Works, create the database. Pick the best form sketch from part (d) and modify the database form to match. Save the database naming it Comic.

   f) Enter information for four different comic book characters.

   g) Save the modified Comic and print a copy.

   h) Use the Find command to display the records of those characters who are villains, and then print only those records.

6. Your insurance agent wants a database of all of your valuable belongings. Examples of the kind of information to include might be: music and computer CDs, calculator, watch, musical instrument, computer, etc.

   a) On a piece of paper create a list of categories that describes the items. Categories could include item name, original cost, and item type (i.e. electronics, art, clothing, jewelry, and equipment).

   b) The insurance agent forgot to tell you to include the age of the item. Add a category to your list that shows the date of purchase.

   c) Using your categories, create a list of field names and types and determine the appropriate appearance of any number, date, and time fields.

   d) Create two different sketches of the database form experimenting with order, groupings, and spacing. Be sure to include appropriate labels.

   e) Using Works, create the database. Pick the best form sketch from part (d) and modify the database form to match. Save the database naming it Insure.

   f) Enter data for four different items.

   g) Save the modified Insure and print a copy.

7. City Zoo needs your help to create a database of animals in the zoo. It may be helpful to refer to Chapter Three, Exercise 14.

   a) City Zoo has determined that the categories of information should include the name of the staff member who cares for the animal, the kind of animal (American Black Bear, Asian Green Boa Constrictor, etc.), number of female animals, animal type (mammal, reptile, bird, etc.), location of animal (aquarium, rain forest, etc.), and number of male animals. Using these categories, create a list of field names and types and determine the appropriate appearance of any number, date, and time fields.

   b) Create two different sketches of the database form experimenting with order, groupings, and spacing. Be sure to include appropriate labels.

   c) Using Works, create the database. Pick the best form sketch from part (b) and modify the database form to match. Save the database naming it Zoo.

   d) The zoo has decided it wants the staff member field to be in the upper-left of the record, above the other fields. Move the staff member field, adjusting other fields as necessary.

   e) Save the modified Zoo.

   f) Enter the following records:

Staff	Animal	Type	Males	Females	Location
S. Smith	American Black Bear	Mammal	0	1	American West
T. Quay	Asian Green Boa	Reptile	1	2	Reptile Garden
S. Smith	Eastern Cotton Tail	Mammal	2	1	Eastern Forest

   g) Save the modified Zoo and print a copy.

   h) Use the Find command to display only the records of those animals that are mammals, and then print only those records.

8. The research scientists have received the grant for the research proposal you helped write in Chapter Three, Exercise 12. They are living on the tropical island of Bashibashi and need a database to keep track of the movements of the island's gibbon population.

   a) The research scientists have determined that the categories of information should include time of sighting, date of sighting, individual gibbon's name, gender (male or female), approximate age, the island's weather (sun, clouds, rain, wind, storm), temperature, location of the sighting, and gibbon's activity (eating, sleeping, grooming, playing, aggression). Using these categories, create a list of field names and types and determine the appropriate appearance of any number, date, and time fields.

   b) Create two different sketches of the database form experimenting with order, groupings, and spacing. Be sure to include appropriate labels.

   c) Using Works, create the database. Pick the best form sketch from part (b) and modify the database form to match.

   d) Save the database naming it My Gibbons and print a copy.

9. In your search for an undergraduate or graduate school, it is helpful to have a database of the colleges and universities you are interested in attending.

   a) On a piece of paper create a list of categories for the college database. Be sure to include the full name, complete mailing address, and phone number for each entry, as well as the school's enrollment, tuition, and room and board fees.

   b) It will be important to know if the school is public or private. Add a category to your list which indicates this.

   c) Using your categories, create a list of field names and types and determine the appropriate appearance of any number, date, and time fields.

   d) Create two different sketches of the database form experimenting with order, groupings, and spacing. Be sure to include appropriate labels.

   e) Using Works, create the database. Pick the best form sketch from part (d) and modify the database form to match. Save the database naming it My College.

   f) Enter information for five of your favorite colleges. If you do not know the exact information concerning address, costs, etc., make up a realistic entry.

   g) Save the modified My College and print a copy.

   h) Use the Find command to display the record of your favorite college, and then print only that record.

10. Fantasy Wheels, Inc. is an automobile dealership that sells exotic used cars and wants to store their inventory of cars in a database. Below is the information to be stored in three records:

   1969 Maserati, blue exterior, black interior, 4-speed transmission, radio, and air conditioning. Originally paid $9,800. Now asking $21,600.

   1984 Ferrari, gray exterior, black interior, 4-speed transmission, convertible. Originally paid $22,000. Now asking $38,500.

   1972 Corvette, red exterior, green interior, automatic transmission, radio, and air conditioning. Originally paid $8,500. Now asking $25,800.

   a) Using the information above as a guide, create a list of categories for the car inventory database on a piece of paper.

   b) Using your categories, create a list of field names and types and determine the appropriate appearance of any number, date, and time fields.

   c) Create two different sketches of the database form experimenting with order, groupings, and spacing. Be sure to include appropriate labels.

   d) Using Works, create the database. Pick the best form sketch from part (c) and modify the database form to match. Save the database naming it Wheels.

   e) Enter the information above for the three cars into the database. Each car should have its own record.

   f) Save the modified Wheels and print a copy.

   g) Use the Find command to display the records of those cars with black interiors and then print only those records.

11. You are to use the survey form created in Chapter Three, Exercise 15 to create a database.

    a) Open Survey Form. Print three copies and then close the file. Have three friends complete the survey.

    b) Using the questions on the survey form as categories, create a list of field names and types and determine the appropriate appearance of any number, date, and time fields.

    c) Create two different sketches of the database form experimenting with order, groupings, and spacing. Be sure to include appropriate labels.

    d) Using Works, create the database. Pick the best form sketch from part (c) and modify the database form to match. Save the database naming it Student Survey.

    e) Enter the data from the completed survey forms into the database. Each survey form should correspond to a separate record.

    f) Save the modified Student Survey and print a copy.

12. Holiday Airlines has weekly flights to the Bahamas and has decided to computerize its reservation system. Holiday owns one airplane which has 20 seats numbered as shown below:

Window			Aisle			Window
1A	1B			1C	1D	
2A	2B			2C	2D	
3A	3B			3C	3D	
4A	4B			4C	4D	
5A	5B			5C	5D	

    a) On a piece of paper create a list of categories for the reservations database. Be sure to include a seat number, location (aisle or window), class (first or coach), and the name and phone number of each passenger on the plane.

    b) Using your categories, create a list of field names and types and determine the appropriate appearance of any number, date, and time fields.

    c) Create two different sketches of the database form experimenting with order, groupings, and spacing. Be sure to include appropriate labels.

    d) Using Works, create the database. Pick the best form sketch from part (c) and modify the database form to match. Save the database naming it Holiday.

    e) Add an empty record for each of the 20 seats on the plane. Enter the appropriate seat numbers. Enter the word "Empty" into the first name field of each record. In the appropriate field, enter the seat's location (window or aisle). Make all seats in rows 1 and 2 the first class section.

    f) Make the following reservations by updating the proper records in the database. Use the Find command to locate seats for passengers with preferences:

Mr. and Mrs. Irplane	Ms. McGuire
Phone Number: (407) 555-6321	Phone Number: (617) 555-5217
Ada Irplane: window seat, first class	Kerrin McGuire: aisle seat, coach
Adam Irplane: aisle seat next to Ada	

    g) Save the modified Holiday and print only the records of Mr. and Mrs. Irplane.

5

13. A database is commonly used to record the data from experiments. A weather observation experiment requires periodic data collection over a long period of time to establish trends and help meteorologists make predictions based on these trends.

   a) The categories for a weather experiment database should include the date, time, temperature, amount of rainfall, and sky conditions for a single observation. Using these categories, create a list of field names and types and determine the appropriate appearance of any number, date, and time fields. Use the following data as a guide:

   b) Create two different sketches of the database form experimenting with order, groupings, and spacing. Be sure to include appropriate labels.

   c) Using Works, create the database. Pick the best form sketch from part (c) and modify the database form to match. Save the database naming it Weather.

   d) Enter the following records.

Date	Time	Temp. (C)	Rain (cm)	Sky
1/8/60	3:00 PM	22	0.0	partly cloudy
11/5/61	5:46 AM	19	0.0	sunny
4/20/62	6:19 PM	14	0.4	cloudy
6/5/65	5:26 PM	−3	0.2	cloudy

   e) Save the modified Weather and print a copy.

   f) Use the Find command to display the records of those days where it did not rain, and then print only those records.

14. You are to use the field names and form sketches you created in the Practices of this chapter to create a database for Mega Music.

   a) Using Works, create a database using the field names you selected in Practice 1.

   b) Pick the best form sketch from those you created in Practice 3 and modify the database form to match. Save the database naming it Mega Music.

   c) Enter records for five of your friends. Save the modified Mega Music.

   d) Use the Find command to display the records of those freinds who like the same kind of music as you do, and then print only those records.

An Introduction to Computing Using Microsoft Works

List

Field Width

Print

Page Setup

Headers and Footers

Filters

Show

All Records

Apply Filter

Insert Record

Delete Record

Sort Records

6

Objectives

After completing this chapter you will be able to:

1. Display, format, and print a database in List view.

2. Modify fields in a database.

3. Update the database.

4. Query the database for records that contain specific information.

5. Modify and delete queries.

6. Create complex queries.

7. Insert and delete records from a database.

8. Sort records based on the data in a key sort field.

6

This chapter describes the steps necessary to modify a Works database and perform some common operations on it: query, update, and sort. Queries will be applied to determine which records meet certain criteria. Records will be ordered (sorted) in different ways to make the database easier to use. Information stored in the database will be changed to keep the database current.

6.1 List View

It is best to display a database in List view when it is important to see the relationship between records, such as when querying a database as described later in this chapter. Selecting the List command from the View menu or clicking the List View button on the Tool bar (⊞) displays the records of a database in *List view*:

The List view screen

In List view, the first few fields for over 20 records are displayed. Each record is displayed as a row of data, and each column corresponds to a field.

In List view, the active field has a solid outline. Pressing the Tab key makes the next field in the record active. The mouse can also be used to select an entry by clicking on it. Scroll bars at the bottom and right of the screen are used to view fields and records not currently visible.

When switching between List view and Form view, the current field of the current record remains active. For example, if the Tuition field in record 3 is selected in List view, switching to Form view displays record 3 with the Tuition field selected.

6.2 Formatting List View

The default field width in List view is about 10 characters. This may not be wide enough to entirely display a field's contents. For example, in the IVY STUDENT database shown on the previous page the Address field entries are not entirely shown because the field is not wide enough.

A field's width is changed by dragging its right column divider bar. To do this, point to the bar separating the field names at the top of the screen. The pointer shape changes to a double-headed arrow with the word ADJUST below it:

Dragging the divider resizes the Address field

Next, drag the divider bar to the right to increase the width of the field. To decrease a field's width, drag the divider bar to the left.

A second way to change a field's width is by executing the Field Width command from the Format menu, typing the desired width in the Field Width dialog box, and then selecting OK. Changing field widths in List view has no effect on field widths in Form view, and vice versa.

The order in which fields appear in List view can be changed by dragging a selected field to a new location. To do this, first click on the field name at the top of the screen to select all its entries. Next, drag the field name which displays a heavy black line to indicate where the field will be inserted. When dragging, the pointer displays the word MOVE under it:

Field order is changed by dragging a selected field to a new location

When the heavy black line is where the field is to be moved, release the mouse button. In the example above, the Middle Name field will be located between the First Name and Last Name fields when the mouse button is released. Moving fields in List view does not affect Form view, and vice versa.

6.3 Printing in List View

A database will be printed in List view if it is displayed in List view when the Print command from the File menu is executed or the Print button (🖨) on the Tool bar clicked. The Print Preview command from the File menu or the Print Preview button on the Tool bar (🔍) can be used to view the database as it will appear when printed. Databases in List view are often too wide to print on a single sheet of paper. In this case Works prints the database on consecutive sheets starting from the leftmost columns and proceeding to the right.

Executing the Page Setup command from the File menu displays a dialog box that contains the orientation options:

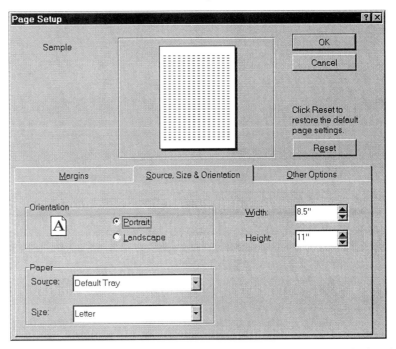

The Orientation options are available from the Page Setup dialog box

Selecting the Landscape option prints the database across the widest part of the page in *landscape orientation*. This is useful when printing a database in List view because more fields fit on a page.

Selecting the Margins tab displays the margin options. Decreasing the top and bottom margins may allow more records to fit on a page, and decreasing the left and right margins may allow more fields to fit on a page.

Printouts can be easier to read if field and record labels and gridlines are included. Selecting the Other Options tab in the Page Setup dialog box displays the Print record and field labels and Print gridlines options.

Headers and footers can be included on the List view printouts to provide more information. To include a header or footer, the Headers and Footers command from the View menu is selected and then the desired text typed in the dialog box.

In this Practice you will format List view of IVY STUDENT and then print it in List view.

1) DISPLAY IVY STUDENT IN LIST VIEW

    a. Start Works. The Works Task Launcher dialog box is displayed.
    b. Click on Cancel to remove the Works Task Launcher dialog box.
    c. From the File menu, select Open. The Open dialog box is displayed.
    d. Open IVY STUDENT.
    e. From the View menu, select the List command. The first few fields of many records are displayed. If necessary, scroll until the Address field is visible.

2) FORMAT LIST VIEW

    a. Point to the divider bar between the Address and City fields. The pointer displays ADJUST below it.
    b. Drag the divider bar about ½ inch (1.3 cm) to the right. The column is widened. Continue to widen the column until all the Address entries are entirely displayed.
    c. Change the widths of the remaining fields so that all of the entries in the fields are displayed entirely. Make fields that are unnecessarily wide narrower, but be sure that field names are displayed entirely. Scroll through the entire database to be sure that field widths are appropriate.

3) CHANGE THE PAGE SETUP OF LIST VIEW

    a. From the File menu, select Print Preview. The List view of the database is displayed on the screen as it will appear when printed. Note that a record will not fit across one the page.
    b. Select Cancel to return to the List view screen.
    c. From the File menu, select Page Setup. The Page Setup dialog box is displayed.
    d. Select the Source, Size & Orientation tab if those options are not already displayed.
    e. Select the Landscape option and then select OK.
    f. From the File menu, select Print Preview. Notice that a record will fit on one page, and that there are now fewer records on the page.
    g. Select Cancel to return to the List view screen.
    h. From the File menu, select Page Setup. The Page Setup dialog box is displayed.
    i. Select the Other Options tab.
    j. Select the Print gridlines and Print record and field labels options and then select OK.
    k. From the File menu, select Print Preview. Notice how much easier it is to read the contents of the database.
    l. Use the Next button to scroll through the print preview. Notice how three pages will be required for the printout.
    m. Select Cancel to return to the List view screen.
    n. From the File menu, select Page Setup. The Page Setup dialog box is displayed.
    o. Select the Margins tab.
    p. Type 0.5 in the Top margin and Bottom margin entry boxes and then select OK.
    q. From the File menu, select Print Preview. Scroll through the print preview and notice how only two pages will be required for the printout.
    r. Select Cancel to return to the List view screen.

4) PRINT THE DATABASE IN LIST VIEW

    a. Save the modified IVY STUDENT.
    b. From the File menu, select Print. The Print dialog box is displayed.
    c. Select OK. The database is printed in List view with the new Page Setup options.

6.4 Modifying the Fields in a Database

Fields might need to be renamed or deleted, or a database may need a new field added. Changes to the fields contained in a database can be made from Form Design view and affect both Form and List views.

Renaming a field

To rename a field, click on the field name to select it, type the new name followed by a colon, and then press the Enter key.

Adding a field

To add a field to the database click the mouse on a blank area of the form to place the cursor. Next, type the new field name followed by a colon, and then press Enter. Works displays the Insert Field dialog box which is similar to the one used when creating the database. In this dialog box, select the type and appearance for the field and then select OK. The new field can then be moved and resized as was done to the fields in the Student database in the last chapter.

Deleting a field

To delete a field, click on the field to select it and then press the Delete key. Works displays the following warning:

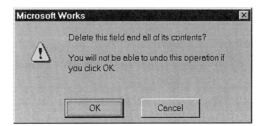

Works warns you when a field is about to be deleted

If OK is selected, the field and any data in that field is removed from every record in the database. Selecting Cancel retains the field.

Practice 2

In this Practice you will modify the IVY STUDENT database by adding, renaming, and deleting fields. Start Works and open IVY STUDENT if you have not already done so.

1) ADD A NEW FIELD TO THE DATABASE

a. From the View menu, select Form Design. The database is displayed in Form Design view where fields can be modified, added, and deleted.
b. Click the pointer in the space below the Tuition field. The cursor is displayed on a blank part of the form.
c. Type Class: and then press Enter. The Insert Field dialog box is displayed.
d. Select Text as the type and then select OK.
e. From the View menu, select Form. The new Class field is displayed on the form.
f. From the View menu, select List. Use the horizontal scroll bar to display the Class field. It has been added after the existing fields.

2) RENAME A FIELD

    a. From the View menu, select Form Design. The database is displayed in Form Design view.
    b. Click on the Class field name. The field name is displayed on the Entry bar.
    c. Type Status: and press Enter to replace the current name.
    d. From the View menu, select Form. The Class field name has been changed to Status.
    e. From the View menu, select List. Use the horizontal scroll bar to display the Status field.

3) DELETE THE STATUS FIELD

    a. From the View menu, select Form Design. The database is displayed in Form Design view.
    b. Click on the Status field and press the Delete key. Works displays a warning dialog box. Select OK to delete the Status field.

4) SAVE THE MODIFIED IVY STUDENT

Display IVY STUDENT in List view and save the database.

6.5 Updating a Database

Changing the information stored in a database is called *updating*. Updates should be done from Form view and include removing old records, changing existing records, and adding new records. Adding a new record was done in the last chapter. Removing old records is discussed later in this chapter. Existing records can be changed by replacing an entry or editing an entry.

The entry in a field can be replaced by selecting the desired field's entry, typing the new data, and then pressing the Tab or Enter key.

You can also edit the entry in a field. After selecting the desired field's entry, click on the Entry bar to display the cursor. The arrow keys and Backspace key can then be used to edit the entry. Pressing Tab or Enter enters the entry.

It is possible to update a record in List view by selecting the desired entry and entering the new data. However, it is usually better to update records in Form view because all of the fields for one specific record are visible.

After updating, the database must be saved to retain the changes. It is important to realize that simply changing an entry on the screen does not change it in the file. Should there be a power failure before you save the file, the change would not appear the next time the file is opened.

Because an update often involves a specific record, a query can be used to display that record. Queries are described in the next section.

A *query* is used to display only specific records in a database. When a query is performed, *criteria* is entered which describes the records to display. For example, in the IVY STUDENT database, it is difficult to immediately determine all the records for students who have not paid their tuition. In this case a query with the criteria "Tuition is equal to U" could be applied so that only the records of unpaid students are displayed. To create this query, execute the Filters command from the Tools menu. At the bottom of the Filter dialog box select the New Filter button to display the Filter Name dialog box. If this is the first query created for the database the Filter Name dialog box is automatically displayed:

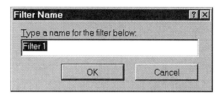

A query must be given a name

In this dialog box type a descriptive name up to 15 characters long. In this case, Unpaid Students would be an appropriate name. After typing the name, select OK to remove the dialog box and display the Filter dialog box where the query criteria is entered. The query criteria field name can be selected from the collapsible Field name list by clicking on the down arrow and then clicking on the desired field name. The comparison is selected from the collapsible Comparison list. The entry is then typed in the Compare To box. For our Unpaid Students query, the Filter dialog box looks like the following:

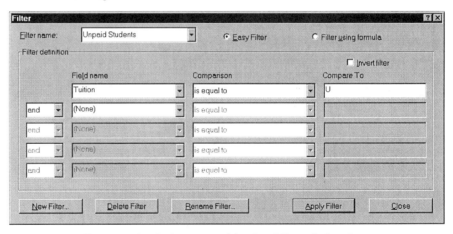

Query criteria is entered in the Filter dialog box

To apply the query select the Apply Filter button. The records that meet the query criteria will be displayed while those which do not are hidden from view. *Hidden records* have not been deleted, they are just no longer displayed. If there are no records that meet the query criteria Works displays a dialog box with the message "No records matched the criteria." To again display all the records in the database, execute All Records from the Show command in the Record menu.

Before applying a query the database should be displayed in List view where it is easier to see the relationship between records.

When a database is saved, any queries are saved with it. To apply an existing query, select the query name from the Apply Filter command in the Record menu.

Practice 3

In this Practice you will update IVY STUDENT by modifying a record. A query will be used to display the record that needs to be updated, and IVY STUDENT will be queried to determine which students have not paid their tuition. Start Works and open IVY STUDENT if you have not already done so.

1) DISPLAY THE DESIRED RECORD

Student Roberta Poston needs to have the spelling of her last name corrected.

a. From the View menu, select List if the database is not already shown in List view.
b. Scroll so that the First Name field is visible on the screen if it is not already displayed.
c. Roberta Poston's last name was entered into the database as Poisson. From the Tools menu, select the Filters command. The Filter Name dialog box is displayed.
d. Type Poisson Record and then select OK. The Filter dialog box is displayed.
e. Click on the Field name down arrow to display the names of the fields in the IVY STUDENT database. Click on "Last Name."
f. The Comparison entry should already be "is equal to."
g. In the Compare To entry box type Poisson and then select the Apply Filter button. Only the record for Roberta Poisson is displayed and the other records of the database are hidden.

2) CORRECT THE STUDENT'S LAST NAME

a. From the View menu, select Form. Roberta Poisson's record is displayed in Form view.
b. Press the Tab key until the Last Name field is selected.
c. In the Entry bar, click the pointer before the second "s."
d. Drag the pointer over the second "s," highlighting just that letter.
e. Type the new character, t. The "t" is inserted at the current cursor position, replacing the highlighted "s" and the entry is now "Poiston."
f. Press the left-arrow key two times so that the cursor is to the right of the "i."
g. Press the Backspace key to remove the "i" and then press the Enter key. The proper last name, "Poston," is shown in the entry box.

3) SAVE IVY STUDENT TO RETAIN THE UPDATE

a. From the View menu, select List.
b. From the Record menu, point to the Show command and then select All Records. All the IVY STUDENT records are displayed.
c. From the File menu, select Save.

An Introduction to Computing Using Microsoft Works

4) DETERMINE WHICH STUDENTS HAVE NOT PAID THEIR TUITION

   a. From the Tools menu, select Filters. The Filter dialog box is displayed.

   b. Select the New Filter button. The New Filter dialog box is displayed.

   c. Type Unpaid Students and then select OK. The Filter dialog box is again displayed.

   d. In the Field name list, select "Tuition."

   e. In the Comparison list, select "is equal to" if it is not already selected.

   f. Type U in the Compare To entry box.

   g. Select Apply Filter. The records of those students who have not paid their tuition are displayed.

5) SAVE IVY STUDENT AND PRINT THE UNPAID RECORDS

   a. Save the modified IVY STUDENT.

   b. On the Tool bar, click on the Print button to print the database in List view. Only the displayed records are included on the printout.

6.7 Modifying and Deleting a Query

To modify, delete, or rename an existing query, select the Filters command from the Tools menu to display the Filter dialog box. Next, select the desired query from the Filter name collapsible list to display its criteria in the dialog box. To modify the query criteria change the entries in the Field name, Comparison, and Compare To entry boxes as desired. To delete the current query, select the Delete Filter button at the bottom of the Filter dialog box. The Rename Filter button displays the Filter Name dialog box where a new name can by typed for the current query.

To remove the Filter dialog box, select the Close button. If changes have been made to any of the exiting queries Works displays a message asking if the changes are to be saved.

6.8 Range Queries

A query can also display records that match a range of values. For example, Ivy University uses its database to determine which students are eligible for the dean's list. For this query, the criteria "GPA is greater than 3.5" would be used to display records with a GPA of 3.6, 3.7, 3.8, 3.9, or 4.0. The comparison "is greater than" is one way to query for a range of records. Other comparisons for range criteria include the following:

     is less than
     is less than or equal to
     is greater than or equal to
     is not equal to

Query criteria can also be defined for a text range. For example, to display the records of those students that come before Lynsey alphabetically, the query "Last Name is less than Lynsey" is used.

Practice 4

In this Practice you will query IVY STUDENT for records that match a range of values. Existing queries will be renamed and deleted. Start Works and open IVY STUDENT if you have not already done so. Be sure IVY STUDENT is displayed in List view with the Student ID field visible.

1) DETERMINE WHICH STUDENTS ARE ELIGIBLE FOR THE DEAN'S LIST

a. From the Tools menu, select Filters. The Filter dialog box is displayed.
b. Select the New Filter button. The Filter Name dialog box is displayed.
c. Type Dean's List and then select OK. The Filter dialog box is again displayed.
d. In the Field name list, select "GPA."
e. In the Comparison list, select "is greater than or equal to."
f. Type 3.6 in the Compare To entry box.
g. Select Apply Filter. The records of those students with a GPA greater than or equal to 3.6 are displayed.

2) CREATE AND APPLY A TEXT RANGE QUERY

a. From the Tools menu, select Filters. The Filter dialog box is displayed.
b. Select the New Filter button. The Filter Name dialog box is displayed.
c. Type Students A-M and then select OK. The Filter dialog box is again displayed.
d. In the Field name list, select "Last Name."
e. In the Comparison list, select "is less than."
f. Type N in the Compare To entry box.
g. Select Apply Filter. The records of those students with a last name that comes before N alphabetically are displayed.

3) DELETE A QUERY

a. From the Tools menu, select Filters. The Filter dialog box is displayed.
b. In the Filter name collapsible list, select "Poisson Record." The query criteria for the query from Practice 3 is displayed.
c. At the bottom of the Filter dialog box, select the Delete Filter button. Works displays a message asking if you want to permanently delete the filter. Select Yes.

4) RENAME A QUERY

a. The Filter dialog box should still be displayed.
b. In the Filter name collapsible list, select "Dean's List." The query criteria for the query from Step 1 is displayed.
c. At the bottom of the Filter dialog box, select the Rename Filter button. The Filter Name dialog box is displayed.
d. Type GPA >= 3.6 and then select OK. A more descriptive name has been assigned to the query.
e. Select the Close button.

5) SAVE THE DATABASE

a. From the Record menu, point to Show and then select All Records. All the IVY STUDENT records are displayed.
b. Save the modified IVY STUDENT.

6.9 Complex Queries

Tools
Address Book...
Dial This Number
Spelling...   F7
Filters...
ReportCreator...
Rename Report...
Delete Report...
Duplicate Report...
Envelopes...
Labels...
Customize Toolbar...
Options...

Complex queries use the logical operators "and" and "or". For example, Ivy University students with a GPA of 4.0 are eligible for the president's list in addition to the dean's list. To omit president's list students and query for only students eligible for the dean's list, the criteria "GPA is greater than or equal to 3.6 and GPA is less than 4.0" would be used. The Filter dialog box for this query looks similar to the following:

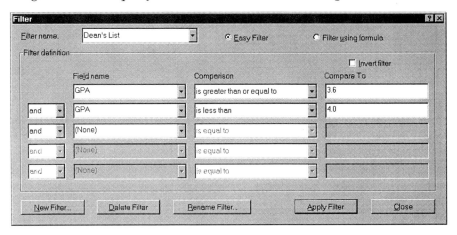

Criteria can include a limited range using "and"

Criteria is entered as before with the "and" available from a collapsible list. When the Apply Filter button is selected, only records with a GPA of 3.6, 3.7, 3.8, or 3.9 will be displayed.

Complex queries can also include the "or" logical operator. For example, to query for students from Maine or Rhode Island, the criteria "State is equal to ME or State is equal to RI" would be used.

The logical operators can combine different fields. The criteria "Last Name is equal to Malfas or GPA is greater than 3.0" would be used to display the records of students with the last name Malfas and the records of students with a GPA over 3.0.

If only the records of students named Malfas with a GPA over 3.0 are to be displayed, the criteria "Last Name is equal to Malfas and GPA is greater than 3.0" would be used.

A query can include both "and" and "or." For example, to display the records of students from Maine and the records of students admitted in 1996 the criteria "State is equal to ME or Admit Date is greater than or equal to 1/1/96 and Admit Date is less than 1/1/97" would be used.

The most important step in querying a database is carefully defining the criteria. Some guidelines to follow when creating query criteria are as follows:

1. **Determine which fields are required in the query.** For example, suppose the college admissions office wants to know which students on the dean's list are from Arizona. The GPA field will be used in this query because dean's list students must have a GPA greater than 3.5. The State field will also be used to determine which students are from Arizona.

2. **Determine which values are required in the query.** Continuing with the example in Step 1, >3.5 is used because we are interested in a range of GPA values. AZ is used to determine the appropriate state.

3. **Carefully create the criteria using the proper relationships.** Because we want student records which contain a value greater than 3.5 in the GPA field and the text AZ in the State field, our criteria is GPA>3.5 *and* State=AZ.

4. **Before applying the query think about the data a record must contain in order to be displayed.** For example, if the criteria is GPA>3.5 and State=AZ, does this mean that a record storing 3.5 in the GPA field will be displayed? What about a record storing 3.6 in the GPA field and RI in the State field?

Practice 5

In this Practice you will apply complex queries. Start Works and open IVY STUDENT if you have not already done so. Display IVY STUDENT in List view with the First Name field visible.

1) DETERMINE WHICH STUDENTS ARE FROM CA OR NV

    a. From the Tools menu, select Filters. The Filter dialog box is displayed.
    b. Select the New Filter button. The Filter Name dialog box is displayed.
    c. Type CA or NV and then select OK. The Filter dialog box is again displayed.
    d. In the Field name list, select "State."
    e. In the Comparison list, select "is equal to" if it is not already selected.
    f. In the Compare to entry box, type CA.
    g. From the collapsible list on the next line, select "or."
    h. In the second Field name list, select "State."
    i. In the second Comparison list, select "is equal to."
    j. In the second Compare to entry box, type NV.
    k. Select Apply Filter. California and Nevada student records are displayed.

2) DETERMINE WHICH STUDENTS WERE ADMITTED IN 1996

    a. From the Tools menu, select Filters. The Filter dialog box is displayed.
    b. Select the New Filter button. The Filter Name dialog box is displayed.
    c. Type 1996 Students and then select OK. The Filter dialog box is again displayed.

d. In the Field name list, select "Admit Date."
e. In the Comparison list, select "is greater than or equal to."
f. In the Compare to entry box, type 1/1/96.
g. From the collapsible list on the next line, select "and" if it is not already selected.
h. In the second Field name list, select "Admit Date."
i. In the second Comparison list, select "is less than."
j. In the second Compare to entry box, type 1/1/97.
k. Select Apply Filter. The records of those students admitted in 1996 are displayed.

3) PRINT FLORIDA STUDENTS ADMITTED IN 1996

a. From the Tools menu, select Filters. The Filter dialog box is displayed.
b. Select the New Filter button. The Filter Name dialog box is displayed.
c. Type 1996 FL Student and then select OK. The Filter dialog box is again displayed.
d. In the Field name list, select "State."
e. In the Comparison list, select "is equal to" if it is not already selected.
f. In the Compare to entry box, type FL.
g. From the collapsible list on the next line, select "and" if it is not already selected.
h. In the second Field name list, select "Admit Date."
i. In the second Comparison list, select "is greater than or equal to."
j. In the second Compare to entry box, type 1/1/96.
k. From the collapsible list on the next line, select "and" if it is not already selected.
l. In the third Field name list, select "Admit Date."
m. In the third Comparison list, select "is less than."
n. In the third Compare to entry box, type 1/1/97.
o. Select Apply Filter. Florida students admitted in 1996 are displayed.
p. Save IVY STUDENT.
q. From the File menu, select Print. Select OK to print the displayed records.

4) SAVE THE MODIFIED IVY STUDENT

Show all records and then save IVY STUDENT.

6.11 Inserting and Deleting Records

It is often necessary to add new records to a database: new students enroll in school, a new item is added to inventory, etc. A new record can be added to the end of a database or inserted between existing records. In both cases, it is usually best to add new records in Form view because all the fields for only the new record are displayed.

In Form view, a blank record is added to the end of a database by clicking on the ▶ record control. To insert a blank record between existing records, the record to follow the new record must first be displayed. Next, select the Insert Record command from the Record menu or the Insert Record (⊞) button from the Tool bar.

Just as it is necessary to add new records to a database, records must often be deleted: a student graduates or transfers out of school, an item is no longer carried, etc. The Delete Record command from the Record menu removes the active record from the database. As with any update, it is best to delete a record from Form view where only the active record is displayed. If a record is deleted by mistake, selecting Undo from the Edit menu before any other command is executed recovers the deleted record.

Practice 6

In this Practice you will insert and delete records. Start Works and open IVY STUDENT if you have not already done so.

1) FIND THE RECORD TO BE DELETED

    a. Display the database in Form view.
    b. Note the Message bar indicates there are 80 records in this database.
    c. From the Edit menu, select Find. The Find dialog box is displayed.
    d. Type Morrison in the Find what entry box.
    e. Select OK. The record for Ian Morrison is displayed.

2) DELETE THE ACTIVE RECORD

    From the Record menu, select the Delete Record command. The current record is removed from the database. Note that the Message bar now indicates there are 79 records in the IVY STUDENT.

3) INSERT A RECORD

    a. Click on the ▶▎ record control. A new, blank record is displayed.
    b. Enter the new record:

        Student ID: PL259
        First Name: Paula
        Last Name: Lutz
        Address: 10 Daniel Drive
        City: Squirrel Island
        State: ME
        Zip: 04570
        Admit Date: 2/19/96
        GPA: 3.5
        Tuition: P

    c. Display the database in List view. Scroll to view the records in the database. Note that Paula's record has been added as the last record.

4) SAVE MODIFIED IVY STUDENT

6.12 Sorting Records

Placing records in a specified order is called *sorting*. In Works, records can be sorted based on the data stored in a specified field called the *key sort field*. For example, it is easier to locate students in the IVY STUDENT database if the records are in order alphabetically by last name. In this case, Last Name would be the key sort field.

Executing the Sort Records command from the Record menu displays the Sort Records dialog box:

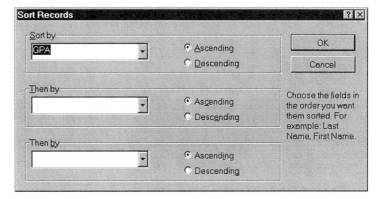

The key sort field is chosen in this dialog box

The key sort field is selected from the Sort by collapsible list. Ascending is then selected to sort records from lowest to highest based on the key sort field or Descending can be selected to sort records from highest to lowest. In the dialog box above, an ascending sort based on the GPA field has been specified. Selecting OK sorts the database. In this case, a record with a GPA of 3.5 will be moved before a record with a GPA of 4.0.

Additional fields can be specified in a sort. If a field is selected in the Then by collapsible list, records with the same Sort by field entries will be sorted on the Then by field entries. This is useful when sorting by a field that commonly has duplicate entries, such as a Last Name field. In this case, the Then by field could be First Name so that records with the same Last Name will be sorted on the First Name field as well. A third field can also be specified in the sort. For example, a Middle Name field could be specified so that records with the same Last Name and First Name will then be sorted on the Middle Name.

Performing a sort reorders all the records in the database, even those that are hidden as a result of a query.

Practice 7

In this Practice you will sort IVY STUDENT. Start Works and open IVY STUDENT if you have not already done so.

1) SORT THE DATABASE IN DESCENDING ORDER BY GPA

    a. Display the database in List view.

    b. From the Record menu, select the Sort Records command. The Sort Records dialog box is displayed.

    c. In the Sort by collapsible list, select "GPA."

    d. Select the Descending radio button and then select OK. The records are sorted from highest to lowest by GPA.

2) SORT THE DATABASE IN ALPHABETICAL ORDER BY LAST NAME

    a. From the Record menu, select Sort Records. The Sort Records dialog box is displayed.

    b. In the Sort by collapsible list, select "Last Name."

    c. Select the Ascending option and then select OK. The records are sorted alphabetically.

3) PRINT A RECORD

    a. Display the database in Form view.

    b. Click on the ◀ record control to display the first record.

    c. Save IVY STUDENT.

    d. From the File menu, select Print. The Print dialog box is displayed.

    e. Select the Current record only option and then select OK. The first record of the database is printed.

4) CLOSE IVY STUDENT

    Close IVY STUDENT and exit Works.

Chapter Summary

The List command from the View menu displays the database in List view, where the first few fields for over 20 records are displayed. List view is best for comparing records and is usually used when querying or sorting a database.

The default field width in List view is about 10 characters. Fields can be widened by dragging the column divider bars or by executing the Field Width command from the Format menu. The order in which fields appear in List view is changed by dragging a field to a new location. Formatting List view has no effect on Form view and vice versa.

When printing in List view, more fields can fit on a page in landscape orientation. To print in landscape orientation, the Landscape option from the Page Setup dialog box is selected. Printouts can be easier to read if record and field labels and gridlines are included. These options are also available from the Page Setup dialog box.

Once a database has been created, new fields can be added, and existing fields can be renamed or deleted while in Form Design view. A field is added by typing the name followed by a colon on a blank space of the form. Selecting a field and then typing a new name followed by a colon changes the field name. A field is deleted by selecting it and then pressing Delete. Modifying the fields in a database affect both Form and List view.

A database is updated by changing the information it stores. This is best done in Form view where all the fields for only one record are displayed. A field entry is changed by selecting it and then typing the new entry. A field's entry can also be edited by selecting it and then clicking the mouse on the Entry bar where the arrow keys and Backspace key can be used to modify the entry. A query can be used to quickly locate the records that need to be updated. A record is deleted with the Delete Record command from the Record menu. A new record is added with the New Record command from the Record menu or by clicking on the ▶ record control. When a change has been made to a database, the database must be saved to retain the changes.

6

A query is used to display only specific records in a database. Criteria is used to describe the records displayed by a query. To query a database, the Filters command from the Tools menu is executed which displays the Filters dialog box. A query can be created, applied, renamed, and deleted from the Filters dialog box. When a query is created it must be given a name. When the query is applied, records that match the criteria are displayed and the remaining database records are hidden. To again view all the records, execute All Records from the Show command in the Record menu.

Comparisons such as "is greater than" and "is less than or equal to" are used to query for a range of records. The logical operators "and" and "or" are used to create complex queries. The most important step in querying a database is carefully defining the criteria.

Placing records in a particular order is called sorting and is accomplished by executing the Sort Records command from the Record menu. The records are reordered in either ascending or descending order based on the data stored in the desired key sort field.

Vocabulary

All Records command - Used to display hidden records.

Ascending order - In order from low to high.

Complex query - A query whose criteria includes the logical operators "and" and "or."

Criteria - Description of the records to be displayed by a query.

Delete Record command - Removes the active record from the database.

Descending order - In order from high to low.

Filters command - Used to create a query.

Hidden records - Records that do not meet the query criteria.

Insert Record command - Inserts a new, blank record before the active record.

Key sort field - Field whose entries are used to determine the order of the records during a sort.

Landscape orientation - A printing orientation that indicates the document is to be printed across the widest part of the paper.

List view - Database view where the records are placed in rows and each field is a column. The active field has a solid outline.

Query - Using criteria to display specific records in a database.

Range query - Using comparisons such as "is less than" to query for records that match more than one value.

Sort - To place records in a specific order based on the data stored in a key sort field.

Updating - Changing the information stored in a database.

Reviews

Sections 6.1 — 6.3

1. List two different ways to switch from Form view to List view.

2. a) How are records displayed in List view?
   b) How can you tell which field is the active field in List view?

3. In List view, what happens when you press the Tab key?

4. a) List two ways to change a field's width in List view.
   b) How can the order of fields in List view be changed?

5. a) How can a database be printed so that more fields fit across the page?
   b) How do you print a database in List view with gridlines and record and field labels?

Sections 6.4 — 6.5

6. a) What are the three ways the fields of a database can be modified?
   b) What view must the database be in to modify its fields?
   c) What happens to a field in List view if it has been modified in Form Design view?

7. List the steps required to change a field's name from Student ID to ID Number.

8. List the steps required to add the field Date of Birth to a database.

9. What does updating a database mean?

10. Sam Adams has moved to 35 Cleve Street in Lawrenceville, NJ, 08618. List the steps required to change his address in the IVY STUDENT database.

Sections 6.6 — 6.10

11. What is a query used for?

12. Give an example of why the Admissions office of Ivy U would query the IVY STUDENT database.

13. What is meant by the term criteria? Give two examples.

14. List the steps required to query the IVY STUDENT database for students from Texas.

15. a) How is an existing query applied?
    b) How is a query renamed?
    c) How is a query deleted?

16. Can query criteria include more than one field? If yes, give an example using the IVY STUDENT database. If no, why not?

17. a) What is a range query? Give two examples.
    b) What is a complex query? Give two examples.

18. a) List examples of the City entries contained in the records displayed by the query "City is greater than Paris."
    b) List examples of the Age entries contained in the records displayed by the query "Age is less than or equal to 14."

Sections 6.11 — 6.12

19. List the steps required to:
    a) delete a record.
    b) insert a record before the third record in a database.
    c) add a record to the end of a database.

20. Ivy University is planning a mailing to its students and wants its database arranged in ascending order by zip code. List the steps required to sort the records of a database in this order.

6 | Exercises

1. Print seven more copies of Survey Form, the questionnaire you designed in Chapter Three, Exercise 15 and distribute them to your friends. The data from your surveys will be entered into the Student Survey database created in Chapter Five, Exercise 11 along with the three previously entered records.

    a) Open Student Survey and enter the data from the completed survey forms. Each form should correspond to a separate record.

    b) Display the database in List view. Format List view appropriately.

    c) Sort the database alphabetically by the favorite course.

    d) Save the modified Student Survey and print a copy in List view using the appropriate Page Setup options.

2. In Chapter Five, Exercise 2 you created an author database named Author Catalog and entered three records. Open Author Catalog and make the following changes.

    a) Enter seven records for books that your friends might someday write. Be sure to use a wide variety of names, states, subject areas, etc. Have at least one friend author a romance.

    b) Display the database in List view. Format List view appropriately.

    c) Create and apply a query named Mystery/Romance that displays the records of mystery or romance books. Print the results in List view.

    d) Show all records, then sort the database alphabetically by the author's last name.

    e) Save the modified Author Catalog and print a copy in List view using the appropriate Page Setup options.

3. Fantasy Wheels would like you to update the database created in Chapter Five, Exercise 10. Open Wheels and make the following changes.

    a) Add these additional records:

    1975 Aston Martin, red exterior, black interior, automatic transmission, radio, and air conditioning. Originally paid $56,000. Now asking $120,000.

    1987 Porsche, black exterior, white interior, 4-speed transmission, and air conditioning. Originally paid $22,300. Now asking $46,000.

    1988 Ferrari, red exterior, black interior, 4-speed transmission, radio, and air conditioning. Originally paid $72,300. Now asking $102,000.

    1985 Porsche, red exterior, blue interior, 4-speed transmission, and radio. Originally paid $31,000. Now asking $62,000.

    1978 Triumph, green exterior, white interior, 4-speed transmission, and air conditioning. Originally paid $4,560. Now asking $7,200.

    1958 Thunderbird, white exterior, red interior, automatic transmission, radio, and air conditioning. Originally paid $14,500. Now asking $31,000.

1969 Maserati, red exterior, black interior, 4-speed transmission, radio, and air conditioning. Originally paid $9,800. Now asking $21,600.

1978 Nova, yellow exterior, orange interior, automatic transmission, and air conditioning. Originally paid $4,200. Now asking $6,600.

b) Display the database in List view. Format List view appropriately.

c) Fantasy Wheels has had a great day and sold the 1985 Porsche. Delete this record from the database.

d) A customer has come into Fantasy's show room and wants to buy her husband a red sports car as a Valentine's Day present. Query for only red cars and then print the results in List view using the appropriate Page Setup options.

e) Fantasy has had the blue 1969 Maserati painted purple, its radio removed, and its asking price raised to $29,000. Update the appropriate Maserati record accordingly.

f) Query the database for all cars with black interiors that originally cost under $25,000. Display these records in List view and then sort by price paid.

g) Save the modified Wheels database and then print the results of the query in part (f) in List view using the appropriate Page Setup options.

4. In Chapter Five, Exercise 12, you created a database for Holiday Airlines. Open Holiday and update the database following the steps below. It may be helpful to refer to the seating chart in Chapter Five.

   a) Make the following reservations by updating the proper records. Use queries to locate seats for passengers with preferences.

Mr. and Mrs. Kemp	Mr. and Mrs. Morawski
Phone Number: (407) 555-2475	Phone Number: (508) 555-3197
Katie Kemp: window seat, first class	Susan Morawski: window seat, coach
Tristan Kemp: aisle seat next to Katie	Steve Morawski: aisle seat next to Susan
Mr. Presley	Ms. Crane
Phone Number: (305) 555-7847	Phone Number: (609) 555-9165
Bruce Presley: aisle seat, first class	Heidi Crane: window seat, first class
Mr. Borelli	Mrs. Wagy
Phone Number: (413) 555-8857	Phone Number: (217) 555-3500
John Borelli: window seat, coach	Ruth Wagy: No preference

   b) Display the database in List view. Format List view appropriately.

   c) The reservation desk at Holiday needs to know the seat numbers of all empty seats. Create and apply a query named Empty Seats that displays the records of available seats. Print the results in List view using the appropriate Page Setup options.

   d) Holiday Airlines has held a promotional contest and you have won five free trips to the Bahamas. Make five reservations using the names and phone numbers of friends. No first class seating is allowed for these free seats.

e) Ms. McGuire has changed her mind and would now like a seat in first class. Query for empty seats in first class. If a seat is available, change Ms. McGuire's record.

f) Query for the records of those passengers in first class who have a window seat.

g) Save the modified Holiday and then print the results of query from part (f) in List view using the appropriate Page Setup options.

5. In Chapter Five, Exercise 13 you created a database for a weather experiment and entered four records. Open Weather and update the database by following the steps below.

a) Add these additional records:

Date	Time	Temp. (C)	Rain (cm)	Sky
12/21/67	10:59 PM	8	0	clear
10/15/69	7:15 AM	27	0.2	windy
3/16/70	4:00 PM	9	0	partly cloudy
7/12/72	1:00 PM	26	0	sunny
12/11/73	12:59 AM	8	0	hazy
7/19/74	6:49 AM	13	0	sunny
10/31/75	9:15 AM	9	0.3	windy
11/16/77	11:50 PM	23	0	clear
1/1/80	3:43 PM	0	4.8	partly cloudy
2/6/81	6:55 PM	−6	0.1	cloudy
2/27/82	8:20 PM	32	1.2	partly cloudy
5/19/84	7:46 PM	17	0	sunny
6/27/85	2:28 PM	20	0.3	cloudy
12/23/86	12:59 PM	2	0	clear
8/24/87	5:33 AM	24	0.5	hazy
11/5/88	6:45 AM	7	0.1	windy
3/2/89	2:33 PM	19	0.7	cloudy
10/22/90	10:15 AM	28	0.2	windy
2/24/91	7:32 AM	26	0	sunny
3/22/91	2:45 PM	22	0.5	windy
5/24/92	5:03 AM	21	4.0	cloudy
8/22/92	9:30 PM	27	0.3	windy

b) Add a record to the database describing today's weather.

c) Display the database in List view. Format List view appropriately.

d) Create and apply queries to answer the questions below. Be sure to name the queries appropriately. Write your answers on a separate piece of paper.

• On which days was it sunny or hazy?
• On which days was the temperature exactly −6 degrees or above 26 degrees?
• On which days was it windy and colder than 15 degrees?
• When the temperature was lower than 10 degrees, what days were not sunny or were not clear?

e) Save the modified Weather and print the results of the last query in List view using the appropriate Page Setup options.

6. Open CAR PRICE which contains information about the prices of new cars.

   a) Sort the database alphabetically by the Make field. Print only the first car record.

   b) The price for a Porsche 944S with sunroof has gone up $200. Find this car and then update the record to reflect this change.

   c) Create and apply queries to answer the questions below. Be sure to name the queries appropriately. Write your answers on a separate piece of paper.

      • How many cars have a base price under $12,000?
      • Your friend needs a new car but does not have much money. How many cars with a stereo cost under $9,000?
      • How many cars have air conditioning for under $6,500?

   d) Save the modified CAR PRICE and print the results of the last query in List view.

7. Open COUNTRY which contains information about the countries of the world.

   a) What country is the fifth most populated? Print only this record.

   b) Create and apply queries to answer the questions below. Be sure to name the queries appropriately. Write your answers on a separate piece of paper.

      • How many countries use the Ruble or the Pound as their currency?
      • Which countries with areas over 3 million use the Dollar as their currency?
      • Which countries have populations under 100,000?
      • Which countries using the Franc have areas less than 15,000?

   c) Save the modified COUNTRY and print the results of the last query in List view.

8. In Chapter Five, Exercise 7 you created a database for City Zoo. Open Zoo and update the database by following the steps below.

   a) Enter the remaining records:

Staff	Animal	Type	Males	Females	Location
L. Wrighte	Blue-faced Angelfish	Fish	1	1	Aquarium
M. Rolls	Barn Owl	Bird	0	1	Aviary
M. Rolls	S. American Fruit Bat	Mammal	2	5	Aviary
W. Carr	Locust	Insect	12	25	Insect Room
T. Quay	Eastern Indigo	Reptile	2	0	Reptile Garden
W. Carr	Egyptian Scarab Beetle	Insect	4	0	Insect Room
S. Smith	Mountain Cougar	Mammal	1	1	American West
L. Wrighte	Nurse Shark	Fish	0	1	Aquarium
W. Carr	Praying Mantis	Insect	3	7	Insect Room
S. Smith	Eastern Red Fox	Mammal	1	2	Eastern Forest
M. Rolls	Zebra Finch	Bird	6	14	Aviary
M. Rolls	Red Shoulder Hawk	Bird	1	0	Aviary

An Introduction to Computing Using Microsoft Works

b) Display the database in List view. Format List view appropriately.

c) Create and apply queries to answer the questions below. Be sure to name the queries appropriately. Write your answers on a separate piece of paper.

- How many mammals and insects are at the zoo?
- What is the total number of animals in the Aviary and American West?
- Which animals have more than 5 females and more than 5 males?
- How many animals are cared for by S. Smith and W. Carr?

d) Sort the database by the animal and then print the results of the last query in List view using the appropriate Page Setup options.

e) A female Red Shoulder Hawk has been added to the Aviary display. Update this record in the database and save the modified Zoo. Print only this updated record.

9. Open COLLEGES which contains information about U.S. colleges and universities.

a) Which college or university is located in Kalamazoo? Print only this record.

b) Based on tuition only, what are the three most expensive and inexpensive schools in the database? Write your answer on a separate piece of paper.

c) Create and apply queries to answer the questions below. Be sure to name the queries appropriately. Write your answers on a separate piece of paper.

- How many public schools are in Massachusetts?
- How many public schools enroll more than 10,000 students?
- How many California and Illinois public schools enroll less than 20,000 students?

d) Save the modified COLLEGES. Find your favorite college and print only that record.

10. Open INVENTOR which contains a list of inventors and their inventions. Answer the questions below on a separate piece of paper.

a) Which French inventors produced their inventions in the 1800s?

b) What inventions did Galileo invent?

c) Which inventions were produced in Russia after 1960?

d) How many inventions were invented in England and Italy between 1600 and 1830, inclusively?

e) Last week your friend Molly McVention from Ireland invented a peanut butter and tuna fish sandwich. Add a new record to INVENTOR which chronicles this event. Resize the Invention field entry box so the entire name contents are displayed.

f) Save the modified INVENTOR.

g) How many inventions were produced in the United States before 1840?

h) Sort the results of part (g) in ascending order by year. Save the modified INVENTOR and then print the database in List view with the query still applied.

11. Open the Address database you created in Chapter Five, Exercise 1.

a) Enter data for at least seven more of your friends.

b) Display the database in List view. Format List view appropriately.

c) Apply a query to display only friends born during the year you were born.

d) Save the modified Address and print the results of the query in List view using the appropriate Page Setup options.

e) You've made a new friend, Amy Eppelman. Add her record to the database:

    Amy Eppelman, 713 Graisbury Avenue, Haddonfield, NJ 08033 (213) 555-1324, Born 7/5/80

f) You have decided that the first person in the file is no longer your friend. Delete that record from the database.

g) Sort the database alphabetically by last name, save the modified Address, and then print only record 5.

12. Open GIBBON RESEARCH which contains a number of gibbons observations.

a) Sort the database in descending order by the age of the animal. Print the record of the oldest gibbon in the database.

b) Create and apply queries to answer the questions below. Be sure to name the queries appropriately. Write your answers on a separate piece of paper.

   • When the temperature was above 80 degrees, which gibbons were observed either playing or eating?
   • How many observations were made from 6 AM to 9 AM? 3 PM to 6 PM?
   • What is the most common activity of the animals when it is raining?
   • How many gibbons under the age of 10 are female?
   • Which male gibbons older than 7 years old have female companions?
   • Which gibbons are under 5 years old?

c) Sort the results of the last query alphabetically by name. Save the modified GIBBON RESEARCH and print the database in List view with the last query still applied.

13. Open ACADEMY AWARDS which contains records about the Academy Award winners since the Awards started in the late 1920s. Each record contains the winners in each category for each year. Answer the following questions on a separate piece of paper.

a) How many winning films has United Artists produced?

b) Which winning movies did Columbia produce between the years 1960 and 1990?

c) What movies won in the 1940s?

d) How many total times did Katherine Hepburn or Bette Davis win the Academy Award for Best Actress?

e) Sort the results of part (d) by Actress. Save the modified ACADEMY AWARDS and then print the database in List view with the last query still applied.

Chapter Seven

Reports and Advanced Database Techniques

ReportCreator

Report

Column Width

Alignment, Font and Style

Number

Insert Row

Field Name

Field Entry

Insert Column

Delete Row, Delete Column

Report Settings

Duplicate Report

Field Summary

Objectives

After completing this chapter you will be able to:

1. Plan and create new reports.

2. View existing reports.

3. Format reports.

4. Modify existing reports.

5. Copy and delete reports.

6. Create and add a calculation field to a database.

7

One of the most powerful features of a database is the ability to produce printed reports that present the information stored in the database. In this chapter the commands necessary to produce such reports are discussed. Special fields that make calculations based on the data stored in other fields are also introduced.

7.1 Reports

A *report* is a printout of records that have been organized and summarized for a specific purpose. For example, the Ivy U student database could be used to generate a report for the dean that details those students eligible for the dean's list. The report would include only the name and GPA fields of those students with GPAs greater than or equal to 3.6. The dean's report would look similar to the one below:

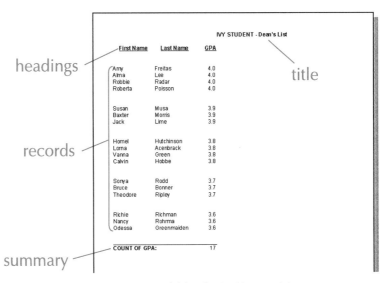

A report could look similar to this

The *title* of a report is printed at the top of the first page and describes the report's contents. Because reports can be several pages long, *headings* are included on each page. The records in a report are printed in rows, similar to List view. However, not every record needs to be included. The number of fields in a report can also be limited. A *summary* is used to total, average, or perform other calculations on the values in a report. A summary can also count the number of records in the report.

7.2 Planning a Report

A useful report is well-organized and contains only the necessary information. To create such a report it must first be carefully planned using the following four steps:

1. **Determine the appropriate layout.** A report should include only the necessary fields. For example, if the dean wants a report listing those students who are eligible for the dean's list, only First Name, Last Name, and GPA fields are needed. Also, a report needs to include an appropriate title that is short but descriptive of its contents.

2. **Determine the appropriate query.** A report should display only the necessary records. For example, because the dean's report is to list students eligible for the dean's list, a query that will display only those students that have a GPA greater than or equal to 3.6 would be used.

3. **Determine the appropriate sort.** A sort should be used to make the report easier to read. For example, the dean's report should list students eligible for the dean's list in order by GPA.

4. **Determine the appropriate summary.** A summary should be used to make a report more informative. For example, the dean's report could display a count of the students eligible for the dean's list at the bottom of the report.

Practice 1

In this Practice you will plan reports for three different IVY STUDENT database users.

a. The accounting department needs to know which students have not paid their tuition. Plan and then make a sketch of the report.

b. The dean wants to know student GPAs. Plan and then make a sketch of the report.

7.3 Creating a Report

The *report definition* is a description of the report's contents. To create a report definition, execute the ReportCreator command from the Tools menu to display the Report Name dialog box:

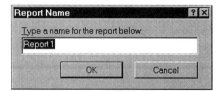

A report definition must be given a name

A report definition must be given a unique name to distinguish it from other report definitions in the database. The report definition name cannot be longer than 15 characters and it is best to use a descriptive name, such as Dean's List for the dean's report definition. After typing a name, select OK to remove the Report Name dialog box and display the ReportCreator dialog box:

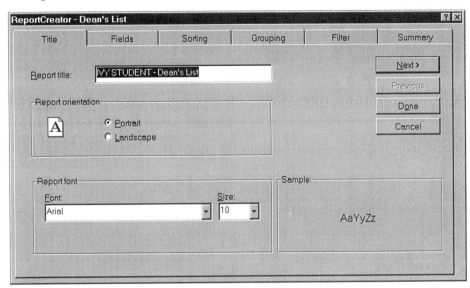

The Title options are used to choose the print orientation of the report

The ReportCreator dialog box contains all of the options necessary for creating a report definition. The Title options are where the report's title can be typed. However, Works automatically creates a report title from the database filename and the report definition name. The print orientation of the report and the font of the report text can also be changed here.

Selecting the Next button displays the Fields options where the fields to be included in the report are selected:

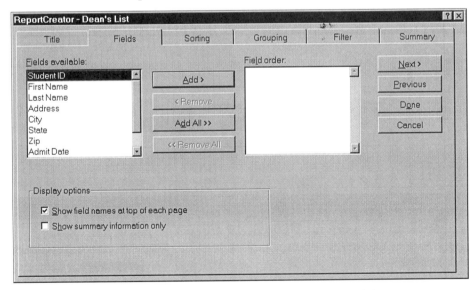

The Field options are used to select the contents of the report

For example, for the dean's report the First Name field is highlighted and Add selected to move the field to the Field order list. This process is repeated for the Last Name and GPA fields. Headings will automatically be included in the report definition for each field in the Field order list.

Selecting the Next button displays the Sorting options. For the dean's report "GPA" was selected for the key sort field and Descending selected as the sort order:

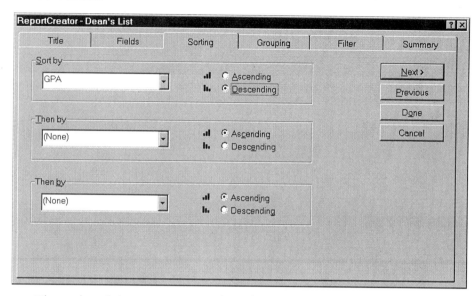

The order of the report's records is designated in the Sorting options

Selecting Next displays the Grouping options. In a report, records can be *grouped* by the key sort field. For example, in the report displayed in Section 7.1 the records are grouped by GPA. Notice that when the GPA changes there is a space between the records so that all the students with a 4.0 GPA are grouped together, students with a 3.9 GPA are grouped together, etc. The When contents change check box in the Grouping options is selected for this kind of grouping:

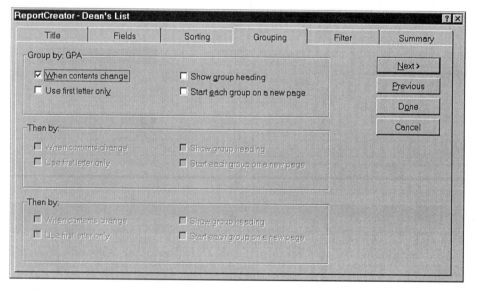

Records can be grouped by the key sort field using Grouping options

Selecting Next displays the Filter options. To display only specific records in a report, a query must be included in the report definition. An existing query can be selected from the Select a filter list or a new query created by selecting the Create New Filter button. For the Dean's List report, the GPA >= 3.6 query will be used:

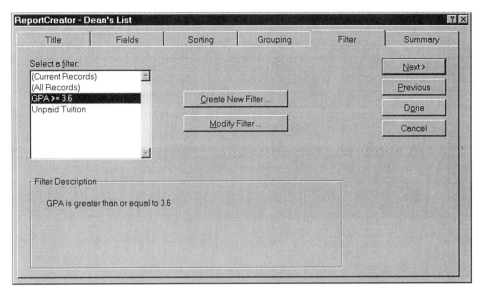

Only specific records are included in a report by selecting a query

Selecting Next displays the Summary options. The Summary options are used to total, average, count records, and perform other calculations on the records in a report. For the dean's report, the records will be counted:

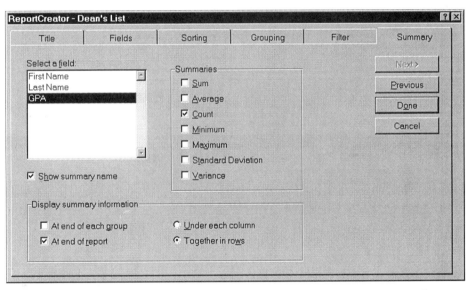

The information in the records of a report can be summarized

After selecting the summary options, selecting the Done button displays the following dialog box:

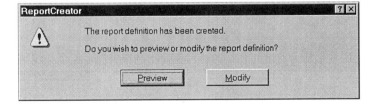

Selecting Preview displays the report on the print preview screen. From here, the report can be printed or Cancel selected to display the report definition. Selecting Modify displays the report definition.

A report definition is displayed on the Report screen. The report defini-tion for the Dean's List report looks like the following:

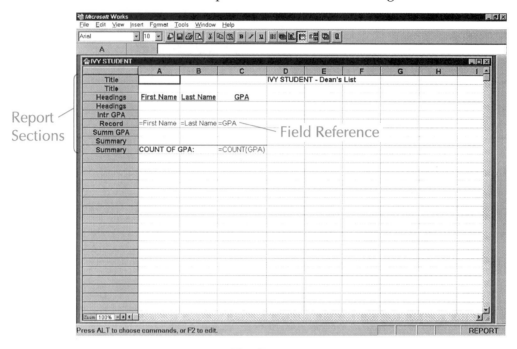

The Report screen

Each column is identified by a letter, and each row is identified by a sec-tion name. The *section names* tell how the information in that row will be printed in the report. For example, any text that appears in the Title row is printed as the report's title.

In the Record row, markers called *field references* indicate where field entries will appear. For example, =First Name shown in the report defini-tion above is replaced by the actual first names from the records when the report is printed or print previewed. Note that a field reference always begins with an equal sign.

Selecting List or Form from the View menu or clicking on the List View or Form View buttons on the Tool bar returns to the database screen.

Practice 2

In this Practice you will create a report which shows the students eligible for the dean's list. Start Works and open IVY STUDENT.

1) CREATE THE DEAN'S LIST REPORT

The dean needs a report that lists in order by GPA only those students with GPAs greater than or equal to 3.6. The report need only contain the name and GPA fields.

a. From the Tools menu, select the ReportCreator command. The Report Name dia-log box is displayed.

b. Type Dean's List and then select OK. The ReportCreator dialog box is displayed with the Title options showing.

c. Notice the title IVY STUDENT - Dean's List is already displayed in the Report title entry box, and Portrait is selected as the orientation option. Select Next to display the Fields options.

d. In the Fields available list, click on First Name to select it if it is not already selected.

e. Select the Add button to move the First Name field to the Field order list.

f. Repeat steps (d) and (e) to move the Last Name and GPA fields to the Field order list.

g. Select Next. The Sorting options are displayed.

h. From the Sort by collapsible list, select GPA.

i. Select Descending and then select Next. The Grouping options are displayed.

j. Select the When contents change option and then select Next. The Filter options are displayed.

k. In the Select a filter list, select GPA >= 3.6.

l. Select Next. The Summary options are displayed.

m. Select GPA and then the Count option to count the records in the report.

n. Select Done. A dialog box is displayed.

o. Select Preview. The report is displayed on the print preview screen.

2) *VIEW THE REPORT DEFINITION*

Select Cancel to go to the Report screen. Notice the field references and section names.

3) *PRINT THE REPORT*

a. Save the modified IVY STUDENT.

b. From the File menu, select Print. In the Print dialog box, select OK. The report is printed.

7.5 Viewing a Report

To view an existing report, the Report command from the View menu is executed to display a dialog box similar to the following:

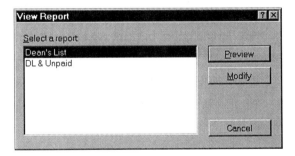

Existing reports are displayed using this dialog box

Selecting the Preview button displays the highlighted report on the print preview screen. Selecting Modify displays the report definition.

The Report View button on the Tool bar can be clicked to display the report definition of the last report created.

7.6 Formatting a Report

The report definition can be formatted to change the way a report is printed. For example, a column's width may need to be changed, a title moved, or important data made bold to draw more attention to it. When formatting a report it is a good practice to use print preview to determine how the formatting will affect the printed report.

When there are more columns in a report than can fit on a single page, Works prints the report over several pages. One way to reduce the number of pages is to decrease column widths so that they are just wide enough to entirely display their entries. Column widths in a report definition can be changed by dragging a column divider as was done to change the column widths in List view. The Column Width command from the Format menu can also be used.

In a report, text field entries are automatically left aligned and numeric, date, and time field entries are right aligned. Headings are automatically centered, bold, and underlined. To change the formatting of a text field entry it must first be selected by clicking on it to display a solid outline. Next, the Alignment and Font and Style commands from the Format menu can be executed to display formatting options. The Bold, Italic, and Underline buttons on the Tool bar can also be used for formatting. The Number command is used to format numeric, date, and time fields.

....

Practice 3

In this Practice you will format the Dean's List report. Start Works and open IVY STUDENT if you have not already done so.

1) DISPLAY THE DEAN'S LIST REPORT

Follow the steps below if the report definition is not displayed, otherwise go to step 2.

a. From the View menu, select the Report command. The View Report dialog box is displayed.
b. Select Dean's List if it is not already selected.
c. Select Modify to display the report definition.

2) LEFT ALIGN THE NAME HEADINGS

a. Click on the First Name heading in column A. A solid outline is displayed around the heading indicating it is selected.
b. From the Format menu, select Alignment. The Format dialog box is displayed.
c. Select Left and then select OK. The First Name heading is left aligned.
d. Follow steps (a) through (c) to left align the Last Name heading in column B.
e. Print preview the report to see the affect of the formatting.
f. Select Cancel to return to the report definition.

3) RIGHT ALIGN THE GPA HEADING

a. Click on the GPA heading in column C. A solid outline is displayed around the heading indicating it is selected.
b. From the Format menu, select Alignment. The Format dialog box is displayed.

c. Select Right and then select OK. The GPA heading is right aligned.
d. Print preview the report to see the affect of the formatting.
e. Select Cancel to return to the report definition.

4) FORMAT THE SUMMARY

a. Click on the summary formula (=COUNT(GPA)) in column C. A solid outline is displayed around the heading indicating it is selected.
b. From the Format menu, select Number. The Format Number dialog box is displayed.
c. Select Fixed and type 0 for the Decimal places.
d. Select OK.
e. Print preview the report to see the affect of the formatting.
f. Select Cancel to return to the report definition.

5) CHANGE THE WIDTH OF THE GPA COLUMN

a. Point to the right column divider bar between columns C and D. The pointer displays ADJUST below it.
b. Drag the divider bar to the left to make the column narrower. Continue to resize the column until it is just wide enough to display the GPA heading.

6) PRINT THE REPORT

a. Print preview the report. Notice the formatting changes. Look carefully at the GPA column.
b. Select Cancel to return to the report definition. If necessary, adjust the GPA column so that all its field entries are entirely displayed.
c. Save the modified IVY STUDENT.
d. From the File menu, select Print. In the Print dialog box, select OK. The Dean's List report is printed.
e. Display the database in List View, show all records, and then save IVY STUDENT.

7.7 Modifying a Report Definition

Sometimes a report needs to be modified to include additional titles, more field entries, or a different query. Modifications to a report are made in the report definition, and then print preview used to display the modified report.

Adding a row

Adding a new row to a report definition is sometimes desired if, for example, a title is to be added below the original or another summary is to be added. A new row is inserted into the displayed report definition by executing the Insert Row command from the Insert menu to display the following dialog box:

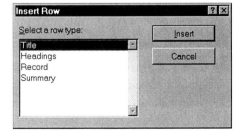

A section can be inserted into a report definition using this dialog box

Selecting a row type and then Insert places the new row in the report definition. New rows are automatically placed in the correct position of the report definition. For example, selecting Title in the Select a row type list and then selecting Insert places a new Title row below any existing Title rows, and the rows below are moved down to make room. A title can then be added by clicking in the Title row and then typing the desired text.

Adding a field to an existing report definition is a two step process. First, the field name must be placed in the Headings row, and second, the field reference must be placed in the Record row.

Adding a heading

To add the field name, click in the column of the Headings row where the field name is to be placed. Next, execute the Field Name command from the Insert menu to display the Insert Field Name dialog box:

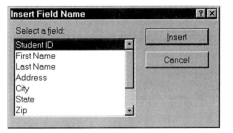

A field heading is added to a report definition using this dialog box

Selecting the desired field name and selecting Insert places the heading in the report definition. The new heading can then be formatted.

Adding a reference

To add the field reference, click in the column of the Records row where the field reference is to be placed. Next, execute the Field Entry command from the Insert menu to display the Insert Field Entry dialog box listing the fields in the database. Highlighting the desired field and selecting Insert places the field reference in the report definition.

Adding a column

A new column must be added to the report definition if a new field is to be placed between existing fields. To add a new column select the Insert Column command from Insert menu. Works adds a new column to the left of selected data.

Deleting rows and columns

A row is deleted by clicking on the name of the desired row to highlight it and then selecting the Delete Row command from the Insert menu. A column is deleted by clicking on its column letter and then selecting Delete Column from the Insert menu.

The Report Settings command from the Format menu is used to change the sorting, grouping, and query options for a report definition. Executing Report Settings displays a dialog box similar to that shown when a report definition is created. A new sort order can be selected from the Sorting options, records can be grouped differently using the Grouping options, and a different query can be selected using the Filter options.

An Introduction to Computing Using Microsoft Works

7.8 Copying and Deleting Reports

When creating a report that has the same kind of information as an existing report, it is usually easier to copy the existing report definition and then modify the copy. A report definition is copied by selecting the Duplicate Report command from the Tools menu to display a dialog box with the names of existing report definitions. Here, the desired report definition is highlighted, the name for the copy typed, and then the Duplicate button selected to create a report definition that has the same contents as the selected report definition. Selecting OK removes the dialog box.

Works allows only 8 report definitions to be saved with a database. Therefore, it is sometimes necessary to delete a report definition to make room for another. A report definition is deleted by selecting the Delete Report command from the Tools menu to display a dialog box with the names of existing report definitions. Here, the desired report definition is highlighted and then the Delete button selected. Selecting OK removes the dialog box.

Practice 4

In this Practice you will create a new report from a copy of the Dean's List report. Start Works and open IVY STUDENT if you have not already done so.

1) COPY THE DEAN'S LIST REPORT

Ivy admissions needs to know which dean's list students have not paid their tuition.

   a.   From the Tools menu, select the Duplicate Report command. The Duplicate Report dialog box is displayed.
   b.   Select Dean's List if it is not already highlighted.
   c.   In the entry box, type DL & Unpaid.
   d.   Select the Duplicate button. The Dean's List report is copied to DL & Unpaid.
   e.   Select OK to remove the dialog box.

2) VIEW THE REPORT

   a.   From the View menu, select Report. The View Report dialog box is displayed.
   b.   Select DL & Unpaid and then Modify to display the report definition.

3) CHANGE THE TITLE OF THE REPORT

   a.   Click on the title of the report to select it.
   b.   Type IVY STUDENT - Unpaid Dean's List Students to replace the title.

4) CREATE AND SELECT THE QUERY FOR THE REPORT

   a.   From the Format menu, select the Report Settings command. The Report Settings dialog box is displayed.
   b.   Select the Filter tab to display the query options. Select the Create New Filter button to display the Filter Name dialog box.
   c.   Type GPA>=3.6&Unpaid for the Filter name.
   d.   In the Filters dialog box, enter the criteria GPA is greater than or equal to 3.6 and Tuition is equal to U and then select OK. The Report Settings dialog box is displayed.
   e.   Select the GPA>=3.6&Unpaid query and then select Done.

<u>Check</u> - Your report definition screen should look like the following:

	A	B	C	D	E	F	G
Title				IVY STUDENT - Unpaid Dean's List Students			
Title							
Headings	First Name	Last Name	GPA				
Headings							
Intr GPA							
Record	=First Name	=Last Name	=GPA				
Summ GPA							
Summary							
Summary	COUNT OF GPA:		=COU				

5) VIEW AND PRINT THE REPORT

a. Save IVY STUDENT.
b. From the File menu, select Print Preview. The report is displayed on the screen.
c. Select Print to print the report.

7.9 Summaries and Subsummaries

For the Dean's List report, a count summary was used to display the total number of records in the report. Other summary options can be used to sum or average the values in a specified field, or find the maximum or minimum value in a specified field.

A report can also include a *subsummary* that displays statistics about each group of records. For example, to further summarize the Dean's List report, a subsummary could be added to count the number of GPAs in each group of records:

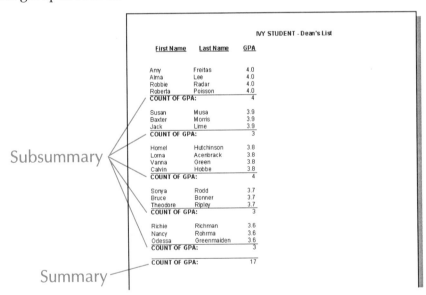

A subsummary makes a report more informative

To include a subsummary in a new report definition the At end of each group check box is selected in the Summary options of the ReportCreator dialog box. For the Dean's List report the dialog box would look like the following:

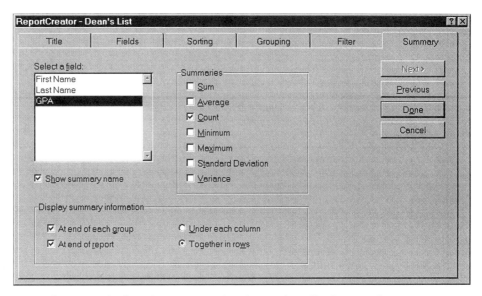

The At end of each group option is used to display a subsummary

The subsummary option is available only when Sorting and Grouping options have already been selected and will display only the same statistics as the summary. For example, in the Dean's List report the summary selected is Count. Therefore, the subsummary will also use Count.

A summary and subsummary can be added to an existing report by first displaying the report definition. To add the summary, click in the Summary row below the appropriate field, or to add a subsummary, click in the Summ row below the appropriate field. Next, select the Field Summary command from the Insert menu to display the following dialog box:

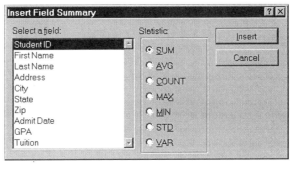

A summary can be added to an existing report using this dialog box

The field to be used in the calculation is selected and then the calculation to be performed selected from the Statistic list. Selecting Insert adds the summary to the report definition. Labels are not automatically added to an existing report definition so it is necessary to type a descriptive label next to the summary.

If necessary, a summary row can be added by selecting the Insert Row command from the Insert menu. A Summ row is automatically added when a Grouping and Sorting option are selected for the report.

Practice 5

In this Practice you will add a subsummary to the Dean's List report and then create a new report that has both a summary and a subsummary. Start Works and open IVY STUDENT.

1) ADD A SUBSUMMARY TO THE DEAN'S LIST REPORT

    a. Select the Report command from the View menu. In the View Report dialog box select Dean's List and then Modify to display the report definition.

    b. In the Summ GPA row, click below the GPA field reference.

    c. From the Insert menu, select the Field Summary command. The Insert Field Summary dialog box is displayed.

    d. In the Select a field list, highlight GPA.

    e. Select COUNT and then Insert. The Summ GPA row now contains =COUNT(GPA).

    f. In the Summ GPA row, click below the First Name field reference and type the title COUNT OF GPA: and then click on the Bold button on the Tool bar.

Check - Your report definition should look like the following:

	A	B	C	D	E	F
Title				IVY STUDENT - Dean's List		
Title						
Headings	First Name	Last Name	GPA			
Headings						
Intr GPA						
Record	=First Name	=Last Name	=GPA			
Summ GPA	COUNT OF GPA:		=COU			
Summary						
Summary	COUNT OF GPA:		=COU			

2) PRINT THE MODIFIED DEAN'S LIST REPORT

    a. Save IVY STUDENT.

    b. From the File menu, select the Print Preview command. Notice the subsummaries in the report.

    c. Print the report.

    d. Display the database in List view, and show all records.

    e. Save and then close IVY STUDENT.

3) CREATE A REPORT FOR IVY BOOKSTORE

The Ivy bookstore needs a report on the number of items in inventory.

    a. Open IVY BOOKSTORE which contains inventory information.

    b. From the Tools menu, select the ReportCreator command. The Report Name dialog box is displayed.

    c. Type Inventory and then select OK. The ReportCreator dialog box is displayed with the Title options showing.

    d. In the Report title entry box, IVY BOOKSTORE - Inventory is displayed. Select Next to display the Fields options.

    e. In the Fields available list, click on Item Name to select it if it is not already selected.

    f. Select the Add button to move the Item Name field to the Field order list.

    g. Repeat steps (e) and (f) to move the Department and In Stock fields to the Field order list.

    h. Select Next. The Sorting options are displayed.

    i. From the Sort by collapsible list, select Department.

    j. Select the Ascending option and then select Next. The Grouping options are displayed.

k. Select the When contents change option and then select Next. The Filter options are displayed.
l. All the records will be used in this report, so select (All Records).
m. Select Next. The Summary options are displayed.
n. Select the In Stock field and then Sum to total the values in the In Stock field.
o. To display a subsummary, select the At end of each group check box in the Display summary information section.
p. Select Done. A dialog box is displayed asking if you would like to preview the report.
q. Select Preview. The report is displayed on the print preview screen.

4) VIEW THE REPORT DEFINITION

Select Cancel to go to the Report screen.

5) PRINT THE REPORT

a. Save IVY BOOKSTORE.
b. From the File menu, select Print. In the Print dialog box, select OK. The Inventory report is printed.

7.10 Calculation Fields

A *calculation field's* entry is automatically calculated by Works as the result of a mathematical statement called a *formula*. The formula usually uses data in other fields of the record to compute the value to display.

The usefulness of a calculation field can be illustrated using the IVY BOOKSTORE database. This database contains records for all items sold at the Ivy bookstore, how many of each are in stock, and the price of each item. A few of the records are shown below:

☑		Item Name	Department	In Stock	Price
☐	1	Dictionary	Books	22	$12.95
☐	2	Thesaurus	Books	12	$15.00
☐	3	Class Ring	Clothing	50	$198.95

If the bookstore manager wanted to know the value of the stock of each item, she would multiply the number in stock by its price. For example, there are 50 class rings in stock priced at $198.95 each. To determine the value of the stock of class rings, 50 would be multiplied by $198.95, producing $9,947.50. An easier method would be to include this operation in a calculation field.

A calculation field is created similarly to other fields. After displaying the database in Form Design view, add a numeric field. Next, in Form view select the entry box of the new field and type the desired formula. For example, the Value field formula would be =In Stock*Price. Formulas must begin with an equal sign (=) and can contain any of the following mathematical operators:

Addition   +
Subtraction   −
Multiplication   *
Division   /
Exponentiation   ^

While the formula in a calculation field remains constant and does not change, the result displayed is updated when any value in the formula changes. For example, if 20 class rings were sold one day and the In Stock field updated to 30, the Value field would automatically display $5,968.50 to reflect this change (30×198.95).

It is also possible to include numeric constants in a calculation field's formula. For example, to display a 5% tax on each item, a new calculation field called Tax that stores the formula =Price*0.05 could be added to the database. Works multiplies each item's price by 0.05 and displays the product in the Tax field. The tax on a class ring, for example, would be $9.95 ($198.95 × 0.05).

Practice 6

In this Practice you will add a calculation field which displays the value of each item in Ivy Bookstore's inventory. Start Works and open IVY BOOKSTORE if you have not already done so.

1) ADD A CALCULATION FIELD

    a. From the View menu, select Form Design. The database is displayed in Form Design view.

    b. Place the pointer in the white space below the Price field and click the mouse to place the cursor.

    c. Type Value: and then press Enter. The Insert Field dialog box is displayed.

    d. Select Number as the type, $1,234.56 for the Appearance, and then OK.

    e. Move the field on the form so that it is aligned with the Price field.

    f. From the View menu, select Form. The database is displayed in Form view.

    g. Click on the entry box of the Value field to select it.

    h. Type: =In Stock*Price and then press Enter.

    i. From the View menu, select List. The database is displayed in List view with the new field added. Note how the value for each record is calculated.

Check - Your database should be similar to the following:

		Item Name	Department	In Stock	Price	Value
	1	Dictionary	Books	22	$12.95	$284.90
	2	Thesaurus	Books	12	$15.00	$180.00
	3	Class Ring	Clothing	50	$198.95	$9,947.50
	4	School Bookbag	Clothing	125	$15.99	$1,998.75
	5	School Jacket	Clothing	100	$34.95	$3,495.00
	6	School Logo T-Shirt	Clothing	250	$9.99	$2,497.50
	7	School Tie	Clothing	15	$17.50	$262.50
	8	School Umbrella	Clothing	26	$10.99	$285.74
	9	Calculator	Electronics	136	$17.88	$2,431.68
	10	Cheetos	Food	280	$0.97	$271.60
	11	Chips	Food	77	$0.65	$50.05
	12	Doritos	Food	145	$2.49	$361.05
	13	Heath Bars	Food	167	$0.97	$161.99
	14	Pepsi	Food	444	$0.65	$288.60
	15	Ball Point Pen	Pens/Pencils	150	$0.89	$133.50
	16	Felt-tip pen	Pens/Pencils	76	$0.98	$74.48
	17	Highlite Markers	Pens/Pencils	158	$1.49	$235.42
	18	Pencil	Pens/Pencils	200	$0.15	$30.00
	19	Asprin	Pharmacy	168	$1.99	$334.32
	20	Band Aids	Pharmacy	12	$1.39	$16.68
	21	Sucrets	Pharmacy	378	$4.39	$1,659.42
	22	Tums	Pharmacy	144	$0.45	$64.80
	23	Legal Pad	Stationery	500	$1.75	$875.00
	24	Three-Hole Paper	Stationery	200	$1.98	$396.00
	25	Three-Ring Binder	Stationery	122	$3.50	$427.00

2) UPDATE A RECORD

    a. Note the current entry in the Value field of the Dictionary record.
    b. Click on the In Stock entry of the Dictionary record and enter 14. Note how the Value entry is automatically recalculated.

3) SAVE IVY BOOKSTORE AND PRINT A RECORD

    a. Save IVY BOOKSTORE.
    b. Print the database in List view with record and field labels and gridlines.
    c. Save the database and close IVY BOOKSTORE.
    d. Exit Works.

7.11 Where can you go from here?

The last three chapters introduced the concepts of databases: their design, creation, and use. The Works database has other options not discussed in this text which you may want to explore using the online help or *The Works Companion* supplied by Microsoft.

A powerful feature of Works is its ability to integrate the information stored in a database with a word processor document to produce personalized form letters. This process is called *mail merge* and is described in Chapter Eleven. Chapter Twelve describes how to add graphics to a database form.

Larger, more powerful database programs have even more options for generating reports and performing various operations with the data. Three of the most widely used packages are Access, dBASE, and FileMaker Pro. Because you have learned how to use the Works database it will be easier to learn a new package.

The knowledge of what a database is and what it can be used for is an important skill. There are many database-related job opportunities, some of which are discussed in Chapter Thirteen.

Chapter Summary

A report is used to present the information stored in a database and can contain titles, headings, records, summaries, and all or some of the fields in the database. When planning a report, the appropriate layout, query, sort, and summaries must be determined.

The ReportCreator command from the Tools menu is used to create a report definition. The report definition contains the elements of the report. To see the report it must be printed or print previewed.

The Report screen displays the report definition which is divided into rows and columns. Each row is identified by a section name which tells how the information in that row will be printed. The Record row contains field references that are replaced by the actual record contents when the report is printed or print previewed.

An existing report is displayed by using the Report command from the View menu. Clicking the Report View button displays the last report definition created.

A report definition can be formatted to change the way a report is printed. Column size can be changed by dragging the column divider bar or by executing the Column Width command from the Format menu. Styles and alignment can be applied by executing the Alignment and Font and Styles commands from the Format menu.

A report is modified by changing its report definition using commands from the Insert menu. In the report definition, a row is added by executing the Insert Row command, a column added by executing the Insert Column command. The Delete Row and Delete Column commands are used to delete rows and columns. To add a field to a report its field name and field reference must be added to the report definition by selecting the Field Name and Field Entry commands. The Report Settings command from the Format menu is used to change the sorting, grouping, and query options.

A report can be copied by executing the Duplicate Report command from the Tools menu. The Delete Report command from the Tools menu is used to delete a report.

Summaries and subsummaries are used to display statistics in a report. They can be used to sum, average, and count the values in a specified field of the records displayed in a report. Summaries and subsummaries can also be used to find the maximum or minimum values in a specified field. The Field Summary command from the Insert menu is used to insert a summary or subsummary into an existing report. A subsummary can only be added to a report that has been grouped and sorted.

A calculation field displays a value that is automatically computed. This value is calculated from a mathematical formula that is stored in the field. For example, the formula =In Stock*Price displays the product of the values stored in the In Stock and Price fields. Calculation fields are created by typing a formula as the entry for one numeric field in Form view.

Vocabulary

Calculation field - Numeric field that displays a value based on a calculation. The calculation can be based on values stored in other fields or constants.

Delete Report command - Deletes a report definition.

Duplicate Report command - Creates a copy of a report definition.

Field Entry command - Adds a field reference to an existing report definition.

Field Name command - Adds a field name (heading) to an existing report definition.

Field reference - Marker in the Record row of a report definition that indicates where field entries will appear. Field references are always preceded by an equal sign.

Field Summary command - Adds a summary or subsummary to an existing report definition.

Formula - A mathematical statement used to calculate a value.

Group - Records in a report that are placed together because they have the same value in the key sort field.

Headings - Field names printed at the top of each column in a report.

Insert Column command - Adds a column to a report.

Insert Field command - Adds a field to a report.

Insert Row command - Adds a row to a report definition.

Report - A printout of records that have been organized and summarized for a specific purpose.

Report command - Displays an existing report.

Report definition - Description of a report's contents.

ReportCreator command - Creates a report definition.

Section name - Describes how the information in a row will be printed.

Subsummary - Displays a summary for a group of records when the database is sorted on a specific field.

Summary - Used to total, average, or perform other calculations on the values displayed in a report. Summaries can also count the records displayed in a report.

Title - A description of a report's contents printed at the top of the first page of the report.

Reviews

Sections 7.1 — 7.5

1. Why would a database have more than one report?

2. Describe a report and what it contains.

3. List the four steps for planning a report.

4. a) What is a report definition?
   b) What command is used to create a report definition?

5. List the steps required to produce a report named Paid Students for Ivy University. The report should be sorted by Last Name and display the number of students who have paid their tuition.

6. The CAR PRICE database stores the make, model, and price for more than 100 different automobiles. List the steps required to produce a report that displays makes and models of cars over $5,000. Include a summary that totals all the car prices.

7. What is a field reference?

8. How can an existing report be displayed?

9. What will the Report View button on the Tool bar display?

Section 7.6 — 7.8

10. a) How can the column widths of a report be changed?
    b) How can a report title be made bold?

11. a) List the steps required to add a new Title row with the subtitle "Fall Semester" to an existing report.
    b) List the steps required to add the First Name field and its heading as the first field in an existing report.
    c) What three options of the report definition can be changed using the Report Settings command?

12. a) List the steps required to copy a report definition.
    b) List the steps required to delete a report definition.

Sections 7.9 — 7.11

13. What is a subsummary?

14. a) List the steps required to add a summary to an existing report?
    b) List the steps required to add a label for the summary in part (a).

15. A database stores each student's grades in fields named Grade 1, Grade 2, Grade 3, Grade 4, and Grade 5. The grades are numeric values from 0 to 100. Explain how a field named Average can be added to the database which calculates and stores the grade average for each student.

16. A bank database contains the following fields:

    First Name
    Last Name
    Acct Number
    Deposit Date
    Withdrawal Date
    Acct Balance

    a) List the steps required to create a calculation field named Interest that calculates the interest in each account as 5% of the account balance.
    b) List the steps required to produce a report named Interest Earned that displays the Last Name and Interest fields. The report should be sorted by Last Name, and include a summary that totals the interest earned.

7 | Exercises

1. The CAR PRICE database stores prices for a number of foreign and domestic cars. Open CAR PRICE which you last modified in Chapter Six, Exercise 7.

   a) Plan and then create a report named Less than $9000 that includes only the Make, Model, and Base Price fields. The records in the report should be sorted in ascending order by Base Price and include only cars with a base price less than $9,000. The report should also include a summary that averages the Base Price.

   b) Format the report appropriately. Save CAR PRICE and print the report.

   c) Plan and then create a report named Price w/Sunroof that includes only the Make, Model, and Price w/sunroof fields. The records in the report should be sorted in ascending order and grouped by Make and include only cars that have a sunroof. The report should also include a summary that counts the makes that have sunroofs.

   d) Format the report appropriately. Save the modified CAR PRICE and print the report.

   e) Plan and then create a report named Cheap Chevs&Ply that includes only the Make, Model, and Base Price fields. The records in the report should be sorted in ascending order and grouped by Make and include only Chevrolets and Plymouths that have a base price under $10,000. The report should also include a summary that counts the makes.

   f) Format the report appropriately. Save modified CAR PRICE and print the report.

2. The Address database stores information about your friends. Open Address which you last modified in Chapter Six, Exercise 11.

   a) Plan and then create a report named Birthdays that includes only the first and last names, birth date, and city fields. The records in the report should be sorted in ascending order by birth date and include all your friends.

   b) Format the report appropriately. Save modified Address and print the report.

   c) Plan and then create a report named Older Friends that includes only the first and last names and birth date fields. The records in the report should be sorted in ascending order by birth date and include only friends that were born before you.

   d) Format the report appropriately. Save Address and print the report.

   e) Plan and then create a report named My Town Friends that includes only the name and city fields. The records in the report should be sorted in ascending order by last name and include only friends that live in the same town as you.

   f) Format the report appropriately. Save modified Address and print the report.

3. Open INVENTOR which you last modified in Chapter Six, Exercise 10.

   a) Plan and then create a report named French Invent that includes only the Invention, Year, and Country fields. The records in the report should be sorted in ascending order by Year and include only inventors from France. The report should also include a summary that counts the number of inventions.

   b) Format the report appropriately. Save modified INVENTOR and print the report.

   c) Modify the report to display only those French inventions from this century. Save INVENTOR and print the modified report.

   d) Plan and then create a report named Inventions that includes only the Invention and Country fields. The records in the report should be sorted in ascending order and grouped by Country and include all the records in the database. The report should also include a subsummary and a summary that counts the number of inventions for each country.

   e) Format the report appropriately. Save modified INVENTOR and print the report.

4. Fantasy Wheels, Inc. would like reports generated from their Wheels database. Open Wheels which you last modified in Chapter Six, Exercise 3.

   a) Create a calculated field named Profit that displays the profit on each sale (asking price minus the price paid). Format the field appropriately and place it below the asking price field in Form view.

   b) Plan and then create a report named Auto Profit that includes only the Make, Price Paid, Asking Price, and Profit fields. The records in the report should be sorted in descending order by Make and include all the records in the database. The report should also include a summary that averages the profit.

   c) Format the report appropriately. Save modified Wheels and print the report.

   d) Plan and then create a report named Asking<$10,000 that includes only the Year, Make, and Asking Price fields. The records in the report should be sorted in descending order by Make and include only cars that cost less than $10,000. The report should also include a summary that averages the asking price.

   e) Format the report appropriately. Save modified Wheels and print the report.

5. Reports can be used to learn more from the temperature data you entered in the Weather database. Open Weather which you last modified in Chapter Six, Exercise 5.

   a) Create a calculated field named Temp. (F) that converts degrees Celsius (C) to degrees Fahrenheit (F). The conversion formula is Fahrenheit=9/5 × Celsius + 32. Format the field appropriately and place it to the right of the Temp. (C) field in Form view.

   b) Plan and then create a report named Sky Conditions that includes only the Date, Sky, and the Celsius temperature fields. The records in the report should be sorted in ascending order by Date and include all the records in the database.

   c) Add the Fahrenheit field to the report. Be sure to include a heading.

   d) Format the report appropriately. Save modified Weather and print the report.

e) Make a copy of the Sky Conditions report named Sunny and >65. Modify the report to include only those records when it was warmer than 65° F and sunny. The records in the report should be sorted in ascending order by temperature (F). The report should also include a summary that counts the days displayed.

f) Format the report appropriately. Save modified Weather and print the report.

6. Open the ACADEMY AWARDS database which contains information about Academy Award winners since 1928. ACADEMY AWARDS was last modified in Chapter Six, Exercise 13.

a) Plan and then create a report named UA Films that includes only the Year, Picture, and Studio fields. The records in the report should be sorted in ascending order by Year and include only the United Artists films. The report should also include a summary that counts the records.

b) Format the report appropriately. Save modified ACADEMY AWARDS and print the report.

c) Plan and then create a report named 1985 to Present that includes only the Year and Picture fields. The records in the report should be sorted in ascending order by Year and include only films from 1985 to the present.

d) Format the report appropriately. Save modified ACADEMY AWARDS and print the report.

7. Open COLLEGES which contains information about U.S. colleges and universities. COLLEGES was last modified in Chapter Six, Exercise 9.

a) Create a calculated field named Total Cost that displays the total cost of attending each school (tuition plus room and board). Format the field appropriately and place it below the Room/Board field in Form view.

b) Plan and then create a report named CO Total Costs that includes only the Name, Enrollment, and Total Cost fields. The records in the report should be sorted in ascending order by Name and include only the schools in Colorado. The report should also include a summary that averages the total cost.

c) Format the report appropriately. Save modified COLLEGES and print the report.

d) Make a copy of the Total Costs report named <8000 & >$15000. Modify the report to include all schools with less than 8,000 students and whose total cost is more than $15,000. The records in the report should be sorted in ascending order name. The report should still include a summary that averages the total cost.

e) Format the report appropriately. Save modified COLLEGES and print the report.

f) Plan and create a new report named CA & MA Schools that includes only the Name, State, and Private/Public fields. The records in the report should be sorted in ascending order and grouped by State and include only California and Massachusetts schools. The report should also include a subsummary and summary that counts the records.

g) Format the report appropriately. Save modified COLLEGES and print the report.

8. Open COUNTRY which contains information about the countries of the world. COUNTRY was last modified in Chapter Six, Exercise 7.

a) Plan and then create a report named Pounds or Pesos that includes only the Country, Capital, and Currency fields. The records in the report should be sorted in ascending order and grouped by Currency and include only countries whose currency is either the pound or peso. The report should also include a subsummary and summary that counts the records.

b) Format the report appropriately. Save modified COUNTRY and print the report.

c) Plan and then create a report named < 1 Million that includes only the Country and Population fields. The records in the report should be sorted in ascending order by population and include only countries whose population is less than 1 million. The report should also include a summary that averages the population.

d) Format the report appropriately. Save modified COUNTRY and print the report.

9. Open GIBBON RESEARCH which contains a number of observations of gibbons. GIBBON RESEARCH was last modified in Chapter Six, Exercise 12.

a) Plan and then create a report named Male Gibbons that includes only the Name, Gender, Age, Location, and Companion fields. The records in the report should be sorted in ascending order by name and include only male gibbons. The report should also include a summary that averages the age.

b) Format the report appropriately. Save modified GIBBON RESEARCH and print the report.

c) Make a copy of the Male Gibbons report named Female Gibbons. Modify the report to include only those records of female gibbons. The records in the report should be sorted in ascending order by name. The report should also include a summary that averages the age.

d) Format the report appropriately. Save modified GIBBON RESEARCH and print the report.

Chapter Eight
Introducing the Spreadsheet

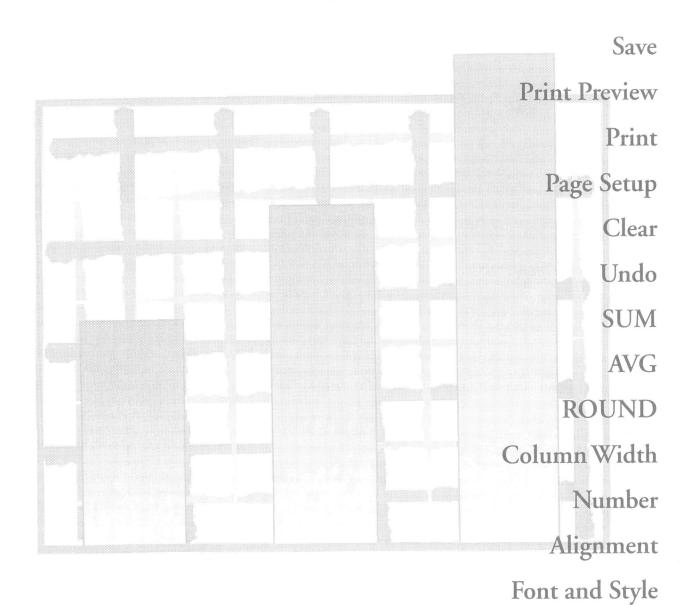

Save

Print Preview

Print

Page Setup

Clear

Undo

SUM

AVG

ROUND

Column Width

Number

Alignment

Font and Style

Objectives

After completing this chapter you will be able to:

1. Define a spreadsheet.

2. Create a spreadsheet, enter data into it, and edit the data.

3. Save and print a spreadsheet.

4. Use formulas and functions to perform calculations.

5. Use cell names in formulas.

6. Use the SUM, AVG, and ROUND functions.

7. Change the width of columns.

8. Format a spreadsheet.

9. Select cell ranges by highlighting blocks of cells.

8

This chapter explains what a spreadsheet is and how to use one. The components of a spreadsheet are presented first, then the commands needed to produce a simple Works spreadsheet are covered. The next chapter explains how to create larger and more powerful spreadsheets.

8.1 What is a Spreadsheet?

A *spreadsheet* is simply rows and columns of data. The term comes from the field of accounting where accountants kept track of business activities on large sheets of paper that spread out to form a "spreadsheet." Accounting spreadsheets contain rows and columns of figures that relate to the flow of money, but spreadsheets can be used to organize any type of numeric data.

Spreadsheets are record keeping tools that work primarily with numbers. An example of a simple spreadsheet is the grade book used by Ivy University's chemistry professor, Dr. Sulfuric. In her grade book, the names of her students run down the left side of the page and labels run across the top of the page to indicate each test and test date:

Name	Test 1 9/12/97	Test 2 10/17/97	Test 3 11/14/97	Test 4 12/12/97
C. Bowser	50	83	68	64
D. Warheit	86	89	78	88
M. Porter	78	100	90	89
B. Presley	45	78	66	78
D. Unwalla	66	76	78	55
T. Hogan	85	74	83	66

Dr. Sulfuric's grade book

The grade book is organized into rows and columns. A row runs horizontally and stores both the name and grades for one student. The name T. Hogan and the grades 85, 74, 83, and 66 form a row. A column runs vertically and stores a title, date, and all of the grades for a single test. The title Test 1, the date 9/12/97, and the grades from 50 to 85 form a column.

Computerized spreadsheets can be set up to automatically perform calculations on data. Dr. Sulfuric could use a computerized spreadsheet to store her grades and calculate grade averages. The spreadsheet will automatically recalculate the average if she changes a grade. This is the primary advantage of a computerized spreadsheet; the ability to perform calculations on data and to automatically recalculate when changes are made.

8.2 The Spreadsheet Screen

To create a new spreadsheet, the spreadsheet button is selected from the Works Task Launcher dialog box. The Works spreadsheet screen has columns, rows, and a few other features:

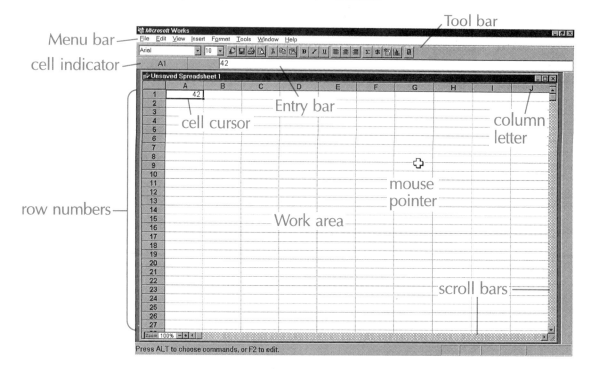

The Works spreadsheet screen

Columns are identified by letters across the top of the screen, and rows are identified by numbers down the left side. In Works, a spreadsheet has letters that run from A to Z, and then AA to AZ, then BA and so on up to IV. Rows are numbered from 1 to 16,384. However, only a limited number of rows and columns can be displayed on the screen at one time. For example, the screen above displays only columns A to J and rows 1 to 27. Other columns and rows can be displayed by scrolling the spreadsheet with the scroll bars.

Data is entered into a spreadsheet on the screen shown above. The intersection of a row and column is called a *cell*. A single cell is identified by its column letter and row number, which together is called a *cell name*. For example, the third cell from the top in column C is named C3. Each cell can store a single item of data. This system is similar to mailboxes at the post office where each box (or cell) has a name and can store information. Be careful not to confuse the name of a cell with the data it stores. The outline appearing around cell A1 is called the *cell cursor*. Data can only be entered into the cell where the cell cursor is located, also called the *selected cell*. The *cell indicator* at the top of the screen shows the current location of the cell cursor, in this case A1.

Commands are accessed from menus in the Menu bar at the top of the screen. Below the Menu bar is the Tool bar. The contents of the selected cell are displayed on the *Entry bar*. Spreadsheet cells and the data they store are in the Work area.

8.3 Types of Data

Spreadsheets can store three types of data in cells: labels, values, and times/dates. *Labels* are text and cannot be used in calculations. *Values* are numeric and can be used in calculations. *Times/dates* are either a time, such as 12:10 PM, or a calendar date such as 6/4/97. A time/date entry may be used in some calculations. In the grade book spreadsheet, student names and titles (e.g., T. Hogan and Test 1) are labels, a grade such as 50 is a value, and a date such as 9/12/97 is a time/date. When planning a computerized spreadsheet it is important to first determine what the data will be stored as: labels, values, or times/dates.

8.4 Moving Through the Spreadsheet

When the mouse pointer is moved onto the Work area, it changes from an arrow shape to a plus sign (⊕). Clicking the plus sign on a cell moves the cell cursor to that cell. If the desired cell is not displayed on the screen, the scroll bars can be used to bring hidden rows and columns into view. Clicking once on one of the scroll arrows moves the spreadsheet one row or column in the direction of the arrow. Holding the mouse button down continues the scroll. Dragging the scroll box within the scroll bar moves the spreadsheet in the window a greater distance.

Another way to move the cell cursor is to use the keyboard. Pressing an arrow key moves the cursor from cell to cell, automatically scrolling the spreadsheet when necessary. Pressing the Home key moves the cell cursor to the first cell in the row. The End key moves the cell cursor to the last cell in the row that contains data. Pressing the Page Up key moves the cell cursor to the cell one screen up while pressing the Page Down key moves the cell cursor to the cell one screen down.

· ·

Practice 1

In this Practice you will create a new spreadsheet, use the mouse to move the cell cursor around, and scroll through the empty spreadsheet.

1) CREATE A NEW SPREADSHEET

    a. Following the directions given in Chapter Two, start Works.
    b. In the Works Task Launcher dialog box, click on the Works Tools tab if the Works Tools options are not already displayed.
    c. Select the Spreadsheet button. A new empty spreadsheet is displayed.

2) SELECT CELL D8

Select cell D8 by pointing to cell D8 and clicking once. Note that the cell indicator in the upper-left corner of the screen displays D8.

3) SCROLL THE SCREEN USING THE SCROLL BARS

a. Click once on the right horizontal scroll arrow. Note how column A moves off the screen and another column moves onto the screen.

b. Click and hold the mouse on the right horizontal scroll arrow until cell Z8 becomes visible. When scrolling with the mouse, the cell cursor does not move from the currently selected cell. Click on cell Z8 to select it.

c. Click once on the down vertical scroll arrow. Note how the top row moves off the screen. Click and hold the mouse on the down vertical scroll arrow until cell Z50 becomes visible. Click on cell Z50 to select it.

4) RETURN THE CELL CURSOR TO CELL A1 USING THE SCROLL BOXES

a. Drag the scroll box to the far left of the horizontal scroll bar. Column A should be visible.

b. Drag the scroll box in the vertical scroll bar upwards to display Row 1. Note that the cell indicator still displays Z50 because scrolling only changes what is displayed, not which cell is selected. Click on cell A1 to select it.

8.5 Entering Data into the Spreadsheet

Data is entered into a cell by selecting that cell and entering the data from the keyboard. When the data is typed, it appears on the Entry bar and in the cell:

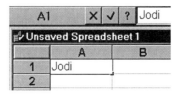

Clicking on the Check box enters the label "Jodi" into cell A1

Clicking on the *Check box* (✓) or pressing the Enter key enters the data and leaves the cell cursor on the selected cell. Pressing the Tab key enters the data and then selects the next cell in the row. Clicking on the *X box* (✗) or pressing the Escape key cancels data entry and restores the cell's original contents.

Typing data and then pressing an arrow key enters the data and then selects the next cell in the direction of the arrow key.

If a mistake is made when entering data, it can be corrected by selecting the cell and entering the correct data. The new data then replaces any previous data. If the mistake is noticed while typing the data, the Backspace key can be used to delete one character at a time.

Works automatically displays values up to 9 digits long in a single cell. When the value exceeds 9 digits it is expressed in scientific notation. For example, the number 333344445555 is displayed as 3.333E+11. However, labels are displayed in their entirety until they encounter another cell containing data.

8.6 Saving, Viewing, and Printing a Spreadsheet

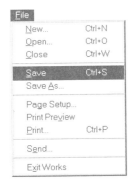

Executing the Save command from the File menu (Ctrl+S) or clicking on the Save button on the Tool bar (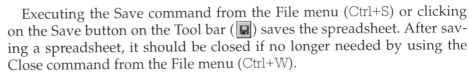) saves the spreadsheet. After saving a spreadsheet, it should be closed if no longer needed by using the Close command from the File menu (Ctrl+W).

The Print Preview command from the File menu or the Print Preview button on the Tool bar ( ) can be used to view the spreadsheet as it will appear when printed. To print the spreadsheet, the Print command from the File menu is selected to display its dialog box. Selecting the OK button prints the portion of the spreadsheet that contains data. A spreadsheet can also be printed by clicking on the Print button ( ) on the Tool bar. When the Print button is used, the Print dialog box is not displayed and one copy of the spreadsheet is printed. Before printing, it is a good practice to first save the spreadsheet.

A spreadsheet printout can be easier to read if row and column headers and gridlines are included. Selecting the Page Setup command from the File menu displays the Page Setup dialog box. Selecting the Other Options tab displays the Print gridlines and Print row and column headers options.

Information such as the creator's name, the date, or the filename can be included in a header or footer in the spreadsheet to provide more informative printouts. To include a header or footer, the Headers and Footers command from the View menu is selected and then the desired text typed in the displayed dialog box.

Practice 2

In this Practice you will enter the data from Dr. Sulfuric's grade book into the spreadsheet created in the last Practice. If the spreadsheet is not open, create a new one following the steps given in Practice 1.

1) ENTER THE COLUMN TITLES IN ROW 1

   a. Move the pointer to cell A1 and click once to select it, if it is not already selected. Type Name and click on the Check box. Cell A1 now contains the label Name. Note that the Entry bar displays the currently selected cell's contents.
   b. Select cell B1 and type Test 1. Press the Enter key.
   c. Press the right-arrow key to move the cell cursor to cell C1, then type Test 2.
   d. Press the Tab key. The label is entered and the cell cursor moved to the next cell in the row, D1.
   e. Continue this procedure to place the headings Test 3 in cell D1 and Test 4 in cell E1.

2) ENTER THE TEST DATES

   a. Select cell B2 and type the date 9/12/97. Click on the Check box. Works right aligns a date when entered into a cell.
   b. Select cell C2 and type the date 10/17/97. Press the Tab key. The cell cursor is moved to the next cell in the row, D2.
   c. Enter the date 11/14/97 in cell D2 and the date 12/12/97 in cell E2.

3) ENTER THE STUDENT NAMES

a. Select cell A3. Type the name C. Bowser and press the down-arrow key. The cell cursor moves to the next cell in the column, A4.

b. Type the name D. Warheit and press the down-arrow key.

c. Continue this process to place the names:

M. Porter	into cell A5
B. Presley	into cell A6
D. Unwalla	into cell A7
T. Hogan	into cell A8

4) ENTER THE GRADES

Move the cell cursor to cell B3 and enter the first grade for C. Bowser, a 50. Continue entering the grades from Dr. Sulfuric's grade book as shown below. If a mistake is noticed before a cell's data has been entered, use the Backspace key to erase data on the Entry bar, then type the correction. Incorrect data that has already been entered may be corrected by moving the cell cursor to the cell and entering new data. When complete your spreadsheet should look like the one below:

	A	B	C	D	E
1	Name	Test 1	Test 2	Test 3	Test 4
2		9/12/97	10/17/97	11/14/97	12/12/97
3	C. Browser	50	83	68	64
4	D. Warheit	86	89	78	88
5	M. Porter	78	100	90	89
6	B. Presley	45	78	66	78
7	D. Unwalla	66	76	78	55
8	T. Hogan	85	74	83	66

5) PREVIEW THE SPREADSHEET

a. From the File menu, select Print Preview. The print preview screen is displayed with the portion of the spreadsheet containing data.

b. Notice how it is hard to read a row in the spreadsheet because there are no gridlines or row and column headers. Select Cancel to return to the spreadsheet screen.

c. From the File menu, select Page Setup. The Page Setup dialog box is displayed.

d. Select the Other Options tab if those options are not already displayed.

e. Select the Print gridlines and Print row and column headers options. Select OK.

f. From the File menu, select Print Preview. The print preview screen is displayed.

g. Notice how much easier the spreadsheet is to read. Select Cancel to return to the spreadsheet screen.

6) SAVE, PRINT, AND CLOSE THE SPREADSHEET

a. From the File menu, select Save. The Save As dialog box is displayed.

b. In the File name entry box, type Grades. Select Save.

c. From the File menu, select Print. A dialog box is displayed.

b. Select OK to print the spreadsheet. The printout contains only the portion of the spreadsheet that contains data.

c. Close Grades.

An Introduction to Computing Using Microsoft Works

8.7 Using Formulas to Perform Calculations

A primary benefit of using a spreadsheet is its ability to perform calculations using formulas. *Formulas* are mathematical statements used to calculate values. For example, entering the formula =25 * 3 will display the value 75 in the cell. Note that every formula in Works must begin with an equal sign (=).

The following mathematical operators can be used in a formula:

Addition	+
Subtraction	–
Multiplication	*
Division	/
Exponentiation	^

Exponentiation means to raise to a power and is represented by the caret (^) symbol. For example, $2^2 = 4$ and $5^3 = 125$.

When Works evaluates a formula, it follows the rules of *order of operations* which indicate the priority of operators. For example, what value is displayed when the formula

=9+12/3

is evaluated? Is the sum of 9 and 12 divided by 3? If so, the answer is 7. Or is the result of 12 divided by 3 added to 9 to produce 13? Entering the formula we discover that 13 is displayed. Division is performed first and then addition because a specific order of operations is followed.

Works evaluates a formula from left to right. If a formula contains two operators of equal priority, the leftmost operator is used first. The following order of operations is used when a formula is evaluated:

Exponents

1. Any number raised to a power is calculated first.

   =4+3^2   produces the value 13

Multiplication & Division

2. Calculations involving multiplication and division, which are of equal priority, are performed next.

   =3+5*6/2   produces the value 18

   Here, Works first computes the product of 5 and 6 to get 30, and then divides by 2 to produce 15. Finally, 3 is added to 15 to produce 18. Operations of the same priority are performed in order from left to right.

Addition & Subtraction

3. Third in the order of operations is addition and subtraction which are of equal priority.

   =7+4*2   produces the value 15

   Here, Works first multiplies 4 and 2 to get 8. The final result is computed by adding 7 to 8 to get 15.

When a formula contains parentheses, whatever operations are within them are performed first. By using parentheses you can change the order of operations. For example, to add 7 and 4 and then multiply the result by 2, parentheses must be used:

$$=(7+4)*2 \qquad \text{produces the value } 22$$

Here are other formulas and their results:

Formula	Resulting value
=2*2+3*2	10
=25*8/4	50
=35+12/3	39
=3+5*8+7	50
=(3+5)*(8+7)	120
=3^2*8-4	68
=6+2^2	10
=(6+2)^2	64

Entering an invalid formula in a cell causes Works to display an error message in that cell. For example, a number cannot be divided by zero because the result is mathematically undefined. Therefore, entering =10/0 displays ERR.

Practice 3

In this Practice you will enter formulas into the cells of a new spreadsheet to perform calculations. Start Works if you have not already done so.

1) CREATE A NEW SPREADSHEET

Use the Works Task Launcher dialog box to create a new empty spreadsheet.

2) ENTER A FORMULA INTO CELL A1 OF THE SPREADSHEET

a. Select cell A1 if it is not already selected.
b. Type =35*12/3. Click on the Check box. The result 140 is displayed in cell A1. Note that the formula is shown on the Entry bar, but the result of the formula is shown in the cell:

A1		=35*12/3

Unsaved Spreadsheet 1

	A	B
1	140	

3) ENTER FORMULAS

a. Select cell B1.
b. Enter each of the formulas shown on the next page by typing the formula and then pressing the down-arrow key to move the cell cursor to the next cell in the column. Note the resulting values:

Formula	Resulting value
=20/50	0.4
=20*50	1000
=20-50	-30
=2+20*5+50	152
=(2+20)*(5+50)	1210
=20/0	ERR
20+50	20+50

In the last example, the result is a *label* because it is not preceded by an equal sign.

4) SAVE THE SPREADSHEET

Save the spreadsheet naming it Example.

8.8 Using Cell Names in Formulas

A cell name may be used in a formula. When Works evaluates the formula, it uses the cell name to locate the value needed in the calculation. For example, if cell B3 stores the value 20 and cell C2 stores the value 50:

Formula	Resulting value
=B3/C2	0.4
=B3*C2	1000
=B3-C2	-30
=2*B3+5*C2	290
=B3+5*C2+8	278
=B3+5*(C2+8)	310
=(B3+5)*(C2+8)	1450

If the cell contains a label, 0 is used for its value.

It is important to realize that a formula cannot reference the cell it is stored in. For example, the formulas above cannot be stored in cells B3 or C2 because this would cause an error.

Formulas are commonly used to sum values. For example, the sum of the values stored in cells C1 to C6 can be calculated using the formula:

=C1+C2+C3+C4+C5+C6

To average the values stored in cells C1 to C6, the following formula can be used:

=(C1+C2+C3+C4+C5+C6)/6

8.9 Editing Entries

A cell's entry can be edited by first selecting the cell to display its contents on the Entry bar. Next, clicking the pointer on the Entry bar or pressing the F2 key displays a blinking cursor and then characters can be entered or deleted. When the entry has been corrected the Check box is clicked or Enter pressed.

Entering an invalid formula displays an error dialog box that may look similar to the following:

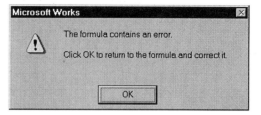

Works displays an error dialog box when an invalid formula has been entered

Selecting OK removes the box so that the formula can be corrected.

The contents of a selected cell can be erased by pressing the Delete key. Selecting the Clear command from the Edit menu also erases a selected cell's contents. If a cell is cleared by mistake, immediately executing the Undo command (Ctrl+Z) from the Edit menu restores the cell's contents.

Practice 4

In this Practice you will enter values and formulas into the cells of a spreadsheet and perform calculations. Start Works and open Example if it is not already displayed.

1) ENTER VALUES INTO THE SPREADSHEET

    a. Select cell C1 and enter the value 20.
    b. Select cell D2 and enter the value 50.

2) ENTER FORMULAS

    a. Select cell D5.
    b. Enter each of the formulas below by typing the formula and then pressing the down-arrow key to move the cell cursor to the next cell in the column. Note the resulting values:

Formula	Resulting value
=C1/D2	0.4
=C1*D2	1000
=C1-D2	-30
=2+C1*5+D2	152
=(2+C1)*(5+D2)	1210
=C1^2+D2^2	2900
=(C1+D2)^2	4900
=C1/0	ERR
C1+D2	C1+D2

In the last example, the result is a *label* because it is not preceded by an equal sign.

3) ENTER A NEW VALUE IN CELL C1

    a. Select cell C1.
    b. Enter 30 to replace the current value. Every formula in the spreadsheet referencing cell C1 is automatically recalculated. A major advantage of using a spreadsheet is that formulas are automatically recalculated when values they reference change.
    c. Enter 20 in cell C1. Note how the values are again automatically recalculated.

4) CLEAR THE CONTENTS OF EACH CELL

a. Select cell D5.
b. From the Edit menu, select the Clear command. The cell's contents are now cleared and the Entry bar is blank.
c. Clear each cell displaying data using either the Clear command or the Delete key. The entire spreadsheet Work area should now be blank.

5) ENTER NEW VALUES

a. Select cell C1 and enter the value 50.
b. Select cell C2 and enter the value 85.
c. Continue entering the values:

   75   in cell C3
   83   in cell C4
   34   in cell C5
   55   in cell C6

6) CALCULATE THE SUM OF THE VALUES IN COLUMN C

a. Select cell C8.
b. Enter the formula:

   =C1+C2+C3+C4+C5+C6

Cell C8 displays the sum of the values stored in cells C1 through C6, 382.

7) CALCULATE THE AVERAGE OF THE VALUES IN COLUMN C

a. Select cell C9.
b. Enter the formula:

   =(C1+C2+C3+C4+C5+C6)/6

The average of the values, 63.666667, is shown in cell C9.

8) EDIT THE FORMULA TO AVERAGE THE FIRST 3 CELLS ONLY

a. Select cell C9, if it is not already selected.
b. Move the pointer to the right of the divisor 6 on the Entry bar and click the mouse to place the cursor. Press the Backspace key to delete the 6. Type a 3.
c. Press the left-arrow key 3 times to place the cursor to the right of the cell name C6.
d. Press the Backspace key 9 times. The formula should now read =(C1+C2+C3)/3. Click on the Check box or press the Enter key. The average of the first three cells only is shown in cell C9. What is it?

Check - Your spreadsheet should be similar to:

C9		=(C1+C2+C3)/3

Example

	A	B	C
1			50
2			85
3			75
4			83
5			34
6			55
7			
8			382
9			70

9) ENTER A NEW VALUE IN CELL C1

    a. Select cell C1.

    b. Enter 20 to replace the current value. The formula in cell C9 is automatically recalculated and a new value displayed.

    c. Enter 50 in cell C1. The values are again automatically recalculated.

10) SAVE AND CLOSE EXAMPLE

8.10 Using Functions to Perform Calculations

To perform common calculations Works contains built-in functions that can be used as part of a formula. A *function* performs a set of calculations and then returns a single value. To better understand this, consider the formula =C1+C2+C3+C4+C5+C6 used in Practice 4. We could have performed this same calculation using a formula that contained the built-in SUM function:

    =SUM(C1:C6)

The SUM function requires the first and last cell names of the cells to be summed. The colon (:) is used to indicate a *range* of cells. For example, C1:C6 refers to cells C1, C2, C3, C4, C5, and C6. Functions are useful because they often make a formula shorter and are less error-prone, especially when a large range of cells is involved.

Values stored in a row of cells can also be added together. For example, the formula

    =SUM(B2:E2)

adds the values in cells B2, C2, D2, and E2 together. It is important to realize that only a section of adjacent cells can be used to define a range.

In Practice 4, we could replace the formula in cell C9 used to average the column of grades with:

    =SUM(C1:C6)/6

Note that we must still divide the sum by 6 to obtain the average. An easier method is to use Works' built-in AVG function:

    =AVG(C1:C6)

The AVG function adds the values of the cells in the range and then divides the result by the number of cells in the range.

Practice 5

In this Practice you will enter formulas to calculate the average grade on each test and the term averages for each of Dr. Sulfuric's students in the Grades spreadsheet created in Practices 1 and 2. Start Works if you have not already done so.

1) OPEN THE GRADES SPREADSHEET

An Introduction to Computing Using Microsoft Works

2) USE A FUNCTION TO SUM THE GRADES FOR TEST 1

   a. Select cell B9.

   b. Enter the following formula:

       =SUM(B3:B8)

   The sum 410 is displayed.

3) ENTER THE FORMULA TO AVERAGE THE GRADES FOR TEST 1

   Dr. Sulfuric needs the average of the grades, not the sum. Move the cell cursor to cell B9 and enter the formula:

       =AVG(B3:B8)

   The average grade on Test 1, 68.333333, is displayed in cell B9.

4) ENTER FORMULAS TO CALCULATE THE OTHER TEST AVERAGES

      =AVG(C3:C8)   into cell C9
      =AVG(D3:D8)   into cell D9
      =AVG(E3:E8)   into cell E9

5) CALCULATE EACH STUDENT'S TERM AVERAGE

   a. Select cell F3.

   b. Enter the formula:

       =AVG(B3:E3)

   The average for C. Bowser, 66.25, is displayed in cell F3.

   c. Repeat this process by entering the formulas:

      =AVG(B4:E4)   into cell F4
      =AVG(B5:E5)   into cell F5
      =AVG(B6:E6)   into cell F6
      =AVG(B7:E7)   into cell F7
      =AVG(B8:E8)   into cell F8

6) ADD TITLES FOR THE NEW INFORMATION

   a. Select cell F1 and enter the label: Average

   b. Select cell A9 and enter the label: Average:

7) SAVE THE MODIFIED GRADES SPREADSHEET

<u>Check</u> - Your spreadsheet should be similar to:

	A	B	C	D	E	F
1	Name	Test 1	Test 2	Test 3	Test 4	Average
2		9/12/97	10/17/97	11/14/97	12/12/97	
3	C. Browser	50	83	68	64	66.25
4	D. Warheit	86	89	78	88	85.25
5	M. Porter	78	100	90	89	89.25
6	B. Presley	45	78	66	78	66.75
7	D. Unwalla	66	76	78	55	68.75
8	T. Hogan	85	74	83	66	77
9	Average:	68.333333	83.333333	77.166667	73.333333	

8.11 The ROUND Function

8

The ROUND function rounds a value to a specific number of decimal places. In the spreadsheet containing Dr. Sulfuric's grades, the test averages are computed to 8 decimal places, but only 2 places are desired. For example, the class average on Test 1 appears as 68.333333, but Dr. Sulfuric wants it computed as 68.33.

To round a stored value, the cell name is used in the ROUND function followed by the number of decimal places that the result is to be rounded. For example, to round the value stored in cell C16 to 2 places, the formula is written:

    =ROUND(C16,2)

If the value stored in C16 is 42.865 the rounded result is 42.87.

To round the result of a formula, the formula followed by the number of decimal places desired is used in the ROUND function. For example, C. Bowser's average can be rounded to 1 place with the formula:

    =ROUND(AVG(B3:E3),1)

To round a value to the nearest integer, a 0 is used to indicate no decimal places:

    =ROUND(AVG(B3:E3),0)

It should be noted that rounding changes the actual value stored in the cell, not just the way the original value is displayed. Therefore, the result of a calculation involving a rounded value may be different from the same calculation using the value before rounding. Works includes a number of other functions which are listed in Appendix A.

Practice 6

In this Practice you will round the averages in the Grades spreadsheet by editing the existing formulas. The modified spreadsheet will then be printed. Start Works and open Grades if you have not already done so.

1) DISPLAY THE RESULT OF A FORMULA TO 2 DECIMAL PLACES

   a. Select cell B9.
   b. Click the pointer on the Entry bar to display the cursor. Place the cursor before the A in AVG and type: ROUND(
   c. Move the cursor to the end of the formula and type ,2) so that the formula on the Entry bar appears:

    =ROUND(AVG(B3:B8),2)

Click on the Check box or press Enter and note that the average is now rounded to 2 decimal places, 68.33.

2) ROUND ALL TEST AVERAGES TO 2 DECIMAL PLACES

Repeat step 1 for cells C9, D9, and E9.

3) ROUND C. BOWSER'S AVERAGE TO 1 DECIMAL PLACE

a. Select cell F3.
b. Place the cursor before the A in AVG and type: ROUND(
c. Place the cursor at the end of the formula and type ,1) so that the formula is:

=ROUND(AVG(B3:E3),1)

Click on the Check box or press Enter and note that the average is rounded to one decimal place, 66.3.

4) ROUND ALL STUDENT AVERAGES TO 1 DECIMAL PLACE

Repeat step 3 for cells F4, F5, F6, F7, and F8.

5) SAVE THE MODIFIED GRADES

<u>Check</u> - Your spreadsheet should be similar to the one below:

	A	B	C	D	E	F
1	Name	Test 1	Test 2	Test 3	Test 4	Average
2		9/12/97	10/17/97	11/14/97	12/12/97	
3	C. Browser	50	83	68	64	66.3
4	D. Warheit	86	89	78	88	85.3
5	M. Porter	78	100	90	89	89.3
6	B. Presley	45	78	66	78	66.8
7	D. Unwalla	66	76	78	55	68.8
8	T. Hogan	85	74	83	66	77
9	Average	68.33	83.33	77.17	73.33	

8.12 Changing a Column's Width

The default column width is 10 which is often insufficient to display a column's data. A column's width is changed by dragging its right column divider bar. To do this, point to the bar separating the column letters at the top of the screen. The pointer shape changes to a double-headed arrow with the word ADJUST below it:

*The width of column G will be changed
when the divider bar is dragged*

Next, drag the divider bar to the right to increase the width of the field. To decrease a field's width, drag the divider bar to the left.

A second way to change a column's width is by executing the Column Width command from the Format menu, typing the desired width in the Column Width dialog box, and then selecting OK.

It is important to realize that the width of single cells cannot be changed, only whole columns. If a cell is not wide enough to display its value, scientific notation is used. For example, the value 123456789012 is displayed as 1.23456e+11. Pound signs (###) are displayed if a cell is not wide enough to display a formatted value.

8.13 Formatting a Spreadsheet

How a spreadsheet is displayed is called its *layout*. Column widths, value formats, and label formats all relate to layout. Choosing a proper layout is important because it makes a spreadsheet easier to use and understand.

Changing a column's width affects every cell in the column. However, other formatting commands affect only the selected cell. To format a cell that stores a number, time, or date, the cell is highlighted and the Number command from the Format menu selected. A dialog box is then displayed:

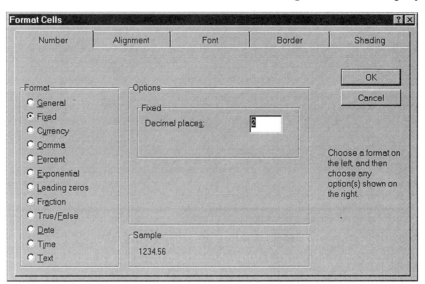

Number formats can be selected from this dialog box

To display the value in the selected cell with a specific number of decimal places, Fixed is selected and then the desired number of decimal places typed in the Decimal places box. Unlike the ROUND function, fixing a value to a specific number of decimal places only changes how the value is displayed, not the value itself. For example, a cell containing a value of 27.8 fixed to 0 decimal places displays 28. Adding 10 to the value of this cell produces 37.8, not 38.

Cells that store dollar amounts should be formatted for currency. When the Currency option is selected, a Negative numbers in red option is available. The Currency button on the Tool bar (🔘) can also be used to format a cell as currency with 2 decimal places and commas.

The Percent option displays the value stored in the cell as a percentage. For example, a cell storing the value 0.15 formatted as Percent with 0 as the Decimal places displays 15%. As with the Fixed format, Currency and Percent do not change the value that is stored in the selected cell, only how that value is displayed.

Unless formatted otherwise, cells containing labels are left aligned, while values and dates are right aligned. For this reason labels and values displayed in the same column do not line up. For example, the Test labels and dates in the Grades spreadsheet do not align in the column. The alignment of a selected cell can be changed by clicking on the desired button on the Tool bar:

A cell's alignment can also be changed by executing the Alignment command from the Format menu and then selecting the desired alignment from the displayed Format Cells dialog box.

The style, font, and font size of cell data in a selected cell can also be changed. The Bold (**B**), Italic (*I*), and Underline (_u_) buttons on the Tool bar are used to apply character styles. The Font Name and Font Size lists on the Tool bar are used to change a cell's font and font size. The Font and Style command in the Format menu may also be used to change a selected cell's font, font size and style.

When a selected cell's font, font size, or style is changed all of the data in the cell is affected. For example, it is not possible to bold just the first letter of a label. Also, more than one style can be applied to a cell. For example, a cell can be formatted as both bold and italic. There are many different ways to use these formats: titles and section names could be bold, important numbers might be italic, and so on.

8.14 Highlighting

Several spreadsheet cells can be selected together to form a *highlighted block*. This is helpful when applying formatting or using the editing commands because all of the cells in the highlighted block are affected. To highlight a block of cells, the pointer is dragged from one cell to another:

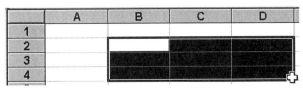

The mouse pointer was placed on cell B2 and then dragged to cell D4 to create this highlighted block

An entire row, column, or block of adjacent cells can be highlighted.

Another way of creating a highlighted block is by first selecting the starting cell, then holding down the Shift key and clicking the mouse on the last cell in the block. To select an entire row click on the row number, and click on a column letter to highlight a column. Clicking in the box above row 1 and to the left of column A selects the entire spreadsheet.

In this Practice you will format the Grades spreadsheet. Start Works and open the Grades spreadsheet if you have not already done so.

1) BOLD THE NAME LABEL

    a. Select cell A1.
    b. On the Tool bar, click on the Bold button.

2) RIGHT ALIGN AND BOLD THE AVERAGE LABEL

    a. Select cell A9.
    b. Enter the label Test Average: to replace the current label with a more descriptive one. The label is truncated because the column is too narrow to display it entirely.
    c. On the Tool bar, click on the Right Align button.
    d. On the Tool bar, click on the Bold button. Cell A9 is now bold and right aligned but its contents is still not entirely displayed because the column is not wide enough.

3) WIDEN COLUMN A BY DRAGGING

    a. Place the pointer on the line separating the column letters A and B at the top of the spreadsheet. The pointer changes to a double-headed arrow.
    b. Slowly drag the line to the right approximately halfway across column B. Column A should be wide enough to display the entire label in cell A9. If not, drag the column divider farther to the right.

4) CHANGE THE AVERAGE LABEL

    a. Move the cell cursor to cell F1.
    b. Enter Student Average replacing the current label with a more descriptive one. Notice how the label extends into the next column because there is no data in the next cell.

5) RIGHT ALIGN AND BOLD THE STUDENT AVERAGE LABEL

    a. Select cell F1 if it is not already selected.
    b. From the Format menu, select the Alignment command. The Format Cells dialog box is displayed.
    c. In the Alignment section, select Right.
    d. Select the Font tab to display the font options.
    e. Select Bold and then OK. Cell F1 is now bold and right aligned but its contents is still not entirely displayed because the column is not wide enough.

6) WIDEN COLUMN F

    a. From the Format menu, select the Column Width command. The Column Width dialog box is displayed.
    b. Type 17 and then select OK. The label is now entirely displayed.

7) RIGHT ALIGN AND BOLD THE TEST LABELS

    a. Place the mouse pointer on cell B1.
    b. Drag the mouse pointer from cell B1 to cell E1. Cells B1, C1, D1, and E1 are highlighted as a block.
    c. On the Tool bar, click on the Right Align button.
    d. On the Tool bar, click on the Bold button. The block of highlighted cells is now bold and right aligned.

8) FORMAT AVERAGES TO DISPLAY 1 DECIMAL PLACE

a. Place the mouse pointer on cell F3.
b. Drag the mouse pointer from F3 to F8. The averages are highlighted as a block.
c. From the Format menu, select the Number command. The dialog box is displayed.
d. Select Fixed. Type 1 for the Decimal places.
e. Select OK. Notice how the value in cell F8 is displayed with a trailing zero in order to display it to 1 decimal place. When the ROUND function was applied to the value in this cell in Practice 6, there was no change in the display because the value remained the same. Fixing the number of decimal places changes the display; the ROUND function changes the value.

9) CHANGE C. BOWSER'S GRADE

a. Select cell C3.
b. An error was made in recording C. Bowser's score for Test 2. Enter the correct test score, 82. Both the Student Average and Test Average have been updated. The trailing zero is displayed in the Student Average because the cell was formatted as fixed to one decimal place.

Check - Your spreadsheet should be similar to:

	A	B	C	D	E	F
1	Name	Test 1	Test 2	Test 3	Test 4	Student Average
2		9/12/97	10/17/97	11/14/97	12/12/97	
3	C. Browser	50	82	68	64	66.0
4	D. Warheit	86	89	78	88	85.3
5	M. Porter	78	100	90	89	89.3
6	B. Presley	45	78	66	78	66.8
7	D. Unwalla	66	76	78	55	68.8
8	T. Hogan	85	74	83	66	77.0
9	Test Average:	68.33	83.17	77.17	73.33	

10) SAVE GRADES AND PRINT THE SPREADSHEET

11) CLOSE GRADES AND EXIT WORKS

Chapter Summary

This chapter covered the basics of creating a spreadsheet. A spreadsheet is simply rows and columns of data, with rows running horizontally and columns vertically. The primary advantage of a computerized spreadsheet is that it has the ability to perform calculations on the data it stores, with the calculations automatically changing to reflect any changes in the data.

In a Works spreadsheet the rows are numbered on the left side and the columns identified by letters which run along the top. Where a row and column intersect is called a cell. A single cell is identified by its column letter and row number, which is called its cell name. For example, C3 is the name of the cell located at column C and row 3.

Spreadsheet cells can store three types of data: labels, values, and times/dates. Labels are text and cannot be used in calculations. Values are numeric and can be used in calculations. Times/dates are either times (12:30 AM) or calendar dates (9/21/95) and both can be used in certain types of calculations.

A new spreadsheet is created by clicking on the Spreadsheet button in the Works Task Launcher dialog box. Data is entered into a spreadsheet by moving the cell cursor to a cell, typing the data, and clicking on the Check box or pressing Enter. The cell indicator in the upper-left corner of the screen shows the current location of the cell cursor. The Entry bar shows the contents of the cell. To move through a spreadsheet, either the scroll arrows or the arrow keys can be used.

A spreadsheet is saved by selecting the Save command from the File menu. It is printed by selecting the Print command from the File menu. The Print Preview command from the File menu is used to display the spreadsheet on screen as it will appear when printed. All of these actions can also be performed by using buttons on the Tool bar.

Formulas are mathematical statements used to calculate values which can be stored in cells. All formulas must begin with an equal sign (=) and may contain cell names. For example, if cell B5 stores the value 12 and cell C8 stores 10, the formula =B5*C8 would display 120.

Works uses an order of operations when evaluating a formula. First it performs exponentiation, then multiplication and division, and finally addition and subtraction. Operations of the same priority are performed from left to right. The order of operations can be changed by using parentheses. For example:

=3+5*8+7   produces the value 50
=(3+5)*(8+7)   produces the value 120

Built-in functions are used to perform some common calculations. The formula =SUM(B3:B8) includes the SUM function. B3:B8 is called a range and defines the cells to be summed.

This chapter covered the SUM, AVG, and ROUND functions. For example, =SUM(B3:B8) sums the values in cells B3, B4, B5, B6, B7, and B8. The formula =AVG(C3:C7) averages the values in cells C3, C4, C5, C6, and C7. The formula, =ROUND(C5,2) rounds the value stored in cell C5 to 2 decimal places. The formula =ROUND(AVG(B7:F7),1) rounds the average of the values in the range B7:F7 to 1 decimal place.

The width of a column can be changed by dragging its right column divider bar. Commands from the Format menu are used to change the layout of a spreadsheet. Cells can be formatted to display currency, percent, or a fixed number of decimal places by using the Number command. The Font and Style and Alignment commands allow the style of labels or values to be changed. Buttons on the Tool bar can also be used to change the style, font, and font size of cell data.

Formatting and editing commands can be applied to a highlighted block of cells. A highlighted block of cells is formed by dragging the mouse from one cell to another cell. A row is highlighted by clicking on its row number, while a column is highlighted by clicking on its column letter.

Vocabulary

Cell - Where a row and column intersect. A cell is identified by its column letter and row number, for example C3.

Cell cursor - Rectangular outline on the screen which is used to indicate the current cell. It can be moved from cell to cell by using the mouse or the keyboard. Data can be entered into a cell when the cell cursor is located on it.

Cell indicator - Location at the top of the screen that shows the location of the cell cursor.

Cell name - The column letter and row number used to identify a cell (i.e., B3).

Check box - A box on the Entry bar containing a check. Clicking on this box moves data from the Entry bar to the selected cell.

Column - Vertical line of data identified by a letter.

Date - Entry in the form of a date (i.e., 9/5/96).

Entry bar - Area at the top of the screen where data entered from the keyboard is displayed before it is entered into a cell. Also displays the contents of the selected cell.

Formulas - Mathematical statements used to calculate values. The statement =C5+D7+E8 is a formula.

Functions - Used in formulas to perform common calculations. =SUM(B3:B8) is a function.

Highlighted Block - A group of highlighted adjoining cells. Formatting commands can be applied to a highlighted block, affecting every cell in the selection.

Label - Words or characters stored in a cell that cannot be used in calculations.

Layout - The way in which cells are formatted and data displayed in a spreadsheet.

Order of operations - The rules the computer uses to evaluate a formula.

Range - Partial row or column of adjacent cells. B3:B8 is a range.

Row - Horizontal line of data identified by a number.

Scroll - Viewing different parts of a spreadsheet.

Selected cell - The spreadsheet cell containing the cell cursor as indicated by a heavy outline.

Spreadsheet - Rows and columns of data on which calculations can be performed.

Time - Entry in the form of a time (i.e., 12:30 PM).

Values - Numeric data that can be stored in cells and used in calculations.

X box - A box on the Entry bar containing an X. Clicking on this box erases data from the Entry bar and leaves the selected cell unchanged.

Reviews

Sections 8.1 — 8.5

1. What is the primary advantage of using a computerized spreadsheet?

2. a) What is the difference between a row and a column?
   b) What is a cell in a spreadsheet?
   c) What is the difference between the cell cursor and cell indicator?

3. What information is displayed on the screen by the:
   a) Entry bar
   b) Cell indicator
   c) Menu bar

4. a) What is the difference between a label and a value entry?
   b) What is a date entry? Give an example.
   c) What is a time entry? Give an example.

5. How many of each of the following types of entries are stored in the Grades spreadsheet shown in Practice 2?
   a) labels
   b) values
   c) dates
   d) times

6. a) How can spreadsheet columns that are off the screen be moved on to the screen?
   b) What is this action called?

7. How can the screen be scrolled to show:
   a) cell A1?
   b) the last cell in a spreadsheet that contains data?

8. a) What is the difference between a cell name and the data stored in a cell? Give an example.
   b) Can the name of a cell be changed? If so, how?

9. Draw a diagram that shows all of the cells in the first three columns and five rows of a spreadsheet. Show the name of each cell and store the value 27 in cell B3.

10. What is the maximum number of digits that may be displayed in a single cell without using special commands?

11. What steps would you take to enter the value 65 into cell C4 of the spreadsheet produced in Practice 2?

12. If a mistake has been made entering data into a cell, how can it be corrected?

Sections 8.6 — 8.9

13. What are two ways to save a spreadsheet?

14. What happens when you print a spreadsheet that is too large to fit on a single piece of paper?

15. How can a spreadsheet be displayed on the screen as it will appear when printed?

16. Briefly explain what a formula is and give two examples.

17. a) What is meant by order of operations?
    b) Which operation is performed first?
    c) Which operation is performed last?
    d) How can the order of operations be changed?

18. If a formula contains 3 operations, all of the same priority, which will be performed first?

19. If 10/20 is entered into a cell, Works considers it a label. How must the entry be changed so that 10 will be divided by 20?

20. What value would be calculated by Works for each of the following formulas?
    a) =2+7*5+4
    b) =(2+7)*(5+4)
    c) =5+10/5
    d) =(5+10)/5
    e) =2^3+4
    f) =15+(12/4)

21. What value would be calculated by Works for each of the following formulas if cell C15 stores a value of 16 and cell D8 a value of 4?
    a) =C15*D8
    b) =C15+5+D8
    c) =C15*5+D8
    d) =C15*(5+D8)
    e) =C15/D8
    f) =C15+4/D8
    g) =C15+(4/D8)

22. Write formulas for each of the following calculations:
    a) The product of the values stored in cells A1, B3, and C4.
    b) The sum of the values stored in cells A3, A4, A5, A6, A7, and A8.
    c) The average of the values stored in cells B5, B6, and B7.
    d) The average of the values stored in cells A1, B3, and C4.

23. If a mistake has been made in a formula what are two ways it can be corrected?

24. How can the value stored in a cell be erased?

Sections 8.10 — 8.14
25. a) What is meant by a range of cells?
    b) Give an example of a range of cells contained in a row.
    c) Give an example of a range of cells contained in a column.

26. What is the difference between a formula and a function?

27. Write a formula that uses a function to calculate the average of the values stored in cells B3, B4, B5, C5, D5, and E5.

28. Write formulas that use functions to calculate each of the following:
    a) The sum of the values stored in cells B4, B5, B6 and B7.
    b) The sum of the values stored in cells B4, C4, D4, and E4.
    c) The average of the values stored in the column of cells D7 to D35.
    d) The average of the values stored in the row of cells F3 to J3.

29. Using functions, write formulas to calculate each of the following:
    a) The sum of the values in cells C5, C6, C7, C8, and C9 rounded to 2 decimal places.
    b) The sum of the values in cells B5, C5, D5, and E5 rounded to the nearest integer.
    c) The average of the values in cells A1, A2, A3, B1, B2, and B3 rounded to 1 decimal place.

30. Is it possible to change the width of only a single cell?

31. Explain how the width of a column is increased.

32. List all of the differences between using the ROUND function or fixing a value to display 2 decimal places using the Number command.

33. List the steps required to perform the following operations:
    a) Format a cell to display a fixed value to 3 decimal places.
    b) Bold and right align the contents of a cell.
    c) Format a cell to display a value in dollars to 2 decimal places.

34. a) Why should the label headings over columns of values be right aligned?
    b) List the steps required to right align all of the column headings in a spreadsheet at one time.

35. List two ways to highlight cells B3 through C12.

Exercises

1. The Ivy U Meteorology department has asked you to create a spreadsheet that converts a Fahrenheit temperature to the equivalent Celsius temperature.

    a) The formula for converting from degrees Fahrenheit (F) to degrees Celsius (C) is Celsius = 5/9×(Fahrenheit – 32). Enter the following data into a new spreadsheet as shown, making sure to enter the appropriate formula into cell E3:

	A	B	C	D	E
1			Temperature Conversion		
2					
3	Fahrenheit Temp:	20.0		Celsius Temp:	-6.7

   Format cell C1 as bold and resize columns if necessary to display all data. Format the cells displaying temperature values as Fixed to 1 decimal place.

    b) Save the spreadsheet naming it Temp Convert.

    c) In row 5 have the spreadsheet convert temperatures from a Celsius temperature entered in cell B5 to a Fahrenheit temperature displayed in cell E5. Be sure to use the correct formula and appropriate labels.

    d) Save the modified Temp Convert and print a copy.

2. The Ivy U Auto Club is testing different sports cars and wants to store the results in a spreadsheet.

    a) In a new spreadsheet, enter the data as shown below. Resize columns as necessary so that all data is displayed entirely:

	A	B	C
1		Track Test	
2			
3	Car	Distance (meters)	Time (seconds)
4	Porsche	37.44	6.78
5	Ferrari	44.18	7.77
6	Lotus	37.51	5.99
7	Aston-Martin	45.19	7.89
8	Corvette	47.42	6.68
9	Jaguar	37.57	5.34
10	Supra	41.55	7.11

    b) Save the spreadsheet naming it Track Test:

    c) In cell D3, enter the label Velocity (m/sec). Velocity is calculated by dividing distance travelled by time. Use a formula to calculate the velocity for each car. Be sure that any change made to a distance or time will automatically change the corresponding velocity. Resize column D as necessary to display all data.

    d) In cell D11 have the spreadsheet calculate the average velocity. Include a label in cell C11 for the average.

    e) Edit the formulas for velocity and average velocity to round the results to 2 decimal places.

    f) Save the modified Track Test and print a copy.

3. Dorothy Sophocles has recently graduated from Ivy University and has decided to keep track of her personal finances using a spreadsheet.

a) In a new spreadsheet, enter D. Sophocles' expenses for three months as shown below. Resize columns as necessary so that all data is displayed entirely:

	A	B	C	D
1		D. Sophocles Expenses		
2				
3	Expense	June	July	August
4	Rent	500	500	500
5	Groceries	120	135	110
6	Transportation	100	90	88
7	Clothes	100	120	150
8	Savings	50	50	50
9	Misc.	80	50	75

b) Save the spreadsheet naming it Expenses.

c) Enter the label Total in cell A11. In cell B11, enter a formula to total the expenses for June. Add similar formulas to total the expenses for July and August.

d) In column E, add a label and the appropriate formulas to display the average for each of the expenses over the three months.

e) Format the values in columns B, C, D, and E as currency with 0 decimal places. Format all the titles to be bold. Right align the month and average titles. Your spreadsheet should be similar to:

	A	B	C	D	E
1		**D. Sophocles Expenses**			
2					
3	**Expense**	**June**	**July**	**August**	**Average**
4	Rent	$500	$500	$500	$500
5	Groceries	$120	$135	$110	$122
6	Transportation	$100	$90	$88	$93
7	Clothes	$100	$120	$150	$123
8	Savings	$50	$50	$50	$50
9	Misc.	$80	$50	$75	$68
10					
11	**Total**	$950	$945	$973	

f) Save the modified Expenses and print a copy.

4. Create a spreadsheet that displays a multiplication table. The table should be set up so that when a number is entered into cell C3, it is automatically multiplied by 1 through 10:

	A	B	C	D
1				Multiplication Table
2				
3	Number:		10	
4	10	*	1	10
5	10	*	2	20
6	10	*	3	30
7	10	*	4	40
8	10	*	5	50
9	10	*	6	60
10	10	*	7	70
11	10	*	8	80
12	10	*	9	90
13	10	*	10	100

a) Resize the columns as shown. The formulas in column D should use cell references for both the multiplier and the multiplicand.

b) Save the spreadsheet naming it Multiply and print a copy.

5. Mr. Hernandez, owner of the Aztec Café, has decided to use a spreadsheet to keep track of the number of hours his employees work.

a) In a new spreadsheet, enter the employee data, resizing the days of the week columns as shown:

	A	B	C	D	E	F	G	H
1			Aztec Cafe Employee Hours					
2								
3	Employee	Sun	Mon	Tue	Wed	Thu	Fri	Sat
4	H. Berry	10	0	0	10	8	8	4
5	G. Diez	0	8	8	8	8	10	0
6	K. Martin	4	4	4	0	4	0	4
7	D. Romani	8	10	9	10	0	10	0

b) Save the spreadsheet naming it AC Employees.

c) In column I, enter formulas to display the total number of hours worked by each employee. Enter an appropriate label in cell I3.

d) Bold all the titles. Format the day and total titles to be right aligned.

e) Save the modified AC Employees and print a copy.

An Introduction to Computing Using Microsoft Works

6. Mr. Horatio von Money, Ivy University's major benefactor, keeps track of his stock portfolio in a spreadsheet named STOCKS. Open STOCKS and note that the spreadsheet displays the price of each stock and the number of shares Mr. von Money owns.

   a) You are to assist Mr. von Money by having the spreadsheet calculate the value of each stock he owns. Title the column Value. The value is calculated by multiplying the price of the stock by the number of shares owned. Add formulas to compute the value of each stock. Format the values appropriately.

   b) Mr. von Money has decided that he will donate one fourth of his portfolio to Ivy University. Add formulas to total the value of all of his stocks and to compute the amount of his donation. Be sure to label both figures.

   c) Format the labels to be right aligned and bold. Format the calculations appropriately.

   d) Save the modified STOCKS and print a copy.

7. Varsity baseball coach Slugger Ryan needs to store his player's statistics in a spreadsheet.

   a) Enter the following statistics into a new spreadsheet, including proper labels:

Player	At bats	Hits	Player	At bats	Hits
Attis	10	3	Fritz	10	6
Baker	11	3	Gold	14	4
Connelly	9	5	Hernandez	12	6
Doucette	12	4	Li	11	5
Enders	15	2			

   b) Save the spreadsheet naming it Baseball.

   c) Batting averages are calculated by dividing the number of hits by the number of times at bat. Add a column to Baseball that calculates and displays each player's batting average rounded to 3 decimal places. Be sure to title the column.

   d) Coach Ryan would like to know the overall team batting average. Use the average function to produce the calculation for him. Be sure to include rounding and an appropriate label.

   e) Bold all the labels and right align the labels describing the At Bats, Hits, and Average columns.

   f) Save the modified Baseball and print a copy.

8. You are to create a spreadsheet to help determine your caloric intake for a week.

   a) In a new spreadsheet, enter data for the calories you consume in a typical week. Include appropriate labels and formatting. Your spreadsheet will have different numbers but should look similar to:

	A	B	C	D	E	F	G	H
1			Calories Consumed in 1 Week					
2								
3		Sun	Mon	Tue	Wed	Thu	Fri	Sat
4	Breakfast	500	0	0	0	0	0	520
5	Lunch	500	510	660	740	590	710	530
6	Afternoon Snack	0	150	0	100	0	0	300
7	Dinner	910	1190	1210	930	1000	1130	1020
8	Midnight Snack	110	0	0	100	0	0	250
9	Other	230	0	0	300	170	0	40

   b) Save the spreadsheet naming it Diet.

   c) Have the spreadsheet calculate the total number of calories consumed each day, the total for the week, and the average number of calories consumed per meal. Round the totals and averages to 0 decimal places. Be sure to include appropriate labels and proper formatting.

   d) It has been determined that aerobic exercise burns 360 calories per hour. Have the spreadsheet calculate the number of hours for a workout to burn off half of the total calories consumed for each day. Round the number of hours to 1 decimal place. Be sure to include an appropriate label and proper formatting.

   e) Save the modified Diet and print a copy.

9. Spreadsheets can be helpful in personal time management. You are to create a spreadsheet to help determine the time spent on different activities during a week.

   a) In a new spreadsheet store the number of hours you spend each day of the week at each of the following activities:

   - school classes
   - athletics
   - extracurricular groups and clubs
   - studying and doing homework
   - eating
   - sleeping
   - watching television or listening to music
   - talking on the phone
   - doing chores at home
   - working at a part-time job

   b) Save the spreadsheet naming it Activity.

   c) Have the spreadsheet calculate the total hours spent for the week on each activity. Also calculate the average number of hours spent per day on each activity for the week.

   d) Most people's schedules do not account for all 24 hours in a day. Add a row that calculates and displays the amount of unaccounted time in your schedule for each day.

   e) Save the modified Activity and print a copy.

An Introduction to Computing Using Microsoft Works

Chapter Nine
Manipulating Data with the Spreadsheet

Function, Formulas

Fill Right, Fill Down

Find

Go To

MAX, MIN, IF

Copy, Cut, Paste, Clear

Insert Row, Delete Row

Insert Column, Delete Column

Create New Chart

Rename Chart

Chart

Titles, Series, Legend/Series Labels

Delete Chart

Objectives

After completing this chapter you will be able to:

1. Plan a large spreadsheet.

2. Enter formulas by pointing.

3. Use the Function command to paste functions into cell formulas.

4. Copy labels, values, and formulas using relative and absolute copying.

5. Display the formulas in cells.

6. Search a spreadsheet for specific text.

7. Use the Go To command to select a cell.

8. Use the MAX, MIN, and IF functions.

9. Expand a spreadsheet properly.

10. Insert and delete rows and columns.

11. Change the margins and print orientation of a spreadsheet.

12. Create charts of spreadsheet data.

13. View and rename charts.

14. Modify and print charts.

15. Delete charts.

9

This chapter discusses how to plan and produce a large spreadsheet on the computer. Techniques for modifying and expanding a spreadsheet are explained, and commands to copy formulas from one set of cells to another are introduced. The chapter ends by teaching you how to produce graphs and charts using the data stored in a spreadsheet.

9.1 Planning a Large Spreadsheet

The spreadsheets produced in Chapter Eight did not require much planning because they were small and easy to understand. In this chapter, planning is more important as we develop large spreadsheets that will be continually modified and expanded.

Before using Works, a spreadsheet should be carefully planned by answering the following questions:

1. **What new information should the spreadsheet produce?**

2. **What data must the spreadsheet store to produce the new information?**

3. **How would the new information be produced without using a computer?**

4. **How should the spreadsheet be organized and displayed on the computer?**

In this chapter we will produce a spreadsheet for Ivy University's accounting department to assist it in calculating the weekly payroll. The first step in producing the spreadsheet is to answer the four questions above as follows:

1. The spreadsheet should produce each employee's gross pay for the week. Gross pay is the pay earned before any deductions (such as taxes) are made.

2. The spreadsheet needs to store the following data:
    - Employee name
    - Pay rate per hour
    - Hours worked per day for each weekday

3. The gross pay can be produced by multiplying the total number of hours worked for the week by the employee's pay rate.

4. The spreadsheet should appear on the computer screen with each employee's data in a separate row. That way, related data will be grouped by columns.

The fourth question is best answered by drawing a sketch of the spreadsheet showing each column heading and the type of data it will store:

Name	Rate/hr	Mon	Tue	Wed	Thu	Fri	Gross Pay
text	dollars	fixed for 1 decimal place					dollars

9.2 Entering Formulas - Pointing

When creating a formula, cell names can be entered by *pointing*. When pointing is used a formula is typed up to where a cell name should appear and then the mouse is used to click on the desired cell to place its name in the formula. Highlighting a block of cells places a range in the formula.

For example, in the spreadsheet below cell H2 was selected and then an equal sign typed. Next, the mouse was used to click on cell B2 which placed its name in the formula. An asterisk (*) and SUM(were then typed. The range was entered by dragging the mouse from cell C2 to cell G2. The colon (:) is automatically inserted by Works:

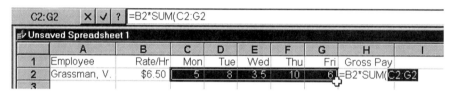

Highlighting a block of cells enters its range name into a formula

To complete the formula, a right parenthesis must be typed and the Check box clicked.

Pointing helps avoid the error of including wrong cell names in the formula. This is especially useful when the cells to be included in the formula are not currently shown on the screen.

9.3 Using the Function Command

An alternative to typing a function name is selecting one using the Function command from the Insert menu. Executing this command displays the Insert Function dialog box. Here, Works lists all of the available functions in alphabetical order:

An Introduction to Computing Using Microsoft Works

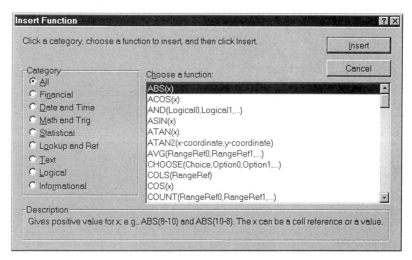

*A function can be inserted into a formula using the
Insert Function dialog box*

Selecting an option in the Category section limits the functions listed. Selecting Insert transfers the highlighted function to the Entry bar. Inserted functions contain *placeholders* which are a reminder that cell names, ranges, or values must be included in the function. In the dialog box above, the word RangeRef0 in the AVG function is a placeholder that must be replaced by a cell name or a cell range.

When the Insert Function dialog box is displayed pressing a letter key scrolls to the first function in the list that begins with that letter. This method of scrolling can be much faster than using the scroll bar.

Practice 1

The Practices in this chapter use the spreadsheet for Ivy University's accounting department. In this Practice you will add a Gross Pay column to IVY PAYROLL.

1) OPEN IVY PAYROLL

    a. Start Works. The Works Task Launcher dialog box is displayed.
    b. Click on Cancel to remove the dialog box.
    c. From the File menu, select Open. The Open dialog box is displayed.
    d. Open IVY PAYROLL. The spreadsheet contains the payroll for Ivy University employees.

2) ENTER THE GROSS PAY HEADING AND FORMAT IT

    a. Select cell H5.
    b. Enter the label Gross Pay.
    c. Select cell H5 if it is not selected. On the Tool bar, click on the Right Align button. The title is right aligned in the cell.
    d. On the Tool bar, click on the Bold button. The title is now bold.

3) CREATE THE GROSS PAY FORMULA

    a. Select cell H6.
    b. Type an equal sign (=).

c. Click on cell B6. Note how the cell reference B6 is inserted into the formula.
d. Type an asterisk (*).
e. From the Insert menu, select the Function command. A dialog box is displayed.
f. Press the S key to display the first function name that begins with an S. Scroll until SUM(RangeRef0, RangeRef1,...) is visible. Click on the SUM function.
g. Select Insert to enter the function into the formula. Note the placeholder, RangeRef0, is highlighted because you are expected to enter a valid cell name or range.
h. Highlight everything between the function's parentheses.
i. Point to cell C6 and drag from C6 to G6. The formula on the Entry bar should appear like the following:

j. Click on the Check box to enter the formula. The calculated gross pay for B. Attis, 192, is shown in cell H6.

4) FORMAT CELL H6 TO DISPLAY DOLLARS

a. Cell H6 should already be selected.
b. On the Tool bar, click on the Currency button ($). The gross pay is now displayed as dollars with 2 decimal places.

5) SAVE THE MODIFIED IVY PAYROLL

Check - Your spreadsheet should be similar to:

	A	B	C	D	E	F	G	H
1			Ivy University Payroll					
2								
3								
4								
5	Employee	Rate/Hr	Mon	Tue	Wed	Thu	Fri	Gross Pay
6	Attis, B.	$8.00	6.0	4.0	4.0	3.0	7.0	$192.00
7	Ball, R.	$4.00	9.5	12.0	9.0	5.5	3.0	
8	Bickle, R.	$6.00	5.0	7.0	0.5	7.0	6.0	
9	Cambell, M.	$4.50	5.0	6.0	7.0	5.0	6.0	

9.4 Using Fill Right and Fill Down

Edit

Undo Typing	Ctrl+Z
Cut	Ctrl+X
Copy	Ctrl+C
Paste	Ctrl+V
Paste Special...	
Clear	
Select Row	
Select Column	
Select All	Ctrl+A
Find...	Ctrl+F
Replace...	Ctrl+H
Go To...	Ctrl+G
Fill Right	Ctrl+R
Fill Down	Ctrl+D
Fill Series...	

The Fill Right and Fill Down commands from the Edit menu are used to copy a cell's contents to an adjacent row or column of highlighted cells. The cell with the contents to be copied is called the *source cell*. Dragging from the source cell selects the cells into which copies are to be made. The Fill Right command (Ctrl+R) is used if the cells are in a row, and the Fill Down command (Ctrl+D) if cells are in a column.

When using the Fill Right or Fill Down commands, a cell's format is copied as well as its contents.

9

9.5 Relative Copying

A useful application of the Fill Down and Fill Right commands is for copying formulas. When a formula is copied using Fill Right or Fill Down, Works automatically changes the cell references to apply to the new row or column. This is called *relative copying*.

For example, in the IVY PAYROLL spreadsheet the formula to calculate B. Attis' gross pay, =B6*SUM(C6:G6) is stored in cell H6. To calculate the remaining employee's gross pay, the formula must be entered into the next 24 rows with the cell names adjusted for the new row numbers. Instead of typing the 24 formulas, the Fill Down command can be used to copy B. Attis' gross pay formula and automatically change the cell references for each employee. For example, because R. Ball's data is stored in row 7, the formula will be automatically changed to =B7*SUM(C7:G7). This approach saves time and avoids the possible errors that could be made if each formula were typed separately.

9.6 Displaying Formulas

It is helpful to view a spreadsheet's formulas at their cell locations. Selecting the Formulas command from the View menu does this. A formula that is longer than the cell width can be displayed in its entirety by increasing the column width.

Printing when formulas are displayed prints the formulas stored in the cells rather than the values. To return to the regular spreadsheet screen select the Formulas command again.

. . . .

Practice 2

In this Practice you will create copies of the gross pay formula in cell H6 for the other employees in the IVY PAYROLL spreadsheet. Start Works and open IVY PAYROLL if you have not done so already.

1) COPY THE FORMULA USING FILL DOWN

a. Highlight cells H6 through H30 by dragging down from cell H6 to cell H30. The screen will scroll as necessary.
b. From the Edit menu, select the Fill Down command.
c. Select cell H7. The formula displayed on the Entry bar shows how the cell names have been automatically changed due to relative copying.

2) VIEW THE FORMULAS ON SCREEN

From the View menu, select the Formulas command. Scroll to the right to view the formulas in column H.

3) RETURN TO THE REGULAR DISPLAY

From the View menu, select Formulas. The formulas are replaced on screen by the values they calculate.

<u>Check</u> - The gross pay has been calculated for each of the employees:

	A	B	C	D	E	F	G	H
1		Ivy University Payroll						
2								
3								
4								
5	Employee	Rate/Hr	Mon	Tue	Wed	Thu	Fri	Gross Pay
6	Attis, B.	$8.00	6.0	4.0	4.0	3.0	7.0	$192.00
7	Ball, R.	$4.00	9.5	12.0	9.0	5.5	3.0	$156.00
8	Bickle, R.	$6.00	5.0	7.0	0.5	7.0	6.0	$153.00
9	Cambell, M.	$4.50	5.0	6.0	7.0	5.0	6.0	$130.50

4) CHANGE THE PAY RATE OF R. BALL

    a. Select cell B7.
    b. Enter 5.5, replacing the current value. $5.50 is displayed in the cell. Note how Works automatically recalculates the gross pay, $214.50.

5) TOTAL THE GROSS PAY

    a. Select cell H32 and enter the formula: =SUM(H6:H30)
    b. Format cell H32 as dollars. The total of all the gross pays, $4,999.51, is displayed.
    c. Select cell F32 and enter and then bold the label: Total:

6) SAVE AND PRINT IVY PAYROLL

    Save IVY PAYROLL and then print the spreadsheet.

9.7 The Find Command

When working with a large spreadsheet it can be difficult to locate the cell or cells that contain a particular value, label, or formula. The Find command from the Edit menu (Ctrl+F) can be used to assist in such a search. Executing Find displays a dialog box where the cell contents to be searched for is typed:

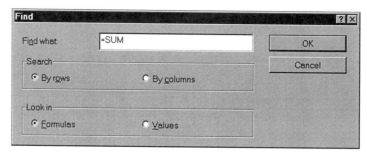

Search text is typed in the Find what box

In this case "=SUM" has been entered. The Search options tell Works to search By rows (from left to right) or By columns (from top to bottom). The Look in options tell Works to search by Formulas (what is stored in the cell) or by Values (what is displayed in the cell). Selecting OK initiates the search from the current cell.

To search from the beginning of the spreadsheet, the cell cursor must be on cell A1 before the search is initiated. A Find can be repeated using the same search text by pressing the Shift+F4 keys. A dialog box is displayed if the search text is not found.

An Introduction to Computing Using Microsoft Works

9.8 The Go To Command

The Go To command from the Edit menu (Ctrl+G) can be used to move the cell cursor directly to a particular cell. Executing the command displays a dialog box where a cell name can be typed:

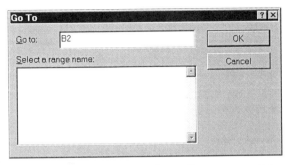

Selecting OK moves the cell cursor to B2

Typing a cell name and selecting OK moves the cell cursor to the indicated cell. This can be faster than scrolling when moving long distances in a spreadsheet.

9.9 The MAX and MIN Functions

Works includes two functions that determine either the maximum or minimum value stored in a range of cells. These functions are useful to the Ivy University accounting department for determining the highest and lowest employee salaries. The MAX function takes the form:

=MAX(<range of cells>)

For example,

=MAX(C2:C9)

displays the maximum value stored in the range C2 to C9. The MIN function takes the form:

=MIN(<range of cells>)

For example,

=MIN(B2:F3)

displays the minimum value stored in the range B2 to F3.

Practice 3

In this Practice you will search IVY PAYROLL and determine the maximum and minimum gross pays. Start Works and open IVY PAYROLL if is not already open.

1) GO TO CELL F34

   a. From the Edit menu, select the Go To command. A dialog box is displayed.
   b. Type F34 and select OK. Cell F34 is selected.

2) DETERMINE THE MAXIMUM GROSS PAY

a. Enter the label Max pay:
b. Format the label as bold.
c. Select cell H34. From the Insert menu, select Function. Press the M key to scroll the list of functions. MAX(RangeRef0, RangeRef1,...) is selected.
d. Select Insert. An equal sign is automatically added in front of the inserted function to create a formula.
e. Highlight everything between the function's parentheses.
f. Point to cell H30. Drag from cell H30 upward to H6. If H6 is not currently displayed, the screen scrolls automatically as the mouse pointer is dragged upward.
g. Stop dragging when cells H30 through H6 have been highlighted. The cell range is inserted into the function. Note that the cell range is entered as H6:H30; the order in which the cells were highlighted makes no difference. Click on the Check box to enter the formula. The gross pay of J. Sowers, 348.25, is displayed as the maximum salary in the cell range used in the function.
h. Format the value as dollars with 2 decimal places.

3) DETERMINE THE MINIMUM GROSS PAY

a. Select cell F35.
b. Enter the label Min pay:
c. Format the label as bold.
d. Select cell H35. From the Insert menu, select Function.
e. Highlight the MIN(RangeRef0, RangeRef1,...) function and then select Insert.
f. Highlight everything between the function's parentheses.
g. Highlight cells H6 through H30 and then click on the Check box. S. Munger's gross pay of 75 has been calculated as the minimum value in the cell range used in the function.
h. Format the value as dollars with 2 decimal places.

4) SEARCH FOR THE TEXT "BALL"

a. From the Edit menu, select the Find command. The Find dialog box is displayed.
b. Type Ball and select OK. The cell cursor is placed in cell A7 which contains the name Ball, R.

5) SEARCH FOR ALL OCCURRENCES OF THE LETTER P

a. From the Edit menu, select Go To. Type the cell name A1 and then select OK to move the cell cursor to cell A1.
b. From the Edit menu, select Find. The previous search text is highlighted in the dialog box.
c. Type a P to replace the old search text and then select OK. The cell cursor moves to the label "Ivy University Payroll" which is the first cell after cell A1 to contain a "p."
d. Press Shift+F4 to repeat the search. The cursor moves to the label "Employee," which is the next cell to contain a P.
e. Continue using Shift+F4 until cell C1 is found again.
f. From the Edit menu, select Find. Type XYZ to replace the search text and select OK. A dialog box is displayed with the message "Works did not find a match." Select OK to remove the box.

6) SAVE THE MODIFIED IVY PAYROLL

An Introduction to Computing Using Microsoft Works

9.10 Expanding a Spreadsheet

Data can be added to a spreadsheet by simply making entries into unused rows and columns, but this should be done with care. If data is added without thought to the overall plan, the spreadsheet will quickly become a jumble of unrelated data.

The Ivy University accounting department has determined that the IVY PAYROLL spreadsheet would be more useful if it could calculate and deduct taxes and social security from each employee's gross pay. Expanding a spreadsheet requires the same careful planning as the initial spreadsheet. Therefore, the four questions answered when originally planning the spreadsheet are again used to determine how the spreadsheet should be modified to incorporate these changes:

1. The new data generated is taxes, social security, and net pay (the actual pay an employee receives after deductions have been made).

2. The modified spreadsheet will need to include the tax rate, which is 15%, and the social security rate, which is 6%.

3. The deductions are calculated by multiplying the tax and social security rates by the gross pay. Net pay is calculated by subtracting the deductions from the gross pay.

4. To display this new data, we need to add three columns titled Taxes, Soc. Sec., and Net Pay. To allow the social security rate to be easily changed, it is stored in a single cell that is referenced in a formula. By doing this, it will only be necessary to change the value in one cell whenever a rate changes, rather than the formulas for each employee.

9.11 Absolute Copying

In some situations we will want to copy formulas without certain cell references changing. To keep cell references constant when copied a dollar sign must be placed in front of both the column letter and row number (i.e., $A$3). Copying these kind of cell references is called *absolute copying*.

For example, if all the employees of Ivy University were to receive a bonus, the bonus amount could be stored in cell A3. Then the following formula could be entered into cell I6 to compute the total pay for one employee by adding his or her gross pay and the bonus:

=H6+A3

If Fill Down was used to copy this formula into cells I7 and I8, A3 would become A4 and A5. To prevent this, the formula must be changed to =H6+$A$3 before copying.

The F4 key can be used to place dollar signs in front of a cell reference. For example, to create the total pay formula with an absolute reference to cell A3, first type an equal sign, click on cell H6, and then type a plus sign. Next, click on A3 and press the F4 key to change the reference to $A$3.

9.12 Copy, Cut, Paste, and Clear

Commands in the Edit menu can be used to copy, move, and clear cell contents. Often the same label, value, or formula needs to be stored in a number of different cells. It can be typed over and over again, or duplicated with the Copy command (Ctrl+C).

Duplicating a block of cells is a four step process:

1. Highlight the cells to be copied.
2. Execute the Copy command. A copy of the cell's contents and formatting is copied to the Clipboard.
3. Select the cell where the data is to appear.
4. Execute the Paste command.

The Cut command (Ctrl+X) removes a selected cell's contents and formatting and places it on the Clipboard. Paste can then be used to paste the contents and formatting into other cells.

The Cut, Copy, and Paste buttons on the Tool bar can also be used to execute the editing commands.

The Clear command removes a selected cell's contents and formatting without placing a copy on the Clipboard. Immediately executing the Undo command (Ctrl+Z) restores the cell's contents and formatting.

Practice 4

In this Practice you will add columns to IVY PAYROLL which calculate taxes, social security, and net pay for each of the Ivy University employees. Start Works and open IVY PAYROLL if you have not already done so.

1) ENTER HEADINGS FOR COLUMNS I, J, AND K

a. Select cell I5. Type Taxes and press the tab key to move the cursor to cell J5.
b. In cell J5 enter the label Soc. Sec.
c. Select cell K5 and enter Net Pay as the label.

2) FORMAT THE HEADINGS

a. Highlight cells I5 through K5.
b. Use the Tool bar to right align and bold the headings.

3) ADD SOCIAL SECURITY RATE LABEL

a. From the Edit menu, use the Go To command to select cell A3.
b. Enter the label Soc. Sec. rate:
c. Bold the label and widen the column as necessary.

4) ENTER SOCIAL SECURITY RATE

a. Select cell B3.
b. Enter 6.00% for the Social Security rate.

An Introduction to Computing Using Microsoft Works

5) ENTER FORMULAS FOR TAXES COLUMN

   a. Select cell I6.
   b. Enter the formula =H6*15% to calculate 15% of the gross pay. 28.8 is displayed.
   c. Format cell I6 as dollars with 2 decimal places.
   d. With the cell cursor on cell I6, highlight the block from cell I6 through I30.
   e. From the Edit menu, select Fill Down to copy the formula into cells I7 through I30. A 15% tax is now calculated for each employee.

6) ENTER FORMULAS FOR SOCIAL SECURITY COLUMN

   a. Select cell J6.
   b. Type an equal sign (=).
   c. Click on cell H6 to enter it into the formula.
   d. Type an asterisk (*).
   e. If necessary, click on the scroll arrows until cell B3 is visible. Click on cell B3 and then press the F4 key once. The absolute reference $B$3 appears in the formula.
   f. Click on the Check box to enter the formula to calculate the social security deduction as 6% of the gross pay, 11.52.
   g. Format cell J6 as dollars with 2 decimal places.
   h. Highlight cells J6 through J30.
   i. From the Edit menu, select Fill Down to copy the formulas into cells J7 through J30. A 6% social security deduction is now calculated for each employee.
   j. Move the cell cursor to cell J7. Note how Works used relative copying for the cell reference that does not use the dollar signs (H7) and absolute copying for the cell reference using the dollar signs ($B$3).

7) ENTER FORMULAS TO CALCULATE NET PAY

   a. Select cell K6.
   b. Enter the formula =H6–I6–J6 to calculate the net pay (gross pay minus the taxes and social security deductions). 151.68 is displayed.
   c. Format cell K6 as dollars with 2 decimal places.
   d. Highlight cells K6 through K30.
   e. Press Ctrl+D to execute the Fill Down command. The formula from cell K6 is copied into cells K7 through K30.

8) CHANGE THE SOCIAL SECURITY RATE

   a. Select cell B3.
   b. Type 6.5% to replace the current value and click on the check box. If necessary, scroll so that columns J and K are visible. Note how Works automatically recalculates all the values in the columns.

9) SAVE THE MODIFIED IVY PAYROLL

Check - Your IVY PAYROLL should look similar to the following:

	E	F	G	H	I	J	K
5	Wed	Thu	Fri	Gross Pay	Taxes	Soc. Sec.	Net Pay
6	4.0	3.0	7.0	$192.00	$28.80	$12.48	$150.72
7	9.0	5.5	3.0	$214.50	$32.18	$13.94	$168.38
8	0.5	7.0	6.0	$153.00	$22.95	$9.95	$120.11
9	7.0	5.0	6.0	$130.50	$19.58	$8.48	$102.44
10	3.0	8.0	7.0	$149.63	$22.44	$9.73	$117.46
11	7.5	6.0	7.5	$203.55	$30.53	$13.23	$159.79

Rows and columns can be inserted and deleted in a spreadsheet. In the IVY PAYROLL spreadsheet, a row is inserted when a new employee has been hired, a row deleted when an employee leaves, and a column to calculate pension plan contributions can be inserted between the Soc. Sec. and Net Pay columns.

To insert a new row, first click on the row number where the new row is to appear, then execute the Insert Row command from the Insert menu. The selected row and all those below it move down to accommodate the newly inserted row. When a column has been selected, executing the Insert Column command inserts a new column. The selected column and all those to the right are moved over. Newly inserted rows and columns are empty and contain no data, formulas, or formatting.

To delete a row, select it by clicking on its row number and then execute the Delete Row command from the Insert menu. All rows below the deleted row move up to fill its position. A column is deleted by selecting it and then executing the Delete Column command. The columns to the right of the deleted column then move to the left. Immediately executing the Undo command restores a deleted row or column.

When cells are inserted or deleted, Works automatically changes the cell references in any formulas. For example, if row 3 is deleted, the formula =SUM(C1:C10) changes to =SUM(C1:C9). If instead a row is inserted between rows 1 and 10, the formula becomes =SUM(C1:C11).

Practice 5

In this Practice, rows will be deleted and inserted into the IVY PAYROLL spreadsheet. Employee H. Crane has left, so her information will be deleted and a new employee's information will be added. Start Works and open IVY PAYROLL if you have not already done so.

1) DELETE THE ROW CONTAINING EMPLOYEE CRANE, H.

    a. Use the Find command to locate the cell storing the name Crane.
    b. Click on the row number of the row containing H. Crane's data to select it.
    c. From the Insert menu, select the Delete Row command. The row is deleted and all rows below move up to fill the space.

2) INSERT ROW AND DATA FOR NEW EMPLOYEE

    a. Select row 21.
    b. From the Insert menu, select Insert Row. A new row is inserted at row 21 and the rows below move down.
    c. Enter the following data into the inserted row:

Nitrate, A.	5.5	6.5	7	8	2	1.5

    d. Format cell B21 as dollars with 2 decimal places. Format cells C21 through G21 as fixed with 1 decimal place.

9

3) COPY FORMULAS TO THE NEW ROW

The new row will require the copying of the four formulas into columns H through K to calculate A. Nitrate's salary and deductions. We can copy all of the formulas at once by highlighting them together as the source.

a. Highlight cells H20 through K21.
b. From the Edit menu, select Fill Down. The new formulas are copied into A. Nitrate's row and the values are automatically calculated.

Check - A. Nitrate's salary and deductions should be:

Gross Pay	Taxes	Soc. Sec.	Net Pay
$137.50	$20.63	$8.94	$107.94

4) SAVE THE MODIFIED IVY PAYROLL

9.14 Using the IF Function

It is sometimes desirable to have a simple decision made based upon the data stored in a spreadsheet. In Works, the IF function makes a decision based on a comparison entered into the function. If the comparison is true, one value is displayed in the cell; if not, a second value is displayed. The IF function has the form:

=IF(<comparison>, <true value>, <false value>)

For example, the formula

=IF(C4<E7,10,20)

displays a 10 if the value in C4 is less than the value in E7. If the value in C4 is greater than or equal to the value in E7, 20 is displayed. What will be displayed if C4 contains the value 35 and E7 contains 30?

The comparison part of the IF function can contain one of the following *relational operators*:

=	equal to
<	less than
>	greater than
<=	less than or equal to
>=	greater than or equal to
<>	not equal to

Examples of formulas using the IF function are:

=IF(N1<=25,50,100)
=IF(B2<K25,0,B2*15%)
=IF(C9>MIN(C2:C7),C11,C14)
=IF(D22<>F25,0,SUM(E1:E10))

For example, the IF function can be used to automatically determine which tax bracket an Ivy U employee's gross pay falls into and then calculate the correct taxes. Ivy U deducts 25% if an employee's gross pay exceeds $250, and 10% if the gross pay is less than or equal to $250. To calculate B. Attis' taxes taking into account the two tax brackets, the formula in cell I6 of the IVY PAYROLL spreadsheet would be replaced with:

=IF(H6>250,H6*25%,H6*10%)

This formula states that if the gross pay stored in cell H6 is greater than 250, multiply it by 25% and display that value. If the value stored in H6 is less than or equal to 250, multiply it by 10% and display that value.

9.15 Printing a Large Spreadsheet

A spreadsheet is often too wide to print on a single sheet of paper. In this case Works prints the spreadsheet on consecutive sheets starting from the leftmost columns and proceeding to the right. Page Setup options can be changed to increase the number of rows and columns that can be printed on a page.

Executing the Page Setup command from the File menu displays the Page Setup dialog box:

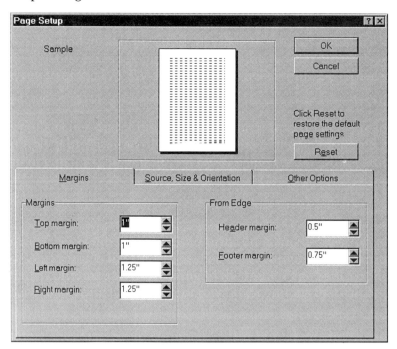

The Orientation option is available from the Page Setup dialog box

Selecting the Margins tab displays the margin options. Decreasing the top and bottom margins may allow more rows to fit on a page, and decreasing the left and right margins may allow more columns on a page.

Selecting the Source, Size & Orientation tab and then the Landscape option prints the spreadsheet across the widest part of the page in *landscape orientation*. In this orientation more columns and fewer rows fit on a page.

An Introduction to Computing Using Microsoft Works

9 | Practice 6

In this Practice you will further expand the IVY PAYROLL spreadsheet to allow for two tax brackets. Start Works and open IVY PAYROLL if you have not already done so.

1) ENTER NEW TAX FORMULA

    a. Select cell I6.

    b. Enter the formula =IF(H6>250,H6*25%,H6*10%). Because the value in H6 is less than 250, the taxes are 10% and therefore the value displayed changes to $19.20.

2) COPY THE NEW FORMULA TO CELLS I6 THROUGH I30

    a. Highlight cells I6 through I30.

    b. From the Edit menu, select Fill Down to copy the new tax formula. Notice how the cells in column I have automatically been recalculated and the new values displayed.

    c. Click anywhere in the spreadsheet to remove the highlight.

Check - Your spreadsheet should be similar to:

	E	F	G	H	I	J	K
	Wed	Thu	Fri	Gross Pay	Taxes	Soc. Sec.	Net Pay
5							
6	4.0	3.0	7.0	$192.00	$19.20	$12.48	$160.32
7	9.0	5.5	3.0	$214.50	$21.45	$13.94	$179.11
8	0.5	7.0	6.0	$153.00	$15.30	$9.95	$127.76
9	7.0	5.0	6.0	$130.50	$13.05	$8.48	$108.97
10	3.0	8.0	7.0	$149.63	$14.96	$9.73	$124.94
11	6.0	5.0	7.5	$173.25	$17.33	$11.26	$144.66

3) VIEW THE SPREADSHEET AS IT WILL APPEAR WHEN PRINTED

    a. From the File menu, select Print Preview.

    b. Select Next. Note how the Taxes, Soc. Sec., and Net Pay columns appear on page 2.

    c. Select Cancel to return to the spreadsheet screen.

    d. From the File menu, select Page Setup. The Page Setup dialog box is displayed.

    e. Select the Margins tab if the margin options are not already displayed.

    f. Change the left and right margins to 1".

    g. Select the Source, Size & Orientation tab to display the orientation options.

    h. Select the Landscape option and then select OK to remove the dialog box.

    i. Print preview the spreadsheet. Note how all the data fits on one page.

    j. Return to the spreadsheet screen.

4) SAVE AND CLOSE IVY PAYROLL

    a. Save IVY PAYROLL and then print a copy.

    b. Close IVY PAYROLL.

Studies have shown that people remember more information when it is presented graphically. For this reason, spreadsheet data can be presented in a *chart* to show the relationship between data. The three most commonly used chart types are pie, bar, and line.

Pie charts show the relation between the parts that make up a whole amount:

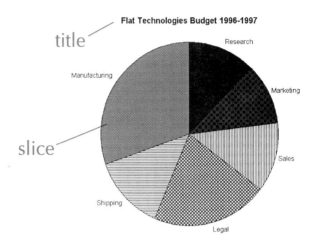

In a pie chart, each *slice* represents one fractional part of the whole. The size of a slice varies with its percentage of the total.

Bar and line charts can display several sets of data where each set is called a *series*. A *bar chart* represents each piece of data by a bar, with taller bars representing larger numbers:

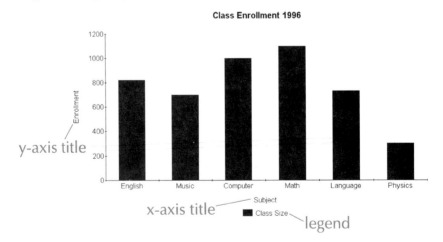

Bar charts are useful for comparing the differences between values. Titles and *legends* may be used to identify what is charted, as shown above.

Line charts show changes in a value over time. For example, the following chart shows two cities' average temperature for each month over the period of a year:

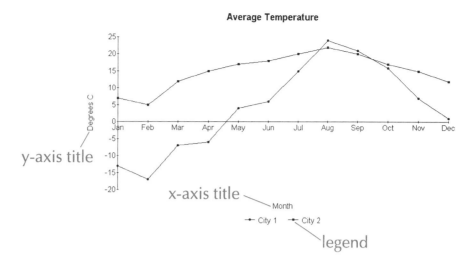

y-axis title

x-axis title

legend

Before creating a chart, you must decide what information the chart is to contain, what type of chart to use, and what titles and legends should be used to make the chart easier to read and understand.

9.17 Creating Pie Charts

A pie chart is created by first highlighting the portion of the spreadsheet that contains the data to be charted. The following spreadsheet data will be used as an example:

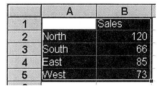

Next, the Create New Chart command from the Tools menu is selected or the New Chart button (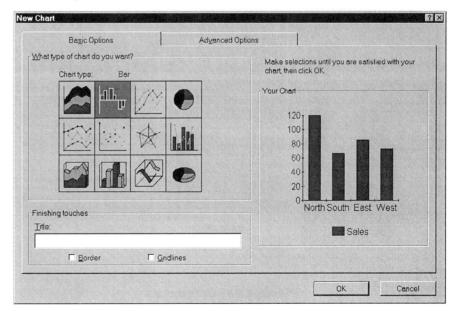) on the Tool bar clicked to display the New Chart dialog box:

The New Chart dialog box shows how the chart will appear. Clicking on the Pie button in the What type of chart do you want? section displays the following:

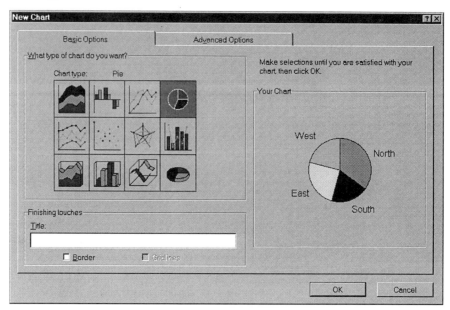

A descriptive title, such as District Sales, can be typed in the Title entry box. Selecting OK displays the new chart in its own window:

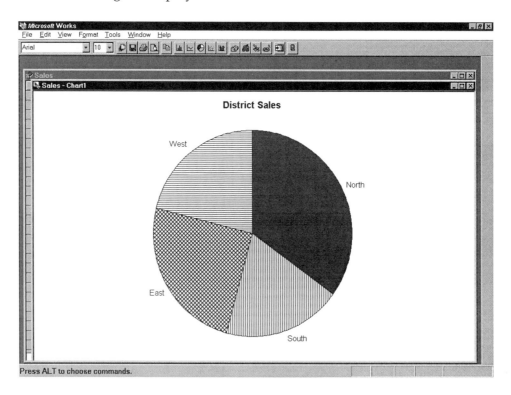

Charts are displayed in their own window

Like other windows, a chart window can be expanded by clicking on its Maximize button (□). After viewing and modifying a chart, it can be closed by clicking on its Close button (✕) in the upper-right corner, or by selecting the Close command from the File menu. Although a chart may not always be visible on the screen, it remains open until it is closed.

An Introduction to Computing Using Microsoft Works

Once created, a chart is linked to the spreadsheet data so that if a number is changed in the spreadsheet, the chart automatically changes. When a spreadsheet is saved, any charts are saved with it. If a range of cells is not selected when the Create New Chart command is executed an error dialog box is displayed.

Practice 7

In this Practice you will create a chart using the data stored in the IVY ENROLLMENT spreadsheet. Start Works if you have not already done so.

1) OPEN IVY ENROLLMENT

Open IVY ENROLLMENT which contains data on the Freshman course enrollment for Ivy University over a period of years.

2) CREATE A PIE CHART

a. Highlight cells A4 through B11. The subject labels and the data for 1993 is selected.
b. From the Tools menu, select the Create New Chart command. The New Chart dialog box is displayed.
c. In the What type of chart do you want? section, click on the Pie button.
d. In the Title entry box, type 1993 Enrollment. Note how the title is displayed above the chart in the dialog box.
e. Select OK. The chart is displayed in its own window.

<u>Check</u> - Your chart should look similar to the following:

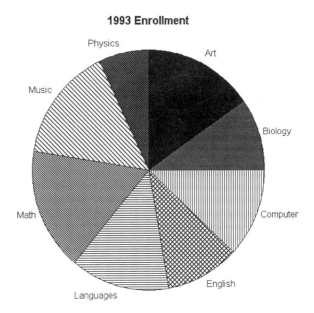

3) CLOSE THE CHART AND SAVE IVY ENROLLMENT

a. From the File menu, select Close. The chart is removed from the screen and the spreadsheet is again visible.
b. From the File menu, select Save. IVY ENROLLMENT now contains a chart.

9.18 Naming a Chart

Up to eight charts can be stored with a spreadsheet. Works uses the default names Chart1, Chart2, etc. to name each chart as it is created. After a chart is created, it should be renamed to reflect the information it displays. For example, a descriptive name such as 1996 Sales could be used to name a chart containing sales figures. It is important to realize that a chart's name is not the title at the top of the chart that was entered in the New Chart dialog box.

A chart is renamed by executing the Rename Chart command from the Tools menu to display a dialog box similar to the following:

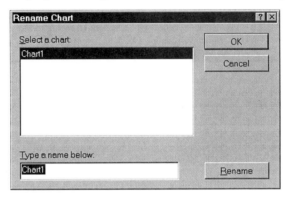

A chart may be given a more descriptive name using this dialog box

The chart to be renamed is highlighted in the Select a chart list and then the new name is typed in the Type a name below entry box. Selecting the Rename button changes the chart name in the list. This process may be repeated to rename other charts. After changing the desired chart names, the OK button is selected.

9.19 Viewing a Chart

To view an existing chart, the Chart command from the View menu is executed to display a dialog box similar to the following:

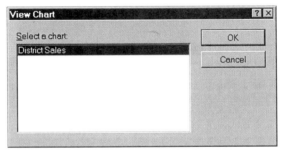

An existing chart may be viewed by selecting it from this dialog box

The desired chart is highlighted and then OK selected to display it.

An Introduction to Computing Using Microsoft Works

9

Since each chart is placed in its own window, multiple charts may be open at the same time. In addition to using the View menu, an open chart can be displayed by selecting its name from the Window menu:

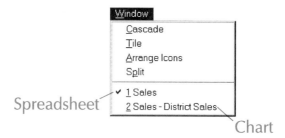

Spreadsheet

Chart

The name of an open chart is displayed in the Window menu

9.20 Printing a Chart

A chart can be printed by first displaying it and then executing the Print command from the File menu, or by clicking on the Print button (📇). Before printing, it is a good practice to use print preview to avoid wasting paper.

The Page Setup command from the File menu is used to change the margins and page orientation of a displayed chart. The Headers and Footers command from the View menu can be used to make the printed chart more descriptive. For example, your name, the date, or the filename can all be included in a header or footer.

Practice 8

In this Practice you will rename and print the pie chart created in the last Practice. Start Works and open IVY ENROLLMENT if you have not already done so.

1) DISPLAY THE PIE CHART

    a. From the View menu, select the Chart command. The View Chart dialog box is displayed.
    b. In the Select a chart list, highlight Chart1 if it is not already highlighted.
    c. Select OK to display the chart.

2) RENAME THE CHART

    a. From the Tools menu, select the Rename Chart command. The Rename Chart dialog box is displayed.
    b. Highlight Chart1 if it is not already highlighted.
    c. In the Type a name below entry box, type 1993 Students.
    d. Select Rename. Chart1 is now named 1993 Students.
    e. Select OK to close the dialog box.

3) CHANGE A VALUE IN THE SPREADSHEET

    a. Note the size of the Art slice in the pie chart. It is about 15% of the pie.
    b. From the View menu, select the Spreadsheet command. The spreadsheet is displayed and the chart hidden from view.

c. Select cell B4.

d. Type a new value of 500 and press the Enter key.

e. From the Window menu, select IVY ENROLLMENT - 1993 Students. The pie chart is again displayed. Note how the Art slice has decreased as a result of the changed value in the spreadsheet.

4) SAVE IVY ENROLLMENT AND PRINT THE PIE CHART

a. From the File menu, select Save. The 1993 Students chart is saved with the spreadsheet.

b. Print preview the chart.

c. Select the Print button from the print preview screen to print a copy of the chart.

d. Close the chart.

9.21 Modifying a Chart

Sometimes a chart needs to have its title changed, a subtitle, x-axis, or y-axis labels added, or its series redefined. For example, a chart should usually contain axes labels. Modifications to a chart can be made only when the chart is displayed.

The Titles command from the Edit menu is used to add a subtitle, x-axis title, and y-axis title to a chart. Executing Titles displays a dialog box similar to the following:

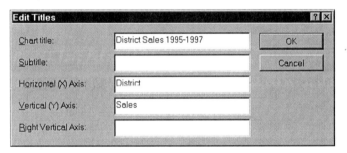

Titles are added to a chart using the Titles command

Typing the desired titles and selecting OK adds them to the displayed chart.

New rows or columns of data can be charted in the displayed chart by using the Series command from the Edit menu. Executing Series displays a dialog box similar to the following:

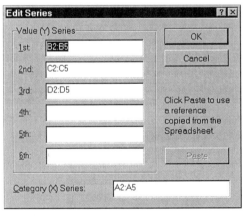

A new series may be added to a chart using this dialog box

An Introduction to Computing Using Microsoft Works

The ranges in the Value (Y) Series section refer to the cells that store the information charted. A new series is added by typing the range of cells into the desired entry box. The range in the Category (X) Series tells Works where the x-axis data labels are stored.

A corresponding legend is normally desired when a new series is added to a chart. To tell Works what cell contains the legend for a series, the Legend/Series Labels command is selected from the Edit menu to display its dialog box. The cell name containing the legend is then typed in the corresponding entry box.

9.22 Deleting Charts

Works allows only 8 charts to be saved with a spreadsheet. Therefore, it is sometimes necessary to delete a chart to make room for another. A chart is deleted by selecting the Delete Chart command from the Tools menu to display a dialog box with the names of exiting charts. Here, the desired chart is highlighted and then the Delete button selected to remove the chart from the spreadsheet. Selecting OK removes the dialog box.

Practice 9

In this Practice you will create a series chart using the data stored in IVY ENROLLMENT. Start Works and open IVY ENROLLMENT if you have not already done so.

1) DISPLAY THE SPREADSHEET

If the spreadsheet is not displayed, select Spreadsheet from the View menu.

2) CREATE A LINE CHART

a. Highlight cells A3 through G6. The year labels and the data for the first three subjects are selected.
b. From the Tools menu, select Create New Chart. The New Chart dialog box is displayed.
c. In the What type of chart do you want? section, click on the Line button in the top row of buttons.
d. In the Title entry box, type Freshman Enrollment.
e. Select OK. A line chart is displayed.

3) RENAME THE CHART

a. From the Tools menu, select Rename Chart. The Rename Chart dialog box is displayed.
b. Highlight Chart1 if it is not already highlighted.
c. In the Type a name below entry box, type Enrollment.
d. Select Rename. Chart1 is now named Enrollment.
e. Select OK to close the dialog box.

4) MODIFY THE CHART

    a. From the View menu, select Spreadsheet. Note that the data for the next subject, English, is displayed in cells B7 through G7 and the label is contained in cell A7.

    b. From the Window menu, select the IVY ENROLLMENT - Enrollment. The Enrollment chart is displayed.

    c. From the Edit menu, select the Series command. The Series dialog box is displayed. Note how each line on the chart has a corresponding series.

    d. In the 4th series entry box, type B7:G7.

    e. Select OK. A new line is added to the chart.

    f. From the Edit menu, select the Legend/Series Labels command. A dialog box is displayed.

    g. In the 4th Value Series entry box, type the name of the cell corresponding to the label for the 4th line, A7.

    h. Select OK. Note the legends at the bottom of the chart.

5) ADD TITLES TO THE CHART

    a. From the Edit menu, select the Titles command. The Titles dialog box is displayed.

    b. In the Subtitle entry box, type 1993 - 1998.

    c. In the Horizontal (X) Axis entry box, type Year.

    d. In the Vertical (Y) Axis entry box, type Enrolled.

    e. Select OK. Note the labels on the chart.

6) SAVE AND PRINT THE CHART

    a. Save IVY ENROLLMENT.

    b. From the File menu, select Page Setup. In the Source, Size & Orientation option select Landscape. Select OK. The chart will now be printed lengthwise on the page.

    c. Preview the chart. Select Print from the print preview screen to print a copy of the chart. Because charts are complex, some printers may require several minutes to print a single chart.

    d. Close the chart and the spreadsheet.

Check - Printed charts vary depending on the printer used, but yours should be similar to the following:

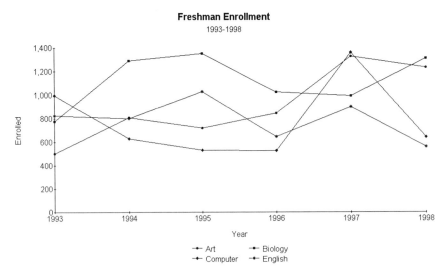

It is important to carefully plan a large spreadsheet before using Works. This is best done by first deciding what new information the spreadsheet will produce, what data it should store, how that data could be produced without a computer, and what the spreadsheet should look like when displayed on the computer. A sketch of the spreadsheet should be done to plan its format. The sketch should indicate column headings and the type of data each column will store.

The cell names that define a range can be entered into a formula by pointing to the cells using the mouse. An alternative to typing a function name is to select one using the Function command from the Insert menu.

To copy a cell's contents into a row or column of cells, the cells are highlighted and the Fill Right command used in a row or the Fill Down command in a column. Both commands are in the Edit menu. One of their most useful applications is in copying formulas. When this is done Works automatically changes the cell names in the copies to reflect the new rows or columns they are in. This process is called relative copying. To view the formulas in a spreadsheet the Formulas command from the View menu is executed.

Cell contents can be searched using the Find command from the Edit menu. The Go To command from the Edit menu can be used to move the cell cursor directly to a specified cell.

The MAX and MIN functions display the maximum or minimum value stored in a specified range of cells.

When expanding a spreadsheet, the four steps for planning a spreadsheet should be used once again so that the modified spreadsheet can easily support further expansion.

To keep cell references from changing when cells are copied, dollar signs ($) are placed in front of the column letter and row number ($A$3). This is called absolute copying. The F4 key can be used to place dollar signs in a cell reference.

The Cut command removes a cell's contents and places it on the Clipboard, and the Copy command places a copy of a cell's contents on the Clipboard. The Clipboard contents can then be placed in selected cells using the Paste command. All three commands are in the Edit menu.

Rows or columns can be inserted into a spreadsheet using the Insert Row and Insert Column commands or deleted using the Delete Row and Delete Column commands, all from the Insert menu. The point of insertion or deletion is indicated by clicking on the appropriate row number or column letter. Works automatically changes the ranges of any involved formulas when a column or row is deleted or inserted.

A decision can be made based on data in a spreadsheet by using the IF function. If a comparison is true the first value in the function is displayed in the current cell, if false the second value is shown. For example, when the formula =IF(A5>B4,30,15) is evaluated, 30 is displayed if the value in A5 is greater than the value in B4, and 15 is displayed if the value in A5 is less than or equal to the value in B4.

The way a spreadsheet is printed can be changed by modifying the margins and changing the print orientation with the Page Setup command from the File menu.

Works can use the data stored in a spreadsheet to produce pie charts and series charts. A pie chart shows the percentage relationship between different parts of a whole quantity. Series charts include bar and line. Generally, a bar chart is used to compare different items and a line chart to track values over time. A new chart is created using the Create New Chart command from the Tools menu. The Rename Chart command from the Tools menu is used to give a chart a descriptive name.

To view an existing chart, the Chart command from the View menu is used. If a chart is already open but not displayed, it can be viewed by selecting its name from the Window menu. The Titles, Series, and Legend/Series Labels commands in the Edit are used to modify a displayed chart.

Vocabulary

Absolute copying - Copying formulas that contain cell references that will not change because dollar signs have been used with the cell name (i.e., $A$5).

Bar chart - Data graphed as a series of bars.

Chart - A graphical representation of numeric data stored in a spreadsheet.

Create New Chart command - Used to create a new chart from spreadsheet data.

Delete Column command - Removes a column from a spreadsheet.

Delete Row command - Removes a row from a spreadsheet.

Fill Down command - Copies a cell's contents to adjacent highlighted cells in a column.

Fill Right command - Copies a cell's contents to adjacent highlighted cells in a row.

Find command - Moves the cursor to the next cell containing specified text.

Formulas command - Displays the formulas in the cells of a spreadsheet instead of the values.

Function command - Supplies a function so that it need not be typed from the keyboard.

Go To command - Used to move the cursor to a specified cell.

Insert Column command - Adds a column to a spreadsheet.

Insert Row command - Adds a row to a spreadsheet.

Landscape orientation - A printing orientation that indicates a spreadsheet is to be printed across the widest part of the paper.

Legend - Identifies data in a chart.

Line chart - Data graphed using a continuous line.

Page Setup command - Used to change the margins and print orientation of a spreadsheet.

Pie chart - Data graphed as segments of a circular pie.

Placeholders - Part of a newly inserted function that are a reminder that cell names, ranges, or values must be included in the function.

Pointing - Clicking on a cell to specify its name in a formula.

Relational operators - Used to compare two values. Operators include =, <, >, <=, >=, <>.

Relative copying - Copying formulas that contain cell references that change to reflect the new rows and columns they are in. The Fill Right and Fill Down commands are used for relative copying.

Series - A set of data displayed in a chart.

Slice - Part of a pie chart that represents one fractional part of a whole.

Source cell - Cell where data to be copied is taken from.

9 Reviews

Sections 9.1 — 9.3

1. What four questions should be answered when planning a large spreadsheet?

2. Sketch the layout for a spreadsheet that will contain an automobile dealership's inventory. The spreadsheet should include model names, quantity in stock, and asking prices.

3. a) What is usually the best method for entering field references in a formula?
   b) What is the advantage of using this method?

4. List the steps required to enter a function name into a formula without typing it.

Sections 9.4 — 9.12

5. What is meant by relative copying? Give an example.

6. List the steps required to copy the formula =AVG(C5:C9) stored in cell C22, into the range of cells D22 to G22 so that the formula correctly calculates the average for each column.

7. How can the formulas stored in the cells of a spreadsheet be displayed instead of the values they calculate?

8. a) List the steps required to find each cell in a spreadsheet that contains the label Harry.
   b) List the steps required to find each cell in a spreadsheet that displays the value 25.

9. What is the fastest way to move the cell cursor from cell A1 to cell Z14?

10. Write formulas that calculate:
    a) the maximum value stored in the range of cells D4 to Y5.
    b) the minimum value stored in the range of cells C1 to C9.

11. Why is it usually not a good practice to keep adding data to a spreadsheet without careful planning?

12. a) When copying formulas how is it possible to keep one cell reference constant while allowing others to change?
    b) Give two examples of when you would need to do this.

13. List the steps required to copy the contents of cell B4 into cells A9, B11, and C15.

14. List the steps required to remove the contents of cells A1, A2, and A3.

Sections 9.13 — 9.15

15. List the steps required to delete the Net Pay column from IVY PAYROLL.

16. List the steps required to insert a column titled Tue into a spreadsheet that follows a column titled Mon and comes before a column titled Wed.

17. a) The formula =SUM(C3:C22) is used to sum the values in cells C3 to C22. If a row is inserted directly above row 20, what must be done to include the new cell in the sum?
    b) If a row is inserted directly above row 23, what must be done to include the new cell in the sum?

18. What will be displayed by the following formulas if cell D4 stores a value of 30 and E7 a value of –12?
    a) =IF(D4<=E7,10,20)
    b) =IF(E7*D4<-5,E7,D4)
    c) =IF(D4-42=E7,D4*2,E7*3)

19. Write formulas that perform each of the following:
    a) Display 50 if the value stored in D20 equals the value in C80, or 25 if they are not equal.

b) Display the value in B40 if the sum of the range of cells C20 to C30 exceeds 1000, otherwise display a 0.

c) Display the value of R20*10 if R20 is less than 30; otherwise display the value in R20.

20. What must be done to print a spreadsheet across the widest part of the paper?

Sections 9.16 — 9.22

21. Would a bar, line, or pie chart best be suited to display:
    a) a student's GPA over four years at college
    b) the percentages spent on different parts of Ivy University's budget
    c) the number of faculty members in each department at Ivy
    d) the number of books sold each day for a month at the college bookstore
    e) the percentage of Ivy's students from each state in the United States

22. What happens to a chart when the data in the spreadsheet is changed?

23. List the steps required to create a bar chart named Emp-Net Pay from the IVY PAYROLL spreadsheet that displays each employee's net pay.

24. Describe two ways to display an existing chart.

25. List the steps required to create a line chart.

26. List the steps required to modify a chart to include an additional series.

27. List the steps required to add a chart title and axis labels on an existing chart.

28. Why might it be necessary to delete a chart?

29. List the steps required to delete a chart named 1998 Enrollment.

An Introduction to Computing Using Microsoft Works

9 | Exercises

1. The Ivy University Alumni Association must determine how much to charge each member attending its annual Homecoming Dinner Dance so that it will not lose money.

   a) Create a spreadsheet like the one shown below that includes the costs for 50 members attending the dance. All of the costs are summed and the total divided by the number of members attending to produce the cost per member.

	A	B
1	Expenses	50 Members
2	Band	$1,500.00
3	Decorations	$185.00
4	Print Tickets	$73.15
5	Electricity	$50.00
6	Advertising	$182.00
7	Clean up	$78.00
8	Appetizers	$56.00
9	Entrees	$111.00
10	Dessert	$34.50
11	Beverages	$150.00
12		
13	Cost/Member	$48.39

   b) Format the column widths and cells appropriately. Save the spreadsheet naming it Dance.

   c) In columns C, D, and E calculate the cost per ticket when 100, 150, or 200 members attend. Consider the following when adding these columns:

   • The expenses for Band through Clean up remain the same no matter how many members attend. Be careful to set up these values in the new columns so that if the value in column B is changed it will also change in the other columns. For example, if Band is changed to $785.50 in column B, it should also appear as $785.50 in the three new columns.
   • The values for Appetizers through Beverages change depending on how many members attend. Therefore, the cost for Dessert for 50 members must be multiplied by 2 to calculate the cost for 100 members, by 3 to calculate the cost for 150 members, and so on. The values for Appetizers, Entrees, and Beverages are calculated similarly.

   d) Save the modified Dance and print a copy. Your spreadsheet should be similar to:

	A	B	C	D	E
1	Expenses	50 Members	100 Members	150 Members	200 Members
2	Band	$1,500.00	$1,500.00	$1,500.00	$1,500.00
3	Decorations	$185.00	$185.00	$185.00	$185.00
4	Print Tickets	$73.15	$73.15	$73.15	$73.15
5	Electricity	$50.00	$50.00	$50.00	$50.00
6	Advertising	$182.00	$182.00	$182.00	$182.00
7	Clean up	$78.00	$78.00	$78.00	$78.00
8	Appetizers	$56.00	$112.00	$168.00	$224.00
9	Entrees	$111.00	$222.00	$333.00	$444.00
10	Dessert	$34.50	$69.00	$103.50	$138.00
11	Beverages	$150.00	$300.00	$450.00	$600.00
12					
13	Cost/Member	$48.39	$27.71	$20.82	$17.37

e) Produce the following charts using the data in Dance. Be sure to name the charts appropriately:

- A pie chart that displays the percent amounts of each cost when 50 members attend. Title the chart Dance Expenses for 50 Members:

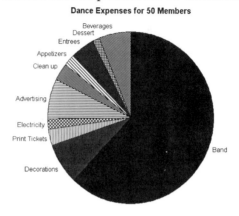

- A bar chart that displays the cost per member when 50, 100, 150, and 200 members attend. Title the chart Homecoming Dance Ticket Cost. (After creating the chart you will need to add the x series labels by using the Series command to specify the range containing the column titles as the Category (X) Series).

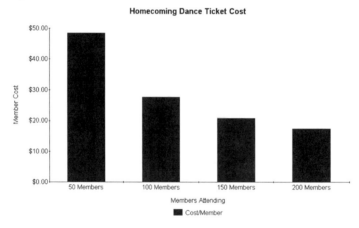

- A bar chart that displays the costs when 50, 100, 150, and 200 members attend. Title the chart Expenses:

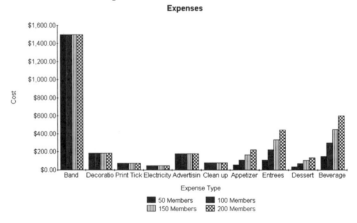

f) Save the modified Dance. Print the spreadsheet and each of its charts in Landscape orientation.

9

2. Mr. Hernandez, owner of the Aztec Café, would like to expand the spreadsheet created in Chapter Eight, Exercise 5 to compute the gross and net pay of each employee.

a) Open AC Employees. The pay rate per hour needs to be in the spreadsheet. In column J, enter an appropriate label and the following pay rates:

Employee	Pay Rate
H. Berry	$2.80
G. Diez	$3.60
K. Martin	$2.80
D. Romani	$10.40

Format the label and values appropriately, and resize the column as necessary.

b) Gross pay is computed by multiplying the total number of hours worked by pay rate. In column K, enter an appropriate label and the formulas necessary to compute the gross pay for each employee. Format the labels and values appropriately.

c) Net pay is computed by making the necessary deductions from the gross pay. Taxes are 12% and social security is 6%. Title column L Taxes and enter formulas to compute 12% of each employee's gross pay. Title column M Soc. Sec. and enter formulas for the deductions. Title column N Net Pay and enter formulas to deduct the taxes and social security from the gross pay of each employee.

d) Save the modified AC Employees.

e) Mr. Hernandez has hired two more employees. Insert the data shown below into the spreadsheet so that the employee names remain in alphabetical order by last name. Add the necessary formulas to the spreadsheet.

D. Roberts	8	8	6	0	10	12	0	$4.20
P. Jorge	0	0	8	8	8	8	8	$3.60

f) Bold and right align titles as appropriate. Resize columns I, J, K, L, M, and N so that they are just wide enough to completely display their titles. The expanded spreadsheet should look similar to the one shown below:

	F	G	H	I	J	K	L	M	N
3	Thu	Fri	Sat	Total Hours	Pay Rate	Gross Pay	Taxes	Soc. Sec.	Net Pay
4	8	8	4	40	$2.80	$112.00	$13.44	$6.72	$91.84
5	8	10	0	42	$3.60	$151.20	$18.14	$9.07	$123.98
6	8	8	8	40	$3.60	$144.00	$17.28	$8.64	$118.08
7	4	0	4	20	$2.80	$56.00	$6.72	$3.36	$45.92
8	10	12	0	44	$4.20	$184.80	$22.18	$11.09	$151.54
9	0	10	0	47	$10.40	$488.80	$58.66	$29.33	$400.82

g) Change the print orientation to Landscape. Save the modified AC Employees and print a copy.

3. The STOCK2 spreadsheet stores the names, purchase price, and number of shares of stocks owned by Grace van Ivy, a relative of Ivy University's founder. You are to assist her by expanding the spreadsheet to produce calculations. Open STOCK2.

    a) Ms. van Ivy wants to know how much money she has made or lost on each stock. In column D add the label Current Price and enter the current price per share:

Campbell's Soup	$41.38	Ford Motor Co.	$50.63
Chrysler	$40.88	General Motors	$31.88
Coca Cola	$40.63	Heinz	$41.50
Disney	$47.00	Hershey	$41.13
Eastman Kodak	$51.88	McDonald's	$14.00
Federal Express	$58.88	Pepsico	$40.63

    Format the label in column D as right aligned and bold. Increase the column width until all data is displayed. Format the values as currency.

    b) Add the label Original Value to column E, then bold and right align it and widen the column to display it. The original value of each stock is calculated by multiplying the shares bought by the purchase price. Enter formulas to compute the original value of each stock. Format the values as currency.

    c) At the bottom of column E calculate the total paid for all of the stock. Include a label for the total and be sure the label and values are formatted appropriately.

    d) Add the label Current Value to column F. Current value is found by multiplying the number of shares by the current price. Enter formulas to compute the current value of each stock. Sum column F to find the current total value of the stocks. Format the label and values appropriately.

    e) Ms. van Ivy wants to know what stocks have gained in value and which ones have lost in value. In column G enter the label Gain or Loss and calculate the gain or loss of each stock by subtracting the original value from the current value. Format the label appropriately. Format the cells for currency.

    f) Save the modified STOCK2 and print a copy.

    g) Produce a bar chart titled Stock Comparisons that displays the Purchase Price and the Current Price. Include axes labels as shown. (After creating the chart you will need to add the x series labels by using the Series command to specify the range containing the stock names as the Category (X) Series).

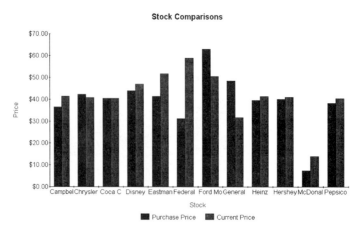

    h) Name the chart Stock Compare. Change the chart orientation to Landscape, save the modified STOCK2, and print the chart.

An Introduction to Computing Using Microsoft Works

9

4. Fantasy Wheels Used Cars wants to use a spreadsheet to keep track of the value of its inventory. The spreadsheet should record the year and model of each car for sale, and the price Fantasy paid for it. In addition, Fantasy typically sells their cars at a 15% markup, and would like to include this information in the spreadsheet.

a) Carefully plan the Fantasy spreadsheet. Take into consideration all of the ways the spreadsheet might be used. In your plan, include a column for the selling price. The year should also be in its own column.

b) Using the plan from part (a), enter the following data into a new spreadsheet:

1972 Corvette, price paid: $8,500	1989 Ferarri, price paid: $22,340
1990 Porsche, price paid: $31,000	1955 Studebaker, price paid: $950
1957 Bel Aire, price paid: $1,250	1980 Aston-Martin, price paid: $56,700
1978 Triumph, price paid: $4,560	1958 Thunderbird, price paid: $14,000
1983 Rolls Royce, price paid: $34,460	1967 Mustang, price paid: $11,230
1958 Cadillac, price paid: $8,895	1948 Bentley, price paid: $49,500
1993 Jaguar, price paid: $24,650	1968 GTO, price paid: $12,000
1985 DeLorean, price paid: $28,999	1978 Bricklin, price paid: $36,200

Add three of your own cars to the inventory.

c) Format all labels and values appropriately. Change the width of any columns if appropriate. Save the spreadsheet naming it Cars.

d) Add labels and formulas to calculate the following in your spreadsheet:

- Total of prices paid for inventory
- Average price paid per car
- The minimum price paid for a car
- The maximum price paid for a car
- Profit for each car when it sells at the 15% markup price
- Total profit if all of the cars were to sell at the 15% markup price

Format all labels, data, and column widths appropriately.

e) The 1972 Corvette has been sold. Delete its row from the spreadsheet. Be sure to modify any formulas that might need to be changed.

f) Fantasy has acquired two new cars. Add the following data to the spreadsheet, being sure to modify any formulas that might need to be changed:

1991 Honda, price paid: $6,500   1989 Jeep, price paid: $5,350

g) Fantasy is having a sale on all cars built before 1970. Add a column titled Sale which displays a 7.5% markup on the price paid if the car is on sale, and a 15% markup if it is not. Format the column appropriately.

h) Add a column titled Sale Profit which displays the profit that Fantasy from the sale prices in part (g). Total this column and format the entire column appropriately.

i) Save the modified Cars and print a copy.

5. Your best friend, Mike Entrepreneur, is opening a lawn mowing service and wants you to set up a spreadsheet for his business.

   a) Plan the spreadsheet so that Mike can enter his customers' names, and the lengths and widths of their lawns in meters. In your plan, include a column for calculating lawn area and the price of cutting the lawn if Mike charges $0.08 per square meter. Also include calculations and labels for the total income Mike receives from mowing all his customer's lawns and the average income per lawn. Be sure to include proper labels for all data.

   b) Using the plan from part (a), create the spreadsheet. Include data for a minimum of 15 customers. Format all data and labels appropriately. Change the width of any columns if appropriate. Save the spreadsheet naming it Lawns.

   c) Mike wants to include his expenses in the spreadsheet so that he can determine his profits. He has determined that his fuel and maintenance costs are $0.07 per 10 square meters of lawn area. Title the next column Expense and use formulas to compute the expense for each lawn. Include formatted calculations and labels for the total and average expenses as well.

   d) Profit is computed by deducting the expense from the price. Title the next column Profit and use formulas to compute the profit made on each lawn and the total and average profit.

   e) Save the modified Lawns and print a copy.

   f) Create a bar chart titled Mike's Lawn Service that displays the price, expense, and profit for each of the first five customers in the spreadsheet. Include axes labels as shown. (After creating the chart you will need to add the x series labels by using the Series command to specify the range containing the customer names as the Category (X) Series).

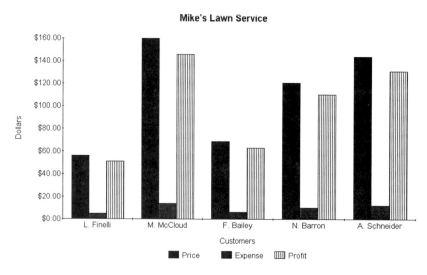

   g) Name the chart Price/Exp/Price. Change the chart orientation to Landscape, save Lawns, and print the chart.

6. In a new spreadsheet, record the average yearly temperature in degrees Celsius for your city for a 50 year period. You can find this information in an almanac, at the library, or use the example data on the next page:

Year	Temp(C)	Year	Temp(C)	Year	Temp(C)	Year	Temp(C)	Year	Temp(C)
1947	18	1957	20	1967	22	1977	18	1987	22
1948	18	1958	19	1968	23	1978	14	1988	18
1949	14	1959	22	1969	21	1979	19	1989	18
1950	19	1960	18	1970	22	1980	20	1990	22
1951	23	1961	18	1971	23	1981	22	1991	21
1952	22	1962	14	1972	22	1982	23	1992	22
1953	23	1963	19	1973	23	1983	19	1993	19
1954	20	1964	20	1974	19	1984	22	1994	22
1955	22	1965	23	1975	22	1985	23	1995	19
1956	23	1966	23	1976	18	1986	19	1996	22

a) Add appropriate labels. To save typing use a formula to calculate and display the year. Format all data and labels appropriately. Change the width of any columns if appropriate.

b) Save the spreadsheet naming it Temp.

c) Add labels and formulas to calculate the following in your spreadsheet:

- The average temperature over the past 50 years.
- The average of the first 25 years only.
- The average of the last 25 years.
- The minimum and maximum temperatures for the first 25 years.
- The minimum and maximum temperatures for the last 25 years.

Format all labels, data, and column widths appropriately.

d) Save the modified Temp and print a copy.

e) Create a chart titled Average Temperature which is a line graph of the temperature for the years 1960 to 1965. (After creating the chart you will need to use the Series command to specify the range with the years as the Category (X) Series and the range with the temperatures as the 1st Vlaue (Y) Series.) Include X and Y axis labels as shown:

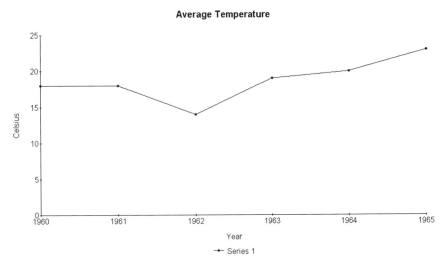

f) Modify the chart to include the data for the first 25 years (use Edit Series and change the 1st Value (Y) Series range).

g) Name the chart Avg Temp. Change the chart orientation to Landscape, save Temp, and print the chart.

7. Dorothy Sophocles would like to modify the Expenses spreadsheet created in Chapter Eight, Exercise 3 to determine her monthly savings.

    a) Open Expenses. Below the monthly totals, add a row labeled Income that stores the monthly net income of $1,420 for June, July, and August. Bold the label.

    b) Savings is computed by subtracting total expenses from income. Below the income row, add a row that computes the savings for each month. Include a bold label.

    c) Save the modified Expenses and print a copy.

    d) Create a pie chart titled June Expenses that displays June's expenses. The chart should be similar to:

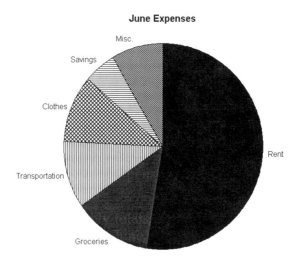

June Expenses

    e) Name the chart June Expenses. Change the chart orientation to Landscape, save the modified Expenses, and print the chart.

8. In a new spreadsheet, enter the data for the last 10 years for Flat Technologies, a one-product manufacturer:

Year	Expenses	Units Sold	Price/Unit
1	$50,000.00	6,000	$14.50
2	$60,000.00	7,500	$15.50
3	$65,000.00	8,000	$16.00
4	$75,000.00	10,000	$17.00
5	$77,500.00	15,000	$17.75
6	$70,000.00	14,000	$19.00
7	$65,000.00	11,500	$19.00
8	$63,500.00	10,250	$18.50
9	$60,000.00	10,750	$18.25
10	$62,500.00	11,000	$18.50

    a) Format all data and labels appropriately. Change the width of any columns if appropriate.

    b) Save the spreadsheet naming it Flat.

    c) Add a column titled Profit which calculates the profit (income minus expenses) for each year. Income is computed by multiplying Units Sold by Price/Unit. Format the label and all data appropriately.

An Introduction to Computing Using Microsoft Works

d) Add a row to the spreadsheet that calculates the average of the yearly expenses, unit sales, price, and profit columns. Include a proper label and format the label and all data appropriately. Change the width of any columns if appropriate.

e) Save the modified Flat and print a copy.

f) Produce a line chart titled Flat Technologies Years 1 to 10 which graphs expenses for years 1 to 10. (After creating the chart you will need to use the Series command to specify the range with the years as the Category (X) Series and the range with the expenses as the 1st Value (Y) Series.) Include X and Y axis labels as shown:

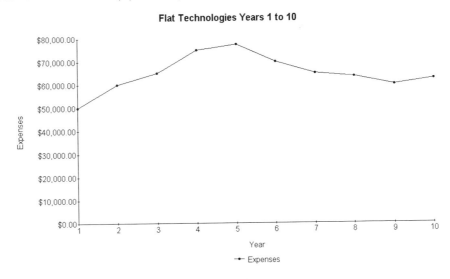

Flat Technologies Years 1 to 10

g) Name the chart Years 1 to 10. Change the chart orientation to Landscape, save Flat, and print the chart.

9. You have been asked to get quotes to have a newsletter printed for your club:

Printer A: $0.25 per copy up to 1000 copies
$0.23 per copy for each copy over 1000

Printer B: $0.27 per copy for up to 900 copies
$0.15 per copy for each copy over 900

Printer C: $0.28 per copy for up to 500 copies
$0.20 per copy for each copy over 500

a) Create a new spreadsheet that shows the cost for printing 500, 1000, and 1500 copies of the newsletter for each of the three printers. Use the IF function in a formula to calculate the prices.

b) Save the spreadsheet naming it Printing Costs.

c) Add a column to the spreadsheet which shows the minimum cost for printing each of the three numbers of copies.

d) The club president would also like quotes for 750 and 1250 copies. Add two rows to the spreadsheet which calculate and display the costs for these numbers of copies. Be sure to copy the appropriate formulas.

e) Save the modified Printing Costs and print a copy.

f) Produce a bar chart titled Price Quotes that displays the cost each printer charges for the different numbers of copies. (After creating the chart you will need to use the Series command to specify the range with the number of copies as the Category (X) Series and the range with the prices as the 1st Value (Y) Series.) Include X and Y axis labels as shown:

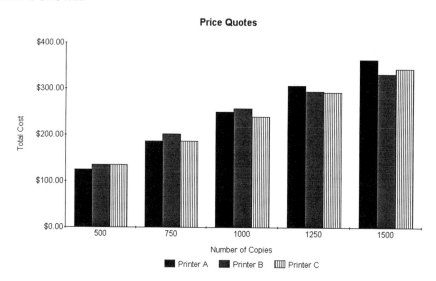

g) Printer C has heard about the other printer's prices and has decided to change his quote to the following:

$0.27 per copy for up to 500 copies
$0.21 per copy for every copy over 500

Change the formulas for Printer C to reflect this new price.

h) Name the chart Printer Charges. Change the chart orientation to Landscape, save Printing Costs, and print the chart.

Sort

CHOOSE

VLOOKUP

Freeze Titles

PMT

Set Print Area

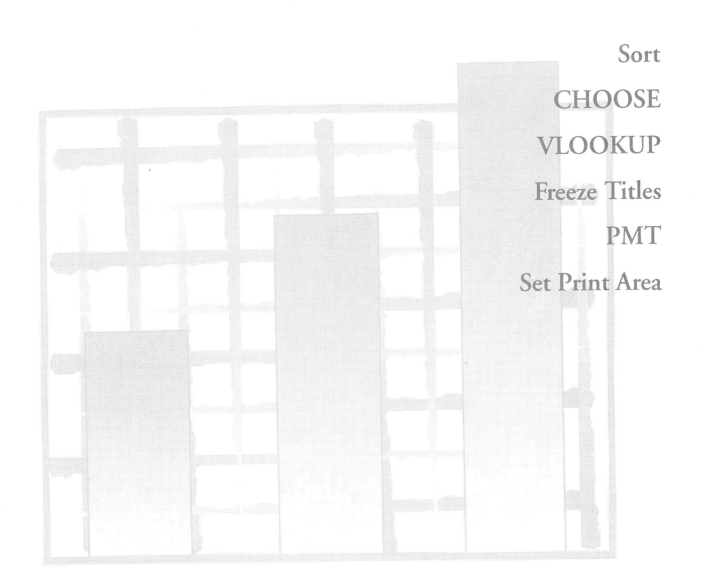

Objectives

After completing this chapter you will be able to:

1. Answer What If? questions using a spreadsheet.

2. Sort the data in a spreadsheet.

3. Use text in functions.

4. Use the CHOOSE and VLOOKUP functions.

5. Freeze selected rows and columns of data.

6. Create an amortization table using the PMT function.

7. Print a specified range of cells.

10

$\mathbf{I}$n Chapter Nine planning was emphasized to make a large spreadsheet easy to modify and expand. In this chapter you will use these skills to answer "What If?" questions.

10.1 Asking "What If ?"

A spreadsheet is often used to answer *What If?* questions. A What If? question is simply a question the user may have and does not require a particular function or formula. For example, a cookie manufacturer may ask: What if the price of sugar increases? How will this affect the cost of my cookies? These questions are easily answered by substituting numbers in a spreadsheet.

A spreadsheet modified to answer What If? questions contains data relating to a particular situation and is called a *model*. For example, consider the cookie manufacturer's spreadsheet model that would include figures related to cookie production such as the cost of the ingredients, packaging, and labor. If the cost of sugar were to increase, the new price could be entered into the model to see how the overall cost of production would be affected. A decision about raising the price of the cookies could then be made based on this model. Many businesses use this technique to help make decisions.

As another example, consider the IVY PAYROLL spreadsheet which models the employee payroll costs. When it is time to give the employees a wage increase Ivy U will be asking: What if the employees receive a 15% increase of their gross pay? What if the employees receive only a 5% or 10% gross pay increase? How much will these increases cost? To answer these questions, three new columns of calculated data will be added to the IVY PAYROLL spreadsheet.

....

Practice 1

In this Practice you will answer the "What If?" questions described in Section 10.1 by adding three columns to the IVY PAYROLL spreadsheet that calculate raises of 5%, 10%, and 15%.

1) START WORKS AND OPEN IVY PAYROLL

2) ENTER HEADINGS FOR THE RAISES

    a. In cell L5, enter the heading: 5% Raise
    b. In cell M5, enter the heading: 10% Raise
    c. In cell N5, enter the heading: 15% Raise
    d. Right align and bold the labels in cells L5 through N5.

3) ENTER FORMULAS FOR THE RAISES

   a. In cell L6, enter the formula: =H6*105%
      This formula multiplies the gross pay in H6 by 105% to calculate a new gross pay which is 5% higher than the original.
   b. In cell M6, enter the formula =H6*110% to calculate a 10% raise.
   c. In cell N6, enter the formula =H6*115% to calculate a 15% raise.
   d. Format cells L6 through N6 as currency with two decimal places.

4) COPY THE RAISE FORMULAS AS A BLOCK

   a. Highlight cells L6 through N30.
   b. From the Edit menu, select Fill Down.
   c. Select cell L30. Note how relative copying was used to change cell names.

5) SUM THE NEW GROSS PAYS

   a. Select cell K32. Enter and then bold the label: New pay:
   b. Select cell L32. Enter the formula: =SUM(L6:L30)
   c. Format cell L32 as currency with two decimal places.
   d. Copy the formula in cell L32 into cells M32 and N32. The model now includes the sums of each of the pay increase columns.

6) CALCULATE THE INCREASED COST OF RAISES

   a. In cell K33, enter and then bold the label: Raise cost: Widen column K if necessary.
   b. In cell L33, enter the formula: =L32–$H$32
      Cell H32 contains the current total pay. We want to make copies of this formula, but we do not want the cell reference H32 to change when copied. This requires the dollar signs in the cell name.
   c. Format cell L33 as currency with two decimal places.
   d. Copy the formula in cell L33 into cells M33 and N33. Because of the dollar signs, the cell reference H32 does not change when copied.

Check - The last rows of the new columns should be similar to:

	K	L	M	N
32	New pay:	$5,180.13	$5,426.80	$5,673.47
33	Raise cost:	$246.67	$493.35	$740.02

7) SAVE THE MODIFIED IVY PAYROLL

10.2 Using Sort to Organize a Spreadsheet

Placing rows of data in a specified order is called *sorting*. In Works, rows can be sorted based on the values displayed in a specified column called the *key sort column*. For example, consider the following:

	A	B
1	Produce	Current Stock
2	garlic	49
3	head lettuce	20
4	potatoes	16
5	apples	50
6	bananas	29
7		
8	Total Stock=	164

Cells from the rows to be sorted must first be highlighted

An Introduction to Computing Using Microsoft Works

The rows to be sorted must first be highlighted. Next, the Sort command from the Tools menu is selected to display the Sort dialog box:

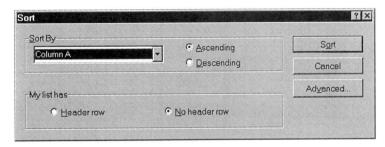

The key sort column is selected in the Sort dialog box

The column in the Sort By entry box identifies the *key sort column*. Radio buttons are used to select ascending (low to high) or descending (high to low) as the sort order. Because we want the rows sorted alphabetically by produce name, Column A and Ascending are selected. Selecting Sort organizes the rows so that they are in order based on the values in column A:

	A	B
1	Produce	Current Stock
2	apples	50
3	bananas	29
4	garlic	49
5	head lettuce	20
6	potatoes	16
7		
8	Total Stock=	164

The highlighted block has been sorted by row

Sorting the same block of cells with Column B as the key sort column results in the following:

	A	B
1	Produce	Current Stock
2	potatoes	16
3	head lettuce	20
4	bananas	29
5	garlic	49
6	apples	50
7		
8	Total Stock=	164

Column B was used to sort the data in ascending order

Practice 2

In this Practice IVY PAYROLL will be updated and sorted. Start Works and open IVY PAYROLL if you have not already done so.

1) INSERT DATA FOR TWO NEW EMPLOYEES

    a. Select row 30 by clicking on its row number.

    b. From the Insert menu, select Insert Row. A new row is inserted. Repeat this procedure to insert a second new row.

    c. In the appropriate cells of rows 30 and 31, enter the following data for the two new employees:

| Hadriano, L. | 7.5 | 8 | 7.5 | 8 | 8.5 | 9 |
| Caxton, C. | 4.25 | 4.5 | 6 | 6.5 | 7 | 8 |

    d. Format cells B30 and B31 as currency with two decimal places. Format cells C30 through G31 as Fixed with 1 decimal place.

2) COPY FORMULAS FOR NEW EMPLOYEES

    a. Highlight cells H29 through N31.
    b. From the Edit menu, select Fill Down.

3) SORT THE DATA

Adding rows can result in a randomly ordered list of employees. Specific employees would be hard to find, so it is best if the employee rows were in order alphabetically by last name.

    a. Place the pointer on the row number for row 6 and drag down to the row number for row 32 to highlight all the rows containing employee data.
    b. From the Tools menu, select the Sort command. Column A is displayed in the Sort By entry box and the order is Ascending. Select Sort to accept these default options. The highlighted rows are sorted alphabetically.
    c. Scroll through the spreadsheet so that the new employee rows are visible. Employee names are now in alphabetical order.
    d. Click anywhere in the spreadsheet to remove the highlight.

Check - Your spreadsheet should look similar to that shown below:

	A	B	C	D	E	F	G	H
5	Employee	Rate/Hr	Mon	Tue	Wed	Thu	Fri	Gross Pay
6	Attis, B.	$8.00	6.0	4.0	4.0	3.0	7.0	$192.00
7	Ball, R.	$5.50	9.5	12.0	9.0	5.5	3.0	$214.50
8	Bickle, R.	$6.00	5.0	7.0	0.5	7.0	6.0	$153.00
9	Cambell, M.	$4.50	5.0	6.0	7.0	5.0	6.0	$130.50
10	Caxton, C.	$4.25	4.5	6.0	6.5	7.0	8.0	$136.00
11	Connelly, B.	$4.75	6.0	7.5	3.0	8.0	7.0	$149.63
12	Fritz, J.	$5.50	5.0	8.0	6.0	5.0	7.5	$173.25

4) SAVE IVY PAYROLL AND CLOSE THE SPREADSHEET

10.3 Using Text in Functions

Text can be used in some functions. Like a label, text can contain letters and numbers. However, the entire label must be enclosed in quotation marks ("). Of the functions discussed so far, the IF function is the only one that can use text. For example, the following formula is valid in Works:

=IF(B3>=70,"Above average","Below average")

This formula displays Above average if the value in cell B3 is greater than or equal to 70. Otherwise, Below average is displayed.

The cell name of a cell storing a label can also be used in the IF function. For example, suppose Above average was stored in cell C1, and Below average in cell C2. The following formula will produce the same result as the formula above:

=IF(B3>=70,C1,C2)

 An Introduction to Computing Using Microsoft Works

Text can also be used in the comparison part of the IF function. When compared, the alphabetical order of the text is determined. For example, the following formula displays True because apple comes before orange alphabetically:

=IF("apple"<"orange","True","False")

Cells that store labels can also be compared. If apple was stored in cell B3, and orange stored in cell B5, the formula =IF(B3<B5,B3,B5) displays apple.

Practice 3

In this Practice the Grades spreadsheet created in Chapter Eight will be modified to determine a student's status and display the appropriate label. Start Works if you have not already done so.

1) OPEN GRADES

2) ENTER A LABEL AND FORMAT IT

    a. Move the cell cursor to cell G1.
    b. Enter the label: Status
    c. Format the label as right aligned and bold.

3) ENTER FORMULA TO DETERMINE A STUDENT'S STATUS

    a. Select cell G3.
    b. Enter the formula: =IF(F3>=70,"Passing","Failing")
       Since the value in cell F3 is less than 70, Failing is displayed in cell G3.
    c. Right align the label displayed in cell G3.

4) COPY THE FORMULA TO CELLS G4 THROUGH G8

    a. Highlight cells G3 to G8.
    b. From the Edit menu, select Fill Down.
    c. Click anywhere in the spreadsheet to remove the highlight.

<u>Check</u> - Your spreadsheet should be similar to:

	A	B	C	D	E	F	G
1	Name	Test 1	Test 2	Test 3	Test 4	Student Average	Status
2		9/12/97	10/17/97	11/14/97	12/12/97		
3	C. Browser	50	82	68	64	66.0	Failing
4	D. Warheit	86	89	78	88	85.3	Passing
5	M. Porter	78	100	90	89	89.3	Passing
6	B. Presley	45	78	66	78	66.8	Failing
7	D. Unwalla	66	76	78	55	68.8	Failing
8	T. Hogan	85	74	83	66	77.0	Passing
9	Test Average:	68.33	83.17	77.17	73.33		

5) SAVE GRADES AND CLOSE THE SPREADSHEET

10.4 CHOOSE

The IF function can be used to create a formula that displays one value if a comparison is true, and another value if the comparison is false. Sometimes it is necessary to select one value from a list of many values. The CHOOSE function can be used to do this.

CHOOSE has the form

$$=CHOOSE(<choice>, <option_0>, <option_1>, ..., <option_N>)$$

where <choice> is a number between 0 and N. CHOOSE displays the value in the list which corresponds to <choice>. If <choice> is 0, CHOOSE displays <option$_0$>, if it is 1 then <option$_1$> is displayed, and so on. For example, given the formula

$$=CHOOSE(A1,10,15,20,25)$$

10 is displayed if the value stored in cell A1 is 0, 15 if the value stored in A1 is 1, 20 if the value is 2, and 25 if it is 3. If <choice> is less than 0 or greater than N (the number of possible values) ERR is displayed, meaning that a corresponding value is not available.

Only the integer portion of <choice> is used to determine which value to display. For example, if A1 stores 1.6, 15 is displayed because only the integer portion of the value, 1, is used. The options (<option$_0$>, <option$_1$>, etc.) in the CHOOSE function can be values, formulas, cell names, or text.

Practice 4

In this Practice you will modify the IVY PAYROLL spreadsheet to include a retirement deduction which allows employees to contribute different percentages of their salaries. This will be calculated using the CHOOSE function. Start Works if you have not already done so.

1) OPEN IVY PAYROLL

2) INSERT COLUMNS TO CALCULATE RETIREMENT CONTRIBUTION

   a. Select column I by clicking on its column letter.
   b. From the Insert menu, select Insert Column. A new column is inserted. Repeat this procedure to insert a second new column. Taxes is now column K.

3) ENTER TITLES

   a. Select cell I5.
   b. Enter the title: Retire Code
   c. In cell J5, enter the title: Retirement
   d. Bold and right align cells I5 and J5. Adjust the column widths as necessary.

4) ENTER THE RETIREMENT CODES

There are five retirement codes numbered 0 through 4 which determine the percentage of gross pay that will be deducted for each employee. Enter the following numbers into column I as indicated:

Cell	Code	Cell	Code	Cell	Code
I6	1	I15	3	I24	1
I7	2	I16	1	I25	2
I8	0	I17	0	I26	0
I9	3	I18	2	I27	3
I10	1	I19	1	I28	2
I11	1	I20	0	I29	1
I12	4	I21	4	I30	1
I13	2	I22	1	I31	4
I14	2	I23	3	I32	0

5) ENTER THE FORMULA TO CALCULATE RETIREMENTS

Each of the codes above corresponds to the following percentages which are used to calculate the retirement deduction:

Code	Percentage
0	0%
1	3%
2	5%
3	8%
4	10%

a. In cell J6, enter the formula: =CHOOSE(I6,0,H6*3%,H6*5%,H6*8%,H6*10%)
   The CHOOSE function first looks in cell I6 which contains the retirement code 1 to determine the value of <choice>. Because the value in cell I6 corresponds to <option$_1$> in the CHOOSE function, Works multiplies the gross pay in cell H6, $192.00, by 0.03 to compute the retirement deduction. Cell J6 displays 5.76, the result of the calculation.
b. Format cell J6 as currency with two decimal places.
c. Highlight cells J6 through J32.
d. From the Edit menu, select Fill Down to copy the formula.

6) RECALCULATE THE NET PAY

a. Select cell M6.
b. Edit the existing formula so that the cell stores the formula =H6–J6–K6–L6
   The amount of $154.56 is displayed. Net pay is now computed by subtracting taxes, social security, and retirement from the gross pay.
c. Highlight cells M6 to M32. From the Edit menu, select Fill Down to copy the formula.
d. Click anywhere in the spreadsheet to remove the highlight.

7) SAVE IVY PAYROLL

Check - Your spreadsheet should be similar to:

	H	I	J	K	L	M
5	Gross Pay	Retire Code	Retirement	Taxes	Soc. Sec.	Net Pay
6	$192.00	1	$5.76	$19.20	$12.48	$154.56
7	$214.50	2	$10.73	$21.45	$13.94	$168.38
8	$153.00	0	$0.00	$15.30	$9.95	$127.76
9	$130.50	3	$10.44	$13.05	$8.48	$98.53
10	$136.00	1	$4.08	$13.60	$8.84	$109.48
11	$149.63	1	$4.49	$14.96	$9.73	$120.45
12	$173.25	4	$17.33	$17.33	$11.26	$127.34

10.5 VLOOKUP

VLOOKUP is a function similar to CHOOSE except that the values to be displayed are stored in cells in the spreadsheet, not listed in the function itself. This is an advantage because the values used are always displayed and can be included in spreadsheet printouts. In addition, the values are easily changed by modifying only the VLOOKUP table.

VLOOKUP has the form

=VLOOKUP(<value>, <range>, <columns>)

where <value> is a number and <range> is the cell range where the VLOOKUP table is stored. VLOOKUP finds the largest number in the first column of <range> which is less than or equal to <value>, and then displays the number stored in the cell <columns> column over. The value of <columns> is usually 1 to indicate that the next column of <range> stores the values to be displayed. This is similar to the manual operation of looking up a value in a two column table: the desired data is searched for in the first column, then the value read from the second column.

As an example, consider the following spreadsheet fragment:

C2		=VLOOKUP(B2,$A$8:$B$11,1)

Jockey Salary

	A	B	C
1	Jockey	Number of Wins	Salary per Race
2	Sam	105	$200.00
3	Rhonda	38	$75.00
4	Franklin	77	$125.00
5			
6			
7	Salary Based on Wins		
8	0	$75.00	
9	50	$125.00	
10	100	$200.00	
11	200	$250.00	

With the formula =VLOOKUP(B2,$A$8:$B$11,1) in cell C2, Works looks in cell B2 for its value, which is 105. Works then looks in the first column of the <range> for the largest value which is less than or equal to 105, in this case 100 (stored in A10). The value in the cell one column over, in this case cell B10, is then displayed in cell C2. Since the value of B10 is $200.00, then $200.00 is displayed in C2. In a similar manner, the function displays $75.00 in cell C3 because cell A8 stores the largest value in <range> which is less than or equal to 38 (the value in B3).

The values in the first column of the <range> must be in ascending order for VLOOKUP to work correctly. If the <value> is less than the first value stored in <range>, ERR is displayed. For this reason it is important to make the first value stored in <range> less than any value that will be looked up. VLOOKUP differs from CHOOSE in that the <value> can be negative or zero as long as it falls within the values stored in <range>.

In the VLOOKUP function, absolute references should be used to define <range> so that the table cell references do not change if the formula containing the VLOOKUP is copied.

VLOOKUP is used in a spreadsheet when a table of information is needed to make calculations. An example of this is when a business needs to calculate tax deductions for the payroll. If tax deduction rates are based on gross pays using the following parameters

Gross Pay	Tax Rate
under $100	0%
$100-$299	8%
$300-$499	10%
$500-up	12%

the VLOOKUP table is created by first determining what the contents of the table must be in order to work with a VLOOKUP function. The table is then entered in an existing spreadsheet, and the necessary VLOOKUP function is placed in an appropriate formula:

C2		=B2*VLOOKUP(B2,$B$8:$C$11,1)		

Employee Taxes

	A	B	C	D
1	Employee	Gross Pay	Taxes	
2	Brown, T.	$365.87	$36.59	
3	Raucher, D.	$98.30	$0.00	
4	Jefferson, P.	$499.23	$49.92	
5				
6				
7		Tax Table		
8		$0	0%	
9		$100	8%	
10		$300	10%	
11		$500	12%	

For employee Raucher whose gross pay is $98.30, $0.00 is the tax deduction because the VLOOKUP function returns 0% which is then multiplied by the value in cell B3.

10.6 Freezing Titles

A problem encountered when working with a large spreadsheet is that as you scroll, rows and columns containing labels that describe the data scroll off the screen. This makes it difficult to determine what columns or rows the displayed cells are in. Works solves this problem by enabling you to *freeze* selected rows and columns so that they cannot be scrolled.

Executing the Freeze Titles command from the Format menu designates every row above the cell cursor and every column to the left of the cell cursor as locked. Before freezing titles cell A1 must be visible for the command to work properly. For example, selecting cell B6 and executing Freeze Titles locks every cell in column A and rows 1 through 5:

	A	B	C	D
1			Ivy University	
2				
3	Soc. Sec. rate:	7%		
4				
5	Employee	Rate/Hr	Mon	Tue
6	Attis, B.	$8.00	6.0	4.0
7	Ball, R.	$5.50	9.5	12.0
8	Bickle, R.	$6.00	5.0	7.0

Locked cells are displayed with solid borders

When rows are scrolled, locked columns remain on the screen. Frozen rows remain on the screen when columns are scrolled. Selecting the Freeze Titles command again unlocks affected cells. When a spreadsheet is printed, any rows or columns with locked cells are printed on each page.

Practice 5

In this Practice IVY PAYROLL will be modified to allow for seven tax rates. Cells will be locked to keep the employee names and column titles on the screen. Start Works and open IVY PAY-ROLL if you have not already done so.

1) ADD A VLOOKUP TABLE TO THE SPREADSHEET

The following tax rates will be used in calculating taxes:

Salary	Tax Rate
under $100	0%
$100-$149	8%
$150-$199	10%
$200-$249	12%
$250-$299	17%
$300-$599	28%
$600-up	33%

a. In cell C39 enter and bold the label: Tax Table
b. Enter the following values into the indicated cells to create the tax table:

Cell	Salary	Cell	Tax Value
C40	0	D40	0%
C41	100	D41	8%
C42	150	D42	10%
C43	200	D43	12%
C44	250	D44	17%
C45	300	D45	28%
C46	600	D46	33%

c. Format cells C40 through C46 as currency with 0 decimal places.

2) FREEZE TITLES

a. Select cell B6. Be sure cell A1 is displayed on the screen as well.
b. From the Format menu, select the Freeze Titles command. Frozen cells are designated by solid borders.
c. Click on the right scroll arrow to scroll columns. Column A remains on the screen while cells not locked are scrolled off the screen.
d. Click on the down scroll arrow to scroll rows. Rows 1 through 5 remain on the screen.

3) CALCULATE TAXES USING THE VLOOKUP FUNCTION

a. In cell K6, replace the existing formula with =H6*VLOOKUP(H6,$C$40:$D$46,1)
   The gross pay stored in H6, $192.00 is multiplied by 10% to compute the tax deduction of $19.20. Dollar signs ($) are needed in the function to keep the cell references for the VLOOKUP table from changing when Fill Down is used.
b. Highlight cells K6 to K32.
c. From the Edit menu, select Fill Down. The old formulas are replaced and new calculations are performed.
d. Click anywhere in the spreadsheet to remove the highlight.

Check - The modified spreadsheet should look similar to:

| K6 | | | =H6*VLOOKUP(H6,$C$40:$D$46,1) | | | | | | | | |

IVY PAYROLL

	A	B	C	D	E	F	G	H	I	J	K
1			Ivy University Payroll								
2											
3	Soc. Sec. rate:	6.50%									
4											
5	Employee	Rate/Hr	Mon	Tue	Wed	Thu	Fri	Gross Pay	Retire Code	Retirement	Taxes
6	Attis, B.	$8.00	6.0	4.0	4.0	3.0	7.0	$192.00	1	$5.76	$19.20
7	Ball, R.	$5.50	9.5	12.0	9.0	5.5	3.0	$214.50	2	$10.73	$25.74
8	Bickle, R.	$6.00	5.0	7.0	0.5	7.0	6.0	$153.00	0	$0.00	$15.30
9	Cambell, M.	$4.50	5.0	6.0	7.0	5.0	6.0	$130.50	3	$10.44	$10.44
10	Caxton, C.	$4.25	4.5	6.0	6.5	7.0	8.0	$136.00	1	$4.08	$10.88
11	Connelly, B.	$4.75	6.0	7.5	3.0	8.0	7.0	$149.63	1	$4.49	$11.97
12	Fritz, J.	$5.50	5.0	8.0	6.0	5.0	7.5	$173.25	4	$17.33	$17.33
13	Gilman, J.	$7.00	8.0	7.8	8.0	8.0	3.5	$247.10	2	$12.36	$29.65
14	Graham, T.	$4.45	8.0	7.0	6.0	7.0	7.5	$157.98	2	$7.90	$15.80

4) SAVE AND CLOSE IVY PAYROLL

a. Save IVY PAYROLL and print a copy.
b. Deselect Freeze Titles from the Format menu.
c. Save and then close IVY PAYROLL.

10.7 Using Text in CHOOSE and VLOOKUP

As with the IF function, text can be used in the CHOOSE and VLOOKUP functions. The actual text enclosed in quotation marks or a cell name which stores a label can be used. The following formula includes a CHOOSE function which uses text:

=CHOOSE(C3,"Freshman","Sophomore","Junior","Senior")

In this function, the word Freshman is displayed if the value stored in cell C3 is 0. If C3 stores the value 1 then Sophomore is displayed, etc.

The VLOOKUP function can be used to display text by storing labels in the range. As an example, examine the following spreadsheet fragment:

| C2 | | =VLOOKUP(B2,$B$8:$C$10,1) | |

Student Status

	A	B	C	D
1	Student	GPA	Status	
2	Jones, H.	3.8	Dean's List	
3	Gruvnurt, L.	1.2	Probation	
4	Werner, S.	2.9	OK	
5				
6				
7		Student Status		
8		0.0	Probation	
9		2.0	OK	
10		3.6	Dean's List	

The formula =VLOOKUP(B2,$B$8:$C$10,1) in cell C2 displays Dean's List because cell B10 stores the largest value in <range> less than or equal to the value in cell B2 (which is 3.8).

Practice 6

In this Practice the Grades spreadsheet will be modified to display each student's letter grade. Start Works if you have not already done so.

1) OPEN THE GRADES SPREADSHEET

2) ENTER AND FORMAT A LABEL

    a. Select cell H1. Enter the label: Grade
    b. Center align and bold the label.

3) ADD A VLOOKUP TABLE

    a. In cell B12, enter and bold the label: Letter Grade Table
    b. Enter the following data into the indicated cells to create the grade table:

Cell	Score	Cell	Grade
B13	0	C13	F
B14	60	C14	D
B15	70	C15	C
B16	80	C16	B
B17	90	C17	A

Note that the scores in the grade table must be in ascending order for the VLOOKUP function to work properly.

4) ENTER A FORMULA TO DETERMINE A STUDENT'S GRADE

    a. Select cell H3.
    b. Enter the formula =VLOOKUP(F3,$B$13:$C$17,1)
    Since the value in cell F3 is less than 70, but greater than 60, D is displayed in cell H3.
    c. Center align the grade in cell H3.

5) COPY THE FORMULA TO CELLS H4 THROUGH H8

    a. Highlight cells H3 to H8.
    b. Use the Fill Down command to copy the formula to the highlighted cells.
    c. Click anywhere in the spreadsheet to remove the highlight.

Check - Your spreadsheet should be similar to:

	F	G	H
	Student Average	Status	Grade
1			
3	66.0	Failing	D
4	85.3	Passing	B
5	89.3	Passing	B
6	66.8	Failing	D
7	68.8	Failing	D
8	77.0	Passing	C

H3 =VLOOKUP(F3,$B$13:$C$17,1)

6) CHANGE C. BOWSER'S SCORE ON TEST 1

C. Bowser has taken a makeup test that replaces Test 4. Select cell E3 and enter 90, the new score. Works automatically recalculates any formulas that refer to the cell containing the test score. Note how C. Bowser's average has been recalculated, the status has changed to Passing, and the grade is now a C. This example demonstrates the computing power of the spreadsheet.

7) SAVE, PRINT, AND CLOSE GRADES

a. From the File menu, select Page Setup. The Page Setup dialog box is displayed.
b. Select the Source, Size & Orientation tab and then select the Landscape option.
c. Select OK.
d. Save Grades, print a copy, and then close Grades.

10.8 Amortization Tables

One of the most useful applications of a spreadsheet is an amortization table. *Amortization* is a method for computing equal periodic payments for a loan such as in an *installment loan*. Car loans and mortgages are often installment loans. Each installment, or payment, is the same and consists of two parts: a portion to pay interest due on the principal for that period and the remainder which goes to reducing the principal. The *principal* is the amount of money owed which decreases with each payment made.

An *amortization table* displays the interest and principal amounts for each payment of an installment loan. For example, the monthly payment on a 30 year loan of $100,000 borrowed at 12% interest (1% per month) is $1,028.61. In the first payment, $1,000.00 pays the interest due (1%×100000) and $28.61 goes to reduce principal (1028.61–1000). In the next payment, $999.71 pays the interest due and $28.90 goes to reduce principal. As payments are made, the interest due decreases because there is less principal to charge interest on. In the final payment, $10.18 pays the interest due and $1,018.43 pays off the principal.

The PMT function is used to calculate the periodic payment for an installment loan. The interest rate, the number of payments to be made, and the amount of the loan (principal) are needed by the PMT function. A formula using the PMT function takes the form

=PMT(<present value>, <rate>, <term>)

where <present value> is the amount to be paid back, <rate> is the interest rate per period, and <term> is the number of payments to be made. As an example, if you borrow $100,000 to purchase a house at an interest rate of 12% for 30 years to be repaid monthly, the formula would be:

=PMT(100000, 12%/12, 360)

Since the payments are monthly, the interest rate must also be monthly. This is computed by dividing the annual rate of interest, 12%, by 12. The number of payments is 360, 30 years × 12 months. This formula computes the monthly payment as $1,028.61.

10.9 Printing a Selected Spreadsheet Area

The Set Print Area command from the Format menu is used to change the printable spreadsheet area. First, the cells to be printed must be highlighted. Next, Set Print Area is executed and OK selected in the verification dialog box. Once the print area is set, only those cells will be included in a printout. Print preview will display only the set print area as well.

To print all the cells in a spreadsheet, the entire spreadsheet must be selected and Set Print Area executed.

Practice 7

In this Practice you will complete an amortization table. Start Works if you have not already done so.

1) OPEN THE LOAN SPREADSHEET

Open LOAN. Notice that the loan information will be stored in cells that can be referenced in formulas.

2) ENTER THE LOAN'S INFORMATION

a. In cell C3, enter the principal: 100000
b. In cell C4, enter the yearly interest rate: 12%
c. In cell C5, enter the number of payments: 360 (30 years × 12 monthly payments)

3) CALCULATE THE MONTHLY PAYMENT

In cell C7, enter the formula: =PMT(C3, C4/12, C5) The division by 12 is needed to convert the yearly interest rate in cell C4 to a monthly value. $1,028.61 is displayed.

4) CALCULATE TOTAL PAID AND TOTAL INTEREST

a. In cell C9, enter the formula: =ROUND(C5*C7,2) This formula computes the total paid for the loan, including principal and interest.
b. In cell C10, enter the formula: =C9-C3 The total interest paid over 30 years is calculated.

5) ENTER THE FIRST PAYMENT DATA

a. In cell A13, enter: 1
b. In cell B13, enter: =C3
c. In cell C13, enter =B13*($C$4/12) to calculate one month's interest on the loan. $1,000.00, which is 1% (12%/12) of the principal, is displayed. The cell reference C4 contains dollar signs because the interest rate will be the same for each payment.
d. In cell D13, enter the formula =IF(C13<0.01,0,$C$7-C13) to calculate the amount of the payment which is applied to the principal, $28.61. If the value in cell C13 is less than 0.01, then 0 is displayed. This comparison must be made because it is not possible to pay less than a penny.
e. In cell E13, enter the formula =B13-D13 to calculate the new principal owed.

An Introduction to Computing Using Microsoft Works

6) ENTER FORMULAS FOR THE SECOND PAYMENT

a. In cell A14, enter the formula: =A13+1
b. To display the new principal, enter =E13 in cell B14.
c. Highlight cells C13 to E14.
d. Use Fill Down to copy the formulas in cell C13 through E13 into cells C14 through E14. This completes the data for the second payment and the principal owed, $99,942.49 is displayed in cell E14.

7) COMPLETE THE TABLE USING FILL DOWN

a. Highlight cells A14 to E372.
b. Use the Fill Down command to copy cells A14 through E14 into rows 15 through 372. Note the value in cell E372. The principal owed is $0.00 which indicates the loan has been paid in full.

Check - Your spreadsheet should be similar to:

Loan					
	A	B	C	D	E
1			Loan Amortization		
2					
3	Principal =		$100,000.00		
4	Interest rate =		12.00%		
5	No. of payments =		360		
6					
7	Monthly payment =		$1,028.61		
8					
9	Total paid =		$370,300.53		
10	Total interest =		$270,300.53		
11					
12	Payment	Principal	Pay to Interest	Pay to Principal	Principal Owed
13	1	$100,000.00	$1,000.00	$28.61	$99,971.39
14	2	$99,971.39	$999.71	$28.90	$99,942.49
15	3	$99,942.49	$999.42	$29.19	$99,913.30
16	4	$99,913.30	$999.13	$29.48	$99,883.82
17	5	$99,883.82	$998.84	$29.77	$99,854.05

8) PRINT A PORTION OF THE SPREADSHEET

a. Highlight cells A1 through E15.
b. From the Format menu, select the Set Print Area command.
c. Select OK to set the print area.
d. Print preview the spreadsheet. Note that only the cells designated as the print area are displayed.
e. Save LOAN and then print a copy with row and column headings and gridlines.
f. From the Edit menu, execute Select All.
g. From the Format menu, select Set Print Area.
h. Select OK to set the print area.

9) CREATE AN AUTO LOAN MODEL

The present values in LOAN represent a house loan. Because the data is stored in cells, it is easy to answer What If? questions. Therefore, the spreadsheet can easily represent a car loan.

a. In cell C3, enter the new principal: 10000
b. In cell C4, enter the new yearly interest: 10%

c. The car loan is a 5 year loan; therefore, the number of monthly payments will be 5 × 12. In cell C5, enter the new number of payments: 60

d. Note how the spreadsheet has been recalculated. Scroll down to row 72 which contains the last payment. The spreadsheet can easily model loans with less than 360 payments.

e. Save LOAN.

10) ENTER YOUR OWN VALUES INTO THE LOAN SPREADSHEET

a. Experiment by changing the principal and interest of the LOAN spreadsheet to any values you like. Change the number of payments to see how that affects the interest paid for the loan.

b. From the File menu, select Close. Click on No in the dialog box when prompted to save the file.

c. Exit Works.

10.10 Where can you go from here?

The last three chapters introduced you to the concepts of a spreadsheet: how one is designed, created on the computer, and used to produce calculations. The Works spreadsheet has other options not discussed in this text which you may want to explore using the online help or *The Works Companion* supplied by Microsoft.

Spreadsheets can be used to store laboratory data to produce scientific and statistical calculations as well as financial calculations. More powerful spreadsheet programs such as Excel and Lotus 1-2-3 have advanced calculating features. These spreadsheet programs have many similarities to the Works spreadsheet. Therefore, you will find it easy to learn and use them.

Chapter Summary

A spreadsheet can be used to answer What If? questions. By including factors that relate to a particular situation, a spreadsheet model can be produced which may then be used to make financial decisions.

The Sort command from the Tools menu can organize the cells in a spreadsheet in alphabetical or numerical order.

Text can be used in functions such as the IF function. For example, the formula =IF(A5<30,"Cheap","Expensive") displays Cheap if A5 is less than 30 and Expensive if A5 is greater than or equal to 30. The cell name of a cell storing a label can also be used in the IF function.

Relational operators can be used to compare text in the IF function. For example, if cell A5 contains George and B12 Andrews then the formula =IF(A5<B12,"Yes","No") displays No since George is greater than Andrews.

The CHOOSE function can select one value from a list of many. When given a choice, 0 to N, the CHOOSE function displays the appropriate option.

The VLOOKUP function selects values from a VLOOKUP table that is stored in a range of cells. When given a numeric expression, <value>, and the cell range where values are stored, <range>, VLOOKUP finds the largest number in <range> which is less than or equal to <value>. It then displays the value stored in the cell <columns> to the right. Both the CHOOSE and VLOOKUP functions can be used to display text.

Works allows rows and columns to be locked using the Freeze Titles command from the Format menu. This feature is especially useful in keeping rows and columns containing labels from scrolling off the screen.

An amortization table displays how much interest and principal make up each payment of an installment loan. The PMT function is used to calculate the periodic payments of an installment loan.

The Set Print Area command from the Format menu is used to print only a portion of a spreadsheet.

Vocabulary

Amortization - A method for computing equal periodic payments for a loan.

Amortization table - Displays the interest and principal amounts for each payment of an installment loan.

Ascending values - Increasing in value from low to high.

Descending values - Decreasing in value from high to low.

Freeze Titles command - Used to designate rows and columns so that they cannot be scrolled off the screen.

Installment loan - Loan that is repaid in a series of periodic payments.

Key sort column - Column containing the data that a sort is based on.

Model - A spreadsheet containing data relating to a particular situation.

Principal - The amount of money borrowed.

Set Print Area command - Used to designate a specific range of cells to be printed.

Sorting - Placing rows of data in a specified order.

What If? question - A question which can be answered using a model.

Reviews

10

Sections 10.1 — 10. 5

1. a) Explain what is meant by a "What If?" question.
   b) How can a spreadsheet be used to answer "What If?" questions?

2. Make a list of 5 "What If?" questions that could be answered using the IVY PAYROLL spreadsheet.

3. Explain how the data in the IVY PAYROLL spreadsheet could be sorted in ascending order based on employee per-hour pay.

4. Write formulas using the IF function for each of the following:
   a) If B3 is less than or equal to C12 display Low, if greater than display High.
   b) If A5 is equal to Z47 display Jonathan, if not equal to display Judith.
   c) If C25 is greater than D19 display Great!, otherwise display Terrible!

5. Give three situations in which the CHOOSE function could be used.

6. Write a CHOOSE function that displays 100 if cell B20 contains a value of 0, 500 if a 1, 900 if a 2, and 1200 if a 3.

7. List three situations in which a VLOOKUP table could be used.

8. The Lawrenceville Widget Company uses the following discount rates when large numbers of widgets are ordered:

Number of Widgets	Discount
100 - 149	10%
1000 - 1999	30%
2000 or over	70%

   Convert this into a VLOOKUP table and make a sketch of the table.

9. Write a formula that uses the VLOOKUP function to display the proper discount percent if cell C12 stores the number of widgets. Use the VLOOKUP table created in Review question 8.

Section 10.6 — 10.10

10. Explain the steps required to keep the row containing the labels that identify the columns in IVY PAYROLL from scrolling off the screen.

11. Write a CHOOSE function that displays Excellent if cell B20 contains a value of 0, Good if a 1, Fair if a 2, and Poor if a 3.

12. Briefly explain what an amortization table is and how it might be used.

13. a) How much interest is paid in the first month of a loan of $5,000 borrowed for 5 years at 12% per year interest?
    b) Show what PMT function is used to calculate the monthly payments on the above loan.

14. Describe the steps needed to print only the values displayed in the cell range A3:D17.

10 – 18   *An Introduction to Computing Using Microsoft Works*

10 Exercises

1. The Ivy alumni are unhappy about plans for their annual dance. Perform the following What If? questions using the Dance spreadsheet created in Chapter Nine, Exercise 1.

   a) Open Dance. The alumni have decided against using the band *The Poison Ivys*. Many of the younger alumni want the *Dreadful Greats* instead, but they will cost $3,500. Update the spreadsheet to calculate the cost per member with the new band.

   b) Many alumni want better desserts. Update the spreadsheet with the cost of desserts doubled.

   c) A group of alumni do not want to hold the dance in Ivy Hall which the University will let them use if they pay for electricity and clean up. These members want to hold the dinner dance at the Leaf County Inn which will cost $7,000. Insert a row that includes the new hotel cost and then delete the rows for Electricity and Clean up because these costs are included in the Inn's fee.

   d) Save the modified Dance and print a copy with row and column headings and gridlines.

2. The STOCK2 spreadsheet modified in Chapter Nine, Exercise 3 contains Grace van Ivy's stock portfolio information. She would like it modified to help her evaluate the portfolio.

   a) Open STOCK2. Ms. van Ivy has decided that it would be best to sell those stocks which have lost more than 30% of their original value. In column H, add the label Stock Status and make it bold and right aligned. Resize the column as necessary. Use the IF function in a formula to display Sell for stock that should be sold or Retain for stock that should be held. Be careful when creating the IF functions. Format the column so that all text is displayed and is right aligned.

   b) Grace van Ivy must pay a commission to her stockbroker when she sells stock. The commission is based on the following scale:

Number of Shares	Commission
0 - 29	5%
30 - 69	4%
70 - 99	2%
100 - 149	1%
150 and over	0.5%

   The dollar amount of the commission is calculated by multiplying the current value of the stock by the appropriate commission percent. In column I, enter the label Commission and make it bold and right aligned. In this column, use the VLOOKUP function in a formula to calculate and display the sales commission on each of Ms. van Ivy's stock. Format the values appropriately.

   c) Save the modified STOCK2 and print a copy with row and column headings and gridlines.

3. Fantasy Wheels Used Cars would like to have the Cars spreadsheet created in Chapter Nine, Exercise 4 modified to determine the markup of its cars based on each car's condition.

a) Open Cars. A rating system of 0 to 4 will be used. The rating for each car is:

Rating	Cars
0	Studebaker, Thunderbird, Delorean, Bricklin
1	Mustang, Jaguar, Honda, Jeep
2	Ferarri, Aston-Martin, Triumph, GTO
3	Bel Aire, Rolls Royce, Cadillac
4	Porsche, Bentley, all other makes

In column H, enter the label Rating. Format the label as right aligned and bold. Enter each car's rating as listed above. Decrease the column width.

b) The percent (%) markup for each rating is as follows:

Rating	Markup
0	10%
1	20%
2	35%
3	50%
4	75%

In column I, enter the label Rating Markup. Format the label as right aligned and bold. Widen the column to accommodate the label. Use a formula that includes the CHOOSE function to compute the price of each car after its markup based on the price paid. Format the column appropriately.

c) Save the modified Cars spreadsheet and print a copy with row and column headings and gridlines.

4. Mike Entrepreneur wants to ask What If? questions about raising his prices for his lawn service. This can be done by modifying the Lawns spreadsheet created in Chapter Nine, Exercise 5.

a) Open Lawns. Modify the spreadsheet so that only one entry needs to be changed to raise the price per square meter. Make any necessary changes to formulas that use this value. Determine what happens to his total profits when he doubles and triples his price per square meter.

b) Mike's customers with large lawns are complaining bitterly about his prices. In response to the complaints he has decided that all customers with lawns of less than 1,500 square meters will pay $0.06 per square meter and those with larger lawns will pay $0.04 per square meter. Modify the spreadsheet so that there is one charge for lawns greater than 1,500 square meters and another charge for lawns with an area under 1,500 square meters. Use an IF statement in a formula to calculate the price for each customer.

c) Mike must pay taxes on the price he charges so he wants the following tax information built into the Lawns spreadsheet:

Price	Tax
$0 - $14	0%
$15 - $29	5%
$30 - $39	7%
$40 - $49	12%
$50 - $59	15%
$60 and above	30%

Add a column titled Taxes that displays the taxes Mike must pay for each of his customers. Use a VLOOKUP table to produce the calculations. Display the total and average tax amounts as well. Format appropriately.

d) Save the modified Lawns and print a copy with row and column headings and gridlines.

5. Mr. Hernandez, owner of the Aztec Café is planning to give his employees a bonus based on their position. He would like to use the AC Employees spreadsheet modified in Chapter Nine, Exercise 2 to compute the bonuses.

a) Open AC Employees and insert a new column after the column that stores the employee names. In the new column enter the label Position. Format the label as bold. D. Romani and D. Roberts are managers. The other employees are servers. Enter the employee positions into the new column. Right align all the positions and label. Format the column widths appropriately.

b) In column P enter the label Bonus. Format the label as right aligned and bold. Mr. Hernandez wants to give managers a bonus of 10% of their gross pay and servers 5% of their gross pay. Use the IF function in a formula to compute the bonuses.

c) Save the modified AC Employees and print a copy with row and column headings and gridlines.

6. Anna Silver needs to borrow $10,000 to purchase a car and would like to ask What If? about different car loans.

a) Open LOAN2 which contains the formulas to compute the monthly payment, total paid, and total interest of an amortized loan. Enter 10000 as the principal in cell B3, 8% as the interest in cell B4, and 48 as the number of payments in cell B5.

b) Copy cells B3 through B10 into columns C, D, and E. Change the interest rate in column B to 7%, column C to 8%, column D to 9%, and column E to 10%.

c) Create a bar chart that shows the monthly payment at different interest rates.

d) Save the modified LOAN2 and print the chart. Print the spreadsheet with row and column headings and gridlines.

10

An Introduction to Computing Using Microsoft Works

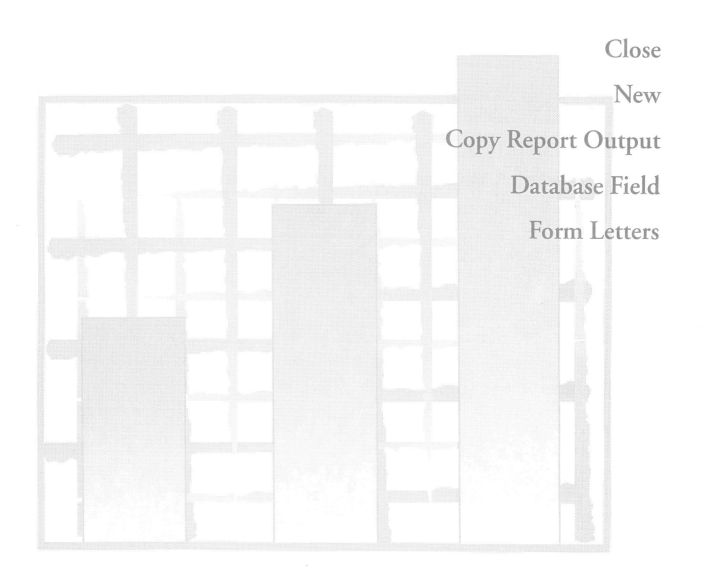

Chapter Eleven

Integrating the Word Processor, Database, and Spreadsheet

Close

New

Copy Report Output

Database Field

Form Letters

Objectives

After completing this chapter you will be able to:

1. Open multiple files and switch between them.

2. Work with multiple windows.

3. Copy text between word processor files.

4. Copy data between spreadsheet files.

5. Copy data between database files.

6. Integrate database and spreadsheet data with a word processor document.

7. Copy data between the database and spreadsheet.

8. Copy data into a new file.

9. Use the word processor to create a mail merge document for use with the database.

10. Copy charts and reports into a word processor file.

11

Works is an *integrated* software package. This means that the word processor, database, and spreadsheet can be used by running one program. There are two important reasons for using integrated packages: data can be copied between applications and it is easy to learn and use each application because they have similar commands. For example, the Save command from the File menu always saves the current file whether you are using the word processor, database, or spreadsheet. Copying data between applications is discussed in this chapter.

11.1 Using Multiple Windows

Works allows many files to be open at the same time. This can include any combination of word processor, database, and spreadsheet files, but the number of files that can be open may be limited by the amount of memory your computer has available.

To open a file, the Open command is executed, the file highlighted in the displayed dialog box, and OK selected. The Open command can then be used again to open a second file. Each file is placed in its own *window*, which is the area on the screen displaying the file. Works displays a list of the open files in the Window menu:

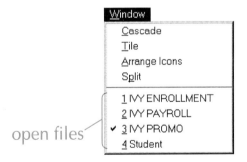

open files

The Window menu displays the names of all open files

The *active file* is designated by a check mark and is the one currently displayed on the screen, usually with a highlighted Title bar. When a file is selected from the Window menu, Works automatically switches to the proper application and displays that file making it active.

There are many reasons for switching between files. For example, you may be writing a letter in the word processor and wish to refer to some figures stored in a spreadsheet. With both files open, you could use the Window menu to switch to the spreadsheet, view the figures, and then switch back to the word processor letter. Another reason is to copy data between applications as described later in this chapter.

Works maintains the current status of each open file in that file's window. This includes any changes made, the position of the cursor, and any options set. For example, a database can be displayed in Form view in one window, and another database displayed in List view in its window. This makes it possible to work with one file, switch to another, and return to the first file, picking up exactly where you left off.

An open file does not have to be saved until you have finished working with it. However, it is a good idea to save modified files from time to time as a precaution. Selecting the Save command from the File menu saves only the active file.

Practice 1

In this Practice you will open several Ivy University files and switch between them.

1) START WORKS

    a. Start Works. The Works Task Launcher dialog box is displayed.
    b. Click on Cancel to remove the dialog box.

2) OPEN THREE FILES

    a. Open IVY CONGRAT. The IVY CONGRAT word processor file is placed in a window and the word processor screen displayed.
    b. Open IVY STUDENT. The IVY STUDENT database is placed in a second window and the database screen displayed. IVY CONGRAT is still open, but may be obscured by the second window.
    c. Open IVY PAYROLL. The IVY PAYROLL spreadsheet is placed in a third window.
    d. Select cell A5.

3) SWITCH TO THE IVY STUDENT DATABASE

    a. Display the Window menu. There are three open files listed at the bottom of the menu. Note the active file (IVY PAYROLL) is denoted by a check mark.
    b. From the Window menu, select IVY STUDENT. The database screen is displayed with the IVY STUDENT window.

4) SWITCH TO THE IVY CONGRAT DOCUMENT AND BACK TO IVY PAYROLL

    a. From the Window menu, select IVY CONGRAT. The word processor screen is displayed with the IVY CONGRAT window.
    b. From the Window menu, select IVY PAYROLL. The spreadsheet is displayed. Note that cell A5 is still selected, where it was placed in step 2 above.

11.2 Close - Removing Files from Memory

When work on an open file is complete, the file should be closed by selecting the Close command from the File menu. Closing a file frees some of the computer's memory which allows Works to perform certain operations faster. Closing windows also avoids accidental changes. When a file is closed, its window is removed from the screen, and Works automatically switches to the next open window.

If you attempt to close a file that has been edited but not saved, Works warns you before proceeding.

11.3 Displaying Multiple Windows

Each window can be resized to allow other windows to be viewed at the same time. While this is not necessary, it is sometimes helpful to see the contents of more than one file on the screen at the same time. When pointing to the corner of a window, the mouse pointer changes to a double-headed arrow indicating that the window will be resized when the corner is dragged:

Dragging the corner of a window changes its size

Dragging towards the upper left makes the window smaller. The window can then be moved to a new location by dragging its Title bar. In the Practices that follow, it is your choice whether to display more than one window on the screen at the same time or not.

11.4 Copying Data Between Applications

In previous chapters you duplicated data by first placing it on the Clipboard using the Copy command then executing Paste to place a copy of the data elsewhere in the document. This method can also be used to copy data from one file to another. When the Copy command is executed, Works places a copy of the highlighted data onto the Clipboard. Works has only one Clipboard, no matter which file is currently active. Therefore, by then making a different file active and executing the Paste command, a copy of the Clipboard contents is pasted into a different file.

11.5 Copying Text Between Word Processor Documents

The ability to copy text from one word processor document to another can save typing and can help to maintain consistency between documents.

To copy text from one word processor document to another, four steps are required:

1. Highlight the text to be copied.
2. Execute the Copy command.
3. Make the file to receive the copied text active.
4. Place the cursor where the text is to be inserted and execute the Paste command.

Copying the text simply transfers a copy of the highlighted block to the Clipboard; the original file remains unchanged. However, pasting data into the receiving file modifies that file, and before it is closed it must be saved to retain the changes.

In this Practice you will copy a paragraph from one word processor document into another. The three files IVY CONGRAT, IVY STUDENT, and IVY PAYROLL should still be open from the last Practice. We will first close IVY PAYROLL and IVY STUDENT, and then copy a paragraph from the IVY HANDBOOK document into the IVY CONGRAT letter.

1) CLOSE THE UNNEEDED FILES

    a. From the File menu, select Close to close the currently displayed file, IVY PAY-ROLL. IVY PAYROLL is closed and the previous window displayed.

    b. From the Window menu, select IVY STUDENT and then Close it. The window containing IVY CONGRAT is again displayed.

2) OPEN IVY HANDBOOK

    Open IVY HANDBOOK which contains a passage from the Ivy University student handbook that is to be copied into IVY CONGRAT. IVY HANDBOOK is placed in another window. Two word processor files are currently open.

3) COPY TEXT TO THE CLIPBOARD

    a. Move the pointer outside the Work area to the left of the paragraph which begins "One of the most...."

    b. Double-click the mouse. The entire paragraph is highlighted.

    c. From the Edit menu, select Copy. A copy of the highlighted text is placed on the Clipboard.

    d. Because IVY HANDBOOK is no longer needed, select Close from the File menu to remove it from the screen. IVY CONGRAT is now displayed.

4) PASTE THE CLIPBOARD CONTENTS INTO THE IVY CONGRAT LETTER

    a. Place the cursor at the position where the text should be inserted, the second blank line after the sentence which reads "To quote the student handbook:"

    b. From the Edit menu, select Paste. The paragraph from IVY HANDBOOK is copied from the Clipboard and placed at the current cursor position.

    c. Save IVY CONGRAT.

Check - The file should be similar to:

```
Dear·Faculty·and·Staff:¶
¶
I·am·proud·to·announce·the·Dean's·List·awards·for·this·semester.·Each·of·these·students·
should·be·congratulated·for·their·exceptional·academic·achievement.¶
¶
As·you·know,·only·students·with·an·exceptional·GPA·are·included·on·the·dean's·list.·To·
quote·the·student·handbook:¶
¶
          One·of·the·most·coveted·academic·honors·is·to·be·included·on·the·dean's·list.·To·
          qualify·for·the·dean's·list,·a·student·must·possess·a·GPA·of·at·least·3.6.¶
¶
The·following·students·are·recipients·of·this·semester's·Dean's·List·award:¶
```

5) CLOSE IVY CONGRAT

11.6 Copying Data Between Two Spreadsheets

Data can be copied from one spreadsheet to another in the same way text is copied between word processor documents. This can save you from retyping data and can be very useful when making spreadsheet models to answer What If? questions.

To copy data between two open spreadsheets, four steps are required:

1. Highlight the cells to be copied.
2. Execute the Copy command.
3. Make the spreadsheet to receive the copied data active.
4. Place the cell cursor where the data is to appear and execute the Paste command.

The pasted cells automatically include all formulas and formatting that they had in the original spreadsheet.

Copied cells can be inserted between existing cells by first making room for the new data. For example, to copy a row from one spreadsheet into the center of another you must first insert a blank row in the receiving spreadsheet. If blank space is not created in the receiving spreadsheet, the pasted data will overwrite existing data.

....

Practice 3

In this Practice you will copy a group of cells from one spreadsheet to another, adding the data for a group of new employees to the IVY PAYROLL spreadsheet. Start Works if you have not already done so.

1) PREPARE THE WINDOWS

    a. Open IVY NEW EMPLOYEE. These are four new employees who need to be added to the IVY PAYROLL spreadsheet.
    b. Open IVY PAYROLL.

2) INSERT EMPTY ROWS IN THE RECEIVING SPREADSHEET

    a. Highlight row 32 by clicking on its row number.
    b. From the Insert menu, select Insert Row. A new row is inserted above the one highlighted.
    c. Use the Insert Row command to insert 3 more rows.

3) COPY DATA TO THE CLIPBOARD

    a. From the Window menu, select IVY NEW EMPLOYEE.
    b. Highlight the four rows containing employee data, rows 2 through 5.
    c. From the Edit menu, select Copy to place a copy of the highlighted data on the Clipboard.
    d. Close IVY NEW EMPLOYEE.

4) PASTE THE CLIPBOARD CONTENTS IN THE PAYROLL SPREADSHEET

a. Select cell A32.
b. From the Edit menu, select Paste. The new employee data is copied into the empty rows.
c. The formulas need to be copied for the new employees. Highlight cells J31 through P35.
d. From the Edit menu, select Fill Down. The formulas are copied into the new rows and recalculated.

5) SORT THE EMPLOYEE DATA

a. After the insertion, the employee names are no longer in alphabetic order. Highlight rows 6 through 36.
b. From the Tools menu, select Sort. In the dialog box, select Sort to accept the default options.
c. Scroll through the data and note how the employees are now in alphabetical order.
d. Save IVY PAYROLL.

Check - The new employees inserted into the spreadsheet automatically change the payroll totals displayed at the bottom of the spreadsheet:

		M	N	O	P
38	New pay:	$6,405.66	$6,710.69	$7,015.72	
39	Raise cost:	$305.03	$610.06	$915.09	

11.7 Copying Records Between Two Databases

Records can be copied from one database to another. This can be helpful when two similar databases need the same data.

To copy records between two open databases displayed in List view, four steps are required:

1. Highlight the records to be copied.
2. Execute the Copy command.
3. Make the database to receive the copied records active.
4. Select the first field in the first empty record and execute the Paste command.

To highlight a record in List view, click on its record number. A group of records can be selected by dragging from one record number to the last in the group.

If the database has previously been sorted, it will need to be resorted after the new records are added.

When records are pasted into a database that has different fields from the original, the entries from the first field in the original file are copied to the first field in the second file and so on, regardless of the field names or field types. However, if fields of different types are copied, the field type of the pasted field is used. If there are not enough fields in the receiving database Works will ask if fields should be added to make room for the new fields.

An Introduction to Computing Using Microsoft Works

Practice 4

In this Practice you will transfer records between two database files. Start Works if you have not already done so.

1) PREPARE THE WINDOWS

   a. Close any open files.
   b. Open IVY STUDENT and display it in List view if it is not already in List view.
   c. Open IVY NEW STUDENT. It should already be displayed in List view.

2) HIGHLIGHT THE RECORDS TO BE COPIED

We want to copy all of the records in IVY NEW STUDENT. Drag from record number 1 to record number 3.

3) COPY THE HIGHLIGHTED RECORDS TO THE IVY STUDENT DATABASE

   a. From the Edit menu, select Copy.
   b. Close IVY NEW STUDENT. IVY STUDENT is again displayed.
   c. Scroll down so that the last record is visible. Click in the first blank Student ID field after the last record in the database.
   d. From the Edit menu, select Paste. The new records are added to IVY STUDENT.
   e. Sort the database in ascending order on the Last Name field. The records are order by last name.
   f. Save IVY STUDENT.

11.8 Copying Spreadsheet Data into a Word Processor Document

Businesses sometimes send memos or letters that contain the data from a spreadsheet. Works allows you to copy spreadsheet data into a word processor document.

When copying spreadsheet data to a word processor document the spreadsheet must remain open until after the cells have been pasted. To copy cells from an open spreadsheet to an open word processor document, four steps are required:

1. Highlight the spreadsheet cells to be copied.
2. Execute the Copy command.
3. Make the word processor document active.
4. Place the cursor where the data is to be inserted and execute the Paste command.

Cells copied into a word processor document are automatically placed in a *spreadsheet frame*:

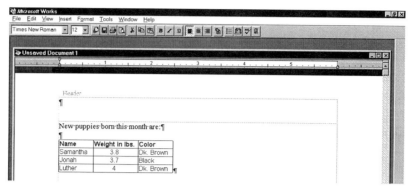

When spreadsheet cells are pasted into a word processor document, they are displayed in a spreadsheet frame

A spreadsheet frame may be selected by clicking on it once. A selected frame displays handles similar to a clip art object (discussed in Chapter Four). Double-clicking on a spreadsheet frame activates it for editing:

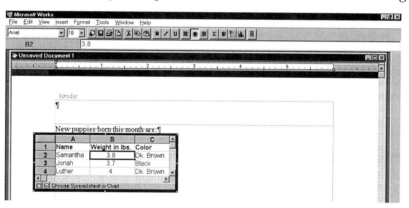

An activated spreadsheet frame shows row numbers and column letters

When a frame has been activated, an Entry bar is displayed and the menus at the top of the screen change to those for the spreadsheet. Data can be entered, edited, etc. in an active spreadsheet frame. Clicking anywhere in the document deactivates the frame and the word processor screen is again shown.

After a spreadsheet frame has been edited, it may be necessary to resize the frame to better display its data. Dragging the handle of a selected spreadsheet frame changes its size.

Practice 5

In this Practice, you will copy part of a spreadsheet into a word processor document. Start Works if you have not already done so.

1) PREPARE THE WINDOWS

    a. Close any open files.
    b. Open the IVY CONGRAT word processor file.
    c. Open Grades. (You created the Grades spreadsheet in the Practices of Chapter Eight.)

An Introduction to Computing Using Microsoft Works

2) COPY THE CELLS TO THE CLIPBOARD

    a. In Grades, highlight cells A1 through E9.

    b. From the Edit menu, select Copy.

    c. From the Window menu, select IVY CONGRAT.

3) PASTE THE CELLS INTO THE DOCUMENT

    a. Move the cursor to the second blank line after the paragraph which begins "Dr. Sulfuric's Chemistry class…."

    b. From the Edit menu, select Paste. The Clipboard contents, the cells from Grades, are placed at the current cursor position. Note how the data is displayed in cells.

4) EDIT AND RESIZE THE SPREADSHEET FRAME

    a. Double-click on the spreadsheet frame to activate it. Row number, column letters, an Entry bar, and spreadsheet menus are displayed.

    b. Select cell B6. Change B. Presley's test score to 100. Note how the test average in row 9 has automatically been recalculated.

    c. Click anywhere in the word processor document to deactivate the spreadsheet frame. Note the handles displayed indicating the frame is selected.

    d. Dr. Sulfuric does not want the text scores for Test 4 shown. Drag the right middle handle of the spreadsheet frame until the scores for Test 4 are no longer displayed.

    e. Save IVY CONGRAT.

Check - Your document should be similar to:

Dr. Sulfuric's Chemistry class once again led the school in highest percentage of dean's list students. Here is a selection from her grade book showing the extraordinary performance of her students:¶

¶

Name	Test 1	Test 2	Test 3
	9/12/97	10/17/97	11/14/97
C. Browser	50	82	68
D. Warheit	86	89	78
M. Porter	78	100	90
B. Presley	100	78	66
D. Unwalla	66	76	78
T. Hogan	85	74	83
Test Average:	77.5	83.17	77.17

¶

Sincerely,¶

¶

Dean Worthington¶

5) CLOSE GRADES

11.9 Copying Database Records into a Word Processor Document

Businesses sometimes include data from databases in letters and memos. Works allows records from a database to be copied into a word processor document.

To copy data from an open database in List view into an open word processor document, four steps are required:

1. Highlight the records or fields to be copied.
2. Execute the Copy command.
3. Make the word processor document active.
4. Place the cursor where the data is to be inserted and execute the Paste command.

List view is useful when copying records because it allows more than one record to be highlighted. Also, only highlighted fields of a record are copied, so the entire record does not have to be selected.

The fields copied into a word processor document are automatically separated by tabs. Tab stops can be set to better align the data.

Practice 6

In this Practice you will copy selected fields from a database into a word processor document. A report will be displayed to limit the number of records and fields. Start Works if you have not already done so.

1) PREPARE THE WINDOWS

IVY CONGRAT should still be displayed from the last Practice. Open IVY STUDENT.

2) APPLY A FILTER

From the Record menu, point to Apply Filter and then select GPA >= 3.6. Only records for students with a GPA greater than or equal to 3.6 are displayed.

3) COPY THE DATA TO THE CLIPBOARD

a. Drag from the First Name entry of record number 1 to the Last Name entry of the last record displayed. Only the first and last name entries for the displayed records are highlighted.
b. From the Edit menu, select Copy.
c. Close IVY STUDENT. Select No when asked to save changes.

4) PASTE THE DATA INTO IVY CONGRAT

a. IVY CONGRAT should already be displayed.
b. Move the cursor to the second blank line after the paragraph which begins "The following students are recipients...."

An Introduction to Computing Using Microsoft Works

c. From the Edit menu, select Paste. The records from the Clipboard have been inserted into the word processor document. Note how tabs are used to separate the fields.

d. Highlight the table of database records and set the following tab stops: left aligned at 2 inches and left aligned at 3 inches. Be sure to clear any preexisting tabs.

<u>Check</u> - Your document should be similar to:

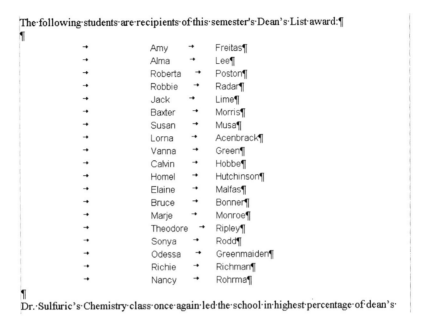

The·following·students·are·recipients·of·this·semester's·Dean's·List·award:¶

	Amy	Freitas¶
	Alma	Lee¶
	Roberta	Poston¶
	Robbie	Radar¶
	Jack	Lime¶
	Baxter	Morris¶
	Susan	Musa¶
	Lorna	Acenbrack¶
	Vanna	Green¶
	Calvin	Hobbe¶
	Homel	Hutchinson¶
	Elaine	Malfas¶
	Bruce	Bonner¶
	Marje	Monroe¶
	Theodore	Ripley¶
	Sonya	Rodd¶
	Odessa	Greenmaiden¶
	Richie	Richman¶
	Nancy	Rohrma¶

¶
Dr.·Sulfuric's·Chemistry·class·once·again·led·the·school·in·highest·percentage·of·dean's·

5) SAVE IVY CONGRAT AND PRINT A COPY

11.10 Copying Data Between the Database and Spreadsheet

What If? questions can be performed on the data in a database by copying fields into a spreadsheet model. In addition, spreadsheet data can be copied into a database so that reports can be generated.

To copy data between an open spreadsheet and an open database in List view, four steps are required:

Edit	
Undo Typing	Ctrl+Z
Cut	Ctrl+X
Copy	Ctrl+C
Paste	Ctrl+V
Paste Special...	
Clear	

1. Highlight the data to be copied.
2. Execute the Copy command.
3. Make the receiving document active.
4. Place the cursor where the data is to appear and execute the Paste command.

When records are copied from a database into a spreadsheet, each record is placed in a row with each column corresponding to a field, similar to a database in List view. This means that entries in the first field are placed in the first column, the entries in the second field in the second column, and so on.

When cells are copied from a spreadsheet into a database, the data in the first column of cells is copied to the first field, the second column to the second field, and so on. However, formulas are not copied—only the values of each cell.

11.11 Copying Data into a New File

So far, we have used the Copy command to copy data into a previously created file. Copy can also be used to transfer data to a new file by creating a new file and then pasting the Clipboard contents into it. For example, to create a new spreadsheet from a database file, four steps are required:

1. Highlight the records to be copied.
2. Execute the Copy command.
3. Execute the New command to create a new, empty spreadsheet.
4. Place the cursor where the data is to be inserted and execute the Paste command.

A new database can be created from a spreadsheet in a similar manner. However, the new database must have fields of the appropriate types for each column of data copied.

Practice 7

In this Practice you will create a new spreadsheet named Books using the information from the IVY BOOKSTORE database. Start Works if you have not already done so.

1) PREPARE THE WINDOWS

    a. Close any open files.
    b. Open IVY BOOKSTORE. Display the database in List view if it is not already in List view.

2) COPY THE RECORDS TO THE CLIPBOARD

    a. Highlight all the records in the database.
    b. From the Edit menu, select Copy.

3) PASTE THE RECORDS INTO THE NEW SPREADSHEET

    a. From the File menu, select New.
    b. Select the Works Tools tab and then select the Spreadsheet button. A new, empty spreadsheet is displayed.
    c. Select cell A2. From the Edit menu, select Paste. The records from IVY BOOKSTORE are copied starting at the current cursor position, each field in a separate column.
    d. Click anywhere to remove the highlight.

4) FORMAT THE NEW SPREADSHEET

    a. Widen columns A and B until all data is completely visible.
    b. Add appropriate titles for each of the columns storing data. Bold the titles and format the titles in columns C, D, and E as right aligned.

An Introduction to Computing Using Microsoft Works

5) COMPUTE THE AVERAGE PRICE OF THE ITEMS

    a. Select cell C28.
    b. Enter and bold the label: Average Price: Widen column C as necessary.
    c. Select cell D28.
    d. Enter the formula =AVG(D2:D26) to determine the average price of the items.
    e. Format cell D28 for dollars.

6) SAVE AND PRINT THE SPREADSHEET

Save the new spreadsheet naming it Books and print a copy with gridlines and row and column headers.

11.12 Copying a Chart into a Word Processor Document

Businesses sometimes include charts of data in letters and memos. Works allows you to paste spreadsheet charts into a word processor document.

To copy a chart from an open spreadsheet into an open word processor document, four steps are required:

1. Display the chart to be copied.
2. Execute the Copy command.
3. Make the word processor document active.
4. Place the cursor where the chart is to be inserted and execute the Paste command.

A chart in a word processor document is much like a clip art object. Clicking on the pasted chart selects it and displays handles for resizing. Paragraph alignment, indents, tabs, and tab stops can be used to position the chart in a document.

Practice 8

In this Practice you will insert a chart into a word processor document. Start Works if you have not already done so.

1) PREPARE THE WINDOWS

    a. Close any open files.
    b. Open IVY REPORT.
    c. Open IVY ENROLLMENT.

2) COPY THE CHART TO THE CLIPBOARD

    a. Display the Enrollment chart created in Chapter Nine.
    b. From the Edit menu, select Copy.

3) PASTE THE CHART INTO THE LETTER

    a. From the Window menu, select IVY REPORT.
    b. Place the cursor in the second blank line after the paragraph that begins "Proof of our continuing...."
    c. From the Edit menu, select Paste. The chart is placed at the cursor position.

4) CENTER THE CHART

The cursor should be just to the right of the chart, in the same paragraph as the chart. On the Tool bar, click on the Center Align button. The chart is centered.

5) RESIZE THE CHART

a. Move the I-Beam pointer so that it is in the middle of the chart and then click once. The chart is selected as indicated by handles.
b. Scroll down if necessary to display the handle in the lower-right corner of the chart. Drag this handle upward and to the left until the chart's size is reduced a lot.

6) SAVE AND THEN PRINT IVY REPORT

11.13 Copying a Report into a Word Processor Document

Database reports can be copied and then pasted into a word processor document. This allows more flexibility in formatting a report.

To copy a report from an open database into an open word processor document, four steps are required:

1. Display the report definition of the report to be copied.
2. Execute the Copy Report Output command from the Edit menu.
3. Make the word processor document active.
4. Place the cursor where the report is to be inserted and execute the Paste command.

Report output is automatically separated by tabs. Tab stops can be set to better align the data and other formatting applied.

. . . .

Practice 9

In this Practice you will insert a report into a word processor document. Start Works if you have not already done so.

1) PREPARE THE WINDOWS

a. Close IVY ENROLLMENT if it is still open.
b. IVY REPORT should already be open.
c. Open IVY DONATION.

2) COPY THE REPORT TO THE CLIPBOARD

a. Display the Donations report definition.
b. From the Edit menu, select the Copy Report Output command.

3) PASTE THE REPORT INTO THE LETTER

    a. From the Window menu, select IVY REPORT.
    b. Place the cursor in the second blank line after "…over the past year:"
    c. From the Edit menu, select Paste. The report is placed at the current cursor position. Note that tabs are used to separate the information.

4) PRINT IVY REPORT

    a. Print preview IVY REPORT. Note the number of pages required. Select Cancel to return to the word processor screen.
    b. If more than one page is required, resize the chart so that it is smaller.
    c. Continue previewing IVY REPORT and reducing the chart size until IVY REPORT fits on one page.
    d. Save IVY REPORT, print the letter, and close the file.

11.14 Mail Merge

One of the most powerful applications provided by an integrated package is the ability to use *mail merge* to create personalized *form letters*. For example, businesses sometimes send letters or advertisements in the mail that include the recipient's name throughout the letter. This is an example of a mail merged form letter.

Mail merge takes advantage of the computer's ability to integrate the information stored in a database with a word processor letter, and print the result. To create such a letter, the letter is first typed into the word processor with special markers where field entries should be inserted. Any data stored in a database can be included in the letter. When complete, executing the appropriate command prints one copy of the letter for each record in the database, printing the indicated field's data from that record in the letter.

The position of field entries in a letter is specified by inserting *field markers* into the document. Executing the Database Field command from the Insert menu displays the Insert Field dialog box:

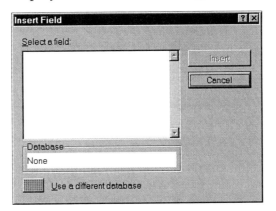

Database files are displayed in this dialog box

Selecting the Use a different database button displays the Use Database dialog box where the desired database is selected. After selecting a database, its fields are listed in the Insert Field dialog box:

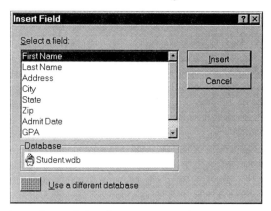

Fields for the selected database are displayed in this dialog box

Highlighting a field name and selecting the Insert button places a marker for that field in the word processor document at the current cursor position. The field marker can then be formatted in the word processor document just like any other text.

Print preview will display the merged letters. To print an unmerged document which shows the field markers, allowing you to review the placement of the fields, the Print command is executed and then the Print Merge check box deselected in the Print dialog box.

To mail merge a letter, the following steps are required:

1. The word processor document is created using the Database Field command to indicate where field entries are to appear.
2. Select the Print command.

When Print is executed, Works generates and prints a personalized copy of the word processor document for each visible record in the database. If there are 50 records visible in the database, 50 personalized documents will be printed.

Practice 10

In this Practice you will modify and print a mail merged letter. Start Works if you have not already done so.

1) PREPARE THE WINDOWS

    a. Close any open files.
    b. Open IVY TUITION.

2) INSERT A FIELD MARKER INTO THE LETTER

a. Place the cursor after the r in "Dear" and type a space.
b. From the Insert menu, select the Database Field command. The Insert Field dialog box is displayed.
c. Select the Use a different database button to display the Use Database dialog box. A list of databases is displayed.
d. Highlight Student. (If Student is not in the list, you may need to select the Open a database not listed here button to change to a different directory or drive.)
e. Select OK. The Insert Field dialog box is again displayed with a list of fields.
f. Highlight First Name in the Select a field list and then select Insert.

3) INSERT THE NEXT FIELD MARKER INTO THE LETTER

a. Highlight Last Name in the list and then select Insert.
b. Select Close to remove the dialog box. The Last Name marker has been inserted into the document. Note how a space was automatically inserted before the Last Name field.
c. Type a colon (:).

Check - The First Name and Last Name markers should be inserted into the letter so that the line appears on the screen as:

Dear·«First Name»·«Last Name»:¶
¶

4) PRINT PLAIN AND MERGED COPIES OF THE TUITION LETTER

a. Save the modified IVY TUITION.
b. From the File menu, select Print. Deselect the Print Merge check box and then select OK to print a plain (unmerged) copy of the letter. Note the position of the field markers in the text. Only one copy of the letter is printed and the word processor screen is again displayed.
c. From the File menu, select Print. Select OK to print merged copies of the letter.
d. A dialog box is displayed asking to Print all records? Select OK. The mail merge copies are printed. Look how the markers have been replaced by the different names from the database.
e. Save and then close IVY TUITION.

11.15 Expanding on Mail Merge

In the previous Practice you created and printed a simple mail merge document. While this document contained the data from only two fields, it is important to realize that any field from the database may be included in a form letter. In addition, it is possible to use a field more than once. For example, the recipient's first name could appear in the form letter twice; once in the address and once in the greeting. Also, field entries may be printed inside other text. That is, a field marker may be inserted inside a sentence and Works will automatically adjust any text following the marker to make room for the merged entry in the form letter printout.

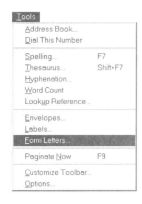

Mail merge letters are usually created with a specific purpose in mind. For example, Ivy University would like to create form letters for only those students with unpaid tuition. To limit the number of letters printed, the Form Letter command from the Tools menu is executed and then the Recipients tab selected:

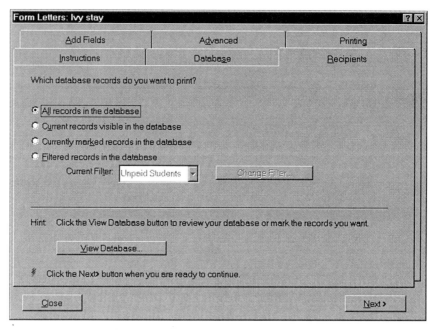

A query can be selected from the Recipients options to limit the form letters printed

Selecting Filtered records in the database, a query, and then Close will limit the letters printed to one for each record that meets the query criteria. For the Ivy U letter, the query Unpaid Students would be selected and then the mail merge letters printed.

....

Practice 11

In this Practice you will modify and print a more complex mail merged letter. A query will be used to limit the number of letters printed.

1) PREPARE THE WINDOWS

    a. Close all open files.
    b. Open IVY STAY. Note that several field markers have already been inserted into the letter.

2) INSERT A FIELD MARKER INTO THE LETTER

    a. Place the cursor on the line below the First Name and Last Name field markers.
    b. From the Insert menu, select Database Field. The Insert Field dialog box is displayed with fields from the IVY STUDENT database.
    c. Highlight Address in the Select a Field list and then select Insert. A marker is inserted into the document.
    d. Select Close to remove the dialog box.

An Introduction to Computing Using Microsoft Works

3) INSERT THE ADDRESS FIELDS INTO THE LETTER

a. Move the cursor to the line below the Address marker.
b. From the Insert menu, select Database Field. The Insert Field dialog box is displayed with the IVY STUDENT fields.
c. Insert a City field marker.
d. Select the Close button.
e. After the City marker, type a comma (,) followed by a space.
f. Use the Database Field command to insert a State field marker.
g. Insert a Zip field marker. Note a space is automatically inserted before the marker.
h. Select the Close button.

4) INSERT A STATE FIELD MARKER INTO THE LETTER

a. Move the cursor into the middle of the first paragraph, between the two spaces after "Students from...."
b. Insert a State field marker. Note how the letter has 2 State field markers.

Check - Your letter should be similar to:

```
6/10/96¶
¶
«First Name»·«Last Name»¶
«Address»¶
«City»,·«State»·«Zip»¶
¶
Dear·«First Name»:¶
¶
Ivy·University·takes·pride·in·having·a·diverse·student·body.·Students·from·«State»,·such·
as·yourself·add·to·this·diversity.¶
¶
Thank·you·for·attending·Ivy·University,·and·do·not·consider·transferring·to·another·
college.·We·need·you·here·at·old·Ivy!¶
¶
Yours·truly,¶
¶
¶
Steven·C.·Munger¶
Assistant·Dean¶
```

5) LIMIT THE LETTERS PRINTED

a. From the Tools menu, select the Form Letters command.
b. Select the Recipients tab to display query options.
c. Select the Filtered records in the database radio button and then select "CA or NV" from the Current Filter collapsible list.
d. Select the Close button.

6) PRINT PLAIN AND MERGED COPIES OF THE TUITION LETTER

a. Save IVY STAY.
b. Print a plain (unmerged) copy of the letter by first deselecting the Print Merge check box in the Print dialog box. Note the number and position of the markers on the printout.
c. Print merged copies of the letter using IVY STUDENT. Note how only letters for the applied query are printed.

Chapter Summary

This chapter presented the commands necessary to copy data between the applications. The ability to copy data between applications is one of the primary reasons for using an integrated package such as Works.

In Works, more than one file can be open at the same time, each in its own window. This can include any combination of word processor, database, and spreadsheet files. An open file can be made active by selecting the filename from the Window menu. When work has been completed on a file, it can be saved and closed using the Save and Close commands.

Multiple windows can be displayed at one time by resizing them. A window is resized by dragging on its corner. The window can be repositioned by dragging on its Title bar.

To transfer data between two open files, four basic steps are required:

1. Select the data to be copied.
2. Execute the Copy command.
3. Make the receiving file active.
4. Place the cursor where the data is to be inserted and execute the Paste command.

This chapter explained how data can be copied between:

- two word processor documents (Section 11.5)

- two spreadsheets (Section 11.6)

- two databases (Section 11.7)

- a spreadsheet and word processor document (Section 11.8 and Section 11.12)

- a database and word processor document (Section 11.9)

- a database and spreadsheet (Section 11.10)

- an open file and a new file (Section 11.11)

- a spreadsheet chart and a word processor document (Section 11.12)

- a database report and a word processor document (Section 11.13)

- a database and word processor document for mail merge (Sections 11.14 and 11.15)

One of the most powerful abilities of an integrated package is producing mail merge documents. In mail merge, a word processor document contains field markers. When the document is printed, the markers are automatically replaced with entries from the database, creating a different copy of the document for each visible record. In this way, the computer can produce personalized form letters. Queries can be used to limit the number of visible records, which affects the number of mail merged documents printed.

Vocabulary

Active file - The file currently being worked on.

Copy Report Output command - Copies the output of a report definition to the Clipboard.

Field marker - Used for a mail merge document, they are placed in a word processor document to refer to a field in a specified database.

Form Letters - A document created using mail merge. Only merged field entries differ from one form letter to the next.

Form Letters command - Contains the Recipient options that allow only records that meet a selected query to be used in a mail merge.

Integrated - One software package that contains multiple applications. Because Works is integrated, data can be copied between its three applications areas.

Mail merge - Using the contents of a database file and a word processor document to have the computer produce personalized form letters.

Spreadsheet frame - An spreadsheet application area in a word processor document.

Window - An area on the screen where an open file is displayed.

Reviews

Sections 11.1 — 11.7

1. a) What is meant by an integrated software package?
   b) What are two advantages of using such a package?

2. a) What is a window?
   b) List the steps required to switch from one window to another window?

3. What is meant by the "active" file when using windows?

4. Give two examples of when you might want to switch between windows. Explain what files would be stored in the different windows.

5. Why should files be closed after you are finished working with them?

6. Explain how three windows can be displayed simultaneously.

7. The word processor file IVY NEWS contains a paragraph that describes the inauguration of Ivy University's new president. Explain the steps required to copy this paragraph into a word processor file named ALUMNI that contains a letter to be sent to all Ivy alumni.

8. List the steps required to copy two columns from a spreadsheet named OWED and insert them between two existing columns in a spreadsheet named ASSETS.

9. Fantasy Cars has just bought out Luxury Autos and wants to add the records from Luxury Autos' inventory database into their own database. List the steps required to do this.

Sections 11.8 — 11.15

10. Give three examples of when you might want to copy part of a spreadsheet into a word processor document.

11. List the steps required to copy part of a spreadsheet to a word processor document.

12. List the steps required to copy the records of a database to a word processor document.

13. Give three examples of where you might want to copy information from a database into a spreadsheet. For each example explain what the spreadsheet's purpose.

14. List the steps required to copy a spreadsheet chart into a word processor document.

15. List the steps required to copy a database report into a word processor document.

16. What does "mail merge" mean?

17. a) List the steps required to mail merge the names and addresses of customers from Fantasy Cars' customer database into a letter sent to each customer.
    b) What additional steps would be required to send the letters to only customers living in Boca Raton, Florida?

18. When printing a mail merge letter, what is printed if the Print Merge check box is deselected in the Print dialog box?

11 | Exercises

1. Ivy University must raise next semester's tuition in order to cover its increasing labor costs.

   a) Create a letter using the word processor which notifies students of the upcoming tuition increase. The letter should be similar to the following:

      > Dear Student:
      >
      > We are sorry to inform you that due to rising costs we are forced to raise your tuition by $1,000. This increase is effective next semester.
      >
      > Sincerely,
      >
      > The Administration

   b) Save the letter naming it Increase.

   c) The administration has decided that students might take the news of a tuition increase better if it came in a personalized letter. Using the IVY STUDENT database, modify the Increase letter to mail merge the students' first name in place of the word "Student."

   d) Save the modified Increase. Print mail merged letters for all students from Texas (TX).

   e) In order to keep its better students from transferring to less expensive schools, the Ivy administration has decided that the tuition increase should be on a sliding scale based on the student's GPA. Every student's tuition will increase by $500, and an additional $100 will be charged for each tenth of a GPA point below 4.0:

GPA	Increase
4.0	$500.00
3.9	$600.00
3.8	$700.00
...	...
0.1	$4,400.00
0.0	$4,500.00

      Modify the IVY STUDENT database to contain a calculation field named Increase that displays the amount of the tuition increase.

   f) Modify the Increase letter to merge the actual tuition increase in place of the "$1,000."

   g) Modify the query created in part (d) to display only students with last names beginning with K.

   h) Save the modified Increase and IVY STUDENT. Print mail merged letters for all for students with last names beginning with K.

2. The Fantasy Wheels preowned car company would like to transfer their inventory database Wheels into a spreadsheet so that they can perform "What If?" questions with the data. This database was created in Chapter Five, Exercise 10.

a) Create a spreadsheet that contains the year, make, original price, and asking price for each car copied from the Wheels database. Format the spreadsheet, adding titles and labels where necessary. Save the spreadsheet naming it Wheels What If.

b) Add two columns to the spreadsheet. Have the first new column calculate a new asking price which is a 10% increase of the current asking price. The second new column should display the additional profit gained by selling the cars at these new prices. Format columns appropriately. Save the modified Wheels What If.

c) Acting as Fantasy's sales manager, use the word processor to write a letter to the owner of Fantasy Wheels describing your plan to raise prices. Save the letter naming it New Price.

d) Place a copy of the Wheels What If spreadsheet data into the New Price letter. Save the modified New Price and print a copy.

3. In Chapter Eight, Exercise 6 Mr. Horatio von Money used a spreadsheet named STOCKS to calculate his donation to Ivy University. Copy the spreadsheet data into a new word processor letter informing the IU Board of Trustees of the donation. Save the letter naming it New Donations and print a copy.

4. Create a new mail merge letter that warns Ivy U students to pay their tuition bill or face expulsion. Save the letter naming it Expel and print mail merge copies for students who have not yet paid their tuition bills and have a GPA less than 1.5.

5. Your friend Jill is searching for a new car and has written to you for information.

a) Using the CAR PRICE database, display all cars with air conditioning that cost less than $9,000. Copy those records into a new spreadsheet. Include proper labels and formatting in the spreadsheet. Save the spreadsheet naming it Cars For Jill.

b) Create a letter informing Jill of her choices. Include the Cars For Jill spreadsheet data in the letter. Save the letter naming it Letter To Jill and print a copy.

6. You have been asked to gather some statistics about car prices for your economics class.

a) Create a new spreadsheet that contains all of the data about new car prices from the CAR PRICE database. Use proper labels and formatting. Save the spreadsheet naming it Prices.

b) Modify the Prices spreadsheet to calculate each of the following:
- average base price of a new car
- average price for a new car with air
- average price for a new car with stereo
- average price for a new car with sunroof
- maximum base price of a new car
- minimum price of a new car with air

An Introduction to Computing Using Microsoft Works

c) Using the word processor, create a report detailing your findings for the class. Include the actual calculated figures from Prices in the report. Save the report naming it Car Stats and print a copy.

7. Use the word processor to create the following memo:

> Memo to: Steve Munger, Asst. Dean
> From: Bob Doucette, Dean
>
> Steve:
>
> The following students have received dean's list status:
>
> Please update their records. Thank you.

Copy the table of Dean's List students from the IVY CONGRAT letter modified in Practice 6 into this memo. Save the file naming it Dean List Memo and print a copy.

8. You have moved. Using the Address database created in Chapter Five, Exercise 1, prepare a personalized mail merged letter to each of your friends which gives your new address. Save the letter naming it New Address and print merged copies. An example is shown below:

> Amy Eppelman
> 713 Graisbury Avenue
> Haddonfield, NJ 08033
>
> Dear Amy:
>
> This is just a short note to let you know I have a new address:
>
> > 1389 Southwest Drive
> > Atlantic, FL 33800
>
> Of course, we'll still get together on your birthday. Call me at (213) 555-1324.
>
> See you soon,
>
> A. Friend

An Introduction to Computing Using Microsoft Works

Chapter Twelve
An Introduction to Desktop Publishing

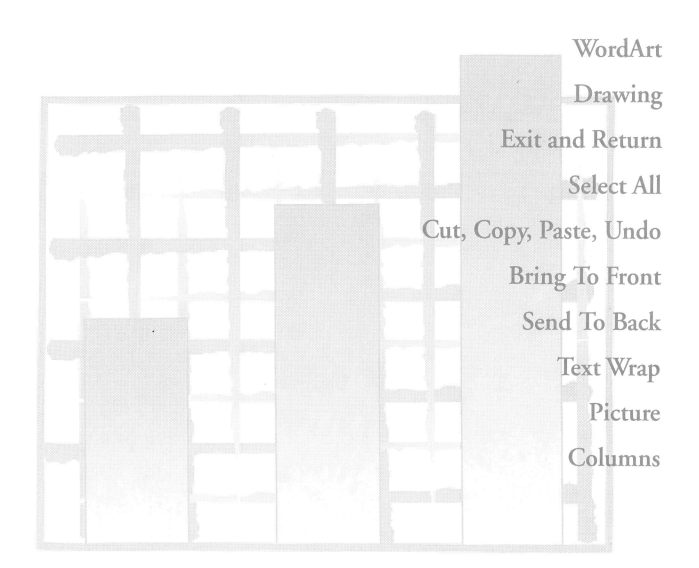

WordArt

Drawing

Exit and Return

Select All

Cut, Copy, Paste, Undo

Bring To Front

Send To Back

Text Wrap

Picture

Columns

Objectives

After completing this chapter you will be able to:

1. Explain what desktop publishing is.

2. Create drawings in Microsoft Draw and WordArt and place them in a word processor or database document.

3. Move and resize objects.

4. Describe and use the Draw tools.

5. Use the Color palettes.

6. Wrap text around an object.

7. Use columns to create a newsletter.

12

W orks' desktop publishing capabilities allow you to manipulate text and graphics using several accessories. With WordArt, text can be manipulated to produce graphic effects. With Microsoft Draw, drawings can be created and added to documents or database forms. This chapter presents WordArt and Draw and how to use them for desktop publishing.

12.1 What is Desktop Publishing?

Combining text and graphics into one single document is called *desktop publishing*. With desktop publishing you can create advertisements, brochures, invitations, newsletters, etc.—you are limited only by your imagination. Desktop publishing can easily be done in Works with WordArt or Microsoft Draw.

12.2 Creating WordArt

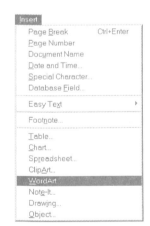

Special effects can be applied to text using the WordArt command from the Insert menu. WordArt is created by first placing the cursor where the text is to appear in the document or database Form Design view. Next, the WordArt command is executed, displaying the WordArt Tool bar and the Enter Your Text Here dialog box:

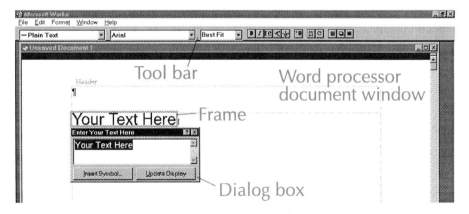

The WordArt screen

Notice the *WordArt frame* around the text. The text is first typed into the dialog box and then added to the frame by selecting the Update Display button. Any desired special effects are then applied using the Tool bar. When the text in the frame appears as desired, clicking once anywhere in the Work area outside of the dialog box places the WordArt in the document and restores the word processor or database screen.

Once WordArt has been placed in a word processor file or database form it can be formatted using features such as alignment options or tab stops. Clicking once on the WordArt object selects it and displays its *handles*. These handles are used to resize the drawing in the same manner as they were used to resize clip art images in Chapter Four.

12.3 WordArt Effects

The WordArt Tool bar offers several special effects to apply to text:

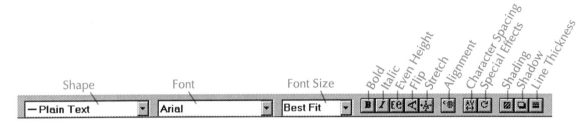

The WordArt Tool bar allows you to format text with many special effects

The first five buttons apply a format, such as bold, when clicked. The Alignment button (▦) displays a menu of alignment commands. The remaining buttons display dialog boxes with formatting options.

The special effects that can be applied from the Tool bar are as follows:

- **Shape** - mold the text into a specified shape.
- **Font** - change the font of the text.
- **Font Size** - change the size of the text.
- **Bold & Italic** - format the text as bold, italic, or bold-italic.
- **Even Height** - format each character to be the same height.
- **Flip** - turn each character onto its side.
- **Stretch** - stretch the text to fit exactly in the Frame.
- **Alignment** - format the alignment of the text in the Frame.
- **Character Spacing** - change the space between characters.
- **Special Effects** - change the shape of or rotate text
- **Shading** - apply different shading to the characters.
- **Shadow** - add a specified shadow to the text.
- **Line Thickness** - change the border of the characters.

Any of the special effects described above can be applied to text in a WordArt frame by clicking a button and selecting an option (if necessary). The text in the frame is instantly formatted with the specified effect. It is important to note that all text in the frame is formatted the same; effects cannot be applied to some characters and not to others.

Most of the tools are used in a similar manner:

1. Select the desired graphics tool by clicking on it in the Tool panel. The pointer changes to cross-hairs (+).
2. Place the cross-hairs at the starting position for the graphic.
3. Drag the cross-hairs to display an outline of the object as it is created.
4. Release the mouse button to place the object on the page.

The Freeform tool () is used to draw closed and open shapes:

Closed shape   Open shape

A closed and an open shape

The Freeform tool can be used in two ways. One way is by dragging. While dragging, the cross-hairs changes to a pencil shape and a line is drawn as the mouse moves. Another way to use the Freeform tool is to draw many-sided objects called *polygons*. To create a polygon, first select the Freeform tool then move the cross-hairs to where you want to start drawing and click once. Next, draw each side of the polygon by moving the cross-hairs to the location of the next corner and clicking once. Each time you click, a line will be drawn connecting that position with the last place you clicked. The last side that closes the shape completes the object. An open shape is created in the same manner, except the mouse is double-clicked when the object is completed.

When drawing objects, holding down the Shift key constrains the drawing to a "perfect" shape. For example, holding down the Shift key while creating a rectangle draws a square, while holding down the Shift key when creating an oval draws a circle. Holding down the Shift key while using the line or freeform tool draws a line at an angle that is a multiple of 45°. When using this technique it is important to press the Shift key before beginning to draw the individual object.

Selecting the Zoom tool changes the pointer to a magnifying glass shape (🔍). Placing the magnifying glass pointer on the Work area and clicking the left mouse button enlarges that area of the drawing. Pressing the Shift key and clicking on the left mouse button again returns the Work area to the normal view. As with the other applications, the scroll bars can be used to view different portions of the Work area.

12.6 Placing a Drawing in a Database or Word Processor File

Once a drawing is completed in the Draw window, the file that it was created for must be updated to include it. To place a finished drawing in a document or database, the Exit and Return command is executed from the File menu of the Draw window. A dialog box is then displayed:

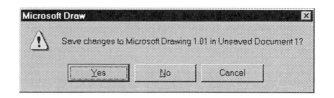

Select Yes to update the word processor or database file with the drawing. The Draw window then closes and the drawing appears at the current cursor position:

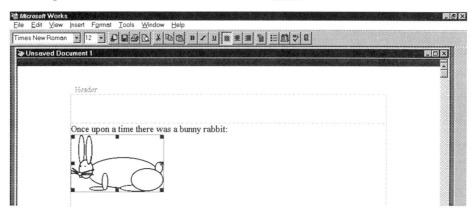

Notice the handles surrounding the drawing, indicating that it is selected.

Once they are placed in a document or database, drawings can be formatted using features such as the alignment options or tab stops.

Practice 2

In this Practice you will create different shapes using Draw and place them into the Shapes Newsletter file. Start Works and open Shapes Newsletter if you have not already done so.

1) PLACE THE CURSOR WHERE THE DRAWING WILL APPEAR

Place the cursor in the upper-left corner of the Work area, to the left of the WordArt.

2) OPEN THE DRAW WINDOW AND SELECT THE OVAL TOOL

a. From the Insert menu, select the Drawing command. The Draw window opens, partially obscuring the word processor document.

b. In the Tool panel, click once on the Ellipse tool (⬭). The tool is highlighted in the Tool panel.

c. Move the mouse pointer onto the Work area. The pointer changes to cross-hairs.

3) DRAW AN OVAL

a. Move the pointer to the upper-left corner of the Work area.

b. Drag the cross-hairs down and to the right. Note the growing outline of the oval. Release the mouse button when the shape is about the size of your thumb print:

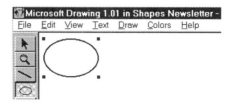

4) DRAW A TRIANGLE AND A SQUARE

a. Select the Freeform tool (⟨⟨⟩⟩) and then move the cross-hairs to the upper-center of the Work area.

b. Click once and then move (do not drag) the cross-hairs straight to the right for about an inch. Remember that when drawing a polygon it is not necessary to drag.

c. Click the mouse button when the line is about 1" long on the screen. Move the cross-hairs straight down, drawing a horizontal line. Click the mouse button when the line is about 1" long on the screen.

d. Move the cross-hairs back to where the polygon started and click once to complete the triangle.

e. Select the Rectangle tool (⟨⟩) and move the cross-hairs to the upper-right corner of the Work area.

f. Hold down the Shift key, then drag the cross-hairs down and to the left. When the square is about 1" wide and 1" tall, release the mouse button and then release the Shift key:

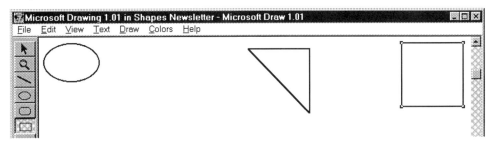

5) DRAW A CIRCLE

a. Select the Ellipse tool (⟨○⟩) and then move the cross-hairs to the bottom-left of the Work area.

b. Press and hold down the Shift key, then drag the cross-hairs up and to the right. When the circle is about 1", release the mouse button and then release the Shift key.

6) DRAW A STRAIGHT LINE AND A SQUIGGLE

a. Select the Line tool (⟨⟩) and then move the cross-hairs to the bottom-right corner of the Work area.

b. Drag the pointer up and to the left, drawing a line about 1" long.

c. Select the Freeform tool (⟨⟨⟩⟩) and then move the cross-hairs in the bottom-center of the Work area.

d. Drag the pointer around and around in a circular motion in that corner of the screen. Notice that the line bends and moves as you draw it. When you are done drawing the squiggle, stop moving the pointer and double-click the left mouse button.

Check - Your document should be similar to that shown on the next page:

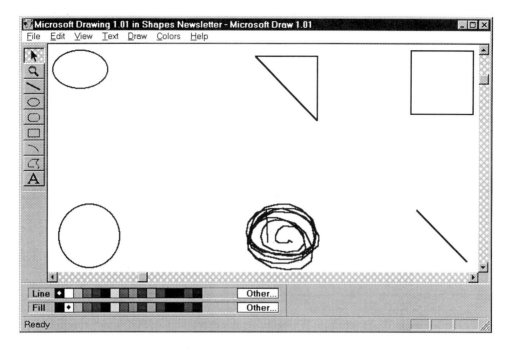

7) PLACE THE DRAWING IN THE WORD PROCESSOR DOCUMENT AND RESIZE IT

a. From the Draw window's File menu, select the Exit and Return command. A dialog box is then displayed. Select Yes from the dialog box to close the Draw window and place the drawing into the word processor document. Note the handles that indicate the drawing is selected.

b. Drag the bottom-right handle of the drawing toward the upper-left to make the drawing smaller. Continue to resize the drawing until it is a little less than half of its current size and the WordArt fits on the same line as the drawing.

Check - Your document should be similar to:

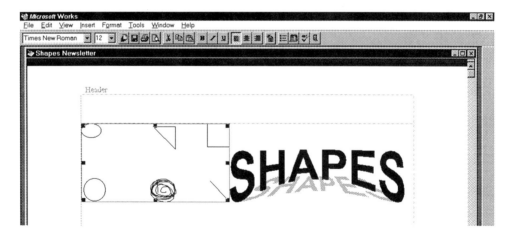

8) SAVE THE NEWSLETTER AND PRINT A COPY

a. Save the modified Shapes Newsletter.

b. Print a copy.

An Introduction to Computing Using Microsoft Works

12.7 Editing Drawings and WordArt

There may be occasions where a drawing or a WordArt object needs to be changed. Editing an object requires that the Draw or the WordArt screen be opened. One way to do this is to first select the object, then choose the appropriate command from the bottom of the Edit menu:

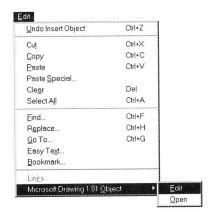

The Edit menu with a drawing selected

The name of the command that appears in the Edit menu will vary depending on what type of object is selected, but will usually be Microsoft Drawing Object or WordArt Object command. Selecting the command will display a pop-out list, and choosing Edit from the list will either display the Draw window and place the drawing in it, or display the WordArt screen and place the WordArt in it.

Another method for starting Draw or WordArt is to double-click on the object that needs editing.

12.8 Moving and Resizing Objects in the Draw Window

In the Draw window, an object can be moved, deleted, resized, or have its basic shape changed. To do any of these, the object must first be *selected* by clicking the pointer tool on it. When selected, an object is displayed with handles that indicate its size:

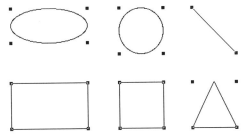

Handles are displayed when an object is selected

To move an object to another part of the Work area, simply drag it to the new location. A dashed-line outline of the object appears while it is being dragged, and when the mouse button is released the object appears in its entirety:

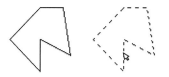

Releasing the mouse button places the object in a new location

When moving an object, it is important not to drag one of its handles because this will change the object's shape. If you do so, immediately selecting Undo (Ctrl+Z) will return the object to its original size and shape.

An object can be reshaped by first selecting it and then dragging one of its handles with the pointer tool. For example, a rectangle could be made wider by dragging a handle on its right side to the right:

A solid line indicates the original size of the object

This action is called *stretching*. Dragging handles in other directions can make the rectangle taller, shorter, or more narrow. Dragging a handle at an angle stretches both the height and width of an object at the same time:

Objects can be resized in both directions by dragging at an angle

12.9 Selecting Multiple Objects

More than one object can be selected at a time by holding down the Shift key when clicking once on each of the objects. This allows multiple objects to be cut, moved, or formatted at the same time. When several objects are selected, one object can be *deselected* by holding down the Shift key and clicking on it again.

Multiple objects can also be selected using *marquee selection*. Dragging the Pointer tool in the Work area creates a box that is visible until the mouse button is released. Creating a box around several objects selects all of the objects that are completely enclosed in the marquee:

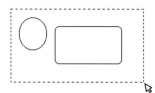

Releasing the mouse selects all of the objects within the marquee

All of the objects in a drawing can be selected at once by executing the Select All command from the Edit menu (Ctrl+A).

An Introduction to Computing Using Microsoft Works

12.10 The Editing Commands

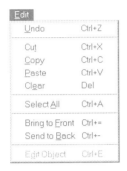

Objects can be copied, deleted, and added to a document using commands from the Edit menu. The Cut command removes a selected object from a draw document and places it on the Clipboard. The Clipboard contents can be placed in the draw document using the Paste command. Executing the Clear command deletes a selected object without placing it on the Clipboard. The Copy command places a copy of the selected object on the Clipboard and leaves the original in the document.

The effect of the last drawing operation can be reversed using the Undo command from the Edit menu (Ctrl+Z). For example, undoing a Clear places the deleted object back onto the draw document. Undoing a stretch returns the object to its original size and shape.

Practice 3

In this practice you will edit the drawing in Ivy's newsletter. Start Works and open Shapes Newsletter if you have not already done so.

1) OPEN THE DRAW WINDOW

Double-click on the drawing in the upper-left corner of the Work area. The Draw window opens and displays the drawing of different shapes. Note that all objects are selected.

2) DELETE THE OVAL

a. Click once on any blank space in the Work area to deselect all objects.
b. In the Draw window, click once on the oval in the upper-left corner to select it. Handles are displayed around the oval.
c. From the Draw window's Edit menu, select Clear. The oval is deleted.

3) REPOSITION THE SQUARE

a. Click the mouse pointer on the square object to select it. Handles appear.
b. Place the mouse pointer on the middle of the square and drag the square straight to the left, until it is in the same location that the oval was. Remember that it is important to not drag one of the handles because this will stretch the object.

4) RESIZE THE SQUIGGLE

a. Click the mouse pointer on the squiggle to select it. Handles appear.
b. Drag the upper-right corner handle upwards and to the right until the dashed-line outline of the squiggle is near the straight line. The squiggle is now bigger.

5) SELECT AND DELETE TWO OBJECTS

a. Click the mouse pointer on the squiggle if it is not already selected. Handles appear.
b. Hold down the Shift key and click once on the straight line. Handles are displayed on both the squiggle and the straight line.
c. From the Draw window's Edit menu, select Clear. The two objects are deleted.

6) PLACE THE MODIFIED DRAWING IN THE WORD PROCESSOR DOCUMENT

a. From the Draw window's File menu, select Exit and Return. A dialog box is then displayed. Select Yes from the dialog box to close the Draw window and place the drawing at the current cursor position.

b. Drag the bottom-right handle of the drawing upwards and to the left until the drawing is a little less than half of its current size.

Check - Your document should be similar to:

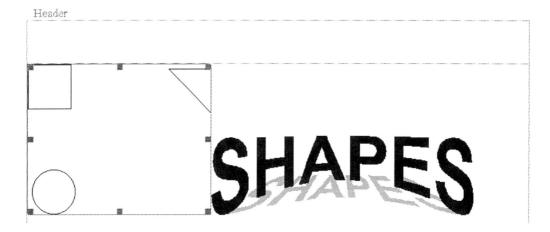

7) SAVE THE MODIFIED SHAPES NEWSLETTER

12.11   The Color Palette

As each object is drawn in the Draw window, it is created with the default line color of black and a default fill color of white. These color selections are indicated at the bottom of the Draw window in the Color palette:

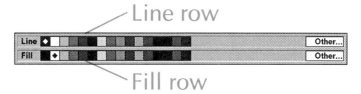

Colors for lines and fills are selected from the Color palette

The colors of the outline and fill of an existing object can be changed by first selecting the object and then changing the line or fill color in the Color palette.

The default colors for the line or fill setting can be changed in the Color palette when no object is selected. Then the new, chosen colors will be the default and apply to all the objects you draw until they are changed again.

12.12 The Bring to Front and Send to Back Commands

As you have seen, it is possible to move objects on the Draw window Work area by dragging them. It is also possible to place an object over another. Because Works keeps track of the order in which objects are created, an object drawn after another will block or cover the first object if it is dragged over the first. It is helpful to think of these objects as being "stacked" on top of each other:

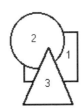 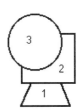

The triangle on the right has been moved to the back of the stack

The order in which objects are stacked can be changed using the Bring to Front and Send to Back commands in the Edit menu. The Bring to Front command (Ctrl+=) moves a selected object to the top of the stack and the Send to Back command (Ctrl+−) moves a selected object to the bottom.

Practice 4

In this practice you will again edit the drawing in Ivy's newsletter. Start Works and open Shapes Newsletter if you have not already done so.

1) OPEN THE DRAW WINDOW

Double-click on the drawing in the upper-left corner of the Work area. The Draw window opens and displays the drawing of different shapes.

2) COLOR THE SQUARE AND CIRCLE RED

a. Click once on any blank space in the Work area to deselect all objects.
b. Move the mouse pointer so that it is slightly above and to the right of the square.
c. Drag the pointer down and to the left, until both the square and the circle are completely surrounded by a dashed line.
d. Release the mouse button. Notice that both the rounded square and the circle have been marquee selected.
e. In the Color palette's Fill row, click once on a bright red color with the pointer. The two shapes are filled with the red color, and still have a black outline as indicated by the Line row in the Color palette.

3) COLOR THE OUTLINE OF THE TRIANGLE BLUE

a. Select the triangle object.
b. In the Color palette's Line row, click once on a light blue color with the pointer. The outline of the triangle is the light blue color.
c. With the triangle still selected, press the Delete key to delete the object.

4) ARRANGE THE OBJECTS

    a. Drag the circle upwards and to the right a little until it covers the bottom-right corner of the square.

    b. With the circle still selected, from the Draw window's Edit menu execute the Send to Back command. The square now covers part of the circle.

5) PLACE THE DRAWING IN THE WORD PROCESSOR DOCUMENT

Select the Exit and Return command from the Draw window's File menu. A dialog box is displayed. Select Yes from the dialog box to close the Draw window and place the drawing into the word processor document. Note the handles that indicate the drawing is selected.

Check - Your document should be similar to:

6) SAVE THE MODIFIED SHAPES NEWSLETTER

12.13 Wrapping Text Around an Object

Once a drawing has been placed in a word processor document, it can be left as a paragraph or repositioned on the page to allow text to flow around it:

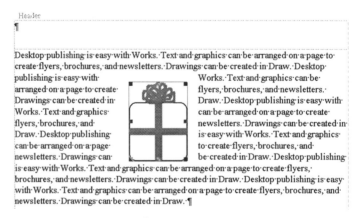

Text can flow around an object

Making text flow around an object is called *text wrap*. Text can flow around a drawing, a spreadsheet frame, a chart, or any other object that has been placed in a document. For example, a chart could be placed into a company report to illustrate the information in a paragraph.

An Introduction to Computing Using Microsoft Works

To wrap text around an object, first select the object and then execute the Text Wrap command from the Format menu. The Format Picture dialog box is displayed with the Text Wrap options:

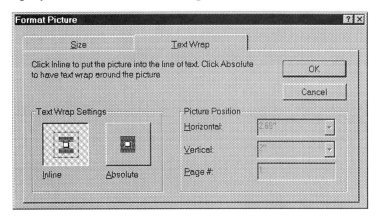

Note that the Inline button is selected, because the object is currently in a paragraph. Selecting the Absolute button makes the Picture Position options active. The position on the page that the object is to be moved to is then entered in the Horizontal and Vertical options. The position coordinates are measured from the top edge and left edge of the page, not from the margins. Selecting OK positions the object and wraps the text around it.

Once the object has had text wrap formatting applied to it, it can be repositioned on the page by dragging the selected object, or by entering new position coordinates into the dialog box.

12.14 Resizing with the Picture Command

The size of an object cannot be precisely controlled by dragging on its handles. However, the Picture command from the Format menu allows you to resize objects to exact dimensions. A selected object can be resized by first executing the Picture command from the Format menu. The Format Picture dialog box is displayed with the Size section:

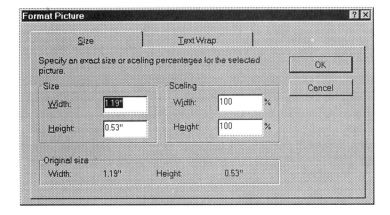

A specific size can then be entered into the Width and Height entry boxes of the Size section, or a desired percentage can be entered into the Width and Height entry boxes of the Scaling section. Selecting OK resizes the object. Note that at the bottom of the dialog box the object's original size is displayed as a reference.

12.15 Desktop Publishing: Layout

The placement of graphics and text on a published page is not arbitrary. The size and location of each element in the document should be carefully planned; this is called the *layout*. For each desktop publishing project the document should be sketched out on paper, then created on the computer. Each time it is printed, the document's design should be reviewed and the design changed as necessary.

It is important to consider three concepts when making the initial sketches of the document: audience, balance, and consistency. The contents of the document must be appropriate for the *audience*—the people who will receive the final product. For example, it would not be appropriate to use an elegant, script font in a newsletter about sumo wrestling. *Balance* refers to how the text and graphics on the page relate to each other. For example, having all the pictures at the bottom of a page is not as effective as having them placed throughout a page. *Consistency* is an important concept in longer documents. It refers to repetitive items such as page numbers. It would be confusing to the reader if the page numbers were placed in a different location and different font on each page.

Only through experience will you discover which layout techniques are most effective for each type of document. For example, 12 point type is usually not used for the text of a newsletter; 11 point or 10 point type is better. Such details can make the difference between a professional-looking document and one that looks amateurish. One way to gain insight into effective layout techniques is to look around you. Open a magazine to an advertisement and scrutinize the ad. What fonts and sizes are used? Where are the graphics placed on the page in relation to the text? What audience is the ad intended for and is it appropriate for them? To fully understand the basics of design, it may help to make sketches of the newsletter pages and advertisements you find around you.

12.16 Using Columns to Create Newsletters

As discussed in Chapter Four, the Columns command from the Format menu can be used to create columns of text in word processor documents. This feature is helpful when creating newsletters, which usually consist of a *nameplate* above columns of *stories*:

12

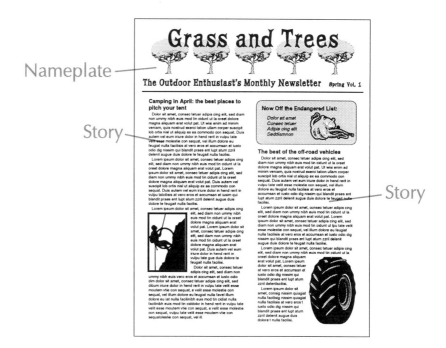

Nameplate

Story

Story

The nameplate is the area at the top of a newsletter's first page. It contains the name of the newsletter, the date of the issue, and other important information. In a Works word processor document, the nameplate is created in the header area. Each story in a newsletter is usually created in separate word processor files and then copied into the final newsletter file. When Graphics are added, the newsletter is complete. Creating a newsletter requires many desktop publishing skills because text and graphics need to be combined to produce the finished publication.

Practice 5

In this Practice you will add text from word processor documents, size graphics and wrap text around them, and complete Ivy's newsletter. Start Works and open the Shapes Newsletter if you have not already done so.

1) COMPLETE THE NAMEPLATE

    a. Move the cursor so that it is after the SHAPES WordArt and press Enter to create a new paragraph.

    b. Type The Ivy University Fitness Newsletter and format the line of text as 20 point Arial italic.

    c. From the Edit menu, execute Select All to highlight all of the text and graphics.

    d. From the Edit menu, select Cut to place the text and graphics on the Clipboard.

    e. Place the cursor in the header area by clicking once with the mouse, then from the Edit menu, select Paste to place the text and graphics in the header area.

    f. Highlight the text and graphics and then click the Center Align button on the Tool bar to center them.

    g. Move the cursor to the end of the The Ivy University Fitness Newsletter line and press Enter once to add a blank line.

2) CREATE COLUMNS IN THE NEWSLETTER

a. Place the cursor in the Work area of the newsletter, not in the header area.
b. From the Format menu, execute the Columns command. The Format Columns dialog box is displayed.
c. Type 2 in the Number of columns entry box and select OK to format the document with two columns.

3) ADD TEXT FROM ANOTHER WORD PROCESSOR DOCUMENT

a. Open LEAD STORY. Notice the large, bold title of the story and the smaller text in the rest of the story.
b. From the Edit menu, execute the Select All command. The entire story, including the title, is selected.
c. From the Edit menu, select Copy to place a copy onto the Clipboard.
d. Close LEAD STORY.

4) PASTE THE TEXT INTO THE NEWSLETTER

a. Display the Shapes Newsletter if it is not already displayed.
b. From the Edit menu, execute Paste. The text fills one column and continues into the second column. This is the first story in the newsletter.

5) ADD ANOTHER STORY

a. Open News Story, a document created in the practices of Chapter Two.
b. Highlight the title and the first two paragraphs of the document, then from the Edit menu select Copy to place a copy onto the Clipboard.
c. Close News Story.

6) PASTE THE STORY INTO THE NEWSLETTER

a. Display the Shapes Newsletter if it is not already displayed and move the cursor to the very end of the text in the second column, where the text reads "—Gabrielle Berni, reporter."
b. Press Enter twice to create a blank line and a new paragraph.
c. From the Edit menu, select Paste. The story fills most of the rest of the second column. This is the second story in the newsletter.

7) ADD A GRAPHIC AND RESIZE IT

a. Move the cursor to the beginning of the first line of the first story that reads "At the March Board of Trustees…" and then from the Insert menu select Drawing. A blank Draw window is displayed.
b. Select the Rectangle tool from the Tool panel, hold down the Shift key and draw a square about 0.75" wide and tall. Release the mouse button and then the Shift key.
c. Select the square if it is not already selected, then click on a light gray color in the Color palette's Fill row to fill the square with gray. This drawing will represent a photograph in the newsletter.
d. From the Draw window's File menu select Exit and Return. A dialog box is displayed. Select Yes from the dialog box to close the Draw window and place the drawing into the word processor document. Note the handles that indicate the drawing is selected.
e. From the Format menu, execute Picture. A dialog box is displayed with the Size options.

    f. Type 0.75 for the Width in the Size options, then type 0.75 for the Height in the Size options. Be sure to type in the Size options and not the Scaling options.

    g. Select OK to apply the formatting. The square in now exactly 0.75" tall and wide.

8) FLOW TEXT AROUND THE GRAPHIC

    a. Select the gray square drawing if it is not already selected. Note how the text in the story has uneven line spacing because the drawing is taller than the text.

    b. From the Format menu execute the Text Wrap command. A dialog box is displayed with the Text Wrap options.

    c. Click on the Absolute button and select OK to wrap the text around the drawing.

    d. Drag the gray square and move it to the left until it is against the left margin guide.

Check - Your document should be similar to:

9) SAVE THE NEWSLETTER AND PRINT A COPY

    a. Save the modified Shapes Newsletter.

    b. Print a copy.

    c. Close the file and exit Works.

12.17 Where can you go from here?

This chapter has presented the basics of desktop publishing and the Works graphics accessories. There are many other commands and options available in both the Draw and WordArt accessories which you may want to explore using the online help or *The Works Companion* supplied by Microsoft.

Computers are powerful graphics tools and many graphics programs exist. Adobe Illustrator, CorelDRAW, and Aldus Freehand are three of the most popular drawing programs. These packages also allow you to manipulate text as you did with WordArt. You will be able to learn any of these programs easily because with Works you have learned the basics of graphics.

This chapter introduced desktop publishing and the Draw and WordArt Graphics accessories. WordArt is created by selecting the WordArt command from the Insert menu. A drawing is created by first placing the cursor in a document at the desired location, then selecting the Drawing command from the Insert menu.

The WordArt graphics accessory allows manipulated text to be placed into word processor documents and database forms. The WordArt Tool bar offers many special effects, including shadowing text, stretching text, and varying space between characters.

The Microsoft Draw graphics accessory has many drawing tools including a pointer, line, rectangle, oval, and freeform tools. Once created, objects can be resized and moved in various ways. Selected objects are displayed with handles. Objects may also have different line and fill colors applied to them using the Color palette.

Both WordArt and Draw objects can be edited after they are placed into a document. Selecting either the Microsoft Drawing Object command or the WordArt 2.0 Object command from the Edit menu will start Draw or display the WordArt screen. Another method for starting Draw or WordArt is to double-click on the object that needs editing.

In the Draw window, multiple objects may be selected by holding down the Shift key while clicking on them. They may also be selected by a method called marquee selection by dragging the pointer. All objects in the window can be selected using the Select All command in the Edit menu.

Objects in the Draw window may overlap one another and are said to be stacked. The order of stacking can be changed using the Bring To Front and Send To Back commands from the Edit menu. Objects may also be manipulated using the Cut, Copy, Paste, Clear, and Undo commands from the Edit menu. The Color palette is used to change the line and fill colors of a selected object.

In a word processor document, the Text Wrap command allows text to wrap around a selected drawing or WordArt object. The Picture command can be used to precisely size a selected drawing or WordArt object.

The three main concepts to consider when determining the layout of a desktop publishing project are audience, balance, and consistency.

Newsletters usually consist of a nameplate above columns of stories. When creating newsletters in a word processor document, the Columns command from the Format menu can be used to create columns of text for stories, and the nameplate can be created in the header area.

Vocabulary

Bring to Front command - Moves the selected object to the top of the stack.

Color palette - Used to change the line and fill colors for a Draw object.

Deselect - Clicking once on a selected object to unselect it.

Desktop publishing - Combining text and graphics into one document.

Frame - WordArt area where the formatted text appears.

Handles - Rectangles displayed around a selected object, used to adjust the size.

Layout - The size and location of each element in a document.

Marquee selection - Selecting multiple objects by dragging to create a box around them.

Nameplate - The area at the top of the front page of a newsletter that contains the title, publisher date, and other information.

Object - Element in a drawing, such as a rectangle or line. Also used to describe WordArt or a drawing that has been placed in a document.

Polygon - A shape with many sides.

Selected object - An object that is displayed with handles.

Send to Back command - Moves the selected object to the bottom of the stack.

Stack - The way in which the objects in a drawing are positioned.

Story - Text in a newsletter that is based on one topic.

Stretching - Reshaping a selected drawing by dragging one of its handles.

Wrapping text - Making text flow around an object.

Reviews

Sections 12.1 — 12.10

1. What is desktop publishing?

2. List the steps required to create WordArt with the text Bargain Hardware and add the WordArt to a word processor document. Include a shadow effect in the WordArt.

3. List the steps required to create a drawing of a rectangle and add that drawing to a word processor document.

4. What is meant by a "perfect" shape and how may one be drawn?

5. List the steps required to edit previously created WordArt that is in a word processor document.

6. List the steps required to edit a previously created drawing that is in a word processor document.

7. Before it is placed into the file, how can the rectangle in Review question 3 be resized?

8. List two ways that a group of objects may be selected.

9. When drawing in the Draw graphics accessory, list the steps required to create three copies of an already drawn square.

Sections 12.11 — 12.16

10. List the steps required to draw a green circle filled with brown. Assume you are already in the Microsoft Draw graphics accessory.

11. If a circle is drawn over a square, how can the objects be reversed so that the square is in front of the circle?

12. What is meant by wrapping text?

13. List the steps required to wrap the text around an object in a word processor document.

14. List the steps required to precisely size an object to 1" high by 3" wide.

15. When designing a document, what three concepts are considered?

16. When creating a newsletter in a word processor document, where is the nameplate created?

An Introduction to Computing Using Microsoft Works

12 | Exercises

1. The Poem word processor file created in the Practices of Chapter Two could be made more interesting by adding a drawing and a title to it. Open Poem.

   a) Place the cursor in a new paragraph after the last line of the poem. Start Draw and use the Tool panel and Color palette to create an appropriate drawing for the poem. Suggested ideas are: a boy and a girl, a pail, two people and a hill, etc.

   b) Place the drawing in the document, resizing if necessary. Add a blank line between the drawing and the poem.

   c) The title of the poem is Jack and Jill. Move the cursor to the beginning of the document. Start WordArt and create an interesting title for the poem using at least three different formats in WordArt. Place the title in the document and resize if necessary. Add a blank line between the title and the poem.

   d) Save the modified Poem and print a copy.

   e) Your neighbors, Jack and Jane, like the poem. Change all occurrences of Jill in the poem to Jane. Edit the WordArt title to incorporate the name change.

   f) Save the modified Poem and print a copy.

2. The Dean List Memo word processor file was created in Chapter Eleven, Exercise 7. Open Dean List Memo so that a letterhead may be added to it.

   a) Create a new logo with WordArt using the words Ivy U and place it at the top of the memo.

   b) Save the modified Dean List Memo and print one copy.

3. Create a new word processor file named Birthday. This document will contain information about you and the year you were born.

   a) Write a short paragraph about yourself. Include your favorite food, music, hobbies, etc. Format the paragraph using different character styles and sizes.

   b) Use WordArt to create a fancy design of your birth date. Place the birth date above the short paragraph created in step 1.

   c) Save Birthday and print a copy.

4. In Chapter Two, Exercise 10 you created a flyer.

   a) Open Grand Opening and add an appropriate drawing to it. Place the drawing in an appropriate place on the database form and resize it if necessary.

   b) Save the modified Grand Opening and print a copy.

5. The Ivy University Center for Environmental Awareness would like you to create a one-page newsletter for them. The newsletter must have a nameplate in the header area, with two columns of articles and pictures below it.

   a) Create a new word processor document with two columns. Save the document naming it Environmental News.

   b) Write one or two short stories appropriate to a newsletter about the environment, endangered species, or recycling programs. Make the headline of each story a different font than the text and 14 point bold.

   c) Place the cursor in the header area, then use WordArt to create the title of the newsletter. Use Green Ivy News as the title. Add a date and any other appropriate information to complete the nameplate in the header area.

   d) Using Draw, create and place at least two drawings appropriate to the newsletter. The drawings could be about recycling, the environment, the current month or season, or an upcoming holiday. Apply text wrap to at least one of the drawings.

   e) Save Environmental News and preview it to make sure that everything appears as you want it to. Make any changes necessary, then save the changes and print a copy.

   f) The editors of the newsletter want to make some changes, including changing the title of the newsletter to Planet Ivy. Edit all of the drawings and the WordArt title at the top. Make at least one visible change to each drawing.

   g) Using ClipArt, place the recycling symbol (♻) somewhere in the newsletter. Wrap the text around the symbol.

   h) Save Environmental News and preview it. It may be necessary to move some drawings around since they have been edited. Make any changes necessary, then save the changes and print another copy.

6. You have decided to make a page-sized poster for your wall that includes special information about you and the year you were born.

   a) In the new word processor document, write a short paragraph about yourself. Include your favorite food, music, hobbies, etc. Format the paragraph using different character styles and sizes. Change the paragraph alignment. Save the file naming it My Birth Year.

   b) Open ACADEMY AWARDS. In this database, display the record for the year you were born. Copy the record and paste it into the word processor document. Format the information appropriately. Use WordArt to create an appropriate title above the awards information in the word processor document.

   c) Open COUNTRY and display the record for the country you were born in. Copy the record and paste it into the word processor document. Format the information appropriately. Use WordArt to create an appropriate title above the country information in the word processor document.

   d) Save the modified My Birth Year and print a copy.

7. Bonster Enterprises, a large company that produces suntan products and beach chairs, has asked you to create a new logo for them and make letterhead stationery with it. Create a new word processor document and then use the Draw graphics accessory to make a logo for Bonster Enterprises. The logo must include a sun and a palm tree, in addition to anything else that you decide to add. When the completed logo is in the word processor document, type the company information below it:

> 1400 Corporate Drive
> Harrisburg, VT 20398
> (302) 555-2940
> (302) 234-2343 fax
> http://www.bonster.sunstuff.com

Right align the graphic and text. Save the file naming it Bonster Letterhead and print a copy.

8. Dr. Jessica A. Nenner, a veterinarian, has asked you to design letterhead stationery for her.

   a) Create a new word processor document. Using WordArt, create an interesting graphic of the Doctor's full name. Use a different font, at least 16 points in size, and at least one other effect.

   b) Save the word processor document naming it Nenner Letterhead.

   c) Below the WordArt, enter Dr. Nenner's information:

   > 32 Glastonbury Avenue
   > Whately, MA 02433
   > phone (413) 555-8876
   > fax (413) 555-9820
   > e-mail nenner@petdoc.lvp

   Format the information in a different font. Center align the graphic and the text.

   d) Save the modified Nenner Letterhead and print a copy.

9. In a new word processor document, create a two-page newsletter on any topic that you wish. The newsletter must contain the following features:

   - A nameplate with the title, date, and name of the group that publishes it.
   - At least four different stories.
   - A table of contents.
   - At least two drawings.
   - All headlines must be bold.
   - Correct spelling.
   - At least two columns per page.

Save the newsletter naming it First Issue and print a copy.

An Introduction to Computing Using Microsoft Works

Chapter Thirteen

Telecommunications and the Social and Ethical Implications of Computing

Communication

Easy Connect

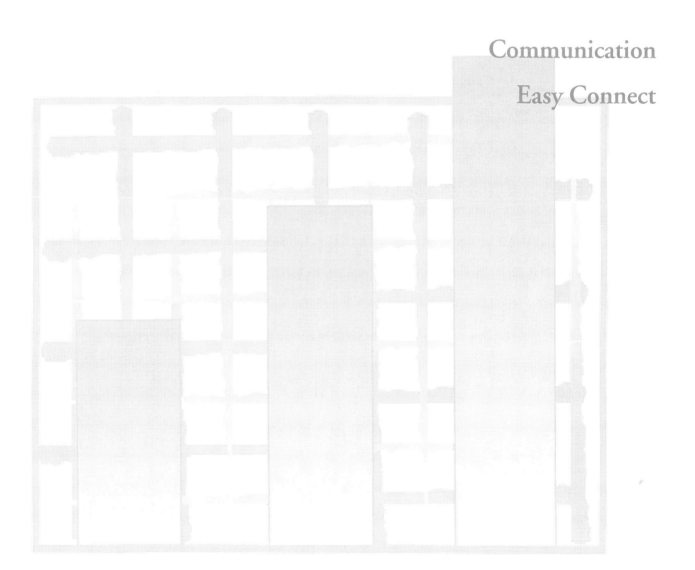

Objectives

After completing this chapter you will be able to:

1. Define telecommunications and describe its uses.

2. Use the Works Communications application to connect to an information service.

3. Describe networks.

4. Understand the Internet, Gophers, and the World Wide Web.

5. Understand Internet addresses.

6. Understand what TCP/IP, HTTP, and HTML are used for.

7. Describe supercomputers, neural networks, and database marketing.

8. Describe artificial intelligence and its use in expert systems and natural language processing.

9. Understand how robots may be used to automate tasks.

10. Understand virtual reality, CD-ROMs, and multimedia.

11. Describe different storage devices and mobile computing devices.

12. Describe different careers in computing and their educational requirements.

13. Understand the ethical responsibilities of computer use and programming.

14. Understand the uses of desktop publishing.

13

In this concluding chapter we discuss telecommunications, career possibilities, and the social and ethical consequences of living in a computerized society. After having studied the previous chapters you should have a good understanding of how useful and powerful a computer is. In the first chapter of this text we stated that computers, unlike people, could not actually think but could store huge amounts of data and process it at very high speeds. This chapter describes these capabilities and how they are being exploited to perform an ever increasing and varied number of tasks.

13.1   Telecommunications

Telecommunications is the sending and receiving of data over telephone lines. With a *modem* a computer is capable of transmitting and receiving data between any two locations connected by phone lines. To send data to another computer (*transmit*), a modem converts the computer's binary data into tones which are then sent over phone lines. To *receive* data, a computer's modem converts the tones from the phone line back into binary form. This process involves what is called signal <u>mo</u>dulation and <u>dem</u>odulation, hence the name modem. In addition to the modem, special telecommunications software is required.

*Modems can be "external" (outside the computer)
or "internal" (built in)*

The rate at which data is sent over the phone lines is measured in *bits per second* (bps). As discussed in Chapter One, a bit is the smallest unit of information in the binary system. Each ASCII character is composed of 8 bits, or one byte. Currently the most common modem rates are 14,400 and 28,800 bps. However, newer modems are being developed that are capable of communicating at even higher speeds.

A modem can be used to access and search large databases which might store financial data, news reports, or travel information. For example, if you go to a travel agent to book an airplane ticket, the agent will most likely use a computer with a modem to connect to an airline's database to check the availability of flights.

Telecommunications makes it possible for people to work at home rather than in an office. This is referred to as *telecommuting*. Writers and news reporters can write their stories at home on a word processor and then transmit their word processor files to their office which might be many miles away. Financial consultants, accountants, and travel agents are able to work at home by accessing databases and other information with a modem. Telecommunications also makes access to the Internet possible as explained in Section 13.5.

Telecommunications allows two computers to exchange information over telephone lines

13.2 Bulletin Board Systems and E-Mail

A popular form of telecommunication is the electronic *bulletin board system* (BBS). People who subscribe to a bulletin board service can *post* messages by calling the BBS's computer and transmitting them. When other subscribers of the service call the bulletin board they can list posted messages. Many companies and organizations maintain bulletin board systems to keep subscribers aware of important events. For example, the Ivy University Alumni Association could have an electronic bulletin board which lists upcoming events such as athletic competitions and alumni reunions.

Some BBSs are run by individual users and are normally free. Others called *information services* are controlled by large companies and offer for a fee a variety of different services such as shopping and international weather forecasts. CompuServe, Prodigy, and America Online are three popular information services.

Electronic mail (e-mail) is a message sent to a person or a small group through an information service or bulletin board system. A message is sent by typing in the name of the recipient and the message. When the recipient connects to the electronic mail service he or she is notified that there is new mail. The primary advantage of this system is speed. When an e-mail message is sent, it can be received in a matter of seconds even to recipients half way around the world.

To keep electronic mail private a password system is usually used. When calling to receive messages, a person is asked to enter a password which must then be verified by the computer before the messages are transmitted.

Messages, files, and graphics can be copied from a BBS or information service to your computer. This is called *downloading* and involves having the system's computer send a copy of the file to your computer, where it will be stored on disk. Once downloaded, you can print or edit the file. Similarly, the process of sending files from your computer to a BBS or information service is called *uploading*.

13.3 Telecommunicating with Microsoft Works

Works has a communication application. If your computer is equipped with a modem, this application allows you to contact electronic bulletin boards and information services to send and receive data.

Telecommunicating can be complex, involving many different options such as parity. In order for telecommunications to take place, both computers must use the same options. New subscribers to an information service normally receive a packet describing the options which must be used to access that particular service. Fortunately, Works allows the options for each different service to be saved in a communications file. Once the options are saved, the user does not have to be concerned about setting the proper options again.

Selecting the Communications button from the Works Task Launcher dialog box displays the Communications screen and the Easy Connect dialog box:

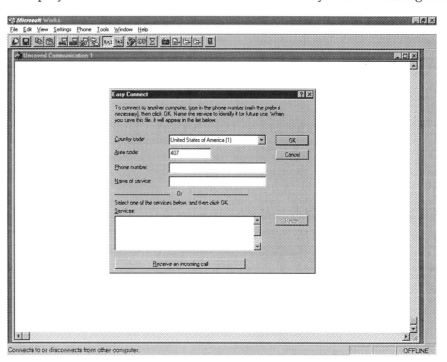

The Microsoft Works Communications Screen

The number of the computer you are dialing and a descriptive name of the service you are connecting to can be entered in the Easy Connect dialog box. Selecting OK saves the settings using the descriptive name as the filename and displays the Dial dialog box. Selecting Dial dials the number. Selecting Cancel removes the dialog box, allowing commands to be executed so that you may choose the communications options.

For two computers to communicate, they both must use the same communication options. The four most important of these are:

Bits per second: The speed at which each computer will send and receive data. 28,800 bps, 14,400 bps, and 9600 bps are common values.

Data bits: The number of bits (binary digits) that make up one piece of data. This is usually 7 or 8.

Parity: How the receiving computer will determine if an error occurred in the transmission of data. Common parity choices are named None, Odd, Even, and Space.

Stop bits: The number of bits, 1 or 2, sent to indicate the end of a piece of data.

These four items are so important that BBSs and information services are classified by the settings that they expect. For example, a BBS may list itself as "9600, 8, None, 1" or "96, 8, N, 1" meaning that its computer communicates using 9600 bps, 8 data bits, None parity, and 1 stop bit. To configure Works, commands in the Settings menu are used. Executing the Communication command displays the following dialog box:

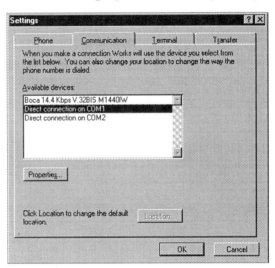

The Communication command controls communications options

Tabs at the top of the dialog box can be selected to display different sets of options. Selecting the Properties button displays options for the selected port:

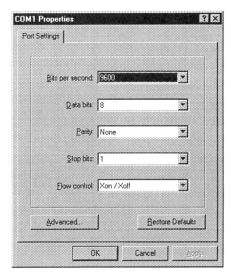

Bits per second, data bits, stop bits, and parity options are set here

Once the proper options have been set, a communications file can be created by selecting the Save command from the File menu which saves your choices on disk. Opening a previously saved communications file recalls the options you have set. In this way, Works simplifies the process of setting communications options by allowing you to create a different communications file for each information service you contact.

After the options have been set and saved, Works can be told to contact the information service using the Easy Connect command from the Phone menu. When executed, the phone number you supplied is dialed to contact the other computer. If a connection is made, the other computer then takes control of your computer, and anything that you type is sent to it. For this reason, the remote computer is often called the *host*. Executing the Hang Up command also from the Phone menu terminates communications with the host and hangs up the phone.

Practice 1 - Connecting to a BBS

In this Practice you will set options to access a BBS and create a communications file for that BBS's options. If you do not have a modem attached to your computer you will not be able to perform this Practice.

Make sure that your modem is connected to a phone line and is turned on. As examples for this exercise we will use the options 7, Even, 1 and the telephone number 800-346-3247. You may be able to get actual information about a local BBS from your computer dealer.

1) CREATE A NEW COMMUNICATIONS FILE

    a. Following the directions given in Chapter Two, start Works.

    b. In the Works Task Launcher dialog box, click on the Works Tools tab if the Works Tools options are not already displayed.

    c. Click on the Communications button. The Communications screen is shown with the Easy Connect dialog box displayed.

    d. We need to set communications options first. Therefore, select Cancel to remove the dialog box.

2) SET THE COMMUNICATIONS OPTIONS

a. From the Settings menu, select the Communication command. A dialog box is displayed. In the Available devices list, select your modem.
b. Click on the Properties button to display options for your modem. Note the defaults for Data bits (8), Parity (None), and Stop bits (1).
c. In the Data bits collapsible list, select 7.
d. Change the Parity to the Even option.
e. Select OK to remove the Properties dialog box, then select OK to remove the Settings dialog box.

3) SET THE EASY CONNECT OPTIONS

a. From the Phone menu, select the Easy Connect command. The Easy Connect dialog box is displayed.
b. In the Phone number entry box, type 1-800-346-3247.
c. In the Name of service entry box, type BBS TEST.

4) INITIATE COMMUNICATIONS

a. Select OK. The Dial dialog box is displayed.
b. Select the Dial button. Works initializes the modem and displays a message:

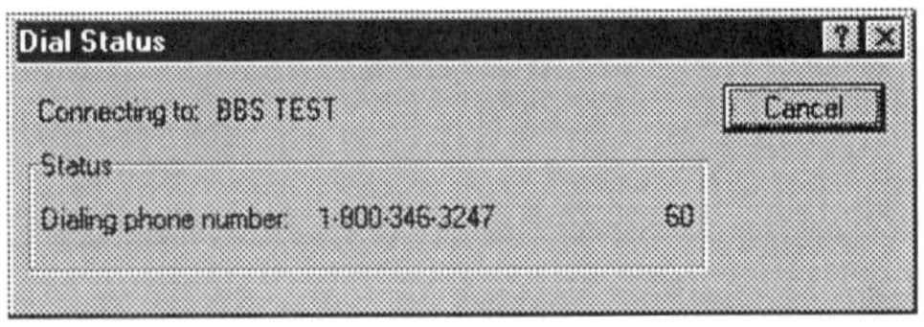

Depending on the type of modem that you have, you may be able to hear the phone as it is dialed.

c. When the host computer answers the phone and establishes communications with your modem, a blinking cursor is displayed. Press the Enter key to initiate communications.

Note: If the host is already connected to another computer, or if your communications options are not set correctly Works display a message such as, Error, Busy, or No Carrier. If this occurs, check your options and tell Works to dial again by selecting the Dial command from the Phone menu.

Check - When communications have been established, the host computer transmits a welcome message. Messages differ from service to service, but most ask for a name or account number. Your screen should be similar to the one shown below:

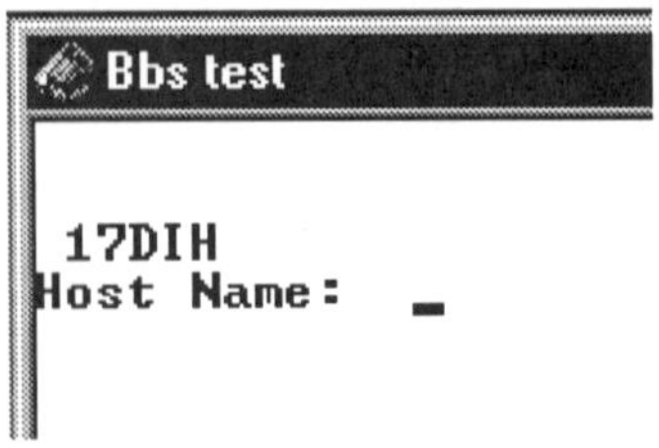

Because you are connected, anything typed on your keyboard will be sent to the host computer. You will next enter a host name and receive information by following the instructions that the host computer sends to your machine.

5) ENTER PHONES AS THE HOST

At the "Host Name:" prompt, type PHONES and press Enter. The other computer responds with a message. You are telecommunicating: your computer sent the message "PHONES" over the modem to the other computer which has now responded.

6) TERMINATE COMMUNICATIONS

From the Phone menu, select the Hang up command to terminate communications. Works displays the message:

Select OK to disconnect from the BBS.

7) EXIT WORKS

13.4 Networks

Organizations such as businesses, government agencies, and universities often *network* their microcomputers. Networked computers can communicate with each other using a transmission medium such as telephone lines, fiber optics, satellites, or digital microwave radio. They can be in the same building, many miles apart, or on different continents. A network allows applications software, files, and devices, such as printers to be shared.

Networks often include an e-mail system so that users can communicate with each other. To maintain privacy and provide security, network e-mail systems require a password for access.

To share data on a network, a file server is used. A *file server* is a computer containing large disk storage to which all other computers on the network have access. A computer on the network can access a file on the server as easily as if it were stored on its hard drive.

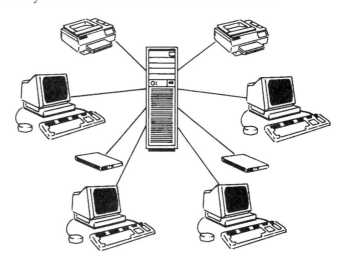

Networked computers can share files and send messages

Suppose that you, as a company employee, are preparing a report with a co-worker. If you are not using networked computers, the report file must be saved on a diskette and carried to the co-worker. On a network, you could both have access to the file at the same time. This is especially helpful for large projects which require files from different departments, such as a spreadsheet from the accounting department, a database from the marketing department, and a letter from the advertising department.

A common network type is the *Local Area Network* (LAN). The computers and other hardware devices in a LAN are usually within a short distance of each other. Rapid developments are being made in the area of the *wireless LAN*, using technologies such as lasers, radio waves, and cellular phones to network the computers. Wireless telecommunications technology, combined with portable computers, will allow users to access their computer data from anywhere in the world.

13.5 The Internet

The *Internet* is a network of networks. It is comprised of business networks, university networks, government networks, and other networks all over the world. Through this vast global network, users are able to access an almost unlimited variety of resources from the most current scientific data to movie reviews. For example, scientists from many countries have conferences online, where they discuss a topic without ever leaving their laboratories. Researchers currently working on the Human Genome Project, the massive effort to identify all the genes in human DNA, are pooling their findings into a single huge database that is available to anyone with access to the Internet. There are thousands of special interest groups available on the Internet, ranging from bungee jumping to particle physics.

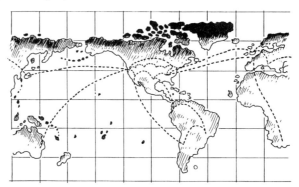

The Internet is a network of networks allowing people from all over the world to communicate

In the 1960s, the Advanced Research Projects Agency was commissioned by the U.S. Department of Defense to build a network called *ARPAnet*. This would become the core of the Internet. The first international connections to ARPAnet were made in the early 1970s, and by 1984 more than 1000 computers around the world were on the Internet. In 1995 the estimate was 30 million computers on the Internet. This includes high schools, universities, individuals, businesses, and government facilities.

An Introduction to Computing Using Microsoft Works

How do all the thousands of networks comprising the Internet communicate with one another? They use a standardized method of communication called a *protocol* that allows different computer networks and computers to talk to one another. The protocol, *TCP/IP* (Transmission Control Protocol/Internet Protocol), is a worldwide standard for the packaging and addressing of computer data so that data can be transmitted to any computer running the protocol software. For example, when e-mail is sent, it is first divided by the Transmission Control Protocol (TCP) into data packets. TCP then adds two pieces of information to each packet. One piece is the data that allows the receiving computer to determine that the data packet has not been altered in transmission, a kind of packing list. The second is the address of the receiving computer. The Internet Protocol (IP) then makes sure that the data finds its destination. With this TCP/IP information, data packets can take different routes and still reach the correct destination. Computers called *routers,* located at the intersections of networks, determine which path is best for a packet's journey.

Data transmitted over the Internet is divided into packets

13.6 Internet Addresses

Internet protocol requires that users have an address. This address is used by TCP/IP for the transmission of data so that other Internet users can communicate. An Internet address takes the form:

username@host.subdomain.domain

The username refers to the person that holds the Internet account. The host refers to the name of the computer running the TCP/IP software. This name was selected when the software was installed. The subdomain refers to the company, organization, educational institute, etc. that owns the computer host. The domain refers to the type of institution. For example, the address:

zmalfas@circa.ufl.edu

is the Internet address for Zoe Malfas whose account is on a host computer named circa located at the University of Florida which is an educational institution.

The following is a list of common domains:

Identifier	Meaning
com	commercial organization
edu	educational institution
gov	government facility
int	international organization
mil	US military facility
net	networking organization
org	nonprofit organization

13.7 Surfing the Internet and Using Gophers

Because the resources of the Internet are so vast it is impossible to know where all of the resources are located. Therefore it can be rewarding to *surf* the Internet. Surfing is when you have no particular resource in mind and no idea of what you might discover; you just access different locations and see what is there. This process is similar to going into a library and just browsing through the books. It is also similar to channel surfing where you switch from one television channel to another to see what is being broadcast.

One way to surf the Internet is with Gopher. *Gopher* makes information on the Internet easily accessible. Gopher displays menus of options. Selecting a menu item may take you to another menu or display a file. By selecting menu items, you are able to travel around the Internet without needing to know the addresses at which the resources are located.

Gopher is a client/server system. A *client* is a program that requests information and a *server* is a program that provides the information. There are many Gopher servers on the Internet. A typical Gopher menu looks like the following:

```
              Internet Gopher Information Client

                         Ivy University


--> 1.   About the Athletics Department.
    2.   About the Education Department.
    3.   About the Liberal Arts Department.
    4.   About the Minor Skin Injury Department.
    5.   Gopher Servers at Ivy University.
    6.   Ivy University Catalog.


Press ? for Help, q for quit, u to go up a menu Page: 1/1
```

To determine if a Gopher client is available through your Internet connection, type gopher and press Enter. Other Gophers are accessed by typing gopher followed by a space and the address of the gopher. For example, typing gopher consultant.micro.umn.ed connects to the CIA World Factbook gopher. Other Gophers include the following:

Gopher	Address	Provides access to:
Academic BBSs	yaleinfo.yale.edu	Internet sites dedicated to academics
Business Statistics	infopath.ucsd.edu	General business indicators, commodity prices, real estate statistics, etc.
CIA World Factbook	consultant.micro.umn.edu	Information about every country and territory in the world
Physics Gopher	granta.uchicago.edu	Information pertaining to physics
Stock Market	lobo.rmhs.colorado.edu	Stock market closing quotes and comments for recent dates
The White House	gopher.well.sf.ca.us	Information on various policies, including links to other government information.

13.8 The World Wide Web

One of the most popular areas of the Internet is the *World Wide Web* (WWW), originally developed at the CERN laboratory in Europe. As with Gopher, the Web can be used to surf the Internet. However, the World Wide Web allows the user to explore Internet resources graphically. Connecting to a Web site displays its *Web pages*. A Web page can contain graphics, fancy text, and easy access to other Web sites.

Because there is so much information on the Web, there are indexes of Web pages to help you find information. These indexes are called *search engines* and contain databases of Web pages. *Yahoo* and *Alta Vista* are two such tools for searching the Web. When a company adds a Web page to a Web site, it can request that the page be added to the Yahoo database. Other programs such as *Lycos* follow links in Web pages all over the Web and automatically add new links to its database. This type of program is called a *robot program.*

Internet sites that provide Web access run HTTP software. *HTTP* is a protocol called HyperText Transfer Protocol. Each Web site, or *Web server*, has an address called a *URL* (Uniform Resource Locator). To view a Web site, both a Web browser and a URL must be used. The URL tells your Web browser to find a specific file at a specific server and then display it. A *Web browser* understands HTTP in order to properly display the graphics and text of Web pages. Popular Web browsers include Microsoft Explorer and Netscape Navigator.

After connecting to a Web site, the first page displayed is called the *home page*. For example, Ivy's home page provides access to information about the school including admissions, athletic schedules, events, and a message from Ivy's president:

Web pages are written in a language called *HTML* (HyperText Markup Language). *Hypertext* is text that contains links to other text. Web pages contain links, usually indicated by underlined words, to other Web addresses. For example, in Ivy University's home page <u>A Message from the President</u> is a link to a page that displays a picture of Ivy's president and a letter written by her. There is a URL associated with the <u>A Message from the President</u> link. When the link is clicked, the Web browser displays the page at that address.

HTML documents can be created using any word processor. Special codes, or *tags*, are placed inside brackets. The Web browser uses these tags to determine how the Web page should be displayed and what should be displayed for each link. A portion of Ivy's home page is shown below:

```
<HTML>
<HEAD>
<TITLE>ivyweb</TITLE>
</HEAD>
<BODY>

<H2><CENTER>Ivy University<CENTER></H2><P>
<IMG SRC="ivy.gif"><P>
<IMG SRC="ivyleaf.gif">
<A HREF ="http://www.ivyu.edu/president/letter.html"><B>A
Message from the President
</B></A><P>

...
```

There are many kinds of tags that can be used in an HTML document. Tags control every aspect of the Web page including text formatting, graphics, and links. In the document above, the <H2> tag indicates a heading will follow. A slash (/) indicates the completion of a tag. For example, in the text above </H2> indicates the end of the heading. The ivy leaves below the Ivy University heading are placed using an image tag. The <A HREF tag tells the Web browser that when the user clicks on the phrase **A Message from the President** the Web page at http://www.ivyu.edu/president/letter.html should be displayed.

The Web makes surfing the Internet fun and easy through interesting and attractive Web pages. Animation, sound, and other special effects can be incorporated into Web pages using a programming language called *Java*. Developed at Sun Microsystems, Java programs can run on any computer. This makes it possible for programs to be sent over the Internet as easily as e-mail. A Web browser called *HotJava*, also by Sun Microsystems, will allow users to create customized Web pages according to their specifications.

Many businesses, schools, and government facilities have Web sites. They often publish their home page address in advertisements, commercials, and printed materials. Popular Web sites include the following:

Web Site	Address
Apple computer	http://www.apple.com
ESPN sports	http://espnet.sportszone.com
Internet College Exchange	http://www.usmall.com/college
The Library of Congress	http://www.loc.gov
The Rock and Roll Hall of Fame	http://www.rockhall.com
USA Today	http://www.usatoday.com
The White House	http://www.whitehouse.gov/
Yahoo search engine	http://www.yahoo.com

13.9 Improved Microprocessors and Software

While the Internet has only recently become widely used, another computer advancement has been utilized in most households around the world. Microprocessors are now found in telephone answering machines, watches, CD players, cameras, television sets, refrigerators, washing machines, and other appliances:

Ordinary household appliances have microprocessors

One example of the use of a microprocessor is in the anti-lock braking system (ABS) found on many cars. As the brakes are applied, a computer connected to sensors on the car's wheels detects when the car begins to skid. The computer then takes control of the brakes, pumping them rapidly to keep the wheels from locking. Other microprocessors increase the efficiency of an automobile engine or control how safety devices perform in an emergency situation.

Microprocessor development has advanced the use of diagnostic systems for complex electronic devices. Many devices such as computers and car engines have become so complicated that it is difficult to determine what is wrong when they malfunction. Therefore, microprocessors have been developed that pinpoint the faulty component and then alert the user. These diagnostic systems are commonly found in automobiles and aircraft.

Another use for microprocessors is in chip-enhanced ATM and credit cards called smart cards. These new cards have a microprocessor embedded in them that records transactions and credits or debits the card's balance instantly.

13.10 Supercomputers and Neural Networks

Considerable effort and money has been committed to developing supercomputers. These computers can perform one trillion (1,000,000,000,000) calculations per second. By comparison the UNIVAC built in 1951 could perform only 1,000 calculations per second. Some supercomputers achieve such speed using a technique called *parallel processing* in which a number of high-speed microprocessors are combined. A problem is first broken into parts and they are then solved simultaneously, or in parallel, on separate microprocessors. Why are such high speeds needed? Because computers are being asked to produce solutions in an acceptable amount of time for problems requiring billions of calculations. In the next two sections we discuss two such problems: the analysis of the data in very large databases and the production of sophisticated graphics to create motion picture effects.

In addition to hardware techniques such as parallel processing, there is software being developed which can substantially increase a computer's ability. Neural-network software, designed to be similar to the pattern of cells in the human brain, can "learn" from analyzing large sets of data. The software is capable of producing a statistical model describing important relationships and patterns in the data. This technique in combination with parallel-processing is especially useful for working with the information stored in large databases.

13.11 Database Marketing

In Chapters Five through Seven you learned how to create and manipulate a Works database. A major problem that confronts the computer industry is how to work with huge databases that have millions of records. For example, the Blockbuster Entertainment Corporation has a database of nearly forty million households and two million daily rentals of its videotapes. This database contains information on the rental habits of Blockbuster's customers that can be used to create effective advertising. Any time you make use of a credit card or fill out a product warranty card you are supplying information that will be stored in a database.

Credit card companies have vast databases which are difficult to store and search because of their size. Marketers developing sales campaigns want to be able to sift through such data in order to discover patterns that will predict consumer behavior. For example, what combination of income, credit-card spending, investments, and geographical location identifies a person most likely to purchase a new automobile? The answer can produce a list of potential customers that is impossible to generate in any other way. Such sophisticated database searches require multiple and interrelated criteria. Currently, this kind of computing ability can only be supplied by very powerful computers which employ advanced technologies such as parallel-processing.

13.12 Computer Generated Motion Picture Effects

Many of the special effects we see in motion pictures are computer generated. By scanning each separate frame from a motion picture into a computer, the image is digitized and stored as a collection of tiny pieces called *pixels*. Once in this form the image can be manipulated pixel by pixel to produce a new image. For example, to create a film that shows dinosaurs in a park, small models of dinosaurs and an outdoor setting are filmed separately and then combined on the computer. Another example is a film that requires an actor to be suspended on wires to give the illusion of flying. If the audience sees the supports the effect will be ruined, but by digitizing the film the wires can be removed frame by frame.

Computers can generate images of models and manipulate them

One of the most exciting computer generated effects is *morphing*, a process by which a photographic image slowly turns into a second image. For example, a human face can be changed to a wolf by digitizing a picture of each face and then changing each pixel of one face into the other.

13.13 Artificial Intelligence

Although computers cannot think, one of the major areas of research continues to be the development of programs that are capable of making increasingly complex decisions. Using computers to make decisions which would normally be made by human beings is called *artificial intelligence*. Herbert Schorr, a computer scientist at IBM, has declared that the development of artificial intelligence is the second wave of the information revolution. The first wave was the development of automated data processing. According to Schorr "the second wave will automate decision making."

In 1950 the brilliant English mathematician Alan Turing wrote a paper entitled "Computing Machinery and Intelligence" in which he raised the question "Can machines think?" To answer that question he invented the "Imitation Game." Briefly summarized, the game involves placing a person and a computer in separate rooms and an interrogator in a third room. Communicating by typed questions and answers, the interrogator questions the human and computer to determine which is the computer. If the interrogator cannot tell the difference between the responses then, according to Turing, the machine has human thought capabilities. Since not even psychologists can agree on a definition of intelligence, this is probably as good a test as any. Currently, no computer or software program has been shown to be capable of consistently passing the *Turing test*. However, when limited to a specific topic, say sports, several programs have fooled their human interrogators into thinking that they were communicating with another human.

One area of artificial intelligence is *expert systems*. An expert system is programmed to produce the same solution a human expert would if asked to solve the same problem.

Another use of expert systems is by U.S. intelligence agents to avert terrorist acts. Programmed with the knowledge of a handful of terrorism agents, the system has proven surprisingly accurate in its ability to predict when and where terrorist activities will occur. Another similar system is used by the FBI to predict the activities of criminals. Both systems have been programmed with rules that human experts have developed based on decades of experience in dealing with terrorists.

The IRS uses an expert system to analyze tax returns and determine if a person is making improper deductions. Programmed to look for suspicious patterns, the IRS computer decides when a human agent should consider initiating an audit.

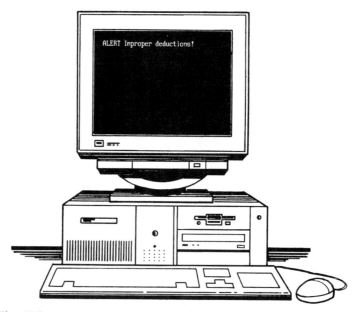

The IRS uses expert systems to find improper tax deductions

An example of such a system is the one used by the credit card division of American Express. If an American Express card holder wants to make a large purchase, for example a $10,000 oriental rug, the computer will decide whether or not to approve the purchase based on the card holder's account history. The expert systems that work the best are those for which a series of rules can be used to make a decision. When specific rules do not apply, as when intuition must be used, expert systems are usually not successful.

13.15 Speech Recognition Software

Designing a computer system that can recognize human speech has long been a goal of computer scientists. Advancements in computer processors and *speech recognition software* have made many such systems available. Speech recognition software uses *natural language processing*, a field of artificial intelligence which translates spoken words into text.

Today speech recognition software has been developed for dictation and command and control. *Dictation systems* are used for voice mail, in the medical field for creating transcriptions, and in many different fields for data entry. *Command and control systems* are often used by those with physical handicaps, including carpal tunnel syndrome, to control their computers by spoken words. Other applications for command and control systems are voice activated car phones and phone menus. For example, many companies today allow you to choose from their menu of choices by saying or pressing the number of the desired menu choice ("Please press or say one").

Another form of speech recognition software that is being developed is for *continuous speech*. Continuous speech refers to normal speaking patterns. However, there are difficulties in producing natural language processing systems for continuous speech. First, many words have different meanings based upon the context in which they are used. The word "change," for example, could mean money as in "Here's your change" or a different order as in "Change my order to a hot dog." Second, there are almost an unlimited number of ways of giving the same instructions. Finally, a speech-recognizing computer needs to be able to understand many different voice patterns and accents.

13.16 Robotics

Another application of artificial intelligence is in *robotics*. To be defined as a robot a machine must be able to both be programmed and move. Most robots, unlike those seen in the movies, are simply moveable arms that can be directed to perform a task. Because they can be programmed, robots can make simple decisions and then act upon them. Some robots are currently "employed" by the automobile industry to spot weld and spray paint cars. As robots become capable of performing increasingly complicated tasks, they are being used in many more industries.

There are a number of advantages to using robots. One advantage is their ability to perform tasks too dangerous for humans. Robots have been developed to remove and defuse bombs, work in highly radioactive environments, or in conditions of extreme noise or temperature. Their use in aiding the physically challenged is also a very promising area of research. A major advantage of robots is that they can perform their tasks tirelessly, willing to work 24-hour days without rest or vacations.

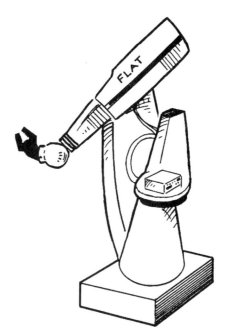

Robots can work 24 hours a day with no rest

However, a task as simple as picking up an egg has proven difficult for a robot to perform. The hand-eye coordination which we take for granted requires an extremely complex set of actions which are difficult to duplicate mechanically. Even a task as simple as moving through a room without hitting objects can be difficult for a robot.

13.17 Virtual Reality

One of the most exciting applications of computing is in creating *virtual reality*. Virtual reality is using a computer to create a world that does not exist. To enter this world the user usually wears a special glove and a helmet with small video displays and earphones. All of the equipment contains motion sensors. This system is *interactive* which means that the actions of the user determine what the computer displays.

Many interactive games have been created using virtual reality. In one popular game the player enters a room displayed in the helmet and moves his or her head looking for a villain. When the villain is spotted a finger in the glove is used to shoot at the villain. The player has the sensation of stalking the villain through different rooms and up and down stairs, in a world that appears startling real.

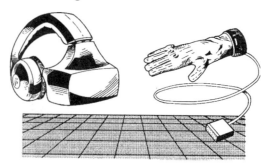

The helmet and glove contain motion sensors that communicate the movements of the wearer to the computer

The worlds created through virtual reality are not limited to games, but also can be used for practical purposes. For example, computers are now used to create a virtual world that allows a pilot to train by landing a jet airliner in a variety of weather conditions without risking a real plane or the pilot's life. Medical students perform simulated operations on patients created by the computer, and architects design buildings through which clients are able to journey without anything being built. Such technology allows customers to experience a "hands-on" demonstration of products or services before they have been actually developed.

It is the convergence of powerful imaging, sensor, and computer technology that has made virtual reality possible. Major improvements in the way that people interact with the computer have made the virtual experience more realistic. Voice recognition software also allows the virtual world to respond to voice commands. This is a field that has only begun to demonstrate its considerable potential.

13.18 Multimedia / Hypermedia

Multimedia or *hypermedia* is where text, graphics, video, and sound are accessible together through a computer:

A multimedia computer system often includes speakers, a joystick, a CD-ROM drive, earphones, and a microphone

An exciting application of multimedia is a computerized encyclopedia where the user can access an entry that includes different types of linked information. When accessing an entry on Ludwig von Beethoven, the user can choose to see a picture of Ludwig, hear a selection from his ninth symphony, or take a video tour of his house in Vienna. With a multimedia computer a user can wear headphones and listen to a CD playing in the computer's CD-ROM drive while watching TV in a small window on the screen and working on a spreadsheet in another window.

13.19 Advanced Storage Devices

The amount of information accessible by a single computer has increased dramatically with the technological advancement of storage devices. These devices use various media to store large amounts of data in easily transportable packages.

One type of storage device is a *tape drive*, which stores data on magnetic tape sealed inside a cartridge. Each cartridge can hold 7 GB or more of data. Another type of storage device is the removable hard drive which uses disks constructed like floppy diskettes but slightly larger. These disks have capacities of 230 MB or more. Two popular styles of the removable hard drive are Bernoulli and SyQuest. A new, smaller version is the Iomega Zip drive that has diskettes similar in size of 3.5" floppy diskettes but with a capacity of 100 MB.

Enormous amounts of data can be made transportable using hard disk arrays. These are towers of several hard drives (not just large diskettes as in the removable hard drives) that combine to equal 72 GB or more. Each hard drive can be removed from the tower and transported to another similar array tower.

Until recently, CD-ROMs were aptly named because the data contained in them was read-only. Now CD recorders are available that write data onto CDs. With a wide range of storage devices available, the exchange of information has certainly increased in society.

13.20 Computing at Home

Personal computers are now inexpensive enough that many people have powerful machines at home. As such, software has been specifically created for the home user. Below we discuss several personal applications for home use.

Entertainment

A popular use for home computers is in the field of entertainment. For example, software is now available that edits home videos and produces graphics which can be added to the video. This allows the home user to produce professional-looking home videos including titles and animation.

The computer can be used by many kinds of artists. Input devices called *scanners* can convert drawings and pictures into a file, which can then be modified using the computer and sent over the Internet to friends. Photographers can use similar software to retouch photographs and produce special effects. Musicians are using a special type of computer output called *MIDI*—Musical Instrument Digital Interface. MIDI permits a computer to control synthesizers, allowing entire scores to be composed, edited, and performed using the computer.

Games

Playing games is another use for computers in the home. There are several different types of games available, but they generally fall into two categories: *simulations* and *role-playing*. In simulations, the computer graphically simulates an action such as driving a car. A popular simulation is Microsoft's Flight Simulator in which the computer is used to fly a plane. By giving different commands, the "plane" can be made to takeoff, accelerate, turn, land, etc. while the cockpit is displayed on the screen. Flight Simulator is so realistic that pilots use it to practice flying techniques at home.

Role-playing or fantasy games involve solving a complex puzzle by directing the actions of a character described on the screen. In these games the user enters commands such as "go west" or "open the door" which the character follows. The player could be looking for treasure, or seeking information about a crime. The sense of player involvement increases when using better systems and software.

An Introduction to Computing Using Microsoft Works

Productivity   Other software helps home computer users be more productive. There are several packages for managing home finances that help develop a budget, keep track of expenses, prepare taxes, and print checks to pay bills. Some allow you to pay bills and receive credit card statements using a modem. Different packages allow the computer to be used as a fax machine or label maker. There are also many database-type programs that keep track of recipes or gardening information or even diet and exercise statistics. Software can also provide opportunities for home study in a variety of different fields like math, science, and specialized courses such as the SAT or real estate examination. This is called *computer based training* (CBT). The ability to learn at home at their own pace gives many people the incentive and opportunity to further their education.

13.21 Mobile Computing

Advancements in computer technology have allowed computer components to become smaller and smaller. This trend is also true of processing chips which can now contain millions of components in an area smaller than a fingernail. Because of this, computers the size and weight of a 5 pound book are now being manufactured with the power of a large desktop model. Usually called *laptops*, these small computers can be powered by batteries and therefore operated anywhere. Business people, newspaper reporters, and students are among the many users who find laptop computers convenient.

The miniaturization of parts through advances in technology has lead to the development of the *personal digital assistant* (PDA). Often using cellular telephone technology and a built-in modem, the PDA creates a computing environment that is *mobile* or *nomadic*:

PDAs are small enough to fit into a shirt pocket

No longer encumbered by either size or wires, the PDA allows its user to travel anywhere and yet have access to e-mail, the Internet, or any information that can be transmitted over a modem. Such technology is of obvious advantage to a salesperson traveling around the world.

Not only are computer systems being adapted to the modern mobile lifestyle, but now there is a system that acts like a smart compass to tell you exactly where you are. The *global positioning system* (GPS) was built by the U.S. government and is composed of a satellite system that periodically sends out signals towards Earth. Anyone wishing to use the system must have a hand-held receiver. The satellite signals are processed by the receiver and result in a very accurate reading of the receiver's current position on the Earth in latitude, longitude, and altitude.

13.22 Careers in Computing

As computers have become more powerful they play an ever increasing role in the world we live in. Consequently most people, no matter what field they are employed in, use computers in some way at work. In this section we discuss some computer careers that you might consider and the education required to enter them.

The area of computing that employs the largest number of people is *data processing*. Data processing involves the electronic entry, storage, manipulation, and retrieval of data. Businesses, governments, educational institutions—almost any organization—require the management of large amounts of data and therefore need employees capable of data processing. Careers in data processing are usually divided into five categories: data-entry operator, system analyst, system developer, system manager, and computer scientist.

Data-Entry Operator   A *data-entry operator* types data into a computer. Data-entry operators may work for banks entering cancelled checks, department stores entering inventory figures, or educational institutions entering student records. A data-entry operator should possess a high school diploma and the ability to type quickly and accurately.

System Analyst   Before a data processing system can be set up a *system analyst* must first analyze and design the system. The analyst must determine how an organization will use the computer system, what data will be stored, how it will be accessed, and how the system is expected to grow in the future. The same planning used in the database chapters of this text have given you an introduction to what a system analyst does.

A system analyst should possess a comprehensive knowledge of data-processing methods, software, hardware, and programming languages. Most system analysts are college graduates who have majored in computer science or information systems or both.

System Developer/ Programmer   After the system analyst has determined what type of system should be installed, the *system developer* provides the necessary software. A programmer should possess a detailed knowledge of the programming language or languages being used as well as an ability to reason analytically and pay close attention to details.

Many businesses employ programmers who have graduated from technical school or community college with a degree in programming. Large or specialized companies, which need highly sophisticated programming, usually require a four-year college degree.

System Manager   Companies with large data processing requirements usually employ a manager who is responsible for running the Management Information Systems department (MIS). The *MIS manager* must organize the computer and human resources of the department in order to best achieve the organization's goals. A system manager should possess a detailed understanding of data-processing methods, hardware, and software. A college degree in business administration with a concentration in information systems is usually required.

Computer Scientist

The study of computer science is a very broad field involving many disciplines including science, electronics, and mathematics. A *computer scientist* often works in research at a university or computer manufacturer developing new computer applications software and hardware. It is computer scientists who first design and develop robots, natural language processors, or the many applications that we have mentioned. A computer scientist usually has both undergraduate and graduate degrees in computer science.

The computer industry careers previously discussed are directed at data processing. There are many computing careers with concentrations in other fields. For example, the computer hardware industry also offers a number of career opportunities including the design, manufacture, service, and sale of computers. Another example is the field of education that employs computer teachers and technology coordinators. A third field is that of maintaining Web sites, including their design.

Computer Engineer

Computer engineers design and manufacture computers. This field is broad and includes engineers who develop new computer applications. Other engineers translate ideas produced by researchers into manufactured products. A computer engineer usually possesses both undergraduate and graduate degrees in engineering.

Manufacturing Worker

The people who help build computer systems usually possess the ability to work well with tools. *Manufacturing workers* usually have earned a high school or community college degree. Good preparation for such a career includes taking courses in mechanical arts as well as science and mathematics.

Technical Support Technician

Working mainly over the phone, *technical support technicians* assist customers of both hardware and software companies. Customers that have questions or problems with any aspect of the company's products, including installation and compatibility call the technical support phone number and speak with a technician who then identifies the problem and offers a solution. A technical support technician is usually a graduate of a technical school or community college.

Computer Sales Representative

A large number of people sell computers either as representatives who travel and visit clients or as salespeople in computer stores. It is important that they possess a thorough knowledge of the equipment they sell and be able to explain how it may be used by each customer. The level of education required for the job will depend on the sophistication of the equipment being sold. Often a high school or community college degree is sufficient. To sell large computer systems, a sales representative may be required to have a four-year college degree.

Computer Teacher

All of the people currently working in a computer-related field are there because of *computer teachers*. In high schools and colleges, teachers and professors do research for and teach all aspects of computing from computer science to ethics. For teaching at the high school level, a four-year college degree in a computer field is sufficient. At the college level, a graduate degree is required for full professorship.

Technology Coordinator

At any school, it is the job of the *technology coordinator* to plan and oversee the acquisition, distribution, and utilization of computer technology. Schools requires such a person to insure that they have working facilities and are keeping up with new advancements in technology. A four-year college degree in a computer field is required.

Webmaster

With the rapid increase in the use of the World Wide Web, there is now a need for *Webmasters*. A Webmaster does everything from designing a Web page to creating the code and graphics for it to maintaining the site with timely updates. A Webmaster possesses extensive Internet knowledge, including programming skills, as well as design experience.

13.23 The Social and Ethical Consequences of Computers

The society in which we live has been so profoundly affected by computers that historians refer to the present time as the *information age*. This is due to the computer's ability to store and manipulate large amounts of information (data). Because of computers, we are evolving out of an industrial and into an information society, much as over a hundred years ago we evolved from an agricultural society into an industrial one. Such fundamental societal changes cause disruptions which must be planned for. For this reason it is crucial that we consider both the social and ethical consequences of our increasing dependence on computers.

We have already mentioned the impact of telecommunications. By allowing people to work anywhere that telephones or satellite communications are available, we have to become a more diversified society. In fact, after the Los Angeles earthquakes in 1994 a computer newspaper had the headline "A not-so-gentle push for telecommuting." Such decentralization could reduce traffic congestion, air pollution, and many of the other consequences of an urban society. Because of this, Alvin Toffler in his book *The Third Wave* called this the age of the "electronic cottage."

In our discussion of robots we mentioned their ability to work 24-hours a day. While this is obviously a major benefit to an employer, it could have a negative impact on employees. Manufacturers are increasingly able to replace factory workers with machines, thereby increasing efficiency and saving money. This trend, however, also leads to increased unemployment of those factory workers who often lack technical skills.

The argument is often used that new technologies such as robotics create jobs for the people who design, build, install, and service them. While this is true, these new jobs require well educated, highly trained people. For this reason it is important to think carefully about the educational requirements needed for employment. As we become an increasingly "high-tech" society, those properly prepared for technical jobs will be the most likely to find employment. In response to this problem many states have instituted programs to train laid-off factory workers so that they may enter technical fields.

Another concern is that the widespread dependence on information services such as the Internet will create two groups; those with access to information and those without. The *National Information Infrastructure* (NII) is a government sponsored version of the Internet created to unite the two groups. One of the goals of the NII is to provide access to the *information highway* at every school, hospital, and public library.

13.24 The Right to Privacy

With computers impacting on our lives in an ever increasing number of ways, serious ethical questions arise over their use. By ethical questions we mean asking what are the morally right and wrong ways to use computers. As human beings we want to insure that our rights as individuals are not encroached upon by the misuse of these machines.

Probably the most serious problem created by computers is invading our right to privacy. Because computers can store vast amounts of data we must decide what information is proper to store, what is improper, and who should have access to the information. Every time you use a credit card, make a phone call, withdraw money, reserve a flight, or register at school a computer records the transaction. Using these records it is possible to learn a great deal about you—where you have been, when you were there, and what you have done. Should this information be available to everyone?

Computers are also used to store information about your credit rating, which determines your ability to borrow money. If you want to buy a car and finance it at the bank, the bank first checks your credit records on a computer to determine if you have a good credit rating. If you purchase the car and then apply for automobile insurance, another computer will check to determine if you have traffic violations. How do you know if the information being used is accurate? To protect both your privacy and the accuracy of data stored about you, a number of laws have been passed.

The **Fair Credit Reporting Act of 1970** deals with data collected for use by credit, insurance, and employment agencies. The act gives individuals the right to see information maintained about them. If a person is denied credit they are allowed to see the files used to make the credit determination. If any of the information is incorrect, the person has the right to have it changed. The act also restricts who may access credit files to only those with a court order or the written permission of the individual whose credit is being checked.

The **Privacy Act of 1974** restricts the way in which personal data can be used by federal agencies. Individuals must be permitted access to information stored about them and may correct any information that is incorrect. Agencies must insure both the security and confidentiality of any sensitive information. Although this law applies only to federal agencies, many states have adopted similar laws.

The **Financial Privacy Act of 1978** requires that a government authority have a subpoena, summons, or search warrant to access an individual's financial records. When such records are released, the financial institution must notify the individual of who has had access to them.

The **Electronic Communications Privacy Act of 1986** (ECPA) makes it a crime to access electronic data without authorization. It also prohibits unauthorized release of such data.

Laws such as these help to insure that the right to privacy is not infringed by data stored in computer files. Although implementing privacy laws has proven expensive and difficult, most people would agree that they are needed.

13.25 Protecting Computer Software and Data

Because computer software can be copied electronically it is easy to duplicate. Such duplication is usually illegal because the company producing the software is not paid for the copy. This has become an increasingly serious problem as the number of illegal software copies distributed by computer *pirates* has grown. Developing, testing, marketing, and supporting software is an expensive process. If the software developer is then denied rightful compensation, the future development of all software is jeopardized.

Software companies are increasingly vigilant in detecting and prosecuting those who illegally copy their software. In recent years, software companies have actually made "raids" on businesses and educational institutions to search their computers. An organization found guilty of using illegally copied software can be fined, and its reputation damaged. Therefore, when using software it is important to use only legally acquired copies, and to not make illegal copies for others.

Another problem that is growing as computer use increases is the willful interference with or destruction of computer data. Because computers can transfer and erase data at high speeds, it makes them especially vulnerable to acts of vandalism. Newspapers have carried numerous reports of home computer users gaining access to large computer databases. Sometimes these *hackers* change or erase data stored in the system. These acts are usually illegal and can cause very serious and expensive damage. The Electronic Communications Privacy Act of 1986 specifically makes it a federal offense to access electronic data without authorization.

One especially harmful act is the planting of a *virus* into computer software. A virus is a series of instructions buried into a program that cause the computer to destroy data when given a certain signal. For example, the instructions to destroy data might wait until a certain time or date is reached before being executed. Because the virus is duplicated each time the software is copied, it spreads to other computers, hence the name virus. This practice is illegal and can result in considerable damage. Computer viruses have become so widespread that there are now computer programs that have been developed to detect and erase viruses before they can damage data.

*Contaminated disks are one way that viruses are
spread from computer to computer*

Most people are becoming aware that the willful destruction of computer data is no different than any other vandalization of property. Since
the damage is done electronically the result is often not as obvious as
destroying physical property, but the consequences are much the same.
It is estimated that computer crimes cost the nation billions of dollars
each year.

13.26 The Ethical Responsibilities of the Programmer

It is extremely difficult, if not impossible, for a computer programmer
to guarantee that a program will *always* operate properly. The programs
used to control complicated devices contain millions of instructions, and
as programs grow longer the likelihood of errors increases. A special cause
for concern is the increased use of computers to control potentially
dangerous devices such as aircraft, nuclear reactors, or sensitive medical
equipment. This places a strong ethical burden on the programmer to
insure, as best he or she can, the reliability of the computer software.

The Department of Defense (DOD) is currently supporting research
aimed at detecting and correcting programming errors. Because it spends
billions of dollars annually developing software, much of it for use in
situations which can be life threatening, the DOD is especially interested
in having reliable programs.

As capable as computers have proven to be, we must be cautious when
allowing them to replace human beings in areas where judgement is crucial. Because we are intelligent, humans can often detect that something
out of the ordinary has occurred and then take actions which have not
been previously anticipated. Computers will only do what they have been
programmed to do, even if it is to perform a dangerous act.

We must also consider situations in which the computer can protect
human life better than humans. For example, in the space program
astronauts place their lives in the hands of computers which must continuously perform complicated calculations at very high speeds. No

human being would be capable of doing the job as well as a computer. Computers are also routinely used to monitor seriously ill patients. Since computers are able to work 24 hours a day without becoming distracted or falling asleep, they probably perform such tasks better than most humans would.

Desktop Publishing and Graphics

The popularity of computers has produced a new generation of software geared to the presentation of information. Computers can now be used to manipulate art work, pictures, and text. These applications allow an organization, educational institution, or individual to produce professional looking documents without the use of artists, designers, or typesetters.

13.27 Printers

Probably the most important advance which made desktop publishing possible was the creation of a low-cost, dependable printer. A *laser printer* uses a beam of light to draw each character on the page, employing a process similar to a photocopier. This allows for smooth characters. A close examination of a character produced by a laser printer illustrates this:

T

A character produced by a laser printer is smooth

Laser printers are also able to produce graphics such as pictures and diagrams with a similar level of clarity. Color laser printers, although much more expensive can print images in full color.

An *inkjet printer* contains an ink cartridge and places very small dots on the paper to form characters and graphics. The output from an inkjet printer is also high quality, but not quite as smooth as the output from a laser printer. Color inkjet printers are also available. They are very inexpensive compared to color laser printers and produce very good color output.

13.28 Desktop Publishing

One of the most popular uses for laser printers is in the field of *desktop publishing* (DTP). As discussed in Chapter Twelve, special software allows persons not trained in art or layout to create professional looking documents using a personal computer and a laser printer. It is the purpose of desktop publishing software to combine text (created in a word processor) with illustrations (created by a graphics program) to produce the final document. Before desktop publishing existed, creating a document such as a brochure was a complicated procedure, involving many people:

1. A writer to create the text of the brochure.
2. An artist to produce the illustrations.
3. A typesetter to print the text.
4. A layout person to combine the text and illustrations into the completed brochure using scissors and glue.
5. A printer to produce the brochure.

Now a single person can perform all of these tasks using a computer. A major advantage of using desktop publishing software is that changes can easily be made to a document instead of cutting and pasting with glue. Illustrations and text can be added or deleted, changed in size, or the whole layout redone—all on a computer screen.

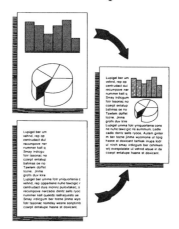

Desktop publishing software combines graphics and text into one file

By laying out a document on the computer screen instead of on paper different layouts can be created and viewed until the desired combination is found. Once completed, the final version can be printed and the document saved so that it can be edited or reprinted at a later time.

Three of the most commonly used desktop publishing programs are PageMaker, FrameMaker, and QuarkXPress. Less powerful and inexpensive programs such as Publish It!, Microsoft Publisher, and PrintShop are also available. Most of these packages contain collections of prepared illustrations called *clip art* which can be included in documents, often eliminating the need for an artist.

13.29 Graphics and Illustration Software

Graphic images can be created and manipulated on the computer with various types of software. Graphic images are non-text items such as drawings, photographs, charts, logos, etc. The advantage of using a computer rather than drawing on paper is that the image can then be manipulated; resized, rotated, etc. and the image can then be stored in the computer's memory. When the final version is created, it can be printed in black and white using a laser printer or in color using a color printer. The graphics you created in Chapter Twelve are simple examples of what can be accomplished using graphics software.

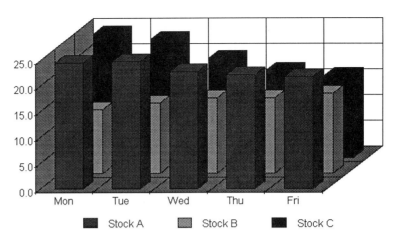

Stock Prices Last Week

Sophisticated graphics programs can easily produce three-dimensional objects, charts, and graphs

There are several powerful programs available for creating and editing graphic images. Two of these are Adobe Illustrator and CorelDraw. Most require the use of a specialized input device to aid in the drawing. The most popular of these devices are the mouse and the drawing tablet. Ready-made images called *clip art* can be purchased in any software store and then manipulated into new images. Clip art is often supplied on CD-ROM that can contain thousands of images.

One advantage to using illustration software is that any graphics produced can easily be placed in a document. Most desktop publishing software packages can read the files produced by illustration software, and place a graphic directly into a desktop publishing document. Some software can even perform basic editing on the image, allowing it to be scaled (resized), rotated, or cropped (only part of the graphic is displayed).

13.30 Graphics and Illustration Equipment

One of the tasks faced by desktop publishers is that of working with photographic images on the computer. There are several ways this can be achieved. One way is to use a scanner to scan an actual photograph, which then sends the digitized information in a file to the computer and the image is viewed. Another way is to use a digital camera, which is much like a regular camera except instead of film there is a microprocessor that creates a file. Currently, digital cameras do not possess the high resolution capabilities necessary for sharp, clear photographs, and therefore better images are obtained with a photograph and scanner.

13.31 Where can we go from here?

In this text we have presented the history of computing, showed you how to use a word processor, database, and spreadsheet, and have considered the future of computing. Our hope is that you are excited by computers and realize the tremendous potential they have to serve us in a wide variety of ways. We also hope that you have been made aware of how computers might be misused. It is therefore the duty of each one of us to ensure that the awesome power computers are capable of be used only to benefit humankind.

Chapter Summary

One of the most important advances in the field of computing has been in telecommunications, which means the sending of computer data over phone lines. Modems are used both to transmit and receive computer data. Because of telecommunications many people may be able to work at home.

A popular form of telecommunications is the electronic bulletin board (BBS) which allows users to transmit and receive messages. A similar form of telecommunications is electronic mail (e-mail) where individual users are able to receive messages meant only for them.

Works has a Communications application that allows access to information services. For two computers to communicate, they must both use the same communication options. Using the Communication command from the Settings Menu, options are entered for the bits per second, data bits, parity, and stop bits. These settings can then be stored in a file. The Easy Connect command from the Phone menu dials the number and attempts to establish communications with the other computer. To terminate the communications, the Hang up command is used.

Networks allow computers to communicate with each other over telephone lines, fiber optics, satellites, or digital microwave radio. Networks allow software, files, and devices such as printers to be shared by many computers. The most common network is the Local Area Network (LAN) which allows files to be shared between a number of computers. These files are usually stored on a file server.

The Internet is a large network of networks linking computers all over the world. Through the Internet personal computer users have access to information resources worldwide. The TCP/IP is a standardized method of communication that allows computers to talk to one another. Each user must have an Internet address. Searching through the vast quantities of information is assisted by specialized software, services, and search tools, including indexes to the numerous databases. Web pages that contain graphics, text, and links to other sites are available on the World Wide Web, a popular area of the Internet.

The continued development of microprocessors has affected many products including automobiles and home appliances. Microprocessors are used in diagnostic systems for electronic devices and in chip-enhanced smart cards such as ATM and credit cards.

Supercomputers are being built that can perform up to one trillion calculations per second. Neural-network software is designed to be similar to the pattern of cells in the human brain and "learn" by analyzing large sets of data. Two problems requiring large amounts of computer power are database marketing and computer generated motion picture effects.

Using computers to make decisions normally made by human beings is called artificial intelligence. Although computers cannot think, they can be programmed to make decisions which, for example, allow them to play chess. Expert systems are a form of artificial intelligence where a computer is programmed with a set of rules that can solve a problem, producing the same solution a human expert would. Credit card companies, the IRS and hospitals are a few of the organizations currently using expert systems.

Recognizing spoken words and translating them into digital form is called speech recognition which involves natural language processing, a field of artificial intelligence that translates a sentence into its separate parts to understand its meaning.

A robot is a machine that can be programmed and also move. Robots are currently used to perform manufacturing tasks. One advantage of robots is their ability to perform tasks 24 hours a day in situations dangerous to humans.

Virtual reality is using the computer to create a world that does not exist. To enter this world the user usually wears a helmet containing small video displays and gloves with motion sensors. Multimedia combines text, graphics, video, and sound together on a computer. Tape drives, hard disk arrays, and CD-ROMs have increased the amount of information accessible by a single computer.

The use of personal computers in the home has become popular and will grow with the increased availability of telecommunications and networks. Home computers are often used to play games, entertain, and help users be more productive. Mobile computing is also increasing with the development of laptops and personal digital assistants.

Careers in computing and the educational requirements needed to pursue them were discussed in this chapter. Careers which require only a high school education as well as those requiring a college education were presented.

Historians refer to the present time as the information age due to the computer's ability to store and manipulate large amounts of data. As the use of computers increases they will profoundly affect society. Therefore, it is important to ananlyze the social and ethical implications of computers.

A problem created by computers is their potential for invading our right to privacy. Laws have been passed to protect us from the misuse of data stored in computers.

Because computer software is easy to copy, illegal copies are often made, denying software manufacturers of rightful compensation. Another problem has been the willful destruction of computer files by erasing data or planting a virus into programs that can spread when the programs are copied.

As computers are increasingly used to make decisions in situations which can impact human life, it becomes the responsibility of programmers to do their best to insure the reliability of the software they have developed. We must continue to be cautious not to replace human beings with computers in areas where judgement is crucial.

Desktop publishing software has made it possible for computers to produce and manipulate art work, pictures and the layout of documents. Laser printers, which employ a beam of light to draw characters on a page, are often used in desktop publishing applications.

Special software is used to create graphics images such as drawings, photographs, charts, etc. on the computer. This software allows the images to be easily manipulated and modified.

Vocabulary

Artificial intelligence - Computers used to make decisions which would normally be made by a human being.

Bits per second - Rate at which characters of data are transmitted in telecommunications. Also called bits per second (bps).

Bulletin board system (BBS) - Telecommunications service which allows subscribers using a computer and modem to transmit messages that can be received by all the other subscribers.

CD-ROM (Compact Disc Read-Only Memory) - An aluminum plastic-coated disc, capable of storing up to 600 megabytes of data, which is read by a laser.

Client/Server - A program requesting information on the Internet/A program that provides requested Internet information.

Clip art - Collection of previously prepared graphics for use in desktop publishing.

Command and Control systems - Computer systems that can be controlled by spoken words.

Communication command - Used to set options for telecommunications.

Computer based training (CBT) - Using specialized software to learn at home, at your own pace.

Data bits - The number of bits that make up one piece of data.

Data processing - Entry, storage, manipulation, and retrieval of information using a computer.

Database marketing - Searching a very large database in order to extract marketing information.

Desktop publishing (DTP) - Using special software to create professional looking documents on a computer.

Dictation systems - A computer system that converts spoken words to text.

Digital - Information expressed as a series of binary digits.

Download - To transfer a message or computer file from a bulletin board system or information service to your computer.

Easy Connect command - Dials the specified telephone number.

Electronic mail (e-mail) - Telecommunications service which allows a person using a computer and modem to send a private message to another person's computer.

Expert system - System programmed to produce the same solution a human expert would if asked to solve the same problem.

File server - A computer containing large disk storage that provides file access to other computers in a network.

Global positioning system (GPS) - A tool that can be used to access information on the Internet.

Gopher - A tool that can be used to access information on the Internet.

Hacker - Person who uses a modem to enter a computer system without authorization.

Home page - The first page displayed after connecting to a Web site.

Host - The computer running a bulletin board or information service.

HotJava - A Web browser that can be used to create customized Web pages.

HTML - Hypertext Markup Language. The language that is used to create Web pages.

HTTP - Hypertext Transfer Protocol. The protocol used by Web sites.

Hypertext - Text that contains links to other text.

Information age - Current historical time characterized by increasing dependence on the computer's ability to store and manipulate large amounts of information.

Information highway - Nickname for a large, publicly accessible computer network, the full name is the National Information Infrastructure. Often applied to the Internet.

Information service - A company that provides different telecommunications services, usually for a fee.

Inkjet printer - A printer that uses an ink cartridge to place small dots on a page to form text and images.

Interactive - Sending information to and receiving information from a computer, which often reacts to your actions.

Internet - A large network linking computers located around the world.

Java - A programming language that will allow programs to be easily sent over the Internet.

Laptop computer - A small computer usually powered by batteries allowing it to be operated in almost any location.

Laser printer - A printer that employs a beam of light to draw characters.

Local Area Network (LAN) - Networking nearby microcomputers so that they can share data.

MIDI (Musical Instrument Digital Interface) - Using computers to control synthesizers.

Mobile computing - A computing environment in which a computer uses cellular phone technology and a modem to send and receive information. Also called nomadic.

Modem - Device which translates binary data into tones and tones back into binary data so that computer data can be sent over telephone lines.

Morphing - A process by which a digitized image turns into a second image.

Multimedia - Graphics, video, text, and sound accessed together. Also called multimedia.

Natural language processing - Using a computer to determine the meaning of words in sentence form. Often used with speech recognition to control the actions of a computer.

Network - Computers that are connected so that data can be transmitted between them.

Neural network software - Software designed to simulate the pattern of cells in the human brain allowing it to "learn" from analyzing large sets of data.

Parallel processing - A computer containing a number of high-speed microprocessors which solves a problem by breaking it into parts and solving the parts simultaneously.

Parity - How the receiving computer determines if an error occurred during data transmission.

Personal digital assistant (PDA) - A very small computer usually containing a modem to allow its user to receive or send electronic information.

Pirate - Person who illegally copies or distributes computer software.

Pixel - A collection of tiny pieces that form a digitized graphic.

Posting - Leaving a message on a BBS.

Protocol - A standardized method of communication that allows computer networks and computers to talk to one another.

Robot - Machine which can be programmed and is also capable of motion.

Robot program - A program such as Lycos that follows links in Web pages and automatically adds new links to its database.

Robotics - The study and application of robots to perform tasks.

Scanner - Input device that can be used to convert drawings and pictures into digital format.

Search engine - Indexes of Web pages that help you find information on the Internet.

Simulation - Where a computer produces information similar to that produced by a real world situation (i.e., flight simulation).

Speech recognition - Using a computer to recognize individual spoken words. See also natural language processing.

Stop bits - The number of bits sent to indicate the end of a piece of data.

Supercomputer - A computer capable of performing billions of calculations per second.

Surfing - Accessing different Internet locations to see what information is there.

Tags - HTML codes used to determine how a Web page is displayed and what will be displayed.

Tape drive - Storage device that uses magnetic tape cartridges to store data.

TCP/IP (Transmission Control Protocol/Internet Protocol) - a standaradized method of communication that allows computers to talk to one another.

Telecommunications - Sending and receiving computer data over telephone lines.

Telecommuting - Using telecommunications to work at home.

Turing Test - "Imitation Game" used to determine how advanced an artificial intelligence program or system is.

Upload - To transfer a message or computer file from your computer to a bulletin board system or information service.

URL - Uniform Resource Locator. The address required to connect to a Web site.

User friendly - Software that is easier to use.

Virtual reality - Using the computer to create a world that does not exist.

Virus - Program which hides within another program for the purpose of destroying or altering data.

Web browser - A program that understands HTTP to display the graphics and text of Web pages.

Web page - Information at a Web site that can include graphics, fancy text, and easy access to other Web sites or pages.

Web server - A Web site.

Wireless LAN - Networking nearby microcomputers without physically connecting them.

World Wide Web (WWW) - A graphical user interface to surf the Internet.

Yahoo - A tool for searching the Web which contains indexes of Web pages.

Reviews

Sections 13.1 — 13.3

1. Describe four databases that you would like to be able to access using telecommunications. State why each of them would be useful to you.

2. Besides those listed in the text, list three occupations where people would be able to work at home rather than in an office using telecommunications.

3. What is the difference between an electronic bulletin board and electronic mail?

4. If all of the students in your class had computers and modems at home, in what ways could they be used by your classmates and instructor?

5. Explain how the bits per second is changed in a Works communications file.

6. What is meant by the term "host"?

Sections 13.4 — 13.8

7. Describe how 3 different organizations might make use of computer networks.

8. Explain how an automobile dealership might use a computer network.

9. Explain what type of files might be stored on the file server in a school computer network.

10. Describe how a Shakespearean scholar might make use of Internet.

11. List 3 different ways in which you might use Internet.

12. Your friend's Internet address at work is cesser@host1.cia.gov. What type of employer does she work for?

13. What is a gopher?

14. How could you use a gopher to find information about Newton's Law?

15. What do the letters HTTP stand for?

16. What do the letters HTML stand for?

17. How could you use the Web to find information that appeared in *USA Today*?

Sections 13.9 — 13.14

18. What tasks do microprocessors perform in automobiles?

19. a) What devices owned by your family contain microprocessors and what are they used for?
    b) What devices would you like to see include microprocessors? Why? What tasks would the microprocessors perform?

20. List three types of problems that would require a supercomputer to solve.

21. Describe a problem that you believe could be solved using neural-network software. Explain how the software will "learn."

22. Describe a marketing problem that can be solved by making use of a very large database. Include a description of the database.

23. List three movies you have seen recently that make use of computer generated effects.

24. What is artificial intelligence?

25. State three questions you would ask to determine which was the human and which the computer when playing Turing's Imitation Game. Asking "Are you the computer?" is not fair!

Sections 13.15 — 13.22

26. List four jobs where you think expert systems could be used to help the people performing the jobs. Explain why the systems would be helpful.

27. List four jobs where expert systems could probably not be used, and explain why.

An Introduction to Computing Using Microsoft Works

28. Would an expert system be helpful to you in selecting clothes to buy? Explain why or why not.

29. Why should we be careful in trusting expert systems? What do they lack that humans possess?

30. What are some of the difficulties being encountered in the development of natural language processing systems?

31. If you could have a robot built to your own specifications, what would you have it be capable of doing?

32. Describe 3 ways in which Ivy University might use virtual reality in educating its students.

33. Describe how multimedia might be used by Ivy University's English Department.

34. Briefly describe a game you would enjoy playing in virtual reality.

35. Describe some of the changes that you believe will occur in the way computers are used in the home over the next ten years.

36. How could you make use of a personal digital assistant that includes a cellular telephone?

Section 13.22

The twelve computer careers mentioned in this chapter include:

    (1)   data-entry operator
    (2)   system analyst
    (3)   system developer/programmer
    (4)   system manager
    (5)   computer scientist
    (6)   computer engineer
    (7)   manufacturing worker
    (8)   sales representative
    (9)   technical support technician
    (10) computer teacher
    (11) technology coordinator
    (12) webmaster

37. Which of the listed careers require only a:
    a) high school diploma
    b) college diploma
    c) college and graduate school degrees

38. For each of the following students list the careers above that he or she should consider:
    a) a student who likes mathematics.
    b) a student who wants to be involved in the management of a business.
    c) a student who wants to work in the development of rocket guidance systems.
    d) a student who likes to think through problems in a methodical, logical way.
    e) a student who likes to work with their hands.

Sections 13.23 — 13.27

39. Alvin Toffler named his book "The Third Wave." What were the first two waves?

40. What is meant by the term information society?

41. a) How do you believe society will benefit from the information age?
    b) What might be the negative aspects of the information age?

42. How can a computer be used to invade your privacy?

43. What can you do if you are turned down for credit at a bank and believe that the data used to deny credit is inaccurate?

44. What is necessary for a federal government authority to access an individual's financial records? What must the authority do after accessing the records?

45. a) What is a hacker?
    b) What is a computer virus?
    c) What is a computer pirate?

46. What ethical responsibilities does a programmer have when writing a program that will be used to design a bridge? Can the programmer absolutely guarantee that the program will operate properly? Why?

47. How does a laser printer differ from an inkjet printer?

48. a) What are 4 advantages of using desktop publishing?
    b) Describe 3 organizations that might make use of desktop publishing.

49. Describe 3 uses you might make of graphics and illustration software.

A | Appendix A - Works Keyboard Commands and Functions

The following keyboard commands are grouped by application area. A complete list is given in *The Works Companion* supplied by Microsoft. A list of functions which may be used in the spreadsheet and database is also included in this appendix.

Word Processor Keyboard Commands

The following keyboard commands can be executed when using the Word Processor.

Function keys

F1 - Switches to Help
F5 - Displays the Go To dialog box
Ctrl+F6 - Jumps to previous window
Ctrl+Shift+F6 - Jumps to next window
F7 - Starts the Spelling Checker
Shift+F7 - Starts the Thesaurus
F8 - Starts or extends a highlight block
Shift+F8 - Reduces the extent of a highlight block

Cursor Movement

Ctrl+Left arrow - Moves the cursor left one word
Ctrl+Right arrow - Moves the cursor right one word
Ctrl+Up arrow - Moves the cursor up one paragraph
Ctrl+Down arrow - Moves the cursor down one paragraph
Ctrl+PgUp - Moves the cursor to the top of the current screen
Ctrl+PgDn - Moves the cursor to the bottom of the current screen
Ctrl+Home - Moves the cursor to the beginning of the file
Ctrl+End - Moves the cursor to the end of the file
Ctrl+G - Displays the Go To dialog box

Selection

F8 (once) - Starts highlighting. Pressing an arrow-key extends highlight
F8 (twice) - Highlights a word
F8 (three times) - Highlights a sentence
F8 (four times) - Highlights a paragraph
F8 (five times) - Highlights the entire document
Ctrl+A - Highlights entire document
Shift+F8 - Reduces highlight to previous level
Shift+Arrow key - Highlights in direction of arrow
Escape - Ends highlighting. Pressing an arrow-key removes highlight
Ctrl+X - Cuts highlighted block
Ctrl+C - Copies highlighted block
Ctrl+V - Pastes a cut or copied block

Text Formatting	Ctrl+Shift+= - Makes highlighted text superscript
	Ctrl+= - Makes highlighted text subscript
	Ctrl+B - Makes highlighted text bold
	Ctrl+I - Makes highlighted text italic
	Ctrl+U - Makes highlighted text underlined
	Ctrl+Shift+F - Displays the Font Name list on the Tool bar
	Ctrl+Shift+P - Displays the Font Size list on the Tool bar
	Ctrl+Spacebar - Removes font style from highlighted text

Paragraph Text Formatting

Ctrl+1 - Single spaces current paragraph
Ctrl+2 - Double spaces current paragraph
Ctrl+E - Centers current paragraph
Ctrl+J - Justifies current paragraph
Ctrl+L - Left aligns current paragraph
Ctrl+Shift+R - Right aligns current paragraph
Ctrl+H - Displays the Replace dialog box
Ctrl+N - Displays the Works Task Launcher dialog box
Ctrl+M - Creates nested indent
Ctrl+Shift+M - Removes nested indent
Ctrl+Shift+H - Creates hanging indent

Editing

Ctrl+2 *or* Alt+Backspace - Reverses previous editing action (Undo)
Ctrl+Enter - Inserts a manual page break
Ctrl+D - Inserts a date stamp
Ctrl+T - Inserts a time stamp
Ctrl+Shift+; (semi-colon) - Inserts current time into document
Ctrl+; (semi-colon) - Inserts current date into document
Ctrl+Shift+N - Inserts filename into document

Database Keyboard Commands

The following keyboard commands can be executed when using the Database.

Function keys

F1 - Switches to Help
F2 - Enters Edit mode for the current entry
F3 - Apply Query
F5 - Displays the Go To dialog box
Ctrl+F6 - Jumps to previous window
Ctrl+Shift+F6 - Jumps to next window
F7 - Starts the Spelling Checker
Shift+F7 - Repeats the last Formatting command selected
F8 - Starts highlight (in List view only)
Ctrl+F8 - Highlights a row (in List view)
Shift+F8 - Highlights a column (in List view)
Shift+Ctrl+F8 - Highlights the entire database
F9 - Switches to Form view
F9 - Switches to List view
F9 - Switches to Form Design view

An Introduction to Computing Using Microsoft Works

A

Cursor Movement	Tab - Moves the cursor to the next field Shift+Tab - Moves the cursor to the previous field Ctrl+End - Moves the cursor to the end of the file Ctrl+Home - Moves the cursor to the beginning of the file Ctrl+PgDn - Displays next record (in Form view) Ctrl+PgUp - Displays previous record (in Form view) Ctrl+G - Displays the Go To dialog box
Formatting	Ctrl+4 - Applies Currency format Ctrl+5 - Applies Percent format Ctrl+, - Applies Comma format Ctrl+B - Applies Bold style Ctrl+I - Applies Italic style Ctrl+U - Applies Underline style Ctrl+L - Applies Left alignment Ctrl+E - Applies Center alignment Ctrl+Shift+R - Applies Right alignment Ctrl+Spacebar - Remove font style
Special	Ctrl+' (quote) - Copies contents of same field from previous record Ctrl+Shift+; (semi-colon) - Inserts current time into field Ctrl+; (semi-colon) - Inserts current date into field Ctrl+X - Cuts highlighted block Ctrl+C - Copies highlighted block Ctrl+V - Pastes a cut or copied block

Spreadsheet Keyboard Commands

The following keyboard commands can be executed when using the Spreadsheet.

Function keys	F1 - Switches to Help F2 - Enters Edit mode for the current entry F4 - Changes cell referencing methods (absolute or relative) F5 - Displays the Go To dialog box Ctrl+F6 - Jumps to previous window Ctrl+Shift+F6 - Jumps to next window F7 - Starts the Spelling Checker Shift+F7 - Repeats the last Formatting command selected F8 - Starts highlight Ctrl+F8 - Highlights a row Shift+F8 - Highlights a column Shift+Ctrl+F8 - Highlights the entire spreadsheet F9 - Recalculate Now
Cursor Movement	Tab - Moves the cursor to the next unlocked cell Ctrl+End - Moves the cursor to the end of file Ctrl+Home - Moves the cursor to the beginning of file Ctrl+G - Displays the Go To dialog box

Formatting	Ctrl+4 - Applies Currency format
	Ctrl+5 - Applies Percent format
	Ctrl+, - Applies Comma format
	Ctrl+B - Applies Bold style
	Ctrl+I - Applies Italic style
	Ctrl+U - Applies Underline style
	Ctrl+L - Applies Left alignment
	Ctrl+E - Applies Center alignment
	Ctrl+Shift+R - Applies Right alignment
	Ctrl+G - Applies General alignment
	Ctrl+SpaceBar - Remove font style
Special	Ctrl+' (quote) - Copies contents of above cell
	Ctrl+Shift+; (semi-colon) - Inserts current time into cell
	Ctrl+; (semi-colon) - Inserts current date into cell

Functions

The following is a partial list of functions that may be placed in a spreadsheet cell or in the formula for a calculated field or query in a database.

In the list of functions that follows:
 <value> may be replaced by:
  a single value (such as 10)
  a cell reference (such as C5)
  an expression that evaluates to a single value (such as C5*2)
  a field reference (such as GPA)

 <range> may be replaced by:
  a list of cells separated by commas (such as A1, B12, D5)
  a continuous range (A1:A10)
  a mixture of both separated by commas (A1, B1:B5, C3, C5:C7)
  a field reference (such as GPA)

Mathematical & Statistical Functions

ABS(<value>)
 Returns the absolute value of <value>: ABS(10) returns 10, ABS(-10) returns 10.

ACOS(<value>)
 Returns the arccosine of <value> in radians. Value must be between -1 and +1.

ASIN(<value>)
 Returns the arcsine of <value> in radians. Value must be between -1 and +1.

ATAN(<value>)
 Returns the arctangent of <value> in radians.

ATAN2(<Xvalue>, <Yvalue>)
 Returns the arctangent in radians of an angle defined by the coordinates <Xvalue>, <Yvalue>.

AVG(<range>)
 Returns the average of the values in <range>. Cells which contain text are treated as 0.

COS(<value>)
Returns the cosine of <value> where <value> is measured in radians.

COUNT(<range>)
Returns the number of non-blank cells in <range>.

EXP(<value>)
Returns *e* raised to the <value> power.

INT(<value>)
Returns the integer value of <value>: ABS(1.9) returns 1.

LN(<value>)
Returns the natural logarithm (base *e*) of <value>.

LOG(<value>)
Returns the base 10 logarithm of <value>. <value> must be positive.

MAX(<range>)
Returns the largest value in <range>.

MIN(<range>)
Returns the smallest value in <range>.

MOD(<value1>, <value2>)
Returns the remainder of <value1> ÷ <value2>. <value2> may not be 0.

PI()
Returns the constant 3.1415…, p (pi). No argument is used.

RAND()
Returns a random number between 0 and 1. No argument is used.

ROUND(<value>, <decimals>)
Returns <value> rounded to <decimals> decimal places. When <decimals> is 0, <value> is rounded to the nearest integer.

SIN(<value>)
Returns the sine of <value> where <value> is measured in radians.

SQRT(<value>)
Returns the square root of <value>. <value> must be positive.

STD(<range>)
Returns the standard deviation of the values in <range>.

SUM(<range>)
Returns the total of the values in <range>.

TAN(<value>)
Returns the tangent of <value> where <value> is measured in radians.

VAR(<range>)
Returns the variance of the values in <range>.

Financial Functions

CTERM(<Rvalue>, <Fvalue>, <Pvalue>)
   Returns the number of compounding periods required for <Pvalue> investment to grow to <Fvalue> at <Rvalue> interest.

FV(<Pvalue>, <Rvalue>, <Tvalue>)
   Returns the future value of an investment where <Pvalue> is a periodic payment, <Rvalue> is the interest rate, and <Tvalue> is the term.

PMT(<Pvalue>, <Rvalue>, <Tvalue>)
   Returns the periodic payment on an installment loan where <Pvalue> is the principal, <Rvalue> is the interest rate, and <Tvalue> is the term.

RATE(<Fvalue>, <Pvalue>, <Tvalue>)
   Returns the fixed interest rate required to turn an investment of <Pvalue> into <Fvalue> when <Tvalue> is the term.

TERM(<Pvalue>, <Rvalue>, <Fvalue>)
   Returns the term required to turn payments of <Pvalue> into <Fvalue> when <Rvalue> is the interest rate.

Date / Time Functions

SECOND(<Time>)
MINUTE(<Time>)
HOUR(<Time>)
   Returns the seconds, minutes, or hours portion of a time.

DAY(<Date>)
MONTH(<Date>)
YEAR(<Date>)
   Returns the day, month, or year portion of a date.

NOW()
   Returns the current date and time. No argument is used.

Special Functions

CHOOSE(<value>, <option$_0$>, <option$_1$>, ...)
   Returns the <option$_0$> if <value> is 0, <option$_1$> if <value> is 1, and so on. <options> may be text.

HLOOKUP(<value>, <range>, <rows>)
   Locates cell in first row of <range> the contains the largest value which is less than or equal to <value>. Returns contents of cell which is <rows> below that cell.

IF(<condition>, <true value>, <false value>)
   Returns the <true value> if <condition> is true, <false value> if false. Both <true value> and <false value> may be text.

VLOOKUP(<value>, <range>, <columns>)
   Locates cell in first column of <range> the contains the largest value which is less than or equal to <value>. Returns contents of cell which is <columns> to the right of that cell.

B | Appendix B - Windows 95 and Backups

Windows 95 is the operating system that is used to run Works. This appendix includes a brief discussion of the Windows 95 Desktop and Windows Explorer. Formatting a diskette and making backups of a file are also discussed.

The Windows 95 Desktop

The Windows 95 Desktop (computer screen) contains features that allow you to easily use Windows 95 applications. The Desktop's three most important features are the Start button, Task bar, and icons:

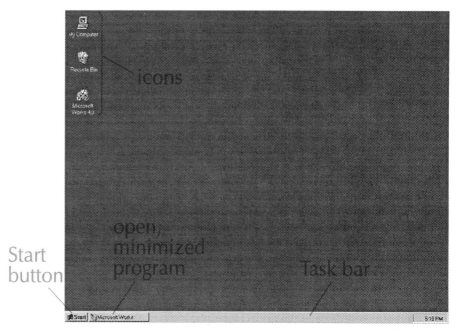

The Windows 95 Desktop

Clicking on the Start button displays a menu of options:

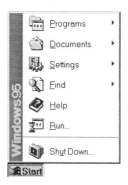

Pointing to a menu option that has a right arrow displays a group of related items. Clicking once on one of the items without a right arrow will execute that item. For example, to start Microsoft Works, first click on the Start button and then point to Programs. Pointing to Programs displays the names of the programs on the computer. Pointing to Microsoft Works 4.0 displays a group of items related to Microsoft Works. Clicking once on Microsoft Works 4.0 in this group starts Works.

The *Task bar*, in the lower part of the desktop, displays a button for every program you have open. This allows you to easily switch between open programs. Clicking on the Minimize button ( ) in the upper-right corner of a program's window removes its window. To restore the window, click once on the Program's button on the Task bar.

The *icons* displayed on the desktop allow you to quickly start a program without using the Start button. For example, double-clicking on the Microsoft Works 4.0 icon starts Works.

Using Windows Explorer

Windows Explorer is used to organize and manipulate files. Clicking on the Start button and selecting Windows Explorer from the Programs menu starts Windows Explorer:

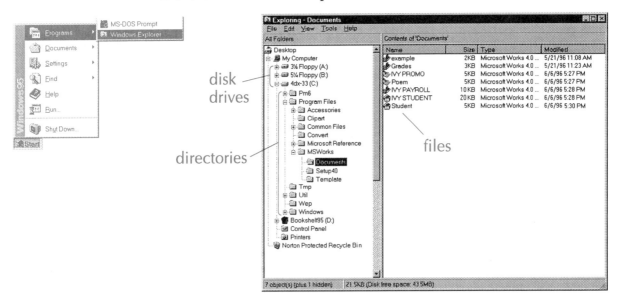

Windows Explorer

The computer's disk drives are represented by their corresponding names and icons in the left section of the window. Clicking on a drive displays the directories it contains. Directories are represented by their name and a folder icon. Clicking on a directory highlights it and displays the files it contains in the right section of the window. Highlighted directories or files are said to be *selected*.

Copying a file

Windows Explorer allows you to copy or move files by dragging them, a method called *drop and drag*. Copying a file leaves the original file in its present location and places an exact copy in the new location. Moving a file removes it from its present location and places it in a new location.

B

To make a copy of a file on the hard disk (the **C:** drive) to a floppy diskette (usually the **A:** drive), the file is dragged to the A: drive icon. This same method can be used to copy a file from one directory to another directory in the same drive while holding down the Ctrl key. Be sure to release the Ctrl key after releasing the mouse button.

Moving a file

To move a file from one directory to another directory in the same drive, simply drag it to the new directory and release the mouse button once the directory is highlighted. This same method can be used to move a file from the C: drive to the A: drive while holding down the Shift key. Be sure to release the Shift key after releasing the mouse button.

Windows Explorer also has commands that allow you to copy or move files. A selected file can be copied to a different disk drive or directory by using the Copy and Paste commands from the Edit menu. A selected file can be moved to a different disk drive or directory by using the Cut and Paste commands from the Edit menu.

Deleting a file or a directory

A file or directory can be deleted by first selecting it and then pressing the Delete key. The Delete command from the File menu may also be used to remove selected files or directories.

Creating a new directory

New directories can be created by pointing to New from the File menu and then selecting the Folder command. When a new directory is created it becomes a sub-directory of the currently selected directory. Therefore, it is important to select the desired directory first before executing this command.

Using My Computer

The My Computer icon on the Windows 95 desktop allows you to format new diskettes and copy the contents of an entire diskette. For example, you may have a new diskette that needs formatting to use it, or you may have a diskette with data file that you wish to make an exact replica of. The procedure for formatting a diskette is as follows:

My Computer

1. Start Windows 95 and double click on the My Computer icon.
2. Select drive A: by clicking once on its icon:

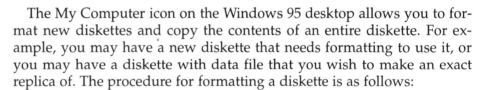

3. Execute the Format command from the File menu to display the Format dialog box.
4. Put the diskette into drive A: and then select Start in the dialog box.

5. If a dialog box appears saying the diskette cannot be quick formatted select OK to accept full format.
6. Select Close to remove the Format Result dialog box and then select Close again to remove the Format dialog box.

All of the files and directories on a diskette may be copied to another diskette by using the Copy Disk command. Note that when using the Copy Disk command, any data on the destination diskette is overwritten. The procedure for copying a diskette is as follows:

1. Start Windows 95 and double click on the My Computer icon.
2. Select a drive by clicking once on its icon.
3. Execute the Copy Disk command from the File menu.
4. Click on the appropriate drive icons in the Copy from and Copy to sections:

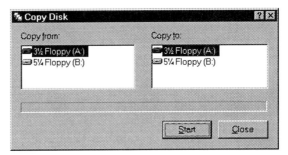

5. Place the diskette to be copied from (source diskette) into the drive and then select the Start button.
6. When prompted, place the diskette that will be copied to (destination diskette) into the drive and then select OK.
7. Select the Close button to remove the Copy Disk dialog box.

Creating Backups of Important Data

Although it is easy to create backups of a file or diskette, many people do not take the time to do so. However, the few minutes it takes to backup a file could save hours if the file is damaged or deleted and must be recreated.

The techniques for copying a file and copying a diskette can be used to create a backup of your Works files. In addition, backup copies of Works data files can also be made from within Works by using the Save As command. To do this open the file and select the Save As command from the File menu. To save the backup copy on a diskette in drive A:, select the appropriate drive from the Save in collapsible list and then select Save. A copy of the current file is saved on the backup diskette in the A: drive. For extra security, you can also save a file under a different name on the same diskette.

It is important to keep backup disks in a different location than the original copies. That way, the chances of both copies being destroyed are low. For example, if you keep you Works data diskette at school, keep the backup copy at home. Businesses often store their backup copies in special fireproof safes, in safe deposit boxes at a bank, or with a company that provides safe "off-site" storage for computer data.

C | Appendix C - Keyboarding Skills

Learning to Touch Type

The ability to *touch type* is especially helpful in using a computer. When touch typing your hands are placed on the keyboard in a position that allows you to strike any of the keys without looking at the keyboard. The advantage of learning how to do this is that you can keep your eyes on the material you are typing. You will also be able to type with greater accuracy and speed than you could using the "hunt and peck" method where you must search for each key before striking it.

Before you begin to type it is important to have your hands and body in their proper positions. Your hands should be placed lightly on the keyboard with the slightly curved fingers of the left hand on the keys **ASDF** and the right hand on the **JKL;** keys. The left pinky is placed on the **A** key while the other fingers of the left hand placed on the **SDF** keys. The right pinky is placed on the semicolon (;) key and the other fingers of the right hand on the **LKJ** keys. The right thumb is placed on the spacebar. With the fingers placed as just described, this is called the "home" position.

Place the chair you are sitting in so that your arms reach out leaving the elbows loosely at your side. Sit in a relaxed but erect position with both feet flat on the floor. Maintaining proper posture will help to keep your body from tensing. Try not to slouch or bend over the keyboard. The proper posture is shown in the diagram:

Always maintain proper posture when touch typing

To touch type it is necessary to memorize the location of each of the keys on the keyboard. This is best accomplished by learning just a few keys at a time which you will do when performing the following lessons. Developing an even, smooth rhythm as you type is important. You want to strike each of the keys with the same pressure using a steady pace. To help you develop speed and accuracy a Timed Practice in most lessons asks you to keep track of how many words per minute you are typing and the number of mistakes being made.

Each of the following keyboarding lessons makes use of the Works word processor. Therefore, we will begin by learning how to access and use the word processor. Read pages 2-1 through 2-10 in Chapter Two and performing the steps in Practices 1 and 2 on the computer to learn how to run Works.

Lesson 1 - The Home Row: ASDF JKL;

Start Works as described in the beginning of Chapter Two and create a new Word Processor document. A blank word processor screen is displayed. You will perform each of the typing lessons on this screen. Note the blinking line at the top left-hand side of the screen which is called the *cursor*. It indicates where characters typed into the word processor will appear.

Place your hands on the keyboard in the *home position* or on the *home row* described above with the left hand on the keys **ASDF** and right hand on the keys **JKL;**. The right thumb is placed on the spacebar.

Type the following letters and when you finish each line, press the Enter key with your right pinky. The cursor will move down one line and to the left side of the screen. Note that the semicolon (;) is normally followed by a space when typing actual material. Do not look at your hands while you type, look only at the picture of the keyboard below.

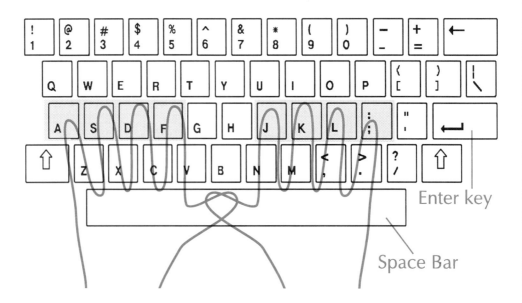

Always place your fingers on the home row when beginning to type

C

Practice 1.1

```
 1   aaa ;;; aaa ;;; sss lll sss lll ddd kkk ddd kkk fff jjj fjf
 2   aaa sss sas asa sss aaa sas aaa sss sas aaa sss sas sss a;a
 3   ddd ada ddd daa dss dad dsd ddd sss aaa ads asd asd dad sls
 4   sss aaa ddd ddd ssa dad dsd dsa dsa dss daa aaa sss dda dkd
 5   fff fff faf fss fss fas fas fad ffd faa fsa ffs fsa fad fjf
 6   fss saf fad sfa fss fad fsa sda fad aff fsd sff ffa sss fjf
 7   jjj jjj jja jaf jfj jdj jfs jja jad jsf jja jda jaf jjj jfj
 8   jad daj fja das saj jjs jsa daf sfj jad faj jjj jad jaa dkd
 9   kkk kka kkk kak kjk kss kkj kak ksa ksk kfk kkf kkk kjj kdk
10   kad dak sak adk sak akk kak jak jak dak ask sak kkk kjk ala
11   lll lll lff llk lak las lad lfl lld lll lsk lfl lkl ljl lal
12   lsl sal fal dsl lsl llf jal all sal lsa fal lll lkl lal a;a
13   ; ; ; ; fa; da; sa; da; fj; sa; da; jl; ; ; ; sa; lad; jak;
14   dad dad lad lad sad sad add add lad ask dad fall fall falls
15   ask ask fad fad ads ads dad lass lass sass sass salad salad
```

Practice 1.2

```
 1   ;;; aaa lll sss kkk ddd jjj fff ;a; a;a lsl sls kdk dkd jfj
 2   sas saa asa asa dfd fdf ffd dfd das sad sad das las das ad;
 3   jjkk kkjj jkjk kjkj jkkj l; l; jkl kjl dakl kald jakl jakl
 4   jjk jjl jj; jaj ksk lal las las kad kad laf laf la; ja; la;
 5   aad aas aaf aaj aak aal aa; fad fad dad dad lad lad sad sad
 6   dask jljl fafa fajk ddl; jadl lads lads dads dads sads jakl
 7   asks asks dads fall lass fads lask fads lads ffjj kkll fkf;
 8   asks dads fall fads lask adds lass fall alls lads dads sad;
```

Repeat the Practices above until you can type the characters without referring to the keyboard diagram.

When you have completed the lesson and want to leave Works select the Exit Works command from the File menu using the mouse as described in Section 2.12. You will then be asked if you wish to save the file. Click on the No button.

Lesson 2 - RTYU

In this lesson you will learn the **RTYU** keys.

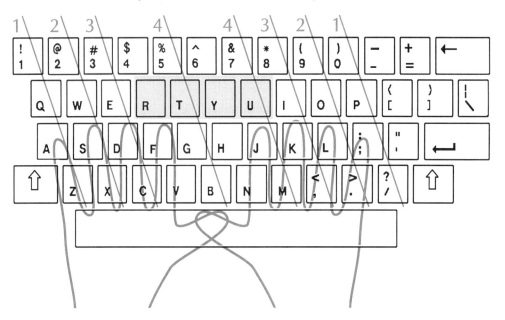

*Press **R** and **T** with the left hand, and **Y** and **U** with the right*

The letters **RT** are typed using the pointer finger of your left hand and **YU** with the pointer finger of your right hand. Note the lines that show which finger is used to type which keys: "1" for the pinky, "2" for the ring finger, "3" for the index and "4" for the pointer.

From this point on, each lesson will begin with a review of the previous lesson. Before proceeding to the new letters, practice this review several times until you feel comfortable. **Remember to press the Enter key at the end of each line with your right pinky.**

Review

```
1   aaa ;;; aaa ;;; sss lll sss lll ddd kkk ddd kkk fff jjj fjf
2   aaa sss lll sas asa ddd das kkk jjj lkl fff fjf jfj klk jas
3   ljl kfk ldf klj kjk ljk fsd sda jkl fsd sad sad lad lad fad
4   dada fada sads jass klas fas; dad; fkal dasd jjkk jaka fada
5   asks lads lass daj; jakl kfkf ladf klds adas fjl; dads lads
```

An Introduction to Computing Using Microsoft Works

C

```
1    fff ffr frf frr frr rrr frr frf rrr frf frr rrr fff frf rrr
2    fff fft ftf ftt ftt ttt ttt ftf ttf ftf ttt ttt fff tff ftt
3    frt frt frt frt fra rta rat rat jar jar far far tar tar far
4    jjj jju juj juu juj jju juj juj uuu juu juj jjj uuu juj juu
5    jjj jjy jyj jyy jyy yyy jyj jyy jyy jyj yyy jyy jyj jyj yyy
6    juu juy jju juy jyu juy jyu jyu jyy juu uuu yyy uyu yuy yuy
7    fujy furt fryt juty rfrt sats fats jakd dar; rats rats sats
8    krad jury safy last last jury tars tars star star duty duty
9    yard jury duty fast just dark dust data klas jars furs yard
10   ruts says lass tar; hats sats rats yard dull tart last dad;
```

Practice 2.2

```
1    juts furs dust suds dart rats sats just just task task fast
2    rats ruts daft rays sats lark jars salt suds suds lads furs
3    yard duty fast lads sad; lass tars hats data tart last dust
4    jar ask fry lad fat dad add sad rut dad add say say far tar
5    dart dull rut; ruts furs asks lass rust just fall star rays
6    dusk last fast lads kart dust sass furs furs just task salt
7    dull darts suds jars lark dusts rust data data rats salt as
8    asks just last fur dark dart says jury task tart tars darts
9    tar rat sally sally last yard dark try; fats lark dark data
10   ruts rudy trudy rust dart just salt dark furs say; dust tad
```

Repeat the Practices above until you can type the keys without referring to the keyboard diagram. When you are finished, exit Works by selecting Exit Works from the File menu. You will then be asked if you wish to save the file. Click on the No button.

Lesson 3 - EGHI

In this lesson you will learn the keys **EGHI**. Rather than pressing the Enter key at the end of each line we are now going to allow the computer to determine where the end of each line is. If there is not sufficient room for a word at the end of a line the word will automatically be moved to the beginning of the next line in a process called *word wrap*. Where your computer breaks a line will differ from what is shown in this text since the break is determined by where the margin is set. Just keep typing the lines on the next page without ever pressing Enter.

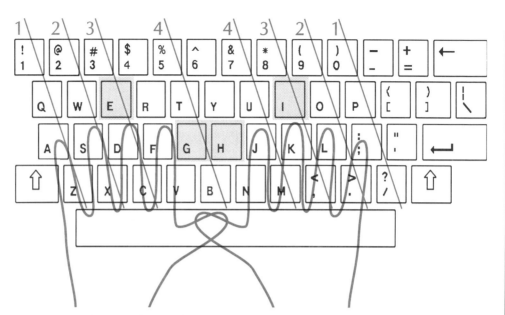

*Press the **E** and **G** with the left hand, and the **H** and **I** with the right*

Review

```
1    fff frr frf frf fft ftf ftt ftf ttt juu juj jju jju juu juj

2    jyy jyy jyj jyj fuy fuy frt fju juy jyy ftt frr jyy juy juy

3    asks jury yard jars arts judy lark rust dust just fast dark

4    trudy dark sally yard daffy salt rat tar fur rays tall fall

5    darts fats sat; us all task lad; salt dust trust last fault
```

Practice 3.1

```
1    ddd ded ded dee dde ded ded ded ddd ded dee dee dee eee ded

2    fff fgf fgf fgg fgf fgf fgg fgf fgg ggg fgg fgf fgg ggg fgf

3    fgd deg fed def fgd deg fed def deg def feg dfe eee ggg ege

4    jjj jhj jhj jhh jhj jjj hhh jhj jhh jhj jhj jjh jjh hhh jhj

5    kkk kik kik kik kii kii kik iii iii kii kik kii kii iii kik

6    jhki jhik kiik kijh kijh khij jhik kihj jhki jhki jhki jjkk

7    did tug lad the she hid set age red red did ask let age the

8    did lug tug hit age yet ask rut elk gas she she did did use

9    rake dirt sake high dirt rail jail kiss jilt hale side said

10   saddle kettle us huddle jerry jail dirt yet little rut side

11   ask rail; kiss jilt hale said elks gas hers juggle rid teds

12   the fight federal fester justify sight satisfy deride kitty
```

An Introduction to Computing Using Microsoft Works

C

Practice 3.2

```
1   did lag elk yes age let rug kiss rake that said; sail hills
2   her; dig a rut age is hill high hear set sail satisfy there
3   erase refer defer agree reset sir differ legal degrees tell
4   satisfy father egret fifes fifth fly leg hedge sell his her
5   gail harsh heart thigh yalta light irish alight; ideal star
6   last jelly judge high kelly jail; kay jest hail to thee jet
7   halts the digs highest eight three furs halt judge judge as
8   lilly ladle legal aisle drill salt the these as; highest to
9   drudge tusk halt fudge last jest hail has gall deak salt as
10  hark yak said sail the less; fastest highest edge all halts
```

Timed Practice 3.3

The next few lessons end with a timed practice which allows you to check your speed. Type for 1 minute and then calculate your speed in words per minute by counting the words typed. Each line contains 12 words. Words in a partial line are calculated using the scale below the lines.

```
1   did yes let rug age rut set ted ask elk yet dad sad lads hit 12
2   sake rail jail dirt side said jails kiss rake that tug; dull 24
3   jilt just fads fife flag fall digs ages rail tell star kills 36
4   fight sight deride just father fifth kettle jelly judge ask; 48
         1    2    3    4    5    6    7    8    9    |    1    2
```

When you are finished, exit Works.

Lesson 4 - CVB MNO

In this lesson the letters **CVB MNO** are added as well as capital letters. Use the finger lines in the diagram to determine which finger is used to type the new letters. To type capital letters use either your left or right pinky to depress one of the Shift keys and type the letter. If the capital letter is typed with the right hand the left pinky is used to depress the Shift key. If it is typed with the left hand the right pinky is used. As in Lesson 3, allow the computer to determine where the end of each line is by not pressing the Enter key.

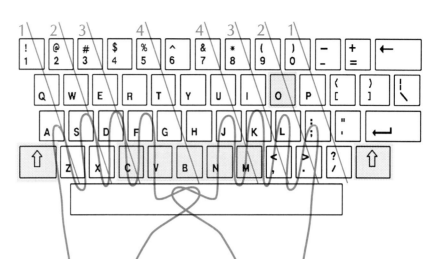

Press the C, V, and B keys with the left hand, and the M, N, and O keys with the right. Use the pinky to press the Shift key

Review

1   ded eee fgf ggg jhj hhh kik iii fge fgf jhj fgh jhi dek deg

2   digs ruts ages hill high sats fads sake rail dirt side said

3   all irish thigh gale takes legal aisle salt eight that flag

4   hail thee; fastest gail sledge haste tasks jet get hail art

Practice 4.1

1   ddd dcd dcc dcd ddc dcc dcc dcc ccc dcc dcd ccc dcc dcc dcd

2   fff fvf fvf fvv fvv vvv fvv fvv fvf vvv fvf fvv fvv fvv fvf

3   fff fbf fbf fbb ffb bbb fbb fbf fbb bbb fbf fbb fbb bbb fbf

4   dcv dcv cfv fvb fvb fbv fbf fvv vdc bdc bbd ccc vvv bbb bvc

5   jjj jmj jmj jmm jjm mmm jmm jmj jmm mmm mmm jmm jmj jmm jmj

6   jjj jnj jnj jnn jnn nnn jnn jnj jnj nnn jnn jnj jnj jnn jnj

7   lll lol lol loo ooo loo loo lol lol ooo loo lol lol loo lol

8   jmn jnm jnm jml jno loj ojn ooj jmn jno loj mno mno bcv bcv

9   Bill odd nod boy Bob night vent Sam avoids mad bite buried;

10 dock mint convert common bimini money none bongo volume vat

11 convince civic conic occur yucca bulb blurb member mayor to

12 ninth linen noun announce mono minds vocation victim vacate

13 kitty Gerry highly Eighty saddle kettle monies Tony convert

14 Jimmy Miami Thomas Fast Kludge Doll Rest Ernest Joan Laurie

15 Satisfy small Father; fight federal Jail tuggle yet Law Jim

An Introduction to Computing Using Microsoft Works

C

Practice 4.2

1 Lara Nina monkey said Gray is art color Has Harry come home

2 Janet will not be at school today It is too late to make up

3 Let us make haste before school starts This is not the time

4 Should you be very good or not This is the universal center

5 George Ferrit was raised in Iowa John Smith in Rhode Island

6 You need to make some money; to be able to go to the movies

7 Bob Cindy Virginia Monica Nina Ollie Barbara Veronica Bruce

8 This is the time for to be verbal Robert is a very nice guy

9 Miami New York Chicago Cleveland Boston Houston Dallas Dent

10 The gain made by becoming a good typist may be considerable

Timed Practice 4.3

Type for 1 minute and then calculate your speed in words per minute by counting the words typed. Each line contains 12 words. The words in a partial line are calculated using the scale below the lines.

1 Come to my house if you need to sell a vacuum cleaner today; 12

2 This is not a good time to help you with cooking the turkeys 24

3 Bill Crane is the secretary at our local offices of the club 36

4 Virginia is a beautiful state; Its capitol city is Richmond 48

     1   2   3   4   5   6   7   8   9 | 1   2

When you are finished, exit Works.

Lesson 5 - WQZX P,.?

In this lesson the letters **WQZX P** are added along with the period (.), comma (,), and question mark (**?**). The question mark is typed by pressing the left Shift key with the left pinky and the question mark key with the right. Note the finger lines for determining which finger to use for each key.

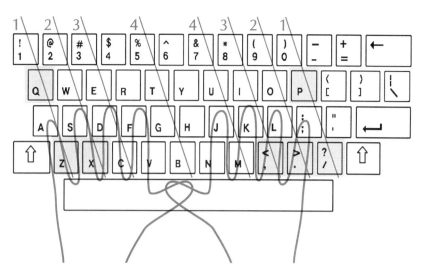

Press the **Q**, **Z**, *and* **X** *keys with the left hand, and the* **P**, *comma, period, and* question mark *with the right*

Review

1 dcdc fvvf fbfb jmmj jnjn Jmnj jnlo loon fvcd Fcvf jmnl Lojn

2 very task dark volt None vast many salt belt bolt none cold

3 Verbal Bimini Bahamas vacuum Nina member announce mist mold

4 members linen Venice Bob Vermont San Antonio convert Melvin

Practice 5.1

1 sss sws sww sww sws sww www sws ssw sww sws sws www sws sws

2 aaa aqa aqa aqq aqq qqq aaq aqa aqq aqq aqq aqa qqq aqa aqa

3 aaa aza azz azz zzz azz azz aza azz azz azz azz zzz azz aza

4 ;;p ;;p ;p; ;p; ;p; pp; pp; ll. ll. l.l lo. lo. la. ll. l.l

5 sss sxs sxx sxx xxx sxs sxx sxs xxx xxx ssx sxx sxs sxx sxs

6 kk, kk, kk, k, kkk, k, k, kk, ; ? ; ? ; ? ; ; ? ; ? ; ? la?

7 aqua, zap? Zeus, want; aqua. quart, extra, quilt. Zoe quill

8 quick query equip quilt quits quote Queen quality paper top

9 apple panel support append popular profess quota quail pops

10 Rudy Penn Paul, plastics proof quart quit? Walter Thomas at

11 Aztec zero, unzip. fuzzy gauze sizes Inez epitomize Prizes?

12 exact axiom vexed Felix, Exxon. Xerox, mixed index exciting

13 dozen Zeke. Brazil, William, hertz gauze dozes? lazy Zurich

14 zonal zooms seize quilt quick prime power opera? allow. Zak

15 Oprah robot Boone, Texas, Portland, Zeus Zola extremely fax

An Introduction to Computing Using Microsoft Works

C

Practice 5.2

1   Jake quit his jobs. What do you want? Exit from the west.
2   Zinc is not really that pretty. Would you please be quiet?
3   I would like to go to Zurich, Brazil, Texas and Queensland.
4   Robert Roodez is a fine person whose qualities are special.
5   In which Texas cities would you like to stay at Quality Inn?
6   The Aztecs had an advanced civilization which disappeared.
7   What equipment would you like to have added to a gymnasium?
8   I have visited Washington, Texas, Arizona, Utah, Vermont.
9   Inez Zola has the qualities that will make her quite famous.
10 Do you have zebras, polar bears, and turtles at your zoo?

Timed Practice 5.3

Type for 1 minute and then calculate your speed in words per minute by counting the words typed. Each line contains 12 words. The words in a partial line are calculated using the scale below the lines. To test your accuracy count the number of letters and spaces missed.

1   There are qualities which are required to become successful. 12
2   The following will come to the front; Bob, Zelda, and Betty. 24
3   Would you please; ask your parents to allow you to visit me? 36
4   Twelve quiet students sat on the wall waiting for the twins. 48
        1   2   3   4   5   6   7   8   9 | 1   2

When you are finished, exit Works.

Lesson 6 - :"/

In this lesson the colon (:), quote marks ("), and slash or division sign (/) are added. The colon is typed by pressing the left Shift key with the left pinky and typing the key containing the semicolon and colon. A space always follows a colon. Quote marks are typed by pressing the left Shift key with the left pinky and the key to the right of the colon key using the right pinky. The slash is typed using the right pinky.

Review

```
1   dozen unzip zesty gauze amaze wants excite explain exhausts

2   prop Perhaps?  personal, profit, operator.  Quality qualify

3   equip quest quicken, proud supports puppy Zanadu?  Exciting

4   quit extra Paul Zak?  Extra qualify pest apple quart quick.
```

Practice 6.1

```
1   : : "abcd" l: "What is that?"  "This is a quote from Jane."

2   "John is the best." The team is: Zeke, Jake, Rob and Quent.

3   ; / / ; / ; abc/de x/y; words/minute nt/m miles/hr, xyz/abc

4   These states are in the west: Utah, Oregon, and California.

5   What person said: "We have nothing to fear but fear itself"?
```

Lesson 7

The two Practices in this lesson are *timed practices*. In the first, type for one minute and then calculate your speed in words per minute by counting the words typed. Each line contains 12 words. The words in a partial line are calculated using the scale below the lines. To test your accuracy, count the number of letters and spaces missed. Record both your speed in words per minute and the number of errors per minute. Repeat the Practice a few times recording the results of each attempt. Your speed and accuracy should improve each time. Note the specific letters which appear as errors and repeat the lesson for that letter. For example, if you often type the letter R instead of T by mistake, go back and repeat Lesson 2. Note that this material is fairly difficult; you should perform all the previous lessons before attempting this one.

Timed Practice 7.1

```
1   dale rail flight word, solve draft general; writers rough at   12

2   Important: work orders going ahead; instead rise part, taken   24

3   gift week disaster creates advantage been skill oral success   36

4   sharpen your smile coal miners desire: insure achieve smiles   48

5   Press exit Zack; suspend flowers: beginning strokes reunite,  60

6   carriage blooms crowd works quite document fashion computer:   72

7   having options print transfer undo; Marcia, Melvin, Samantha  84

         1    2    3    4    5    6    7    8    9    |    1    2
```

C

Timed Practice 7.2

The Tab key is located on the upper left of the keyboard, next to the Q key. Rather than using spaces, Tab is used to indent paragraphs and to begin lines which do not start at the left margin. In the Practices below, you will press Tab once with the left pinky to indent each paragraph.

In this Practice type for five minutes and then calculate your speed in words per minute by counting the words typed and dividing by 5. The total of words is given at the end of each line. To test your accuracy count the number of letters and spaces missed. Repeat the Practice typing for ten minutes and then calculate your speed and accuracy. Repeat this Practice several times, over several days. You should note an increase in both your speed and your accuracy.

1	Many of the advances made by science and technology are 12
	dependent upon the ability to perform complex mathematical 23
	calculations and to process large amounts of data. It is 34
	therefore not surprising that for thousands of years 44
	mathematicians, scientists and business people have 54
	searched for "computing" machines that could perform 65
	calculations and analyze data quickly and accurately. 76

2	As civilizations began to develop, they created both 87
	written languages and number systems. These number systems 99
	were not originally meant to be used in mathematical 109
	calculations, but rather were designed to record 119
	measurements. Roman numerals are a good example of this. 130
	Few of us would want to carry out even the simplest 140
	arithmetic operations using Roman numerals. How then were 151
	calculations performed thousands of years ago? 162

3	Calculations were carried out with a device known as 173
	an abacus which was used in ancient Babylon, China and 186
	Europe until the late middle-ages. Many parts of the 196
	world, especially in the Orient, still make use of the 207
	abacus. The abacus works by sliding beads back and 217
	forth on a frame with the beads on the top of the frame 228
	representing fives and on the bottom ones. After a 239
	calculation is made the result is written down. 249

         1   2   3   4   5   6   7   8   9 | 1   2

Lesson 8

C

In this lesson you will make use of the top row of keys that contains both numbers and symbols. Note which finger is used to press each key. The right Shift key is used to type the symbols at the top of the keys 1 through 5 and the left Shift key for the symbols on the top of keys 6 through =.

Practice 8.1

```
1    aqa aq1 aq1 aq1 a1a a1a a11 sws sw2 sw2 sw2 s2s s2s s22 ss2
2    ded de3 de3 de3 d3d d3d d33 de3 frf fr4 fr4 f4f f4f ff4 fr4
3    fr5 fr5 fr5 f5f f5f f55 ff5 juj ju7 ju7 ju7 j7j j7j ju7 j77
4    jyj jy6 jy6 jy6 j6j j6j jy6 j66 kik ki8 ki8 k8k k8k ki8 k88
5    lol lo9 lo9 l9l l9l lo9 l99 ;p; ;p0 ;p0 ;p0 ;0; ;0; ;;0 ;p0
6    aq1! aq1! aq1! aq!! sw2@ sw2@ s2s@ Sw@@ s@@s de3# de3# d#3d
7    fr4$ fr4$ fr$$ fr$f f$4r fr5% fr5% f5%% f5%5 f%f% jy6^ jy6^
8    ju7& ju7& ju7& j&j& ju&j ki8* ki8* k**k k*8* k8*8 lo9( lo9(
9    L(990); : L( ; 0) ; )0 )) (9923) : ; 00) 19(00)  ; – – __ ;
10   ; + +567 – 342 =$45.60 + ; " ' ;+ ; + = – ; ___ -- +1895.00
11   $435.00; = 389* (873) &23 $35.89@ 380.23! 89 + 78 = $382.00
12   Mary has bought a dress that costs $145.67 plus 6.0(%) tax.
13   (A) 3^2 = 9 & $12@ for 5 items = $60.00. 89 * 34 = 3026 47%
14   If I win the Florida $10,000,000.00 lottery I must pay tax.
15   Jack & Jill went up the 3,450 m hill to fetch 12# of water.
16   23 & 79 are odd numbers! (34 + 78) / (245 * 12.8) = 0.00035
```

An Introduction to Computing Using Microsoft Works

C

Timed Practice 8.2

In this Practice type for five minutes and then calculate your speed in words per minute by counting the words typed and dividing by 5. The total of words is given at the end of each line. The words in a partial line are calculated using the scale below the lines. To test your accuracy count the number of letters and spaces missed.

1   Hortense Bargain has decided to reduce the price of   11
    stock items #3485 (paint), #7431 (electric saws) and #2945   23
    (lawn furniture) by 45%. The new prices will be $38.50@,   35
    $72.95@ and $14.98@.   39

2   Ivy University is having a book fair and charging the   51
    following for books and supplies: pens $0.45@, note books   62
    $3.78@, and boxes of paper clips $0.67@. "An Introduction   74
    to Computing Using Works" is specially priced   85
    with a 10% reduction (plus 6% sales tax). The stock number 97
    of this text is #34-2578 (for paperback) and #34-2580   108
    (hardcover). Heidi Crane's new novel "Old Houses in New   119
    Jersey" is specially priced at $12.45 after a 25% discount. 131

3   Please be advised of the addition of the following   142
    courses to the Ivy University catalog: #126 Advanced   153
    Computing (2 credits), #365 Very Advanced Computing (7   164
    credits), #782 Computing for the Exceptionally Intelligent 176
    (12 credits). The tuition for each course is $45.00@.   187
    What a bargain!   190

        1   2   3   4   5   6   7   8   9 | 1   2

Lesson 9

In this lesson type for five minutes and then calculate your speed in words per minute by counting the words typed and dividing by 5. The total of words is given at the end of each line. The words in a partial line are calculated using the scale below the lines. To test your accuracy count the number of letters and spaces missed. Repeat the Practice typing for ten minutes and then calculating your speed and accuracy.

1   One of the most important advances made in computing   11
has been in the field of telecommunications. By   21
telecommunications we mean the sending of computer data   32
over telephone lines. To do this an additional piece of   43
hardware called a "modem" is required to translate the   54
binary data of the computer into waves which can then be   65
transmitted over phone lines. To receive, data a modem   76
must also have the capability of translating the waves back 88
into binary form.   92

2   With a modem a microcomputer is capable of transmitting 104
and receiving data between any two locations connected   115
by telephone lines. The rate at which the data is sent   126
over the phone lines is measured in bits per second   136
(bps), where eight bits are equivalent to one character.   147
Currently the most common rates are 9600, 14400, and   157
28800 bits per second. However, newer modems are being   168
developed which are capable of communicating at 34400   179
bps and higher.   182

3   In a recent newspaper article the Internal Revenue   193
Service (IRS) defined artificial intelligence as "the   204
science of making machines do things that would require   215
intelligence if done by man." As an example, there are   226
currently computers which can play chess so well that they 238
can beat all but the best players. Universities actually   250
challenge each other's computers to play chess to determine 262
which has the best chess playing program. Are these   272
computers really intelligent? Most computer scientists   283
would say no. They are simply programmed to make a series 295
of decisions in response to the moves made by their   305
opponents. It is merely their speed and ability to access 317
huge amounts of stored data which make them appear to be   329
intelligent.   331

        1   2   3   4   5   6   7   8   9 | 1   2

I Index

C

E

F

I

H

I

J

K

An Introduction to Computing Using Microsoft Works

I

I

W

X

Y

Z

I

An Introduction to Computing Using Microsoft Works